STUPA AND SWASTIKA:
Historical Urban Planning Principles in Nepal's Kathmandu Valley

MOHAN PANT

and

SHUJI FUNO

KYOTO UNIVERSITY PRESS
Japan

in association with

NUS PRESS
Singapore

Kyoto University Press
Kyodai-Kaikan (Kyoto University Hall)
15-9 Yoshida-Kawaramachi, Sakyo-ku
Kyoto-city 06-8305
Japan
www.kyoto-up.gr.jp

ISBN 978-4-87698-720-7 (Case)

Ridge Books
an imprint of NUS Press
National University of Singapore
AS3-01-02. 3 Arts Link
Singapore 117569
www.nus.edu.sg/npu

ISBN 978-9971-69-374-9 (Case)
     978-9971-69-372-5 (Paper)

National Library Board Singapore Cataloguing in Publication Data

Pant, Mohan.
    Stupa and swastika: historical urban planning principles in Nepal's Kathmandu Valley / Mohan Pant, Shuji Funo. – Japan: Kyoto University Press in association with NUS Press, c2007.
    p. cm.
    Includes bibliographical references and index.
    ISBN: 978-9971-69-374-9 (NUS Press)
    ISBN: 978-9971-69-372-5 (NUS Press: pbk.)
    ISBN: 978-4-87698-720-7 (Kyoto University Press)

    1. City planning – Nepal – Patan. 2. City planning – Nepal – Patan – Religious aspects – Buddhism. 3. Religious architecture – Nepal – Patan. 4. Stupas – Nepal – Patan. 5. Swastikas – Nepal – Patan. I. Funo, Shuji, 1949– II. Title.

HT169
307.1216095496—dc22   SLS2007004753

Typeset and Printed in Singapore

Contents

PART IV. THE FOUR STUPAS AND THE PLANNING GRID OF PATAN

APPENDICES

List of Figures

List of Plates

List of Tables

Acknowledgements

We would like to thank a number of institutions and individuals who made possible our research on the settlement patterns in Patan, one of three principal cities in the Kathmandu Valley of Nepal.

The Japan Society for the Promotion of Sciences (JSPS) provided financial support to this study of settlement patterns in Patan in the form of a Postdoctoral Research Fellowship from April 2002 to March 2004, which allowed Mohan Pant to extend his doctoral research on Thimi, a town in the Kathmandu Valley, to Patan. JSPS has also supported this publication with Grant-in-Aid for publication of Scientific Research Result. Kyoto University, Graduate School of Engineering, supported the research program as the host institution. To both of the institutions we express our sincere gratitude.

We are grateful to the members of the Funo Research Laboratory for their generous help, in particular to Dr. Sato Keiichi, Dr. Yamada Kiyouta, Mr. Miwa Tetsuya, Dr. Park Chung Sin, and Dr. Nawit Ongsavachai. We were also fortunate to have Dr. Samitha Manawadu's advice regarding various aspects of our research.

Many persons helped in the survey work in Nepal both directly and indirectly. We owe much to Professor Sudashan Tiwari for his inspiring discussions and to Sudha Shrestha and Badri Pradhananga, lecturers at the Pulchok Engineering Institute, Tribhuvan University who organized our survey team. We also would like to thank Vinaya Shrestha and Naresh Tamrakar for their steadfastness during our survey work in Patan.

Our thanks are also due to the Senior Architects at the Department of Housing, Building and Physical Planning, Ministry of Housing and Physical Planning, Government of Nepal—Balakrishna Shrestha, Naresh Amatya, and Purusottam Dangol—for their help in making drawings and other source materials available to us.

Ghana Raj Lohani, Pant's brother-in-law, provided Pant with logistical support during his visits to Nepal. Later he furnished missing data and searched out answers to our inquiries that cropped up as we analyzed our data in Japan. To him, we express our profound gratitude, as well as to the other members of our respective families for their support during our years of work.

We owe a considerable debt of gratitude to earlier researchers' work on the Kathmandu Valley towns. We especially acknowledge the team from the Nippon

Institute of Technology whose work has made certain aspects of our research much richer than they would have been otherwise. The present research project on Patan owes much to Mohan Pant's Masters thesis supervisor, Professor Yu Min Fei of the Department of Architecture, Tongji University, Shanghai, who suggested the cities of the Kathmandu Valley as the topic for his Masters thesis in 1990. To Professor Yu we also express our gratitude.

Our expression of thanks would not be complete without mentioning the residents of Patan who not only opened their doors during our intruding survey works but also handed out the key to unlock certain planning aspects of the city.

Last, but not least, our gratitude is also due to Mr. Tetsuya Suzuki, the managing editor of Kyoto University Press who looked after the project from the beginning to its publication. We would also like to thank Dr. Paul Kratoska and his staff at NUS Press for overseeing the editorial details of the publication.

Mohan Pant
Shuji Funo

Preface

The towns of the Kathmandu Valley are the hallmarks of Newar civilization. Many historical studies of the towns' art and architecture begin with two questions: what are the origins of the Newar people and what are the origins of the Kathmandu Valley towns? In a way, they are one and the same question, but they do not necessarily lead to the same answer.

Cultural historians agree that the Newar community is an amalgam of different ethnic tribes which settled in the Kathmandu Valley from prehistoric times to the late medieval period. It is, therefore, not surprising that many anthropologists and art historians explain the development of culture and art in the Kathmandu Valley towns in terms of cultural diffusion from other areas of the Indian subcontinent and regions bordering the valley from which migrating communities came. However, cultural diffusion does not completely account for the development of the Newar culture because there are features that are indigenous to the Kathmandu Valley as well as features, which developed quite early in the process of cultural amalgamation.

The valley's inhabitants have been following Buddhist and Hindu religious traditions from ancient period to modern times. Scholars have long recognized the influence of religion on the development of culture in the Kathmandu Valley. Underlying this recognition there also exists a questionable assumption of religious exclusivity. In historical records as well as in the descriptions of the chronicles, one can read that, at certain points in history, antagonisms existed between the two religions; but in the end the two faiths intermingled in such a way that a clear cut division between the two faiths does not do justice to the religious practices of the valley inhabitants. Within this complexity, while one is able to discern certain social forms and institutions including the settlement forms as Buddhist and others as Hindu, there are also social and religious traditions that constitute the common and essential heritage of all the Newar inhabitants of the valley.

The development of the religious traditions in the valley and the ethnic background of the ancient inhabitants are naturally connected to the greater cultural zone of the subcontinent and the regions it borders. For many anthropologists and art historians, therefore, the culture of Kathmandu Valley is a regional or local manifestation that could be explained or deduced from models derived from elsewhere in the region. It is true that the task of theory building often requires a larger zone to validate the proposition. However, features of Kathmandu Valley towns, more than the Newar anthropological origin, raise questions that cannot be explained by a theory of cultural diffusion. Unique features of Newar architecture and urban forms are noted by many scholars of Nepalese architectural and urban history. The uniqueness of Newar culture is not manifested by the inventory list of artifacts but rather in the shapes of these artifacts and their assemblage. Patan is one such great assemblage that represents the Newar cultural identity.

Although architectural and urban historians have noted the uniqueness of Newar architecture and urban forms, it is often assumed that the *Vastusastras,* classical Hindu architectural texts, guided settlement planning in the Kathmandu Valley. It is true that the Kathmandu Valley houses a rich store of ancient Hindu and Buddhist scriptures. The copying of such manuscripts was important both for rulers in the palace and the priests in the monasteries. However, architectural historians will find settlement patterns of the valley's cities hard to understand if they only compare these patterns with the ideal geometries of *mandalas,* and they will find an even more bewildering and complex task in discerning from the social and religious order of the cities the stellar universe mapped by these mandalas.

A large number of towns of the valley existed by the seventh century and among them the three cities—Patan, Kathmandu, and Bhaktapur—have prehistoric origins. Therefore, many Kathmandu Valley settlements, like the cities of Indus civilization, probably existed before the compilation of the *Vastusastras.* Applying the principles of the *Vastusastras* to these towns would be most likely a matter of modifying existing settlement patterns that were built on indigenous or some earlier planning tradition. This suggests that a study of the principles of settlement planning in the Kathmandu Valley means looking beyond the knowledge of the *Vastusastras.* More importantly, the study of settlement planning first of all requires the data from the field itself. Social structures and settlement traditions have logics that cross the boundaries of religious faith and, therefore, cannot be understood purely in terms of certain religious concepts or ethnic traditions. Instead, they need to be seen as the rationale for organizing settlements in particular ways. It is in this belief that this book explores the planning principles of Patan.

The title of this book presents two symbols—the stupa and the swastika, symbols that have been sacred in Buddhist and Hindu cultures from the time the two religions came into existence. However, we should not forget that the origin of these two symbols predate both of Buddhism and Hinduism. The swastika was in use in the Indus culture, 5000 years ago. The stupa began as a tumulus, which we find far back in time and in other cultures such as in East Asia at the period when they were not yet informed by Buddhist sotoreological ideas.

The swastika has been used as an auspicious symbol both in Hindu and Buddhist traditions. It is the *Dharmacakra,* the ever-rolling wheel of the Buddhist religion; one of the signs of Buddha cast in his footprints. This particular sign is manifested in the plan of Buddhist monasteries and in the hand gestures and sitting postures of the Buddhist deities. In the *Vastusastras,* the swastika is described as one of the model plans for town settlement as well as buildings.

On the other hand the stupa has grown to become a monumental symbol that embodies Buddhist philosophy itself. The symbolism of the axis and orientations inherent in stupa symbolism are like the cosmic pillars of Hindu tradition. In Buddhist cultures, stupas are built at places to mark entry points and centers, and also to mark axis and directions.

This book doesn't explore the form of the stupa and its symbolism, which has been the topic of great scholarly interest. And likewise the iconography of swastika is better studied by art historians. We here take up these two symbols to discuss how the two icons are the principles of settlement planning in Patan, a city known to have a long Buddhist tradition among the three cities of the Kathmandu Valley. This is not to suggest that planned settlement in the valley began after the establishment of the two religions in the valley. As mentioned earlier, the book attempts to show how the planning tradition of the valley has a background of Indus civilization that long predates both the high traditions of Hindu and Buddhist cultures. As to the antiquity and importance of Patan, Baburam Acharya, one of the great historians of Nepal, marks the city as the first civilized centre of the Kathmandu Valley.

This study thus goes beyond the guidance of the *Vastusastras*, and does not hold any presumptions and concepts of these texts to the study of the city. This is an unconventional approach in the study of ancient cities of the region. But then it has discerned a connecting thread from the prehistoric times of Indus culture to the period of the Arthasastra of Kautilya of the fourth century BCE and later to medieval times in the planning of cities and architecture. Now it is laid in posterity that this thread was, without break, held high in the hands of Newar of the Kathmandu Valley.

Pl. A. Column style of Manimandap, Patan Palace Square

Pl. B. The Southern Stupa (Lagan stupa)

Pl. C. The Northern Stupa (Yampi stupa)

Pl. D. Patan Palace Square

Pl. E. Sundarichok, Patan Palace (17th c)

Pl. F. Distribution of communities

PART I
Patan and Kathmandu Valley Towns

1
Introduction

Patan is one of three principal cities in the Kathmandu Valley along with Kathmandu and Bhaktapur, all of which have served as capitals of Nepal at different periods of its history. Besides these cities, the valley's radius of roughly 15 kilometers is dotted with numerous small towns and village settlements (Fig. 1-1). The inhabitants belong to a number of different ethno-linguistic communities of which the Newar, who primarily live in town settlements, have been identified with the valley's cultural development since ancient times. While all these towns share a number of features that categorize them as Newar settlements, certain differences also exist between them. Patan is distinguished by having the largest Buddhist population and Buddhist monasteries among the cities of the valley. However, the city is much more ancient than its Buddhist heritage as indicated by historic evidence. This study focuses on these aspects of Patan and attempts to shed light on the plan and structure of the city.

The pattern of town settlements and the architecture in the Kathmandu Valley is considered to be unique even within the cultural zone of South Asia. This distinctness can be discerned in the form of individual dwellings, in the organization of neighborhood and urban squares, and also in community buildings such as temples and monasteries. Visitors can readily observe the uniqueness of the valley towns' architecture and settlement patterns. The Newar of the Kathmandu Valley show a gregarious living pattern with houses clustered along streets or around courtyards. All the neighborhoods of the town have a community square with a well or a fountain, rest houses, and shrines. After entering a city gate, visitors pass through a series of neighborhood squares and taking an almost straight route they reach the centre of the city with a large square and a palace behind it. The palace square is similar to the neighborhood squares but is larger in scale and has numerous temples, fountains, and other artifacts. When entering a lane from

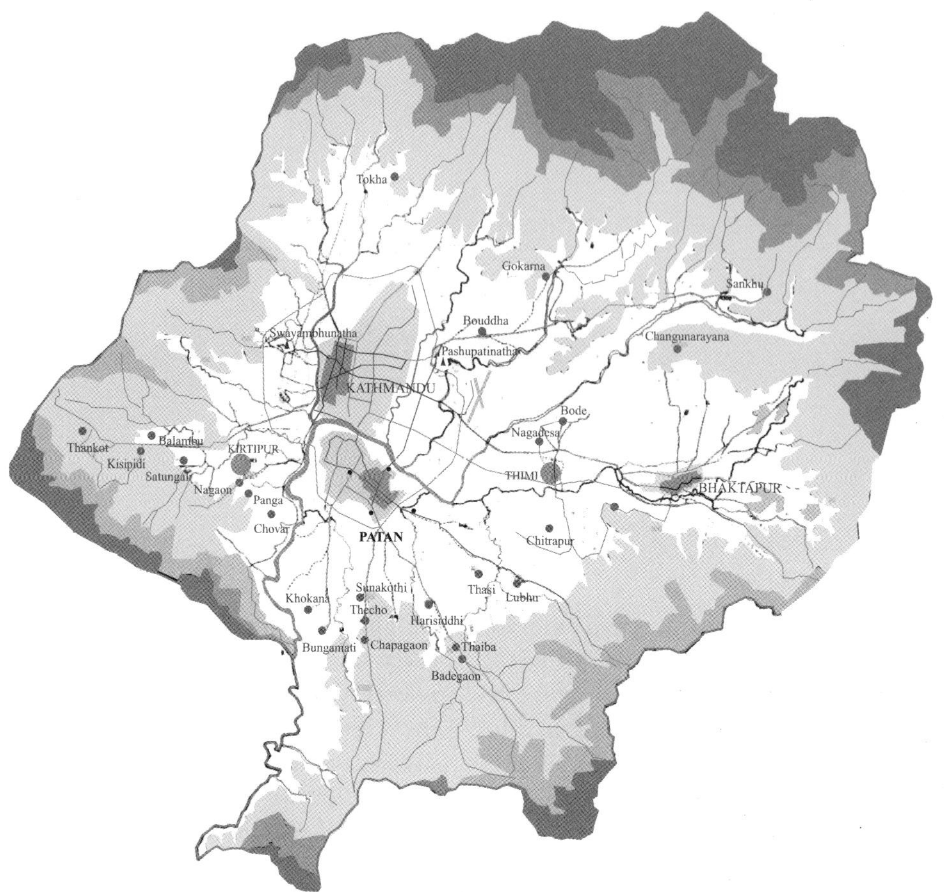

Fig. 1-1. The town settlements of the Kathmandu Valley

a street, visitors may find a gate to a quarter with an open courtyard large enough to accommodate more than 100 dwellings around it or only small enough for a few dwellings. Large or small, there are shrines at the centre of the courtyard. In not a few cases the courtyard has a Buddhist monastery with residential dwellings and their courtyards clustered around it.

If the visitors make a simple sketch plan of the city, it will show regular geometric lines and shapes that indicate a planned settlement. But, modern scholars have not described the towns of the valley as planned when the towns were built. Nor have they determined the principles underlying their planning. To most scholars, the regularity in the urban pattern on the one hand and the complex network of streets and apparent irregular size of settlement blocks on the other suggest both the possibility of planned and organic growth. Only in the last few years, have some scholars described the cities as planned, but answers to questions about the uniqueness of town settlements in the Kathmandu

Valley, their architecture, and the principles of their planning are not readily available, particularly, on the question of settlement pattern.

At the beginning of our research, Patan did not readily appear as a planned city. But the shape of the large quadrangular courts with a *caitya* or a monastery at the centre and the regular arrangement of the individual dwellings around it strongly suggested some kind of planning principle behind the settlement structure as did the placement of four stupas at the northern, southern, eastern, and western peripheries of the city as well as the palace at a central location of the city. The arrangement of the four stupas and the central location of the palace make Patan rather unique among the three major cities of the valley and have appeared to both the inhabitants and scholars to be signs of a planned city. The Buddhist community believes that the city was planned in the shape of the *dharmacakra*, the Buddhist Wheel of Law, which recalls to mind the swastika, a sacred symbol, the form of which was employed in Buddhist monastery plans and recommended as one of the models for buildings and town planning in ancient architectural texts.[1] However, other than these symbolic statements, no concrete descriptions of the planned forms of the city were available to us.

Thus, standing at one corner of a residential courtyard, we asked a simple question: what are the planning principles of such residential quarters? This question naturally expanded to the following questions. What are the planning principles of Patan and the other Kathmandu Valley towns? How does Patan's physical and social structure reflect its history as an ancient centre of

Buddhism whose existence predates the introduction of Buddhism? In answer to these questions, it was necessary to describe the city not just as it appears but also as it is. These questions always surface whenever we study the urban history of traditional cities in the region of South Asia. Further, only answers to such questions can lead us to see the historic links of Patan to other ancient cities in the region, which so far are unclear. This book makes these inquiries into Patan's social and physical structure and its history in an attempt to discover the planning principles of the city.

On the question of whether the cities and town settlements of the valley are planned or organic, there are no priori conclusions or convincing hypotheses to begin with. But, a settlement is often considered as planned if its elements exhibit regularity and the uniformity in its layout (that is, in its size, shape, and orientation). A fixed boundary demarcating a settlement is also an important feature of a planned settlement. Lastly, the planned or controlled development of a settlement sustained over a long time period of decades or generations presumes a continuous administrative power. On the other hand, a possible indication of a settlement as organically developed is the apparent difficulty in identifying a regular geometry in its layout. Organic forms develop without the rigidity of geometric frames or the presence of a continuous central administrative power. Historic towns often exhibit both planned and organic features.

While we may accept such distinctions between planned and organic forms, planning principles are not necessarily only reflected by the regularity in physical features discussed above. The difference between planned and organic forms is a difference in the degree of control exerted over both the social and physical aspects of a settlement or a town. The greater this control, the more the planned form of a settlement is revealed. Therefore, a strict boundary between instances of planned and organic settlements is difficult to draw. This being the case, we may ask what are the planned features revealed in the patterns of Patan and other towns of the valley. There are a number of problems to face when attempting to study the features of planning exhibited by the towns of the valley.

Firstly, we know that all settlements in the world, whether towns or villages, have an "identifiable pattern" in their layout including the distribution of communities within their geographic areas. Descriptions of physical patterns such as neighborhood squares, temples, city gates, courtyard forms, typical dwelling forms, and the distribution pattern of the communities as concentric or sectoral do not always help to categorize a settlement as organic or planned. However, there is one particular physical pattern that shows the settlement as "planned" although it may not be the only one. This is the grid pattern in the shape of a square, rectangle, or other shape defined by geometric principles. Grids have certain fixed modular measures that may span a whole city or a sector of a city, which give shape to settlement quarters. These settlement quarters may include a number of neighborhoods with diverse communities. The existence of such physical and social patterns must invariably be the result of a conscious planning effort. Grid plans may range from a simple division of urban blocks to the planning of residential quarters that determines the

division pattern of individual plots. Some cities of South Asia exhibit this pattern as has been shown by Shuji Funo in his recent work, *Mandala Toshi* [The city as mandala] (2006).[2] However, most of the existing traditional cities in the region do not present us such a picture of regular geometric patterns. The grid patterns with regular block divisions are also not readily apparent in the plan of valley towns even to the careful observer.

Another approach to identifying the planning features of a city is to examine its physical layout and social distribution in the light of the standard principles given by authoritative texts, such as the Vastusastra, which are classical works on architecture and town planning. In the South Asian context, there has existed from ancient times a number of texts that describe various patterns of town and village settlements. A comparative analysis could be based on a description of ideal planning forms in the classic texts and a description of forms built after these texts were written. However, there are three problems in carrying out such a comparative analysis. First, ancient cities have long histories. For example, the cities in the Kathmandu Valley have existed for more than a millennium and manifest layers of development from different periods. Second, as a consequence of these cities' long development, the ideal shapes described in the Vastusastra are rarely apparent in the cities' present physical forms. Earlier elements need to be distinguished from elements superimposed on them at later periods in order to determine which planning concepts were used at which periods of history.

Third, there is a lack of historical documentation to construct a reliable urban history in the South Asia region

(Nepal 1998, 83–93)[3] which raises a question of whether it is possible to successfully compare descriptions from historical documents and the results of present-day research. Aside from a lack of archive records, researchers have to contend with continual changes to the physical face of cities and towns that are eroding the past at an ever-increasing speed and on an ever-increasing scale. In the end, unless we can tally field data with those given by historical documents, the application of town planning principles as described by the Vastusastra or other such texts in the world of practice cannot be explained.

Related Research

To put our inquiry on Patan in the wider context of the scholarship on the urban history of the Kathmandu Valley towns, this section presents an overview of existing research on the social and physical structure of the Kathmandu Valley towns. The studies reviewed here come from disciplines such as architecture and town planning, art and cultural history, sociology and anthropology, conducted since the 1950s. They provide valuable source material on the Newar social structure, religious institutions, and history, and they provide insights to the development of the Newar settlements. Besides this review on modern research, other relevant accounts on the building of towns given in historical documents is separately presented in Chapter 2 along with the historical background on the peoples and towns of the valley.

There is little published research dealing exclusively with the urban history of the Kathmandu Valley towns from the perspective of settlement planning.

The earliest work on town planning was done by the Nepal Department of Housing and Physical Planning and published as *The Kathmandu Valley Plan* (His Majesty's Government of Nepal 1969). This document includes introductory material on the individual valley settlements with selected maps from a physical planning perspective. It provides statistical data on population and community structures, the public utilities of each settlement, and historical sites including a calendar of traditional festivals. Following this project was the two-volume *Kathmandu Valley* (Pruscha 1975). This publication reports extensive documentation work on the historic settlements of the valley. It gives a brief introduction to all 29 historic Newar settlements of the valley, including the three major cities— Kathmandu, Patan, and Bhaktapur (Fig. 1-2). It classifies artifacts such as temples, Buddhist monasteries, and other sites of historic importance. And, it also includes maps, photographs, and brief notes on each settlement. While this document does not give an analytical history of the valley towns, it is still an invaluable guide to conduct preliminary survey of the valley's historic settlements.

Religious monuments are often important signposts that reveal the history and structure of the town settlements. In this respect, we particularly benefit from studies done on Buddhist monasteries, to which we will often refer in our study. Hemaraj Sakya, an epigraphist, has been publishing a series of monographs on individual monasteries since 1956 mostly in Newari. His work provides a brief account of the history, legends, ritual calendar, and historic records pertaining to each monastery.[4] Another contribution in this field is John Locke's *Buddhist*

Fig. 1-2. The traditional city core of Kathmandu

Monasteries of Nepal (1985). It inventories the various types of monasteries to be found in the valley and documents their religious traditions, rituals, and artifacts with photographic illustrations. In addition, he provides maps showing locations of the monasteries in the three major cities. Compared to Hindu temples, Buddhist monasteries have a tightly knit social and religious organization, and they are recognized as the custodians of past historic records. Documents from Rudravarna Mahavihara, by Kolver and Sakya (1985) has brought into light large number of land deed documents from the medieval period that help to know localities and monasteries of Patan.

One of the earliest works with illustrated drawings of *vihara* 'Buddhist

monastery' in the valley is Wolfgang Korn's *Traditional Architecture of the Kathmandu Valley* (1979). More detailed analytical work has been done by a team from the Nippon Institute of Technology (NIT) on architectural types, in particular, on the palace quadrangles and Buddhist monasteries of the valley. The team was involved in a study of architecture in the Kathmandu Valley from 1982 to 1997, which ended with a project to restore a Buddhist monastery, I baha bahi, in Patan. The team published *The Royal Buildings in Nepal* (Nippon Institute of Technology 1981) and *The Royal Buildings and Buddhist Monasteries of Nepal* (Nippon Institute of Technology 1985). Another publication, *Buddhist Monasteries of Nepal* (Watanabe 1998a), is an important document on Buddhist monasteries and Nepalese architecture. In addition, there are a number of research papers in Japanese by Katsuhiko Watanabe and Takayuki Kurotsu, members of the NIT research team, on the module measures and planning principles of the palace quadrangles of Patan (Kurotsu and Watanabe [1990] and Kurotsu [1991a; 1991b]). Their studies on palace quadrangles and Buddhist monasteries are landmark documents of the architectural preservation work in the Kathmandu Valley. The detailed drawings in these works provided invaluable data to our own study.

The Bhaktapur Development Program (BDP), undertaken from 1974 to 1991 with the assistance of the German Agency for Technical Cooperation, began an important chapter in the study of traditional towns in the Kathmandu Valley. The project is now widely recognized to have had a long-lasting exemplary impact on the conservation and development

Fig. 1-3. The traditional city core of Bhaktapur

work of a traditional town. One of the scholarly outcomes of the project was the work of Gutschow and Kolver (1975) on Bhaktapur, *Ordered Space Concept and Functions in a Town of Nepal.* It is the first study that attempts to describe the features of a historic town in Nepal. This work draws attention to some of the characteristic structures of the town, such as the neighborhood unit (*tole*), the neighborhood square as the center of community activity, and the distribution pattern of communities. These elements of physical, social, and ritual significance constitute basic themes along which Gutschow develops his later discourse on the urban history of the valley.

In his later study on the historic development of the valley towns, Gutschow (1981a, 1981b) suggests that the western part of Bhaktapur is a planned extension of the old city while Kathmandu shows a combination of a gradual organic development of the early settlements and planned development during the medieval period (Fig. 1-3). As for Patan, he suggests the northeast street that runs obliquely to other streets in the present street network could have been the axis of an early settlement. He also considers this area as an example of organic growth. Gutschow's observations are derived from the apparent structure of the street pattern, but these observations need to be verified with relevant analytical data.

Book-length studies have also been published on individual settlements in the valley. One such earlier work is Barre and Toffin's 1980 study of Panauti, a small town in the eastern part of the Kathmandu Valley. Written in French, the book was a result of a decade of involvement in a French conservation project of the town. M. Shokohy and N. H. Shokohy's 1994 work on Kirtipur brings together articles by a number of authors on the art, architecture, and other aspects of Kirtipur's urban development. In this work, S. Shrestha describes religious monuments and illustrates them with photographs while M. Barani provides a case study of two neighborhoods with ground floor plans highlighting the relationship between public and private space (Shrestha 1994; Barani, 1994). On Kirtipur, there is yet another study, Reinhard Herdick's 1982 doctoral dissertation in which he notes the town is organized into two halves and suggests the ritual and cosmological meaning of this bipartite division represents the primordial androgyny of Siva and his female consort Sakti (Fig. 1-4). He postulates that the form of the town was organized in the sacred shape of the swastika. Although the form of Kirtipur follows the contour of the hill on which town is built and the hill and the streets do not exhibit regular geometrical patterns, he interprets Kirtipur as developed in accordance with a plan that reflected Hindu cosmology. Herdick's later study (1993) makes a special contribution to the knowledge of large stupas in the valley. According to him, these stupas are structured in axes oriented to the points of the moonrise or sunrise of particular periods of the year. This system also includes two of the four large stupas situated at the periphery of Patan.

There are other studies on small town settlements that have contributed to the study of Newar settlements. Muller (1981) mapped the distribution of communities in Thimi's building clusters for the first time, which provided valuable material

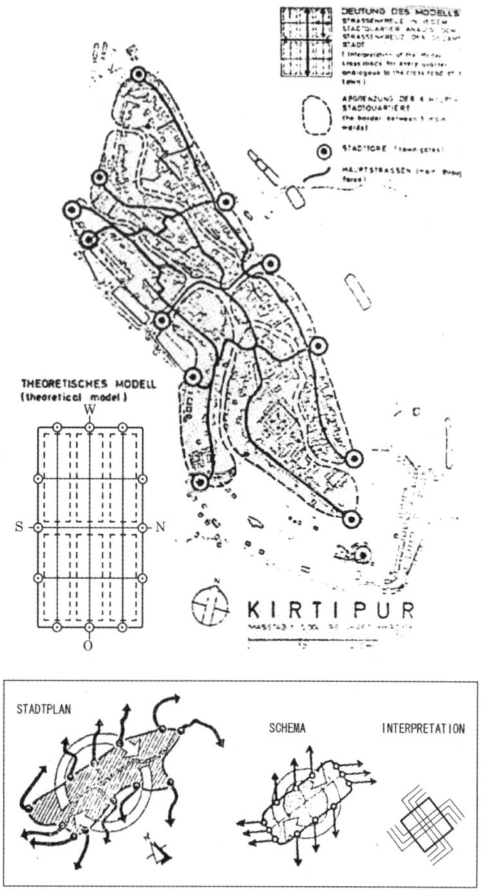

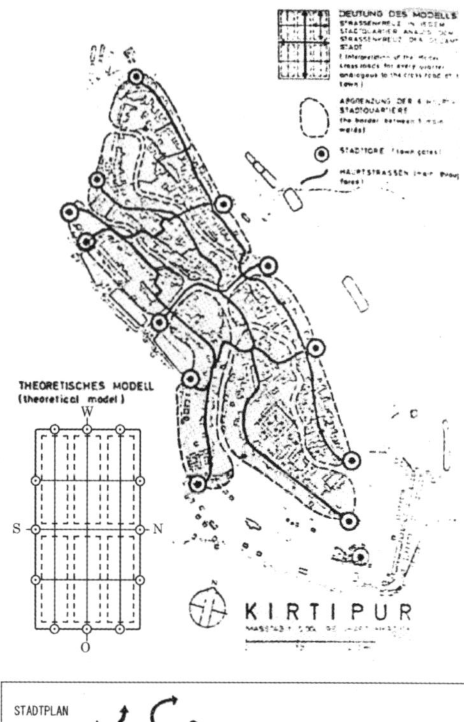

Fig. 1-4. Kiritipur (Herdick 1985)

to the study of the relationship between the spatial and social structures in a traditional settlement of the valley. M. Pant's dissertation (2002) on the same town makes a detailed study of this settlement's social, spatial, and ritual dimensions (Fig. 1-5). Furthermore, a series of papers by Pant and Funo (2001a; 2001b; 2003) shows the crucial importance of clan structure and the ancestral cult, known as dewali, to the understanding of the town's spatial structure.

Of relevance to the valley settlements are some of the works by anthropologists. One valuable reference is G. S. Nepali's

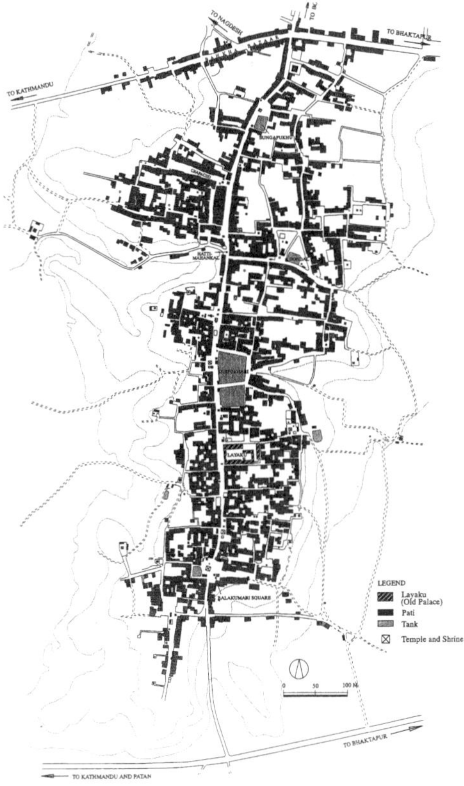

Fig. 1-5. Thimi (Pant 2002)

The Newars (1965), which describes the structure of Newar society in terms of caste, kinship, social customs, rituals, and community festivals. The author focuses on Panga, a village near Kirtipur. Although the work describes little on the physical form of the settlement and provides no maps, it introduces the general structure of Newar society, rituals, and ritual artifacts that have an important bearing on the organization of the settlement. Gellner (1992) gives a more detailed account of religious ritual in the traditional social structure of two Buddhist communities, namely the Sakya and Vajracharya of Patan in his *Monk, Householder and Tantric Priest*. Likewise, Ishii (1980) focuses on the finer structural details of

Newar society as manifested in its traditional rituals. In particular, Ishii relates oral tradition to the precedence of residency of certain communities in Satungal, a town to the west of the valley vis-à-vis their role in conducting the festival of the town goddess, Vishnudevi. Intermigration between the towns of the valley has occurred since ancient times, and traditional rituals hold vital clues to understanding the distribution pattern of the community as demonstrated in M. Pant's 2002 study on Thimi.

Toffin has extensively studied the ethnography of the Kathmandu Valley towns. His 1994 study on Kathmandu's Jyapu community investigates the social as well as the territorial cohesiveness of this community through traditional music associations and neighborhood temples dedicated to Ganesa and Nasa-dyo, the god of music and dance. He also shows the importance of this community in understanding the neighborhood and settlement structure of the city with its division into an upper and lower town. Toffin (1996), citing the instances of Theco and other towns, argues that bipartite divisions in the structure of the settlements are more representative of the Kathmandu Valley towns than the hierarchical divisions of a concentric order described in the Hindu texts on the ideal town plan. A number of other studies show that the cult of the town deity is one symbolic aspect which indicates the social and spatial organization of Newar settlements of the valley. One of such study that centers on the cult of town deities is Zanen's 1986 study of Sankhu, a town in the northeast corner of the valley. It highlights the relationship between the spatial organization of the settlement and the festival of Vajrajogini, a supreme goddess in the Vajrayana pantheon,[5] and eight mother goddesses.

Gutschow, Herdick, and several other authors including the urban anthropologists Toffin and Ishii, take urban ritual as the central focus of their research on the settlement structure of the Kathmandu Valley towns. Occasional references to historical data are made to connect a ritual tradition to its past. These works generally assume that once a ritual is instituted it tenaciously preserves its historic past and thus reflects the medieval or even earlier structure of the town.

There is also a body of scholarship that uses available historical materials to enrich or substantiate the study on the settlement culture of the valley. For example, Slusser and Vajracharya (1973a; 1973b; 1974a) deserve special note. Slusser with her background in art history has attempted to build her research on firm ground supported by historical documents and the iconography of arts and sculptures. Following her intensive research work in Nepal for more than a decade, she published her two-volume *Nepala Mandala*, of text and photographs, in 1982. The book is a panorama of the cultural history of Nepal that introduces the development of religion and religious cults, art, festivals, and political history from ancient times to the beginning of the modern period. The photographs illustrating the text are selective and well researched. Although her topical interest is not on settlement patterns as such, one will benefit from this almost encyclopedic work that makes innumerable references to artifacts, places and historical characters in the Kathmandu Valley.

Lainshing Bangadel's 1982 seminal work sheds light on the prehistoric culture of the Kathmandu Valley from the perspective of art history. His detailed study of the iconography of religious artifacts in the valley brings into light the prehistoric Buddhist and Hindu culture in Nepal and suggests that the artists from the valley were in contact with the work of artists from the Gandhara and Mathura regions during the period of the Kushana. Comparable studies in architectural styles and forms have lagged behind the work done in art history. This is mainly due to the dearth of materials from the ancient period. Yet, architectural historians point out that the layouts of existing ancient Buddhist monasteries show similarities with the cave monasteries of Southwest India, the earliest of which date back to the second century BCE, and monastic cells in Gandhara which are organized around a courtyard or a hall. These similarities are evident in the characteristic layout with an open court and cells around it in all the cave monasteries and other ancient monastery foundations.

Another work that makes exclusive use of historic documents is Sudarshan Tiwari's *The Ancient Settlements of Kathmandu Valley* (2001), which covers the prehistoric, Licchavi, and Thakuri periods before the beginning of Malla rule (thirteenth to eighteenth centuries CE) in Nepala Mandala. The research primarily uses the inscriptional records of the Licchavi period and legends of the valley to identify the places mentioned in those inscriptions. It is the first work to give a spatial interpretation to the texts of the inscriptions through an examination of topographical features and artifacts associated with sites. Tiwari locates 97 place names mentioned in these inscriptions on a map of the valley, some of which identify with presently existing localities. He agrees with other scholars that the settlements gradually moved from the higher elevations in the mountains surrounding the valley to the lower plateaus on the valley floor beside the river basins by the Kirata period, so named for the dynasty that is said to have ruled Nepal prior to the second century CE. While the Kirata's planning principle was to divide town settlements into upper, middle, and lower sectors—a layout found in a number of valley settlements, Tiwari observes that the towns of the Licchavi period, which followed the Kirata period, appear to have been planned according to the Hindu dictates of planning and that the same system, with appropriate Sakta modifications, appears to have been carried over into the Malla period.

Upon observation, it is evident that the Sakta influence on settlement culture prevailed after the cult of the mother goddess came to be supreme in most of the valley settlements and shrines to the eight mother goddesses were established in the settlements for ritual protection (Pant 2002). However, the planning of a settlement according to the principles of the classical Hindu Vastusastra still remains to be demonstrated through extensive fieldwork on physical, social, and ritual structures. In this respect, Kurokawa's study of Hadigaon (1998) suggests a square of nine blocks in Vishalanagara, a prehistoric town according to the chronicles such as the Bhasavamshabali, that narrate events of historic and prehistoric Nepal. According to Tiwari (2002), Vishalnagara was a square mandala of prastara form[6] that is mentioned in classical Hindu architectural

Fig. 1-6. Planning grids of Vishalnagar (Tiwari 2002)

texts, with the palace, Managriha, at the center of the city (Fig. 1-6). The nine-square plan (3 × 3) model with two streets crossing each other with a palace at the center is also a classic model of ancient Chinese cities. However, Tiwari (2002, 202) argues from the layout of certain shrines that Vishalanagara was planned according to Hindu Vastusastra texts in 9 × 9 square blocks (*pada*) which were later extended to south and west making 12 × 12 squares (pada) divisions by Manadeva in the fifth century CE. Block divisions require more detailed measurement analysis and chronological assessment to determine their form and examine the possibility of their existence prior to the Licchavi period, which could then explain the extent of the use of Vastusastra principles in the planning or reorganization of Vishalanagara. In this respect, further research work is needed to demonstrate the validity of this often assumed hypothesis.

Sharma (1997) also makes use of historic documents written before the fifteenth century to study the structure of Newar society during the early medieval period. He analyzes Newar social and communal structures such as lineage, rituals, and festivals of that period to establish a link between current traditions and those mentioned in the early medieval documents and literature.

It has been noted that the Newar community of the Kathmandu Valley is an amalgam of various ethnic communities. The traditional professions, social status, and the religious orientation of the inhabitants are closely related to their ethnic roots. In particular, one has to take note that the Jyapu and Buddhist communities are distinct from other communities of Newar, such as the Shrestha community (Chaps. 2 and 3). The work reviewed above generally discusses the Newar town in its entirety and treat the different communities within Newar society as one unit in its social hierarchy. However, this assumption does not reflect the way that settlement patterns developed historically in the Kathmandu Valley. There are instances of different patterns of settlements in different sectors of the city. There are also instances where the distribution of community quarters does not follow the principle of proximity to the center reflecting their respective status in the social hierarchy.

While the study of rituals remains an important way to uncover various social, religious, and physical aspects of urban structure, we also have to take note that besides religious ritual, the fabric of a settlement is another important resource in the study of past history. The study of this physical fabric is central to analyzing and describing a settlement culture. Settlements have their signs embedded in the existing fabric. Street layouts, plot sizes, modular measures, and the measurement system hidden in the layout of a settlement all form a city's "elements of iconography," to borrow a term from art history. Urban historians know these elements to be the palimpsest of a settlement, and urban morphology is a science devoted to this study. In urban history, the morphological analysis of settlements reveals how their physical structures reflect different historical periods. This research methodology has been widely applied in urban historical studies since the 1960s by urban geographers. This approach analyses the existing fabric of the city, that is, the streets and lanes, the dwelling plots, the quarter blocks of neighborhoods, their layout, and the layout of the town itself. The approach can be equally applied to the study of the archaeological remains of past settlements.

There is a body of urban history work on English medieval towns following this approach of urban morphology. For instance, Conzen (1968) outlines some of the concepts of the approach such as genetic plan unit, morphological regions and fringe belt in his study of Ludlow, a medieval town founded in the twelfth century. Since the 1970s, a number of studies have analyzed the system of plot division, the burgage of medieval Europe. These studies are concentrated primarily on settlements or sites that are still visible in the form of boundaries above ground or whose remains have been discovered by archaeological excavations.

This method of research, long established in urban geography, is also useful for research on architectural and town-planning history but it has not been widely used for this purpose. However, with respect to Asian cities, Shuji Funo and his research associates have made significant contributions through their study of Cakranegara in Indonesia (2002b), Jaipur in India (1997b and1998b), and Beijing (cf. Deng, Yi et al. 2002). All these three cities are living settlements. Funo shows that Cakranegara was planned using a regular grid pattern and divided by a hierarchical structure of streets called *marga-sanga*, *marga-dasa*, and *marga*. Marga-sanga are two central streets that divide the city into four quadrants while marga-dasa divide the quadrants into settlement blocks. Further divisions into neighborhood units are made by marga. The residential plots are divided into regular sizes of 25 m × 25 m, and 20 such households form one neighborhood unit, known as a marga. The quarter block, surrounded by marga-dasa, is 250 m × 250 m and consists of four marga units. These dimensions are related to the local standard of measurement called *tonga* which is 2.5 m long. Funo further describes the distribution of shrines and communities to demonstrate that the city was planned according to Hindu planning principles. Regarding Jaipur, he analyses the physical structure of the city and community distributions and shows specific dimensions employed according to the hierarchy of streets, settlement blocks, and residential quarters. The city is divided in regular grids and the residential quarters show a typical block of 106 m × 75.5 m. Likewise, in the study of Beijing, Deng and Funo show through the analysis of a drawing made in 1744 a division pattern of neighborhood units called *hutong*, which consisted of a number of 10 × 2 plots, each of which was 44 *bu* × 44 *bu* (a measure that corresponded to 8 *mu*, the standard size allowed to an aristocratic family). Plots of 8 *mu* were further divided into 10 plots, each of which amount to 8 *fen*, the traditional measure of land allotted to commoners according to Yuan dynasty (1271–1368) regulations. Thus, urban blocks of Peking were divided into neighborhood units of between 20 and 200 households depending upon the status of the residents. Likewise, M. Pant's study of Thimi (2002), an ancient town in the Kathmandu Valley, shows evidence of town planning based on dividing the town into settlement blocks governed by particular planning modules that correspond to ancient measures known as danda and rajju.

It can be seen that the measuring rod is an important tool in morphological studies. Therefore, relevant records of standard measuring units are studied to uncover the principles of planning for a given cultural period. However, the analysis of plot divisions can also yield the standard measuring units used at a particular historical period. Such standards used in settlement planning are also common in the division of agricultural fields and may have well been the precursor of town planning. In this respect, land deed documents showing units employed in measuring fields are helpful in the study of settlements.

Regular patterns of land division go back to prehistoric times. An example is coaxial planning, which is thought to have been employed in the divisions of tribal territories and fields from as far back as the third millennium BCE (Fleming 1987). The line of divisions would run parallel for several kilometers and continue despite the topographical features like rivers, hills, or valleys. The remains of this type of planning are still to be found in the landscapes of England. Similar field division patterns are found in Japan, where the divisions were made during the seventh and eighth centuries CE following a decree which declared that the land and people belonged to the state. However, the division was not based on a principle of coaxial planning but rather on a grid pattern known as *johrisei,* where one lot could cover tens of square kilometers of land. This ancient division pattern of fields was often used for the layout of new settlements and cities. For instance, ancient capitals of Japan, Fujiwara-kyo, Nara, and Kyoto, were planned using a reference axis based on an earlier field planning pattern (Takahasi et al. 1993, 36). Likewise, agricultural fields in China were managed through the well-known *jing-tian-zhi* 'well-field system' during the Shang period

(sixteenth to eleventh centuries BCE) and the Zhou dynasty (eleventh to third centuries BCE). In this system, the land was divided into grids of nine square units, which were distributed to eight families. Each family received one plot and their plots surrounded a central plot that all families would farm to generate the income to be paid as tribute to the state. The grid of nine square units became a classical model for planning cities during the Zhou dynasty.

Based on available historical records, morphological studies assume that the particular fabric of a settlement is the product of a particular cultural period. The development of cultural changes over time creates fractures and disjunctions between different development phases at their zones of contact (Conzen 1988). Thus, historical data such as chronologies are independent sources to demonstrate the validity of such analysis.

Morphological studies of settlements are distinct from other contemporary approaches that use models, such as the "ceremonial center" (Wheatley 1971) for ancient cities and concentric ordering of medieval or pre-industrial cities (Sjoberg 1960) because the morphological approach does not proceed from paradigm constructs of the settlement under investigation. Instead, the morphological approach is only a method of drilling and analysis of physical data. The material brought to the surface through drilling determines what the results of the study will be. The analysis may indicate whether the material was part of a ceremonial center, a palace-centered hierarchy, a segregated settlement with a class hierarchy, a market town, or some other complex form brought about by changes in different historical periods.

Study Area

Although Patan houses one of the World Heritage Sites of the Kathmandu Valley, namely the Patan Palace, and is considered as one of the earliest cities founded in the valley, there has been no substantial research that focuses on the planning or developmental history of the city. The present study explores Patan in light of our existing knowledge of the Kathmandu Valley towns using the methodological approaches of urban history.

Like all other town settlements in the valley that are characteristically situated on a higher terrace over a river basin, Patan is located in a plateau south of the Bagmati River that flows from the middle of the valley in a northeast to southwest direction. The plateau, which is elongated in a north-south direction, is a spur between two tributaries of the Bagmati, that form the eastern and western sides of the spur. The spur has a widened head giving a conspicuous bend to the Bagmati (Figs. 1-7). The plateau was irrigated by a canal which drew water from the Nakkhu (Prabhavati), the western tributary of the Bagmati, which also provided water for Patan's water fountains through a system of reservoirs and underground channels, a legacy from ancient times.

The northern edge of the plateau is about 30 meters above the river basin, but it gradually rises as one moves southward. Historical records and legends suggest that Patan is located on what was once a major north-south trading route going into Tibet. The route linked Patan with the settlements north of the Bagmati such as Deupatan (Sanskrit: Devapattan) and Vishalnagara, which is thought to have been a Licchavi capital at one time, and then to the northeast region of the Kathmandu Valley and beyond to Tibet. Towards the south, the route connects a number of village settlements, most of which existed by the Licchavi period (Vajracharya 1968). Patan and the settlements east of it were linked to the old town of Kathmandu in the northwest by direct routes running across the northern edge of the plateau. The historic city area of Patan is located at the eastern part of the spur overlooking the Bagmati River, and where the above two routes pass through.

The street structure of Patan features two main streets that cross almost at the centre of the city and deviate about 20 degrees clockwise from cardinal directions. The existing palace of Patan occupies a quarter right at the crossing of these main streets. The quarter block at the northwest of the existing palace is said to be the palace site of a prehistoric ruling dynasty of Kirata (Fig. 1-8). The four stupas at the periphery of the old town are located on the main streets crossing the city center and leading to the outlying regions of Patan. In medieval times, the city had gates at its boundaries, some of which still remain. These gates are also the markers of the old city's perimeter. While the expansion of Patan in modern times has extended it beyond its old boundaries to the new metropolitan area of Kathmandu, the old city area is distinct in both of its social and physical features from the surrounding new developments. The old city is a dense cluster of dwellings arranged around courtyards (Pl. 1-1 and Fig. 1-9). The community clusters of clans that may be identified with a traditional occupation are still distinct. Although modifications to traditional dwellings have led to replacing traditional tiled roofs

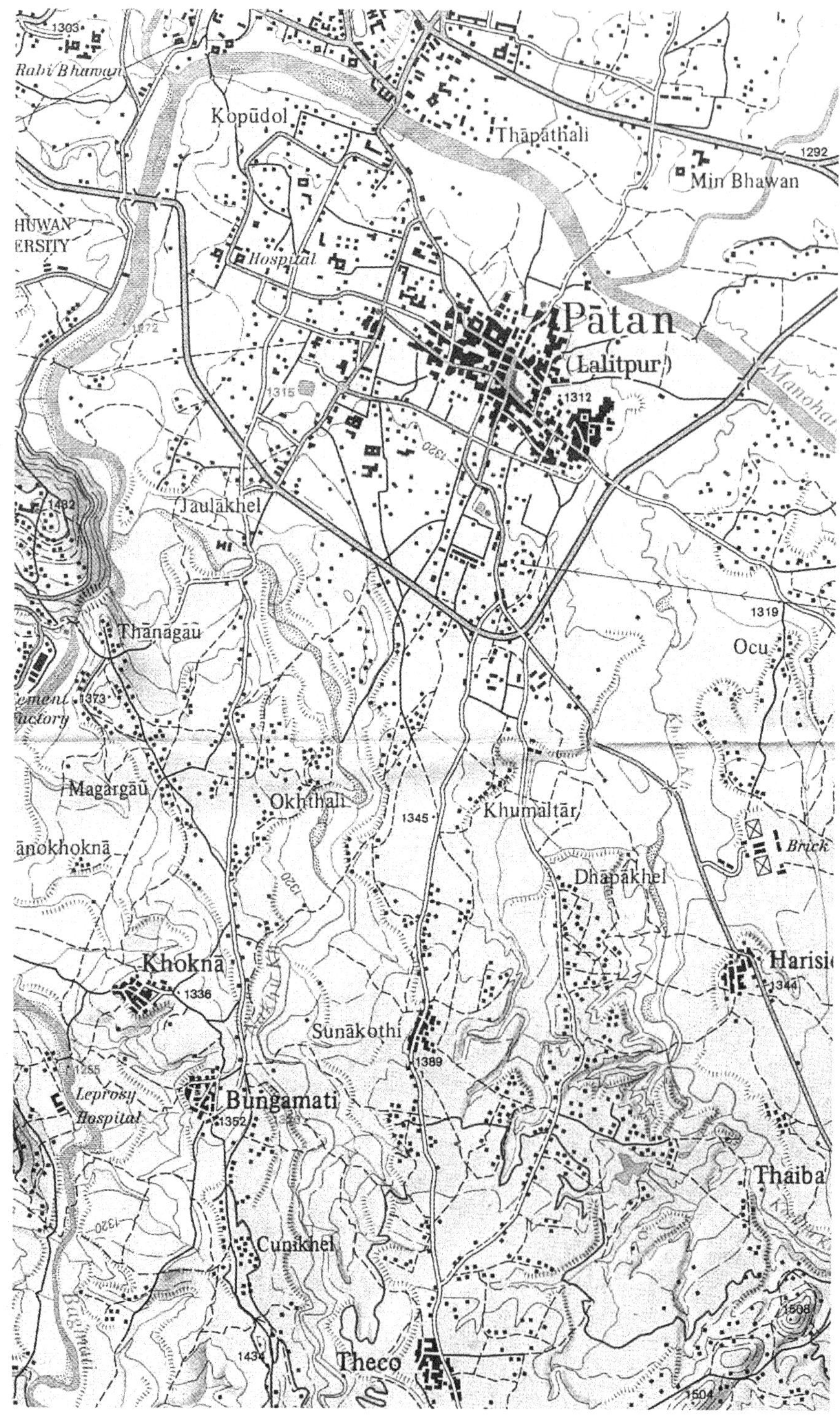

Fig. 1-7. The terrain of Patan Plateau

Fig. 1-8. Patan City

with flat concrete roofs, the physical fabric of Patan has not undergone changes that are characteristic in situations where large-scale redevelopment occur in core city areas. Development in modern times has neither erased nor added a single major lane in any quarter of the city. However, it is possible that the construction of new dwellings and courtyards has blocked some internal access lanes, which connect the open courts of housing clusters, or has resulted in new internal access lanes as studies of Thimi have shown (Pant and Funo 2001b).

Numerous existing quarters of Patan are identified by Licchavi period inscriptions, the earliest of which in Patan is of the fifth century. Three water fountains from the Licchavi period are still functioning in their respective localities.[7] Religious artifacts, such as *caitya* (Buddhist shrines) and images of the deities from this period, are found in both Buddhist and Hindu temples found in numerous quarters and squares of the city. A seventeenth century court poet, Kunu Sharma, describes the city as composed of 24 neighborhoods. Since the neighborhoods still exist with the names mentioned by Sharma, the old city area had been formed already by that time (Sharma 1961). The present layout of the city goes further back in time when one considers that the 35 main vihara, most of which existed

Pl. 1-1. Aerial photograph of Patan (Dept. of Land Survey 1979)

Fig. 1-9. Built up area of historic core of Patan redrawn from Cadastral Survey Map (Dept. of Land Survey 1979)

by the twelfth century, are distributed in all quarters of the city (Chap. 2).

Patan was called Lalitabruma and Lalitakrama in land deed documents from medieval times. The suffixes, *-bruma* and *-krama,* were used to denote the whole town area in these documents (Kolver and Sakya 1985), but the name Lalitabruma was more commonly used than Lalitakrama. The suffix, *-bruma,* is of non-Sanskrit origin. It is older than the suffix, *-krama,* which some scholars consider to be a Sanskrit form of *-bruma.* Numerous localities preserve names of non-Sanskrit origin, which scholars consider to be the legacy of the Kirata, the prehistoric dynasty preceding the Licchavi who used Sanskrit as their official language.

Population of Patan is as diverse as that of other major cities. The Jyapu, one of the Newar communities, comprise the major part of Patan's population followed by the Vajracharya and Sakya. The Jyapu also constitute the majority population in other towns of the valley as well.[8] In Patan, Buddhism is the common faith of all these communities. Traditionally the majority of Jyapu were farmers while the Vajracharya and Sakya served as priests and engaged in making jewelry and religious arts and crafts.

The existing pattern of settlement in all Newar communities shows dwellings organized in contiguous clusters along streets and lanes and around courtyards. Detailed studies can show specific forms in the settlement structure of each of the three above-mentioned communities, but Newar culture generally prevails and characterizes Patan as a typical traditional Newar urban settlement. The present study of Patan will focus on the Jyapu, Vajracharya, and Sakya communities and their respective pattern of settlements that give shape to Patan city.

Method of Research

The study of urban ritual is a fertile ground to understand the urbanism of the Kathmandu Valley towns. This area remains far from exhausted if one considers the diversity of the innumerable festivals that color the months, seasons, and years of the valley. Nevertheless, the approach is limited when describing the city in physical terms. It is unable to give a diachronic perspective due to a lack of historic documentation. Notwithstanding the considerable past research, our question about the planning principles of Patan has remained unanswered.

We were led to this question from our earlier work on Patan and other towns in the Kathmandu Valley, particularly Thimi, a town located five kilometers east of Patan (Pant, 2002). The study on Thimi analyses the ritual of ancestral worship called dewali and the festival of the town goddess in conjunction with the morphological analysis of the settlement. It has brought forth a number of findings on the social and spatial structure of the town, one of which was the discovery of the planning module employed in the layout of the settlement. The module was based on a system of measure described in the Arthasastra of Kautilya who lived in the fourth century BCE. The Thimi study demonstrated for the first time an unambiguous instance of town planning used in the Kathmandu Valley towns during ancient and medieval times. At present, Thimi has a population of around 20,000 in an area of less than one square kilometer. The social and spatial structures of larger, older cities such as Patan, are naturally more complex. The research on Thimi, however, provided a new tool for analyzing other towns in the valley like Patan.

This study primarily makes use of a morphological analysis of the physical fabric of the city to examine the unit of measures, modules, and spatial configurations in the organization of a settlement. It analyzes the spatial structure of the city at different levels—the town and its periphery, town settlement, settlement block, settlement quarter, dwelling plot, and palace and monastery courtyard. The precincts of Hindu and Hindu-Buddhist temples, however, are not included within the scope of present study.

In the analysis of the division of the settlement blocks and patterns of street grids, this study explores a methodology that attempts to explain the existing complex network of streets that do not appear to be in a planned and regular geometric order. This methodology has been developed on a concept, which in this study is referred to as "grid topography" and which has been useful in identifying historic layers and spatial links between different sectors of the town and its periphery.

Our study demonstrates that the city was planned using Patan's four large peripheral stupas as pivots. The city is oriented to the five main mountain summits around the Kathmandu Valley, four of which are sacred Buddhist sites. The swastika, one of the sacred symbols in Buddhist traditions, is employed in the configuration layout of the town at different hierarchical levels. This finding confirms the relevance of the legend about the arrival and meditation of prehistoric Buddhas on the five mountains and the oral tradition that the city is in the form of the dharmacakra, the Buddhist Wheel of Law.

In the end because of the Patan's great age and its connection to the ancient system of measure, our curiosity about whether or not such planning methods existed in other areas pushed the inquiry further back in time. Here again we have the background accounts of chronicles (Chap. 2) about the communities of the Kathmandu Valley that connect them to ancient centers of civilization in the Gandhara region and Indus Valley. We examined Taxila, a town that flourished during the second half of the first millennium CE. A considerable amount of material about this town is available from John Marshall's excavation of the city from 1911 to 1932. Taxila was also the town where Kautilya is said to have worked in fourth century BCE. A preliminary study following our findings on Thimi suggested the possibility of a link between Taxila and the towns of the Kathmandu Valley. This investigation led us further back to Mohenjodaro, so far known as the earliest planned city, and other towns of the Indus civilization that flourished in the third millennium BCE. Some of the conclusions of this investigation are reported in Pant and Funo (2005).

Taxila and Mohenjodaro are the two early cities on the Indian subcontinent for which considerable data is available. There are maps and drawings as well as extensive literature pertaining to diverse aspects of the Indus civilization. An analysis of these materials shows that the planning modules employed in the Kathmandu Valley were also used in the Indus city of Mohenjodaro, and later in Taxila.

This book is divided into five parts. The first part introduces the general historical background of the Kathmandu Valley towns, particularly on the events and documents related to town planning. The second part presents case studies describing the social and spatial structure of two community groups—the Vajracharya-Sakya and the Jyapu community. The third part focuses on the system of measure and planning modules at different levels of the urban spatial hierarchy from the planning of settlement quarters to the analysis of columns in *bahil*, one of the two main types of Buddhist monastery in the Kathmandu Valley. The fourth part studies the planning grid of the town and its peripheral farmland. Finally, the fifth part—the Appendices—compares our research findings on the Kathmandu Valley towns with the planning traditions of Sirkap in Gandhara and the Indus city, Mohenjodaro.

An explanation on the survey data utilized in this study is necessary. One of the primary data sources used in the present study is the cadastral map of Patan's city area made in 1979 by Nepal's Department of Land Survey and Management, and drawn in a 1 : 500 scale. Others include an unpublished 1 : 2000 scale map of the valley settlements done by the United Nations Development Program in 1975[9] made available from the Department of Land Survey and Management and Finsterwalder's 1 : 7500 scale map of Patan (1980) and his 1 : 50,000 scale map of the valley (1989). Aerial photographs, made by the Department of Land Survey and Management, HMG of Nepal in 1978, have also been used in conjunction with the above survey maps. In the study of Buddhist monasteries and Patan Palace, we utilized measured drawings published in scale of 1 : 200 made by the Nippon Institute of Technology. We crosschecked all these data during our fieldwork. In addition to these drawings and maps, we surveyed the distribution of the Jyapu, Vajracharya, and Sakya communities in Patan and neighborhood boundaries including detailed physical plans of the areas selected for the study. Our chronological data come from published work, particularly Vajracharya (1973) for the Licchavi period and Locke (1985) for Buddhist monasteries. For the medieval period, primary sources are *Palm Leaf Documents from Rudravarna Mahavihara, Patan* by Kolver and Sakya (1985) and *Abhilekha*[10] which is regularly published by the Department of Archaeology of Nepal, and Vajracharya (1999) for medieval inscriptions.

The data from our own survey work and those drawn from other sources for the purpose of analytical study constitute primary data that may be independently verified. However, occasional epigraphic errors in the transcription of the age-old documents cannot be ruled out. The discussions in the chapters that follow naturally cross the boundaries of the survey data, but the authors believe that the research work and its findings are essentially built on and explained by these materials.

A Note on The System of Measure

Measurement data and their analysis constitute the backbone of this study. All the measurements in the drawings are given in metric measures. However, to meaningfully analyze the use of particular dimensions in planning or construction of a city, it is necessary to relate the metric values to the prevailing system of measurement. Historical documents on transactions of the sale of houses in the Kathmandu Valley always give measurements in units of *hasta* (cubit) and its division *angula* (digit).[11] The system of measure based on hasta and angula is ancient. The Puranas, which devote chapters treating architecture and sculpture, all give measurement units in hasta and aṅgula. Probably the most ancient text so far that mentions this system is the Arthasastra of Kautilya from the fourth century BCE (Kangle 1972). The system can be traced further back to Panini, the celebrated Sanskrit grammarian of the fifth century BCE (Agrawala 1953).

In this system of measure, there are larger units that are multiples of hasta—*danda, rajju, goruta* and *yojana*. There are a number of problems in making a correct correspondence between metric measure and the hasta standard. One difficulty is that a hasta measured in aṅgula varies according to the type of the hasta standard. Depending upon the documentary source, other higher multiples such as danda and rajju also vary in their length with respect to hasta units (Dutta 1995, 40; Nakagawa and Tsuchiya 2000; Tiwari, 2002, 203 and Raju and Mainkar, 1963, 1964). A second difficulty is the uncertainty of the width of the aṅgula itself.

The Manasara and Mayamata are two texts that deal exclusively with architecture, town planning and sculpture and devote a chapter on measurement units. The Manasara according to Acharya (1979) is a work of the period between the fifth and seventh centuries CE while Dagen (1985) assigns the composition of the Mayamata to some time between the ninth and twelfth centuries. Both of these works mention four types of hasta—*sishu hasta, prajapatya hasta, dhanurmusthi hasta*, and *dhanurgraha hasta* with lengths from 24 to 27 aṅgula respectively. This differs from the Arthasastra, which mentions prajapatya hasta, dhanurgraha hasta and dhanurmushti hasta to be 24, 28 and 32 aṅgula respectively. It also mentions another hasta of 54 aṅgula for the measurement of forest produce. Further,

according to the Arthasastra, 4 *aratni* (hasta) make 1 danda, 1 *dhanusa*, 1 *nalika*, and 1 *paurusa* for householders. A *paurusa* of 84 aṅgula is also given for measuring moats. This paurusa is also a measure for the fire altars. Again 108 aṅgula make one *dhanusa*, a standard measure for roads and city walls. It is also to be noted that Kautilya treats danda, dhanusa, nalika, and paurusa as synonyms to when they are related to a householder.

On the other hand, the Manasara recommends the dhanurgraha hasta and prajapatya hasta for other kinds of mansions, the dhanurmusthi for monuments, and the *kishku hasta* for all kinds of objects. It states that 4 dhanurmushti hasta make 1 danda, and 8 danda make a rajju. But then dhanurgraha hasta is given for the planning of villages and towns suggesting a danda of 108 aṅgula for this purpose. Thus, according to both the Arthasastra and Manasara, the scales are relative to the kind of object measured.

However, when the statements of the Manasara and Arthasastra are taken together, 108 aṅgula make one danda (dhanusa) for the planning of settlements. The number of aṅgula units for the four different hasta given in the Mayamata accord with the Manasara.

The next multiple of danda is rajju. The Manasara notes a rajju is 8 danda while it is 10 danda in the Arthasastra. The Arthasastra, in addition, gives two other units, paridesha and nivartana with their sides of two and three rajju respectively. These units are not mentioned in the Manasara and Mayamata.

Raju and Mainkar (1963; 1964) have discussed at length various standards of measure mentioned in the ancient texts and compared them with the existing traditional standards in the context of commercial scales prevalent in South India. The authors, estimating the width of añgula from measurements of 20 individuals' fingers, relate the data to the prevalent commercial scales that measured in average about 49.8 cm, which is said to be the 'dhanurgraha hasta' of 28 añgula mentioned in the Arthasastra. While the authors thus suggest the possibility of using of the standards mentioned in the Arthasastra, the argument becomes difficult in the context where the measure of an añgula itself is varyingly suggested anywhere from 17 mm to 30 mm (Raju and Mainkar 1964).

Notwithstanding this variability in the traditional system of measures, the study of Thimi suggested a possible link with the system mentioned in the Arthasastra. In this study, the measures in metric dimensions are analyzed to examine if they could be related to such ancient systems of measure. It was discovered that the modular measures found in the division of farm plots, settlement blocks and width of streets did accord with a system of danda, rajju and paridesha

mentioned in the Arthasastra if a danda is assumed to be 1.92 m. The study of Patan also agrees with this where further detailed studies show the division of a danda into 4 hasta and a hasta into 27 añgula.

Various authors have suggested the length of a hasta that ranges from 41 cm to 71 cm depending upon the context of analysis (Raju and Mainkar 1963, 1964; Dutta 1995, 40; Nakagawa and Tutsiya, 2000; Tiwari 2002, 203). However, taking together the measurement standards given by the Arthasastra, Manasara, and Mayamata and comparing them with the modular measures of Thimi and Patan, we consider the description of the Arthasastra relevant to our study.

In this system of measure, a hasta is 48 cm. This value is close to the results of some of the other studies including that of Raju and Mainkar (1963) and Rangarajan (1992). Watanabe (1998b) and Kurotsu (1998a) suggest a cubit of 42.06 cm was employed in the planning of the Buddhist monastery, I baha-bahi, in Patan. This value corresponds to a sishu

Table 1-1. Correspondence of hasta system of measures to metric standard

		Units (hasta system)	*Units (metric)*
Hasta standards	Sishu hasta (h)	24 añgula	42.7 cm
	Prajapatya hasta	25 añgula	44.5 cm
	Dhanurmusthi hasta	26 añgula	46.2 cm
	Dhanurgraha hasta (H)	27 añgula	48.0 cm
Multiples of hasta (H)	1 danda (d)	108 añgula (4 H)	192 cm
	1 rajju (r)	10 danda	9.60 m
	1 paridesha	2 rajju	19.20 m
	1 nivartana	3 rajju	57.60 m
	sata hasta (s)	100 hasta	48.00 cm
Areal measures	1 paridesha	2 rajju × 2 rajju	
	1 nivartana	3 rajju × 3 rajju	

hasta when derived from our standard where 24 añgula make one sishu-hasta thus giving 42.7 cm as its length and accords with the result of Pant's study of dwelling sizes of Thimi (Pant 2002). On the other hand Nakagawa and Tsuchiya (2000) find a unit (cubit) of 48.5 cm to have been used in Northern and Southern Libraries of Angkor Wat.

Table 1-1 shows the metric equivalent of various units in the hasta system to aid the readers as a ready reference to the measurement analysis in this study of Patan. In addition to the measurement units described in the Arthasastra, the table gives a unit of 100 hasta (dhanurgraha hasta) that this study finds to be significant in the division of settlement blocks of the town. It should be noted that the relationship given in this table is one of the aspects the present study will examine in detail.

2

Patan: Legends and History

The documented history of the settlement of the Kathmandu Valley begins from the fifth century when we begin to find inscriptions on stele that primarily record the administrative edicts of the rulers.[1] Literary information on the settlement and culture of the valley prior to this period are the accounts of the chronicles and Puranas.[2] These sources along with linguistic evidence from the later records of epigraphs, and works from art history and archaeology point towards extensive settlement activities in the valley during the early centuries of the Christian Era. The chronicles write that the valley in the prehistoric period was ruled by a number of dynasties in succession. They belonged to the Naga, Gopala, Mahisapala, and Kirata. The migration of other communities into the valley continued in later periods of which the Licchavi and Malla became politically prominent in ancient and medieval Nepal. Licchavi and Malla republics were also known in North India by the time of Gautam Buddha while the rule of Naga

clans are recorded in the Puranas and historic documents (Joshi 1998, 38-45).

Cultural historians, taking note of historical evidence and accounts in the chronicles, are unanimous that the Newar community, as we know today, is an amalgam of various ancient ethnic tribes that settled in the valley from prehistoric times. The most prominent of these tribes were the Kirata. Gopalarajavamsabali, a fourteenth century chronicle states that the Kirata came to the valley from east. Now they inhabit in the eastern hills of Nepal (Vajracharya and Malla 1985, folio 18, 74). Ancient inscriptions also mention the Kirata by name and suggest their habitation of the valley (Vajracharya 1973, 374). In addition, a number of legends and rituals suggest the presence of the Kirata not only as a historical event but also as a deeply rooted culture presence in the valley. The Kirata are still one of the major ethnic communities of Nepal, and scholars are of the opinion that the Newar have a genealogical link with the Kirata of ancient times. In addition to the historical links, often-cited evidence is the similarity of the physical structure between the two communities and their language. The Kirata belong to a Mongoloid stock, and the facial structure of the Newar also reveals Mongoloid or Mongoloid-aryan features. And, the Newari language also belongs to the Sino-Tibetan family.

The Kathmandu Valley continued to be the seat of the capital for all the dynasties both in later historical periods as well as in prehistoric times. Linguistic studies of the place names and the accounts of the chronicles suggest that early settlements were situated in the higher hills but later moved to the lower river basins (Vajracharya 1968). The pattern of settlement of moving towards the valley basin recalls the legend of the draining of the valley lake[3] and the beginning of agriculture at later periods (Poudel 1963, 85).

According to the chronicles, the change of rulers or dynasties was often accompanied by a shift of the ruling court from one place to another. The last pre-historic dynasty of the Kirata is also said to have moved its palace to a number of places within the valley. Among the three principal cities that have been Nepal's capital at various times, the chronicles identify Patan as having the closest association with the Kirata. Place names, rituals, and legends also suggest a connection between the inhabitants of Patan and the Kirata of the past.[4] While there is no available archaeological evidence to suggest the time span of the Kirata rule, historians estimate that their rule may have covered as much as a millennium going back to seventh or eighth century prior to the beginning of the Licchavi period.

As we move further back in time from the Kirata period, we have to take note of legends in the Puranas that are retold in later chronicles. These accounts often move freely between the spiritual world of deities and historic reality weaving myth and historic incidents together. The description become increasingly sketchy as the periods they record recede into the distance. Nevertheless, these chronicles' accounts provide the only source of information about the prehistory of the Kathmandu Valley. Further, modern historical research has demonstrated the value of texts like the chronicles, which contain grains of truth even if they are not always precise in identifying the time and historical persons related to remote events (Vajracharya and Malla 1985, xi). With limited archaeological information, we probably cannot ignore these sources if we wish to construct the prehistoric past using sources from the Kathmandu Valley. Therefore, it is relevant to review the chronicles' legends about the people and settlement of the valley for clues that connect the people and the city of Patan with their past and with the wider geographical region.

The Prehistoric Period: Creation Myths of the Valley

The chronicles describe the Kathmandu Valley as originally being a lake, and it is the creation myths about this lake that reveal the connection between faith, festivals, and settlements in the valley. The accounts are told to show the greatness of the two primary cult centers of Nepal–Swayambhu Stupa, a Buddhist religious centre and Pashupatinath Temple of the Saiva cult.

Fig. 2-1.　Kathmandu Valley: Swayambhu and surrounding mountain summits

The Buddhist legend states that four Buddhas preceding Siddhartha Gautam visited the Nepal Valley.[5] The first was Vipaswi Buddha who came from Vandhumati nagar to the valley during Satyayuga (the Age of Truth). The valley was then known as Nagadaha, the lake of the Naga (the holy serpents). Vipaswi Buddha built a shelter for meditation on a hill, Jama-cho (Jatamatroca in present-day Nagarjun), northwest of the lake. He sowed a lotus seed in the lake. The lotus bloomed after six months, and Swayambhu, the Self-born, became a glowing light in the calyx of the blooming lotus.

On hearing of Swayambhu's birth, Sikhi Buddha came from Arunapura during the same age, and prayed to and meditated on the Self-born in a shelter he built on Dhyano-cha (present-day Champadevi), a mountain southwest of the lake. He then incorporated himself into the divine light of Swayambhu.

Later in Tretayuga, the next age following Satyayuga, Viswabhu Buddha came from Anupam nagara and lived on Phuloccha (present-day Phulchoki [Newari: Phu-cho] at the southeast of the valley) to pray and meditate (Fig. 2-1). Viswabhu told his disciples of the coming of Manjusri and the draining of Nagadaha. He then returned to Anupam nagara.

Following Vishwabhu in the same age, Manjusri Bodhisatva came to the valley from Mahachina and lived on Mahamandala (present-day Manjusri-sthan), a hill located east of Bhaktapur in Nagarkot to devote himself to Swayambhu. He then settled his two consorts, Varada and Moksyada, on two mountains (Phuloccha and Dhyano-cha) and himself on a lower hill at the southern part of the lake. He studied the geography of the lake and drained its waters by cutting a gorge through Katuwal, a hill at the southwest corner of the valley, thus making the land suitable for habitation. He settled a town named Manjupattan between present-day Swayambhu and Guyhesvari, a sacred site at the eastern part of the valley. Krakucchanda Buddha visited the valley with his disciples during the next age, Dvapar. He built his shelter on Satarudra Mountain (present-day Sivapuri) to the north of the valley and meditated on the Lord Swayambhu. He created the Bagmati River to draw sacred water needed to ordain his disciples (Wright 1972). Besides the four Buddhas mentioned above and Manjusri Bodhisattva, three other human Buddhas are mentioned in the legend as having visited the valley–Kanakamuni, Kasyapa, and Siddhartha Gautam.

On the summits of Nagarjun, Champadevi, Phulchoki, and Sivapuri, annual festivals are held to commemorate the key events related to the visits of the Buddhas and their parts in the Buddhist creation myth of the Nepal Valley.

The above legend conveys the message that Buddhism is at the heart of the beginning of civilization in the Kathmandu Valley. On the other hand the Hindu legend, Pradhyumna-Prabhavati, describes Krishna as draining the valley and making it fit for habitation.[6] This legend relates his heroic acts in which he defeated the Naga ruler, Danasur, and established the rule of his followers, the Gopala (the cowherd clans), in the Nepal Valley.

The two legends seem to present contradictory creation myths about the Kathmandu Valley. The Buddhist legend presents the coming of Buddhism as the beginning of civilization in the Kathmandu Valley while the Hindu legend, as related in the Nepala Mahatmya, hails the arrival of Krishna and the Gopala in Nepal and the defeat of Naga as the beginning of civilization. Although each legend has reshaped the events of history reflecting the influence of different religious faiths that have existed in Nepal since prehistoric times, we find accounts in these legends that can be fruitfully examined for a better understanding of the settlement of the valley.

A comparison of the sequences of ruling tribes in the Buddhist and Hindu legends shows them describing same events. Both legends list the prehistoric tribal rulers of the Kathmandu Valley in the following order–Naga, Gopala, Mahisapala, and Kirata, and the legends herald the Licchavi as the first historic rulers of Nepal.[7] The Naga and Kirata tribes inhabited the hills and mountains south of the Himalayas all the way from Kashmir to Burma and Cambodia. One Naga tribe is said to have ruled the city of Taxila (Takshasila) in Gandhara (present-day Uttarpradesh) (Dani 1999). The Gopala (the cowherd clan) and the Mahisapala (the buffalo-herd clan) originally belonged to the same tribe, and they are thought to have flourished in the plains of Sindhu, the Indus River (Nepal 1998, 18). Their primogenitor, Krishna, originally lived in Mathura in Gandhara, but he later moved to Dwaraka (West Gujarat). The name "Nepala" is said to be derived from the Nipa tribe who belonged to the Gopala clan.[8] Historians think that the Nipa tribe migrated to the Kathmandu Valley from southern Indus Valley crossing the Churia hills and following the Mahabharat range in the foothills of the Himalayas.[9]

Following the Naga and Gopala, the Kirata become the next prominent group in prehistoric Nepal. The Gopalaraja-vamsavali lists 32 Kirata rulers who governed Nepal from the eighth century BCE to the second century CE. During this period, the Nepal Valley was already a melting pot of various communities—Naga, Kirata, Gopala, Mahisapala, Abhira, Sakya, and Koliya. Except for the Naga, all other communities are known from ancient Nepalese stone inscriptions. These communities were non-Aryan, and their habitation and cultural inter-actions encompassed Indus and Gangetic plains. For example, the Mahabharata mentions the cooperation between the Kirata and Pandava in the war against the Kaurava. Buddhist sources, such as the Mulasarvastivadi vinaya, describe the visits of itinerant merchants to the valley and religious personages like Ananda, one of the two main disciples of Gautam Buddha (Acharya 1997, 16). The Arthasastra of Kautilya (the prime minister of Chandragupta) during fourth century BCE notes woolen and herbal products coming from Nepal. The style of religious images found in the Kathmandu Valley resemble images from the Mathura and

Gandhara schools of art that flourished during the Kushana era (first to third centuries CE) suggesting a close, ongoing relationship between these two areas.[10]

The legends also tell us something about the settlement of the Kathmandu Valley. The Gopala initially inhabited the higher elevations of the valley's western rim in places such as Kirtipur and Thankot. During the Kirata rule, the chronicles note that the site of the ruling court within the Kathmandu Valley changed from one place to another with Patan as the last palace site. The chronicles also note that Nepal's first planned town, Vishalanagara in the northeast section of the Kathmandu Valley, was an expan-sion of the legendary town Manjupattan credited to Manjusri himself.[11] However, we get little detail about the town's layout except that it extended from the Bagmati River in the south to Sivapuri, a mountain to the north. Archaeological excavations around Hadigaon in Vishalnagar have shown bricks from the second century BCE with indications to settlement planning (Verardi 1988). Religious artifacts, such as images of Srilaxmi and Gajalaxmi, belonging to the period from the second century BCE to the pre-Licchavi period have been found in Patan (Bangadel 1982).

The most ancient event related to the building of a town is probably the story related to Sarvananda. A chronicle men-tions that there was a city named Dipavati where a virtuous king, Sarvananda, known to be one of the previous incarnations of Buddha, lived (Wright 1972, 87–8). He built a vihara adjacent to his palace for *bhikshu* (monks) and a caitya in front. This legendary place is now remem-bered in rituals and is the name of a neighborhood in the east of Patan. There exist two stupas at east and at north in axis with the monastery courtyards at the boundary of the neighborhood, a pattern that is not found in other areas of the city.

The four stupas of Patan could belong to this prehistoric period, which according to the chronicles are monuments built in memory of Asoka's visit to the Nepal Valley. Researchers have not yet ascertained when the four stupas of Patan and other well-known stupas in the Kathmandu Valley were first built and what their original purposes were. But, the presence of such early religious artifacts, such as stupas and statues of mother goddesses, have led scholars to generally agree that the valley inhabitants followed Saivism (a religion based on the cult of Siva), Buddhism, and the mother goddess cult during the Kirata period.

Although no written documents of the Kirata period have been found to shed light on their social system during the prehistoric period, the legacy of the Kirata rule continued to live until modern times. Their presence is reflected in the Licchavi dynasty's preservation of Kirata names for the valley's geographical features, settlements, the administration system, and even the titles of officials.[12] Although we do not have specific information on the pattern of settlements or their planning principles, we can assume that the society of that period was familiar with the idea of town planning since their contact with areas such as Pataliputra, Vaishali, Mathura, and the Indus Valley are amply demonstrated from ancient literature and religious artifacts. On the other side, their contact with the northern region is reflected by their legends, language, and physiognomy.

The Early Historical Period: The Licchavi Dynasty (Fifth to Ninth Centuries CE)

Although historians have not yet been able to confirm the exact end of the Kirata dynasty and beginning of the Licchavi dynasty, it is generally accepted that the Kirata dynasty yielded to the Licchavi sometime around the second century, but the Licchavi regnal period and activities appear in history only from the fifth century. The Licchavi's arrival did not push the Kirata heritage into oblivion. Their rise in Nepal, however, formally introduced Sanskrit and Brahmanic culture as shown by the official court language and script of the period. Scholars are of the opinion that the Licchavi themselves were of Mongoloid stock and belonged to the Kirata tribe, but had adopted the Hindu *varna* system that differentiated social classes in a rigid hierarchical structure (Joshi 1998). The maintenance of the Kirata administrative system and titles may reflect the Licchavi's closeness to the Kirata, or else it could be a superior administrative system, which the Licchavi found advantageous to preserve.

During the Licchavi period, events concerning town settlement become more frequent in the accounts of the chronicles. More details on the nature of artifacts, places, and their contexts are given, which can be compared with other historical references. Probably the earliest accounts about town settlement concern the building of Devapattan by Sivadeva near Pashupatinath in the eastern part of the Kathmandu Valley. We have two accounts that describe the extension of settlement in Patan. The first of this account states that

This king (Amsuvarma) following the palace of Devapattan (at the east of Kathmandu), began to build a town (*vamanagar*) by clearing the suvarna-forest in the area called Lagankhel south of Sankhamul (at the bank of the Bagmati). In this town, beautifully built with a palace, he settled ministers, officials and commoners by building houses according to their ranks. And he himself also lived in the same town. The city was thus populated with twelve thousand inhabitants ... and following the advice of Brahmana astrologers established a shrine to Batuka Bhairava nearby the palace following Vedic, Tantric and Buddhist rituals (Poudel 1963, 84–5 [Our translation]).

This chronicle describes Amsuvarma as the nephew (*bhanij*) of Sivadeva (512–526/535CE), a Licchavi ruler, whose kingdom he inherited. It also describes him as loving grammar. Both these attributes accord with historical records. The Lagankhel area is the southern part of Patan, where there is an ancient shrine to Batuka Bhairav with an inscription dating from 665.[13]

The second account describes the extension of the town towards the north by the second ruler after Amsuvarma:

King Viradeva consulting Brahman astrologers and Bauddha pundits expressed his strong desire to build a city extending to Sankhamul at the south bank of the Bagamati River. He had employed a grass-cutter named Lalita to tend his horse. Lalita was a man of great talent, and he earned the respect of the king and the love of the queen, and rose to become a great personality. Lalita was thus given the chief responsibility to plan and settle a town after clearing the forest, Lalita-

ban. Lalita accepted this responsibility and choosing an auspicious hour began to build the town. The king spent a great amount of money, and a city was formed by joining the older town of Matilinagara and the new town with its nine thousand dwellings. The city was then marked by five mounds. Because the city was built according to the standards of sastras (authoritative texts) by clearing the forest known as Lalita-ban, the city was formally named Lalitapura. It is also said that the city takes this name from its chief planner, Lalita. Then, in the reign of this king, twelve chariots of the gods including that of Minanatha and Lokanatha were built and an annual chariot festival to these gods was instituted. The festival, incorporating both the old and new tole (neighborhoods), was held from the eleventh day of the bright half of Vaisakh to the full-moon day in order for the gods to grant well-being to the king and townspeople (Lamsal 1966, 1–2 [Our translation]).

The above accounts are particularly interesting because they show that Patan continually expanded from its earlier settlement zones and that the city also had a palace court. Matilinagara is the Matingrama that a Licchavi inscription shows to have been a settlement to the east of the existing palace area.[14] Another important aspect is the mention of its planner, Lalita. In another version of this legend, Lalita is mentioned to be a *jyapu* (farmer). It also describes the construction of a fountain and shrine beside the palace and identifies the palace as Manigal, a name that first appears in historic documents in 1065 (Kolver and Sakya 1985). The Tandukar clan of Patan's Jyapu community presently takes care of the monuments commemorating Lalita and rituals honoring him. We do not know if the term, jyapu, existed by that time or not. At present, however, the Jyapu community constitutes the largest single group within the Newar population of the Kathmandu Valley including Patan. Historians generally agree that it is in the Jyapu community that one should seek the roots of the Kathmandu Valley civilization and its links to the Kirata and Naga. Lalita may well be taken as the symbol of the Kirata's influence on the Licchavi rulers and society at that time.

The continued influence of tribal groups such as the Naga and Kirata in the region and on the court is also illustrated by the fact that the queen of Manadeva, the celebrated fifth century Licchavi king, was from a Naga clan. Such matrimonial ties with the Naga existed in the court of the Gupta rulers of North India as well.[15] Thus, from prehistoric times to the Licchavi period, the indigenous Naga and Kirata tribes did not lose their hold on the Nepal Valley despite changes in the ruling dynasties.

Five mounds mentioned in the above chronicle are also an important feature of the structure of Patan. These mounds, without doubt, point to the existing four stupas at the periphery and one within the settlement area of the city.[16] When we map the boundaries of the earlier town of Matilinagara to the east, Bamanagara to the south, and the area expanded by Lalita, we almost get the outline of the present settlement area that lies within the area marked by the four stupas. Matilinagara's existence is attested by Licchavi period stone inscriptions, which call the area Matingrama. Likewise, the inscription of Rudradeva-Bhojadeva dated 1012 (NS 132) which calls Patan by its earliest name, Lalitapura, indicates the

town's boundaries encompassed all the above settlement clusters (Regmi 1965, 511). On the other hand, Yalan, the Newar community's popular local name for Patan, is also mentioned in official documents of medieval times. It is thought to have been derived from the name of the first Kirata king, Yalambara. Cultural artifacts, toponyms, stone inscriptions, and even the chronicles all indicate that the settlement of Patan goes back at least to the Kirata period.

The four stupas of Patan seem to hide a key to the city's history. Archaeologists have not yet attempted to explore their contents, nor have these stupas been studied from the perspectives of art or architectural history. Some scholars consider them to be a Kirata funerary monument while others regard them as Buddhist monuments marking the founding of Patan.[17] Snellgrove and other researchers point out the similarities between Patan's stupas and other early stupas found in Sanchi and Bharhut, which are thought to be tumuli erected as memorial monuments. In view of the antiquity of these stupas, Snellgrove thinks that

> It is likely therefore that Buddhist communities established themselves in this Valley well before the beginning of the Christian era. It seems also that a very special sanctity was associated with Patan, which at that early period was certainly the chief and perhaps the only settlement there. Four great Stupas were constructed at the four points of the compass and one in the center of the town. All five are still standing and Patan may well claim to be the oldest Buddhist city in the world, which has retained its Buddhist character to the present day. It seems likely also that

the name Patan means a royal city, and remembering what was said above concerning the notion of universal sovereignty in buddhahood, one may well wonder what special associations with the idea of a Buddha caused Patan to be thus singled out.

It is possible of course that the early Buddhist cities of India, Pataliputra, Vaisali, Rajagrha and Sravasti, were marked out with four great stupas in this way; thus the arrangement at Patan would be explained as the recognized sign of a Buddhist city, which had been borrowed from earlier model … (Snellgrove 1957, 93–4).

Snellgrove's view corroborates a popular legend handed down in oral tradition. According to this tradition, the city is said to have been planned in the shape of the dharmacakra, the Buddhist Wheel of Law. However, it reflects, in part, its historic past and to a large extent its present social and spatial structure that centers on Buddhist monasteries. We do not know whether erecting the four stupas was a conscious plan to sanctify the city from its early beginning or they were later foundations. Likewise, it will not be known whether such sacred configurations were also present in early Buddhist cities, such as Vaishali and Rajgriha, unless they are revealed by archaeological research. However, the arrangement of four stupas in four directions to sanctify a city is found as late as the seventeenth century in the city of Shenyang in Northeast China.[18]

The chronicles give an impression that early Licchavi were strong promoters of Buddhism in the Nepal Valley. Brikhadev, the grandfather of Manadeva is given credit for the foundation of the Swayambhu Stupa and the Bauddha Stupa. This king ruled in the fourth century CE, according to inscriptional records. Besides such religious edifices, the Licchavi period is known to be a remarkable age of urban construction. Although there are no documents noting the foundation of a town, land donations by the rulers to Buddhist monasteries and temples, maintenance of canals and fountains are noted in inscriptions that were posted as administrative decrees in relevant localities. However, most of the monasteries of the period remain un-identified making it difficult to connect the existing structures with those ancient institutions. In these matters too, the chronicles are the only source of information to suggest the antiquity of the existing institutions.

The Medieval Period (Thakuri and Malla Periods: Ninth to Eighteenth Centuries CE)

Epigraphic documents such as stone inscriptions in the Thakuri period (ninth to twelfth centuries) suddenly become rare, and this period is still known as the dark age of Nepalese history. Little is known about the development and planning of the towns. However, from the tenth century onward, palm leaf documents on land deeds and manuscripts provide a reliable source of information on the activities of monasteries and a link can be established between currently existing monasteries and those mentioned, in the documents.[19] From these records, we can glean changes in the monastery structure leading towards the Vajrayana period that began a process of change in the relationship of the monastery with the settlements of the common people (Sharma 1997). The documents show that the clergy began to have families, and the vihara began to be the center of family clans.

During this period, exchanges of Buddhist scholars in the region were frequent, and a large number of Buddhist manuscripts were copied in Patan, which found their way into Tibetan monasteries. The Buddhist arts and crafts of Patan were popular both in Nepal and Tibet. The records also show that the majority of the principal vihara in Patan were already established by this period, and the noble class is known to be living in such vihara. The network of these vihara appears to have grown to such an extent that it was a means to administer the city. This can be inferred from the division of the city by the *mahapatra* (feudal lords of Patan) according to the area of vihara (Bhandari 1989, 184).

With the rise of the Malla dynasty in the Kathmandu Valley in the thirteenth century, Sakta, a cult that centers on feminine energy, came into the fore. According to the chronicles, Bhaktapur was sanctified with the establishment of eight mother goddess shrines forming an internal and external ring to protect the settlement. The mother goddess cult in the valley had a prehistoric origin, but by this time, the mother goddesses become the symbol of Bhaktapur and most of the other towns as well (Pant 2002). During the Malla rule, while Tantric Hindu priests officiated in the rituals of the palace, there was a gradual disintegration in the earlier monasteries that followed the celibate *bhiksu* (religious mendicants) tradition. However, Buddhism remained a major faith in the Kathmandu Valley under the new banner

of the Vajrayana sect of Buddhism with festivals and rituals that served not only the family life cycle but also the town and state. The light festival, Mataya, and the festival of Machendranath of Patan are examples of such events. In the latter festival, the Jyapu and Vajracharya play the central role in the ritual pulling of the chariot as well as in conducting and managing the festival. The ritual role of the Jyapu in these two festivals can be interpreted as their link to ancient Kirata and Naga tribes.[20]

Thus, ritual traditions, legends, and history depict Patan as an ancient city with its horizons receding far back into the prehistoric past. The ancestors of its inhabitants belonged to various indigenous communities of the region that extended along the lap of the Himalayan range, towards north and east, and to other tribal communities from the Indus Valley and North Gangetic plain that migrated to the Kathmandu Valley. When legends and historical records are connected to the existing Newar settlements they suggest a preeminence of Buddhist communities that includes the Jyapu community among the Newar. How is this particular history manifested in the form of settlements and cities in the Kathmandu Valley where those inhabitants dwelt and where their descendants continue to live? Patan is a city that continued its existence and development at all periods of the history. This study attempts to answer this question by reading the city like a book to see what it has inherited from the past and what the principles were behind the existing shape of the city.

PART II

The Settlement of Communities

3

Community and Neighborhoods

Patan can be described as a settlement of communities where particular communities inhabit certain sectors of the city. Individual families from these communities belong to a number of traditional organizations that link the residents in a variety of social networks. Such organizations, known as *guthi* (Sanskrit: *gosthi*), are based on territorial propinquity, clan relationships, or membership in a religious association. In each neighborhood, there are a number of shrines or traditional public facilities such as wells, fountains, and community houses that are maintained by a local guthi formed by the local residents. There are also responsibilities associated with traditional festivals and rituals that residents of a locality fulfill through their guthi organizations. These responsibilities often need preparation, training of the young, and economic support from all the residents in the locality. Such community obligations are handed down as family traditions. Therefore, it is the clan relationship that has the most important bearing on the social and spatial organization of Newar town settlements.

In Patan, as in other Newar settlements, one may identify such a clan community group by a common surname. These surnames, in many instances, signify a traditional occupation or indicate a link between the inhabitants at a certain point in the historic past. Sociologists and anthropologists have traditionally described these communities in terms of caste, a division of traditional Hindu society into a social and religious hierarchy. The Bhasavamsabali chronicle notes that caste was codified during the reign of Sthiti Malla in the fourteenth century. The code mentions certain ritual obligations as well as the professional duties of each caste in the socio-religious hierarchy. The long existence of various community groups and classes within Hindu social divisions can be gleaned from Licchavi period inscriptions (Vajracharya 1973, 102–4).[1] We do not know how communities were socially organized prior to the fifth century. We only know of the existence of various ethnic groups such as the Naga, Gopala, Mahisapala, Kirata, Sakya, Koliya, Brijji, and Licchavi during the ancient and prehistoric periods of the Kathmandu Valley. The change in the ruling dynasties, close interaction between the communities, and changing economic fortunes during the course of many centuries dissolved these ethnic identities, and it is difficult to establish a definite link between any of the present day community groups and the ethnic tribes of ancient times since there are no detailed comparative studies of the traditions of these tribes and the existing communities.

Community Distribution

Plate F (see p. xxi) shows the distribution of communities according to the clan structure identified in our survey using the common surname that the residents use in modern times. Around 50 such surnames were identified in the survey. Table 3-1 shows that communities such

Table 3-1. Distribution of Communities, Patan.

	Surnames	No. of dwelling units	%
1	Acharya	9	0.10
2	Amatya	118	1.34
3	Awal	298	3.38
4	Barahi	15	0.17
5	Bhatta	8	0.09
6	Chitrakar	39	0.44
7	Dangol	55	0.62
8	Dhaubadel	3	0.03
9	Jha	11	0.12
10	Joshi	206	2.34
11	Kapali	7	0.08
12	Karanjit	21	0.24
13	Karmacharya	20	0.23
14	Khadgi	263	2.98
15	Khosa	4	0.05
16	Kullu	6	0.07
17	Kusle	2	0.02
18	La	16	0.18
19	Lakhe	11	0.12
20	Maharjan	3086	35.00
21	Malla	10	0.11
22	Manandhar	27	0.31
23	Mishra	13	0.15
24	Mulmi	30	0.34
25	Muslim	8	0.09
26	Nakarmi	27	0.31
27	Napit	29	0.33
28	Nawkhwa	2	0.02
29	Newa	3	0.03
30	Nhyachyo	25	0.28
31	Pradhan	71	0.80
32	Rajak	1	0.01
33	Rajbhandari	54	0.61
34	Rajkarnikar	43	0.49
35	Rajopadhyaya	32	0.36
36	Ranjitkar	9	0.10
37	Sakya	1820	20.67
38	Sharma	46	0.52
39	Shrestha	949	10.77
40	Sikarmi	3	0.03
41	Silpakar	116	1.32
42	Sinya	4	0.05
43	Sthapit	25	0.28
44	Tamrakar	305	3.46
45	Tandukar	52	0.59
46	Thakuri	8	0.09
47	Upadhyaya	1	0.01
48	Vaidya	16	0.18
49	Vajracharya	655	7.44
50	Vyanjankar	219	2.48
	Subtotal	8806	100.00
	Unidentified	903	

as the Maharjan, Shakya, and Vajracharya constitute around 70 per cent of Patan's population. It would not be unreasonable to assume that the present spatial distribution also reflects a picture of the past. This assumption will be further elaborated in the following sections and chapters. Of these diverse clan communities, we focus on the Jyapu community (including the Maharjan), the Vajracharya community, and the Sakya community for reasons that we have explained in preceding chapter and which will become more evident from the case studies that follow.

We know from medieval stone inscriptions and palm leaf documents that most of the surnames of people in the communities we find today were used as titles by the sixteenth century (Sharma 1997, 66; 85–6).[2] However, some surnames, such as Vajracharya, can be traced to honorific titles used in the eleventh century. Sakya, another surname of importance in Patan, is probably linked to Sakyabhikshu, a title used in the tenth century (Sharma 1997, 66; 85–6). Other titles on stone inscriptions represent a person's social status. Some examples are Vaidya 'the doctor,' Sakya-vamsa and Patra-vamsa 'of noble family,' and Amatya 'minister or official of higher rank.' Maharjan (meaning uncertain), a major Jyapu community, is also known to have existed by the sixteenth century. It is noteworthy that until the nineteenth century, present-day surnames were used as titles placed before a name. However, there are rare exceptions when, for instance, we find one Lumadi Vajracharya in a sixteenth century document. Most earlier records also note honorific titles such as "Bharo" at the end of the person's name. Bharo was used for persons belonging to a wide range of social classes—from nobles to craftsmen

of various professions and social statuses. Early medieval documents record this title as "Bhalloka" while some later documents record it as "Bharoka" (Kolver and Sakya 1985).

In general, Vajracharya and Sakya Buddhist clergy have the title, "Jusa," following their names (Kolver and Sakya 1985). There are many instances where the early residents of the present tole with a primarily Maharjan population were addressed as Bhavo in place of their surname (Locke 1985, 56). It thus becomes clear from medieval documents that all surnames in present-day Patan do not represent a family clan, but rather the title of a profession. In Pant's study of Thimi (2002), clans are represented by special surnames called *bina*. The shift of title to surname occurred much later, during the modern period in Patan, when its inhabitants began to use surnames as they do today. Thus, as we trace the history of the clan communities, we observe that the social differentiation commonly described as "caste" in modern times was much more diffused as diverse clan members were addressed by common occupational titles like "Jusa" for Sakya and Vajracharya Buddhist clergy, by general honorifics like "Bharo" for craftsmen as well as nobles, and "Bhavo" for others.

Surnames that probably link back to the Licchavi period are family clan names Varma and Gupta. These were the names of ruling families during the Licchavi period and later in early medieval times when the Varma clan continued to rule. Varma is used as a surname and abounds in early land deed documents that are under the custody of Uku Bahal of Patan (Kolver and Sakya 1985). In these documents Bharo and Varma are also identified as Vaisyas, a merchant or craftsmen class in the four classic divisions of Hindu society that consist of Brahmins (priests), *kshetriya* (warriors), *vaisya* (merchants and craftsmen), and *sudra* (menials). The Varma clans, which had such a notable presence in medieval times, were not found in our survey. The probable reason for this is explained in the section on Buddhist monasteries in Chapter 4. In the same documents, nowhere do we find sudra or kshetriya, the other two classes that indicate the status of the inhabitants, although Brahmins were noted in a few instances.

Different clan communities that practice similar professions or have a parallel social status form a larger community group, which may be called a maximal community.[3] The Jyapu with individual clans, such as the Maharjan, Vyanjankar, and others, is a maximal community. Traditionally maximal communities are endogamous. Thus, the 50 different surnames identified in the present survey of Patan make up a number of maximal communities, the exact number of which needs more detailed inquiry. For the purpose of the present study, the Jyapu community includes the Maharjan, Dangol, Vyanjankar, Awale, and Tandukar. If we align it with the Bhasavamsabali chronicle, which relates each community to its profession, *kisan* 'tenant farmer' most probably refers to the Maharjan who continue to be the major farming population in the valley; *tepe* 'grocer' probably refers to the Vyanjankar who are often grocers; the surname, Dangol, is associated with land surveyors; Kumhal, a common surname among the Awale and Prajapati, means potter and reflects the fact that many Awale now work as brick and tile makers;

Table 3-2. Percentile distribution of three communities—Jyapu, Sakya and Vajracharya, Patan.

Community	Surname	No. of dwelling unit	%
Jyapu	Maharjan	3086	35.00
	Awal	298	3.38
	Vyanjankar	219	2.48
	Dangol	55	0.62
	Tandukar	52	0.59
	Total	3710	42.09
Sakya		1820	20.67
Vajracharya		655	7.44
	Total	6185	70.20

and the surname, Tandukar, is associated with rice cultivators. Present-day Jyapu communities still engage in these traditional occupations which are also mentioned in the chronicle.

In the present grouping of communities the Sakya and Vajracharya belong to one maximal community, but we will refer to them separately because both have sizeable populations in Patan and their own distinct settlement clusters. In the Bhasavamsabali chronicle, the Sakya are *banda* (Sanskrit: *vandhya*) 'metal craft artisans' and the Vajracharya are priests. However, the Vajracharya also practice metal craft, particularly in silver and gold. We can see from Table 3-2 that a majority of the inhabitants of Patan (around 70 per cent) belong to the Jyapu, Sakya, and Vajracharya communities.

Besides the occupational categories, the communities may be further differentiated by patrilineal descent. Such patrilineal groups are called *fuki* in Newari. Members of a fuki are exogamous and have ritual obligations to each other, such as participation in the rites of passage for their members. The ritual obligations are regulated by a number of community trusts known as *guthi*. The guthi system is a ubiquitous social organization that goes back to Licchavi times or even earlier. It binds the Newar to their places of origin and places them in their community's socio-religious hierarchy vis-à-vis a system of elders.

The *si-guthi* or *sana guthi* that organize funerary rituals and *dewali guthi* that organize rites of ancestral worship have the most stringent regulations. Dewali (ancestral worship) is an annual ritual wherein all the residents of the community are obliged to attend and offer worship to their ancestral deities. The features of the buildings and places where these social organizations hold their rituals differ from community to community. For instance, the Jyapu have *chapat* for funeral ceremonies and the dewali sites out in the fields for ancestral worship. The Vajracharya and Sakya have *digi*, halls for community functions in monastic courtyards and caityas are offered worship during their dewali rituals. The Shrestha house their ancestral deities in *agan-chhen* courts, and similarly the Manandhar house their ancestral deities in courtyard wings known as *wanjala*.

In Plate F, we see that each of the communities in Patan clusters around particular areas of the city. Such clusters are identifiable not only in terms of their maximal community but also in terms of their constituent clan communities. For instance, the Maharjan are mainly in the eastern and northern parts of Patan. They are also the primary community in a separate clustered settlement near Pulchok Stupa, a few hundred meters west of the city. The Awale and Vyanjankar live in the northeastern part of Patan while the Sakya and Vajracharya cluster in the southeastern and western quarters of the city. Other community groups in similar manner cluster around particular quarters of the city.

The Neighborhood Quarter—Tole

The settlement clusters of the previously mentioned communities are social and spatial units known as *tole* (Newari: *twa*) —the neighborhood quarter. In Patan, our survey identified 57 tole (Fig. 3-1). Identifying a tole is not always as simple as it seems. Each tole bears a name and all inhabitants may identify the tole to which they belong. However, as tole are not a present-day administrative unit, there are no maps delineating their boundaries. In fact, their boundaries appear to change with the buying and selling of the land that lie at the boundaries between the neighboring tole. The boundaries often do not run along the streets but through the plot boundaries within the settlement blocks. In many cases, inhabitants note the location of their dwelling in terms of a particular locality that seems to be just a section of a tole, yet they refer to it as a tole. Thus, tole in one sense simply denotes a locality well known to the residents in their neighborhoods, and labeling a particular area as a tole—as a coherent socio-spatial unit—becomes a sociological and anthropological exercise. To delineate tole boundaries in our survey, we considered the presence of a Ganesa shrine as the prime symbol of a tole. Ganesa is addressed as *tole-devata* 'the deity of the tole' in medieval inscriptions, indicating the symbolic association of Ganesa with the territory of a tole. Other deities are not so addressed.

Kunu Sharma's description of Patan in his *Kirtipataka* (1961) indicates that during the reign of Srinivasa Malla (1661–1684) the city was composed of 24 tole.[4] It is most probable that these tole included the 57 present-day tole because there is evidence of settlements in all these areas during that period. The present number thus appears to be the result of a re-division of the 24 earlier tole territories, a process which may be presumed because there are a number of localities, which call themselves tole although they are not included in our division, that already far exceeds the number given by Sharma. The building of a shrine to Ganesa or *pati* 'wayside rest house' and wells in a square are indicative of a civic-minded community. Such actions could have been a requirement for a locality to exist as an independent tole. A recent example of an emerging tole in Patan is Nohala, where a new Ganesa temple has been built in the vicinity of Wonla tole, which is situated in a quarter east of the palace. Such a requirement could have only been formalized with an increasing population and a rise in local governance.

Historical records from the Licchavi period indicate that the *gvala* preceded the tole as a local settlement unit. The records of this period mention numerous settlement localities with the suffix *-gvala* while making no reference to tole (Kolver and Sakya 1985). By the tenth century the term, tole, or alternatively *sthana* 'locality,' was sometimes used in conjunction with gvala to identify a local area. Gvala appears to be of ancient origin and it is not Sanskrit. The term is thought to be derived from Kirata. We do not know what constituted the gvala and tole territories during those times, but Licchavi records indicate that the gvala was one of several local administrative units or place names of a settlement. Interestingly we find numerous localities in the southeastern quarter of Patan with forms of the suffix -gvala incorporated into their names. These are Tangal, Haugal, Saugal, Yanamungal, and Tyagal. All these localities now exist as tole units. According to early medieval palm leaf documents, the localities of Tanigval, Hatigval, Satigval, Yangval, and Tyagval were situated to the east of Manigval. Thus, there is no doubt that they are the forerunners of the above tole. The central area of Patan, where the royal palace is located, was known as Manigal, which has been abbreviated to the current name Mangal 'bazaar.' Licchavi inscriptions also mention local areas with the suffix *-grama*, a Sanskrit term for a village settlement. It is probable that grama is the Sanskrit equivalent of gvala or that a grama included several gvala to form a higher single administrative unit. In an edict of Jisnugupta (624–633) Thambu grama is noted and it continues as Thambu tole in medieval documents (NS 762) in the southwest of Manigval (Vajracharya, 1973, 404; 1999, 86).

In the records of Patan, the term "tole" first appears in a palm leaf document written in 1090 (NS 211). This document refers to Ravivarmana as *srinogola tolake-pradhana-purusha* 'the head of Nogal tole,' suggesting that the tole was an administrative unit of the town. However, we hear of tole from much earlier documents like the Yanwalottaratole, which is mentioned in colophons of 919 (NS 40) (Joshi 1996, 1).[5] Medieval inscriptions until the late Malla period (1200–1768) provide numerous instances of titles such as *twala-pramukha* and *twala pramana* for the representative head of a tole.

A record dated from 1716 (NS 837) mentions 24 *pramana*, the chiefs of the localities, in connection with the death of Riddhinarasing Malla, the king of Patan (Vaidya and Vajracharya 1998, 91).[6] The tole as a unit is considered to be a later development of the Licchavi *grama-panchali*, the 'village committee,' which exercised considerable autonomy as local administrative units. While gvala continues to be used only in the name of certain localities today, tole became common as the local unit of town settlements from the early medieval period and has persisted as such to modern times. Joshi (1996) writes that tole originated as education centers run by Hindu religious teachers and Buddhist monasteries, which eventually developed into settlement clusters and whose names became the names of neighborhood localities (Joshi, 1996, 1–3).[7] However, the historic origins of tole in the Kathmandu Valley towns are not yet known.

By the medieval period, tole were frequently referred to as part of the hierarchical structure of town settlements. Documents make reference to toponyms that name levels in a nested hierarchical organization of space in settlements, such as tole, *nani*, and *chhen* following the name of the city itself. Chhen, at the lowest level, indicated individual dwellings, while a nani indicated a cluster of dwellings whose inhabitants were generally members of the same clan. A group of nani made up a neighborhood quarter—the tole. *Desha* was the term for a small town settlement before the Sanskritization of place names took place. After Sanskritization *-pura* became the common suffix to indicate the status of a town. Thus, Patan in the early medieval period was at different times known as

Lalitabruma, Lalitakrama, Lalitapattana, and Lalitapura.

In Patan, we still find a significant number of tole localities with the suffix -chhen. It may be presumed that such localities derive their names from the dwellings of the first inhabitants who had some social standing.

Of significance in the toponyms of neighborhood localities is *bahal*—the Buddhist monasteries. Like gvala and chhen, *-bahal* is a common suffix in tole names of Patan. The distinction of these bahal-tole is that they are exclusively settlements of the Sakya and Vajrachaya, who constitute the two major segments of Buddhist population after the Jyapu, and occasionally of the Maharjan. Most of these bahal-tole are concentrated in the southeastern and western sectors of the town with two significant clusters in the east, occupying about one-third of the town area. The Sakya are found in the southeastern and northeastern sections of the city while the Vajracharya are concentrated in the west.

Bhimsensthan, in front of the Malla Palace towards the west, derives its name from the temple of Bhimsen at the northwest corner of the palace square. The temple was built in the seventeenth century, and the locality was probably known as Manigval before it became known as Bhimsensthan because of the temple's popularity among trades people. In this particular quarter, the Amatya and Pradhan communities are more numerous. *Amatya* was a ministerial title during the Licchavi period while the *pradhan* (Newari: *pramanas* or *pama*) were administrative chiefs of towns and localities during the medieval times. If the city of Patan shows a community spatial distribution based on proximity to

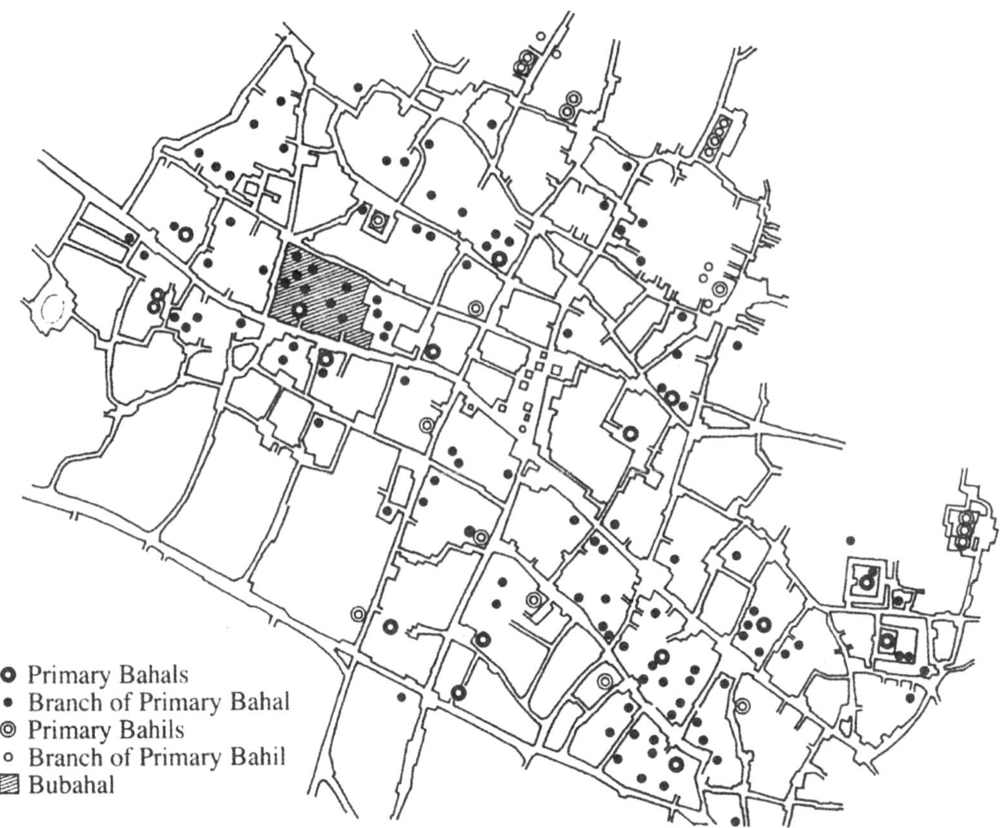

Fig. 3-2. Distribution of Buddhist monasteries (bahal and bahil)

the center of power, it is to be found in the strip towards the west of the palace. In other directions, such a concentric structure is not apparent. The formation of the present socio-spatial structure of Patan will be described in terms of community distribution in the following section where we discuss the development of Buddhist monasteries.

The Buddhist Monasteries

The evolution of Buddhist monasteries in the Kathmandu Valley is one of the determinants of the socio-spatial organization of the settlement quarters in the valley towns in general and of Patan in particular. In Patan, there are presently 163 Buddhist monasteries within the old city limits (see Fig. 3-2).[8] These monasteries are known either as *bahil* or *bahal.* Bahil are thought to be earlier forms of the monasteries while bahal are the result of later developments. Sakya (1998) and Korn (1979) have outlined the differences between these two types of monasteries with respect to their architectural forms. Locke (1985) has further described their ritual traditions. The monasteries not only differ in their architectural forms, but also in their pattern of distribution. Although the exact historical origins of bahil and bahal are still not clear, it is generally believed that bahal are the result following the adaptation of Vajrayana that sanctioned a married Buddhist clergy while bahil maintained Mahayana celibate traditions. It is this difference that brought changes to the social and urban structure of Patan, and bahal consequently became identified with the residential neighborhoods of clan communities.

Medieval documents identify members of bahil as *brahmacharya bhikshu* 'the celibate monk.' Although they too began to marry and live a married life in the later medieval period, Vajrayana rituals were not introduced into the bahil. In the *agan* (shrine of an esoteric deity or ancestor) of a bahal, which is on the second storey, Vajrayana tantric ritual deities are enshrined and a secret initiation ceremony for the title of Vajracharya is performed. In the agan of a bahil, a different deity—*gandhuri-dyo*—is enshrined and no secret rituals are performed. This difference has continued until present times. Further, bahil are exclusively in the care of the Sakya while the bahal community includes both Sakya and Vajracharya.

The hold of Vajrayana on the Kathmandu Valley probably began in the late Licchavi period. However, it is only in later centuries that we get a document dated 1114 (NS 235) that details the right to the respective share by the families of the members of a *Manipurajaiba Mahavihara sarvasangha (Tegvala)* to the income of the monastery. This confirms that by that time the vihara had already been transformed from an earlier monastic structure housing monks who had renounced family life (Sharma 1997, 69). Present-day Vajracharya and Sakya can be traced to the same socio-religious status

of the Sakyabhikshu of ancient times. This is indicated by the title, Sakyabhikshu Vajracharya, which was used by a person called Harshendravudi of Tegvala of Patan in a document dated 1151 (NS 262) (Kolver and Sakya 1985, 115). Another such instance from the fifteenth century is the use of the same title, Sakyabhikshu Vajracharya, by a person named Luntabhadra. Thus, we think that the use of titles, surnames, and professions reflects the formation of the Vajracharya community from the separation of the bahil and the bahal in the Buddhist monasteries of the valley.

From the early seventeenth century, there were clear organizational divisions between the two types of institutions. According to a chronicle, during the period of Siddhinarasingha Malla (NS 731-71) the Buddhist monasteries of Patan were divided into two groups— bahal and bahil (Wright 1972, 234–6). Among the bahal, 15 were identified as primary while the rest were classified as branch bahal of the primary bahal. Likewise, 18 of the 21 bahil in Patan were classified as primary bahil. Three more primary bahal were added later, one of which is within the old city area. That such a division existed earlier is also mentioned by the same chronicle, which states a single senior of the vihara sarvasangha (grand association of viharas) of the main bahal, located at the eastern part of the city. The main bahal, at the western sector did have separate individual sanghas only.

A study of available records prior to the thirteenth century before the beginning of the Malla period shows the existence of 36 vihara in Patan, of which 28 are known from Okubahal documents alone (Table 3-3). The discovery of similar documents stored in other monasteries

Table 3-3. List of Buddhist Monasteries mentioned in available medieval documents (879–1768). 879, Oct 20 = Beginning of Nepal Era (NS)

	Viharas	Date	Source		Viharas	Date	Source
1	Mahavatigvala vihara	40	Petech	31	Chitra Vihara	293	Petech
2	Parinirvana Mahavihara	103		32	Daksina Vihara	306	
3	Jayabhimana Mahavihara	121		33	Dathau Vihara	306	
4	Vi[jva-]gupta vihara	121		34	Yithau Vihara	306	
5	Guita bahi	144	Locke	35	Talinagesvora Vihara	309	
6	Yamgvala Mhavihara	159		36	Livi Vihara	309	
7	Dukavamhan Tejamati Mahavihara	189		37	Manasimha Mahavihara	330	
8	Maharaja vihara	192		38	Ka Vihara(?)	330	
9	Vagini madhyama Mahavihara	192		39	Manako Vihara	331	
10	Udayalaxmi-harsakaragupta mahavihara	194		40	Niva Vihara	331	
				41	Nyaipi Vihara	331	
11	Raghava vihara	198		42	KoVihara	403	Regmi
12	Cakavati Mahavihara	202	Petech	43	YaipimVihara (Yampi?)	340	
13	Kwa baha	202	Locke	44	Naka Vahara	456	
14	Vu vihara	218		45	Guji Baha	373	
15	Vandhavu Vihara	235		46	Puco Bahi	372	Locke
16	Sivadeva Sanskarita Rudravarna Mahavihara (Uku Bahal)	237		47	Pula Bahiri	448	GV
				48	Nhu Baha	457	Locke
				49	I baha bahi	470	Locke
17	Tanga Baha	245	Locke	50	Pim Baha	479	Locke
18	Vr Vihara	**250**		51	Yokhaccha Vihara	476	Petech
19	Varttakalyana Vihara	252		52	Karanda Vihara	494	Petech
20	Visnuchhen Mahavihara	261		53	Sri-Bahal	509	
21	Ca Vihara	262		54	Pintu Bahi	511	Locke
22	Matigalaca Vihara	262		55	Uku Baha bahi	511	Locke
23	Ha(dh)ko Vihara	262		56	Punesvara Vihara	515	Petech
24	Manikajeva Mahavihara (Tegvala)	262		57	Dhanisva Vihara	515	PL
25	Salako Vihara (Su Bahal)	262 (182)	Locke	58	Cakala Vihara	515	PL
				59	Nakhacuk	520	Locke
26	uttara Vihara	262		60	Chwaja Vihara	520	
27	Yangala Vihara	272		61	Khwata Vihara	520	
28	Gagana Vihara	273		62	Yotha Vihara	535	Petech
29	Sri Mahendravarma Mahavihara	273		63	Cikan Bahi	536	Locke
				64	Kinu Bahi	538	Locke
30	Srisivadeva Sanskarita Srimanidharajiva Mahavihara	273		65	Ta-Baha	547	Locke
				66	Ikha chen Baha	553	Locke
				67	Om Baha	561	Locke
				68	Nag Baha	577	
				69	Ekata Vihara	595	GV
				70	Jyestha Vihara	619	
				71	Okha-chuka Vihara	619	

Table 3-3. *Continued*

	Viharas	Date	Source		Viharas	Date	Source
72	Athado Vihara	620		85	**Jya Vahala**	778	
73	Pitho Vihara	620		86	Satigla Bahara	788	
74	Tava-duchhen Vahara	628		87	vatsa Vahara	792	
75	Komati Vihara	636	PL	88	Yanta Vihara	798	
76	Yi Vihara	649		89	Gada Vahala	804	
77	Chupi Vihara	654		90	Metakha Vahara	809	
78	Dhvaka Vahara	665	PL	91	Naridva Vahala	810	
79	Valacchen (Calachhen?)	680	Regmi	92	Hatigla Vahara	812	
80	Gangul Vihara	685		93	Nuguji Bahala	845	
81	Vanasri Vihara	685		94	Na-Bahal	846	
82	**Gvachhen vahara(Cakra)**	708		95	Tavagane Bahal	866	
83	Vam Bahal	718		96	Caitra Bahal (citra?)	878	
84	Yitachhen Vahara	736		97	**Cakra Bahal**	878	

1. The vihharas in shade are either non extant or remain unidentified with the existing bahals or bahils.
2. The sources for the chronology are: Locke (1985); Petech (1984) and Regmi (1965-6, 1969) referred by Locke; GV (Gopalarajavamsabali, 1985). PL (Palm leaf documents: Abhilekh issues, see Biblography). All others are from 'Land Deed Documents from Rudravarna Mahavihara' (Uku Bahal) (Kolver and Sakya, 1987) unless noted.
3. Viharas in bold are Mahavihara or primary bahals (mubaha).

would certainly increase this number such that Patan could be labeled as a city of monasteries. Among these 36 vihara, 11 are identified as *mahavihara*—grand monasteries—while the rest are simply known as vihara. Oku bahal records identify Oku bahal, Hathko bahal, Bhinche bahal, and Subahal as mahavihara, all of which are recorded as primary bahal during the reorganization of monasteries in the seventeenth century. Kwa bahal and Tanga bahal are the other two main monasteries with records available from this early period. Further, in the seventeenth century division, Ta bahal and Tanga bahal were given special status as they were the earliest mahavihara in Patan.

In addition, a collation of monasteries made by Locke (1985) identifies 42 vihara in Patan (including the mahavihara) that are mentioned in known medieval historical documents before the end of the sixteenth century, although they cannot be located at present. However, it is also quite possible that, due to the lack of historical documents, some of them remain unidentified in present-day bahal, which are now known by names that are often truncated to the monosyllabic Newari tongue. For instance, the Jayadeva vihara is now known as Jati-bahal, which makes it difficult to identify it with the original even by the inhabitants of the bahal themselves (Sakya 1994). This list of 42 vihara excludes the ones mentioned by the Licchavi period inscriptions and whose locations are yet unknown.

From NS 456 onward, the Buddhist monasteries that were described as vihara in documents begin to be called *bahara* (*vahara*) or *bahala*. Moreover, by about the same time we also take note of the word *bahiri* being used for those vihara that have become known as bahil in modern times. It was probably the increasing use of the Newari tongue in official documents instead of Sanskrit that accounts for such changes, and it suggests that the common people called the two types of monasteries by different names by that time. This difference in wording occurred in the fourteenth century which marks the beginning of Newari literature (Malla 1982; also see Sharma 1997, 11). In early medieval or Licchavi documents, all main bahal and bahil had the status of mahavihara. For this reason, within the limitations of available data, we can not ascertain whether any particular bahal or bahil of today existed as a kind of monastery different from bahil at the time of its foundation. It is only from titles such as *Brahmacharya-bhikshu* and *Sakya-bhikshu* for members of early vihara or bahil of medieval times and *Vajracharya-Sakyabhikshu* and *Vajracharya* for members of bahal that we can deduce an upward genealogical link between bahal and bahil members.

Besides the primary bahal and bahil, another group of monasteries in Patan comprise the branch bahal known as *kaca-baha*. Moreover, a document dated NS 262 (1141 CE) also mentions a *ca-vihara*. The Newari suffix *ca* means 'minor,' which is said to indicate a branch monastery (Kolver and Sakya 1985, 115). Vajracharya cites an inscription of Guita bahil dated NS 399 (1278 CE), which states that someone called Bhikshu Gautamasri had asked permission from a sangha to establish a new vihara. This suggests that the tradition of establishing

branch vihara existed from early medieval times. The existence of such branch bahal by the beginning of the seventeenth century is evident from palm leaf documents where a number of vihara are mentioned as belonging to particular mahavihara.

Distribution of the Monasteries

The distribution of monasteries throws light on the development pattern of Patan's settlement quarters and on certain relationships between the bahal and bahil and the town settlement. Figure 3-3 shows the spatial distribution of these bahil and bahal within the old city area of Patan. The figure shows that bahil are located at the periphery of the settlement while bahal are distributed within the settlement quarters. We consider that this is one of the indications of the earlier history of bahils compared to bahals in Patan. The locations of early monasteries noted in the chronicles, such as Yampi bahi near the North Stupa and Guita bahi in Guita tole at the eastern border of the city, also point to a similar chronological sequence between bahil and bahal. The dates of each monastery given in the Table 3-3 are the available dates referring to their existence; the foundation dates for both bahal and bahil could be much earlier.

The bahal and bahil are not concentrated in any particular area of the city. However, close observation will show certain differences between their patterns of distribution. In a number of instances, several bahil are situated near or next to each other. Bahal, however, are separated by an interval of a quarter block. No two primary bahal are located in a single quarter block, or even within one tole. Haka bahal and Bubahal now belong to

◼ Primary Bahals:

1. Kwa-bahal (Bhaskaradeva sanskarita Hiranyavarana)
2. Dhum-bahal (Gunalaxmikirti)
3. Om-bahal (Suryadharma sanskarita Vajrakirti)
4. Jyo-bahal (Rudradevanam Gopala sanskarita Jetavarana)
5. Su-bahal (Indradeva sanskarita Jayamanohara Ratnajaya)
6. Bhinche- bahal (Jayasrimisra sanskarita Mayuravarna)
7. Yachhu -bahal (Baladharagupta sanskarita)
8 Guje-bahal (Amritavarna Vaisravana)
9. Uku-bahal (Sivadeva sanskarita Omkuli SriRudravarna)
10 Chuka-bahal (Manadeva sanskarita Chakravarna
11. Tanga-Minanatha bahal (Balachandra sanskarita Jyesthavarna)
12. Tah-, Machhindra -bahal (Bhuvanakaravarma sanskarita Dharmakirti)
13. Dau-bahal (Rudradeva Gargagotravarma sanskarita Dattanama)
14. Haka-bahal (Laksmikalyanavarma sanskarita Ratnakara)
15. Bu-bahal (Vidhyadharavarma sanskarita Yasodhara)
16. Si-baha (Srivatsa)

▣ Bahils:

1. Pintu bahil (Gopichandra)
2. Duntu bahil (Gobardhanmisra sanskarita)
3. Konti cidhangu bahil (Kasyapamisra sanskarita lalitavarna)
4. Konti bahil (Kasyapamisra)
5. Yampi bahil (Yampi yanta)
6. I bahil (Sunyasrimisra)
7. Cikam bahil (Saptapura)
8. Guita cidhangu bahil (Gustala)
9. Guita dhatu bahil (Vasucasila-dipavati)
10. Guita tadhangu bahil (Dipavati padmocasri)
11. U baha bahi (Omku bahil)
12. Thapa bahil (Sthavirapatra)
13. Jyaba bahil (Jyesthavarna)
14. I baha-bahil (Simhavarna Rajasri)
15. Kinu bahil (Lokakirti)
16. Nhyakam bahil (Suraschandra)
17. Khwaya cidhangu bahil (Khvati)
18. Khwaya bahil (Khvati)
19. Nak-bahil (Lokakirti)
20. Dhapaga bahil (Manimandapa)

Fig. 3-3. Main (Primary) bahals and bahils

one Bubahal tole, but Hakabahal's present location is not its original site, which was somewhere in the vicinity of the palace. Historical documents show that the existing primary bahal were either established by, or had close links with, the aristocrat class of the time. Eight of these bahal were founded by the Varma clan mentioned in preceding sections. Undoubtedly, they were linked to Thakuri and Licchavi rulers. The Varma were not only the founders or guardians of the bahal. Their clan members were also the residents of these bahal as shown by palm leaf documents (Kolver and Sakya 1985). A legend of Uku bahal traces its foundation to Sivadeva, a Licchavi king in the eighth century who, upon his retirement, expressed a desire to lead the life of a Buddhist monk, but in the company of his family. The bahal were probably built as a religious retreat for retiring nobles living in the quarter (Wright 1972). The disappearance of the Varma from the communities of Patan suggests the possibility of their absorption into the bahal which belonged to communities of the Vajrayacharya-Sakya, which had been a socio-religious status rather than a clan identity in medieval times.

The distribution of bahal and bahil within the city area almost corresponds to the structural net of the city. In other words, the spatial frame and the settlement nucleus of Patan were already complete by the twelfth century. Later developments revolved around these primary bahal with an increasing number of branch bahal built in the quarters where the primary bahal were located.

Among the 16 main bahal in Patan today, 10 are located in the eastern section of the city. If we include Haka (Hathko) bahal, whose original location is said to have been in the vicinity of the palace complex, the eastern sector would show a much greater concentration of bahal. When we see that there is also a considerable number of tole with the suffix -gvala (mentioned in the Licchavi and early medieval documents) in the eastern sector, it is clear that the four quadrants of Patan did not develop in a uniform manner. The eastern sector shows a much earlier and more concentrated development than the western sector. In the west, the northwest quadrant was developed much more extensively than the southwest quadrant. The limits of the old city area shown by the existing dwelling clusters completely coincide with the distribution pattern of bahal.

The spatial distribution of communities and the features of tole broadly outline the importance of two types of communities. One is the Jyapu community and the other is the Sakya and Vajracharya community. These two communities and their respective neighborhoods also show particular features in their spatial structures. As these communities constitute most of the population of Patan, the urban form of the city is basically represented by their neighborhoods. Therefore, in order to understand the social and spatial structure of Patan, we will analyze in detail the spatial and social structure of these two types of neighborhoods and their planning principles in the chapters to follow.

4

Neighborhood Quarters I: Buddhist Monasteries

Buddhism has been one of the two main cultural vehicles of urban civilization in the Kathmandu Valley. The effects of Buddhism on the development of the valley's culture over the last two millennia are evident through the art, architecture, and urban forms found in the valley towns. As we have seen in the preceding chapter, the communities associated with Buddhist monasteries constitute one major group among the population of Patan. Among the many facets of the valley's heritage, the Buddhist monastery–bahal and bahil (Sanskrit: *vihara*)–represents a genre that eloquently expresses the history and culture of the people. Increasing scholarly study of these monasteries has pointed out their importance in the history and urbanism of the valley. In particular, the works of Hemaraj Sakya[1] and John Locke (1985) are notable contributions to the wealth of material that

has increased our knowledge of the Kathmandu Valley monasteries.

The present chapter will analyze one bahal settlement quarter, the Bubahal tole, situated in the western part of the city. This quarter still preserves its traditional physical structure wherein monasteries constitute the social and religious centers of the communities around them. The quarter derives its name from the monastery, Bubahal, which is one of the 16 primary monasteries of Patan. While there are more of these monasteries in the eastern sector of the city, we find a greater concentration of Buddhist communities in the west. In the preceding chapter, we pointed out the references to ancient place names in the eastern part of the city, which suggests that the western sector was developed after a much earlier and more concentrated development in the east. This development followed the evolution of Buddhist schools from the early Theravada to the Mahayana and then to the Vajrayana, when married life for the Buddhist clergy became sanctioned and the early tradition of monastic austerity was no longer followed. It was during the Vajrayana transformation of Buddhist doctrine that Buddhist monasteries or vihara were gradually adapted to the needs of household life and housing clusters began to develop around them. The transformation brought changes both to the physical form of the vihara itself and the social composition of the settlement. The Bubahal quarter exemplifies the process of transformation of an individual monastery into a monastery settlement quarter.

Spatial Structure of Bahal and Bahil

Of the two types of Buddhist monasteries—bahal and bahil—it was the bahil that until recently maintained the older tradition of Mahayanic monachism; the bahal is a later adaptation related to Vajrayana Buddhism. At present, there are more bahal than bahil in the Kathmandu Valley towns. For example, in and around Patan where 166 Buddhist monasteries have been recorded, 137 are bahal. Of these, 16 are known as *mulbahal* (Newari: *mu:baha*) or primary bahal[2] (Fig. 3-2 in Chap. 3). All the other bahal are associated with a mulbahal and considered as its branch bahal, or *kachabahal*. Still other bahal are independent of any mulbahal or they are branches of bahil. The mulbahal and branch bahal form a system of relationships in the ritual hierarchy and symbolically represent the identity of the settlement quarter. Their names are also often the toponym of the neighborhoods.

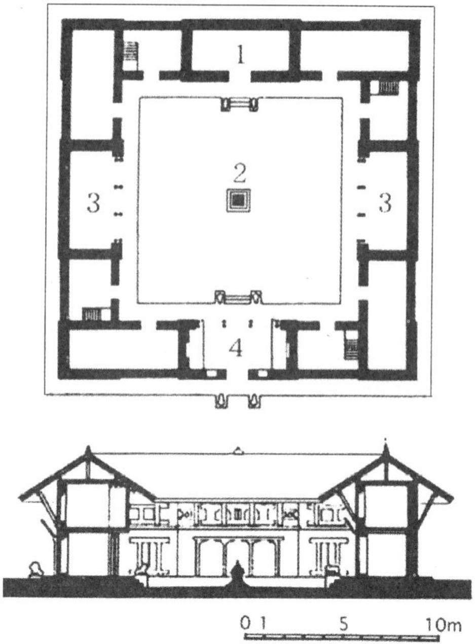

1.Main Shrine 2.Caitya 3.Dalan 4. Phalacha

Fig. 4-1. The plan of a typical bahal:
Chusya bahal

The typical bahal is a quadrangular structure with an open court in which there are Buddhist shrines and artifacts. It is enclosed on its four sides by a two-story courtyard building (Fig. 4-1 and Plate 4-1).[3] Within the open quadrangle, the main shrine of the bahal is situated opposite the main entrance. At the central section of the left and right wings, there is an open porch consisting of three bays known as *dalan,* which are used for periodic ritual activities. On the second floor above the main shrine is found the sanctum of the tantric deity—the *agam* of the Vajracharya community. The *digi* (the hall above the main entrance hall) is used for community festivals and ritual gatherings. There are staircases at the four corners of the quadrangle. These independently serve four groups of chambers.

Pl. 4-1. Chusya bahal, facing the south wing

Pl. 4-2. Cha bahil, Kathmandu (Nippon Institute of Technology, 1985)

Some of these chambers are used as dwelling units by the families who belong to the bahal community while the rest are used as store rooms, kitchens, and auxiliary spaces. The blocks of the four wings are laid out such that each meets only one end of the quadrangle thus creating a cyclic order which, according to the classical Vastusastra, is *Sarvatobhadra* (Sanskrit: all auspicious) or the swastika pattern.

Votive elements such as caitya, mandala, and a sacrificial altar are characteristic ritual artifacts of a bahal. They are arranged in a sunken court about 50 centimeters below the ground level along a longitudinal axis that runs through the entrance gate and the main shrine. The entrance area has raised platforms of wooden planks or *phalacha* built on both sides. Images of the guardian deities, Ganesa and Mahankal, are placed on each sidewall of the entrance hall.

A bahal is invariably linked to a number of residential courts clustered behind its walls. These constitute the living quarters of the bahal community. In medieval land deed documents, the bahal was usually the reference point when giving the location of a house. Examples are *yata-chhen* 'the southern house' and *ukuli-chhen* 'the house at the northeast corner.' The open court of a bahal is called a *mulchok* or the main court. In classical bahal architecture, the size of the court is relatively uniform. For instance, the Chusya bahal measures 12.4 m × 12.1 m at the courtyard side.

All the primary bahal of Patan are in the interior section of their quarter. Thus, they do not directly open to the major streets of the city. A lane, or in most cases an entry access lane, leads up to the entrance gate of the bahal while the branch bahal have one of their entries linked to their primary bahal. Among the 16 primary bahal of Patan, 11 have a northern orientation. This preference for the north is also found in Kathmandu. There are no primary bahal with a southern orientation.

Chusya bahal has an inscription from 1648 (NS 769), but it is believed to have existed before the fourteenth century. The building of bahal in the classical form apparently continued until the beginning of the sixteenth century. This is shown by a 1591 inscription in Pinche bahal (also known as Khun baha) in Kathmandu, which is an example of a complete bahal structure.[4] There are no available records that indicate the building of bahal in the classical form from this time onwards.

Compared to bahal, bahil are relatively simpler in their plan, structure, and decorative motifs. Both the ground floor and upper floors are open with rows of wooden columns supporting the floor and roof structure. Brick masonry is used only for the exterior wall (Pl. 4-2). The floors are partitioned with light latticed panels to make rooms and halls with a continuous balcony projecting from the four wings around the courtyard. The two floors are connected by a single staircase. Cha bahi, thought to be one of the earliest Buddhist monasteries in Nepal, has individual rooms on the ground floor partitioned with brick walls. The size of the rooms and the layout of the ground floor are reminders of Cha bahi's close similarity to the early monasteries of India, such as the cave monasteries of Ajanta or the remains of monasteries in Gandhara. In later times, when the members of a vihara began to live in bahal or in separate dwellings, the cell-like rooms for the monks lost their function. Consequently, these rooms were converted into common halls with movable partitions that provided space for the community members during various ritual ceremonies. Hatano divides the bahil form into three types based on characteristic variations in their partitions with the bahal as a fourth type (Hatano 1998, 2-4).

Besides the two typical monastery types—bahal and bahil in Kathmandu Valley, there exists yet another form, which belongs to the bahal category. These are bahal with large open courts on the four sides lined with individual residential dwellings. In Patan, such large bahal courts are concentrated in the western quarter of the town, and they occupy a substantial part of the city area. How such bahal courts evolved and what the significance of the change is in the organization of the community quarter are still unanswered questions. Existing research work is limited to areas within the precincts of bahal. Moreover, these have not explored the morphological link of the bahal to urban structures.[5] Thus, in the following section, we present a case study of Bubahal, a typical large bahal quadrangle. We analyze the evolution and form of the community settlement clusters around it and its link with the historical forms of bahal architecture.

Social and Historical Background of Bubahal

Bubahal is located in the western quarter of the city to the north of a major east-west street that crosses the palace square (Fig. 4-2). On the north, it is bordered by a three-meter wide lane and on the west by a street-lane with considerable traffic. This street-lane connects the

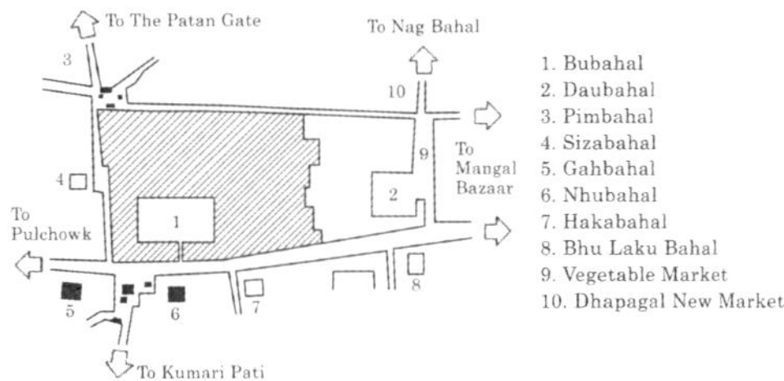

Fig. 4-2. Bubahal and its neighborhood

north and south of the western quarter of the city. Its northern terminus is the Patan City Gate, a transportation node, while the southern boundary of the quarter is a major transportation artery that separates the traditional city from the area of modern developments. On the east, Bubahal borders Daubahal, a younger and smaller community.

Bubahal is one of the 16 main bahal of Patan. Its formal Sanskrit name is Vidhadhara Varma Sanskarita Yasodhara Mahavihara. A legend describing its history states that Bubahal was originally founded by Vidyadhara-Varma. It later became known as Yasodhara-mahavihara as well as Buyabahal, when a bramhani widow settled in the vihara to lead a Buddhist life there with her son, Yasodhara. With respect to the period of its foundation, the legend also mentions Shankaradeva as the ruling king. According to the historical sources, a king with this name ruled in 920 CE (Tewari et al. 1963, 15). The earliest definite historical record that refers to Bubahal's existence comes from a palm leaf document dated NS 218 [1097 CE] (Sakyabhikshu 2002, 58).

Bubahal has eight branch bahal within its quarter. Among these branch bahal two are recognized as official while the rest are private foundations. There are three other official branches of Bubahal,

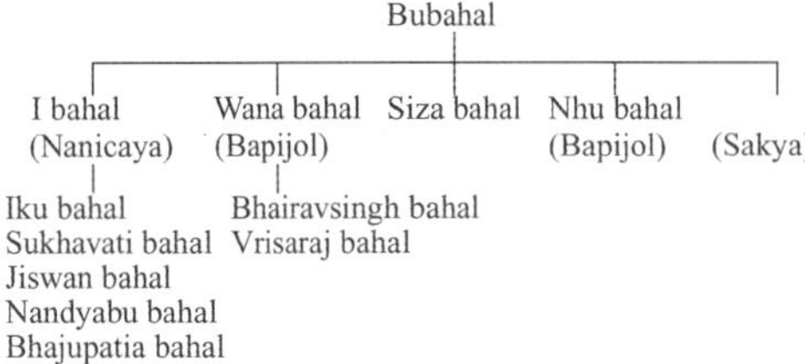

Fig. 4-3. The lineage structure of the
Bubahal community

but they are located in the adjoining neighborhood quarters. The hierarchical relationship among these bahal is shown in Figure 4-3. This hierarchy can be observed in various religious rituals such as the one where the attendant of the main shrine of Bubahal visits only the official branches for the daily worship early in the morning.

At present, most of the people residing within the Bubahal quarter are Vajracharya, a hereditary priestly class. This community consists of three agnatic lineages known as the Nanicaya, Bapijol, and Rajguru. Members of Nanicaya and Bapijol link these lineages to the foundation period of Bubahal. The Bubahal quarter residents belong to the first two lineages. The last lineage, the Rajguru, is said to have been assimilated into the Bubahal community at the beginning of the seventeenth century. They reside in Haka bahal, the area across the street south of Bubahal. Accordingly, the branch bahal of Bubahal are associated with the above agnatic clan system.

The Court of Bubahal

Like all main bahal, the Bubahal quadrangle is connected by a 4 m wide, 15 m deep lane to the main street south of the quarter. At the end of the lane opening into Bubahal, there is a gate guarded on both sides by two griffins. Auspicious symbols are painted on the sidewalls. Above the doorway an epitaph reads Yasodhara Mahavihara, the formal Sanskrit name of the bahal's founder.

The bahal quadrangle is a rectangular space of approximately 60.6 m × 33.8 m,

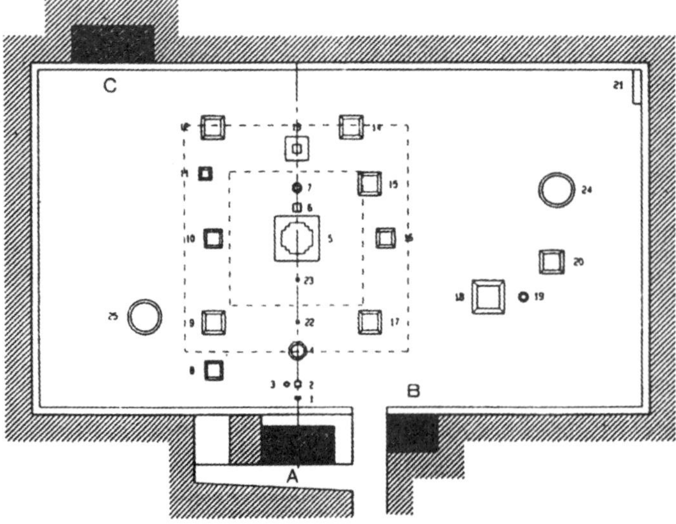

Fig. 4-4. The courtyard of Bubahal

Pl. 4-3b. Main Shrine

Pl. 4-3c. Central caitya

Pl. 4-3a. The courtyard facing east wing

Pl. 4-3. Votive artifacts in the Bubahal courtyard

which contrasts the narrow streets around the quarter (Pl. 4-3 and Fig. 4-4). The central section of the quadrangle has numerous shrines and votive artifacts. The main shrine of the bahal, Kwapadyo, a seated image of Amitabha facing north, is located just at the left of the entrance. It is a two-tier temple that is now the tallest in the quarter. The primary ritual artifacts of the Vajrayana are arranged on a central axis with the main shrine as the apex of the organization. Religious activities held here make the bahal the social and ritual center of the Bubahal community. These activities include sermons, initiation ceremonies and other rites of passage, observance of the anniversary of the main shrine's foundation, and other rituals held daily or at certain times of the year.

Among the 16 primary bahal in Patan, there are three with open courts that lack the super structure of the classical courtyard architecture within the open court. These are Bubahal, Tabahal, and Tangabahal, all with large bahal courts. While Tabahal and Tangabahal still have a section of the southern wing housing the main shrine, Bubahal, has no such structure. Thus, it is not possible to link it to its earlier form on stylistic grounds. At present, the typical spaces constituting a bahal such as the phalacha, dalan, and digi, and the main shrine in the Bubahal court are arranged in a way such that it is difficult to find a link between them and construct a coherent architectural unit. However, given the ritual importance of primary bahal and the evidence of its standard architectural form that has been so extensively employed in all the towns of the Kathmandu Valley, it is unlikely that the present form of the Bubahal quadrangle reflects its original form. This is because the Bubahal quadrangle does not have the typical forms of monastery architecture that already existed in the region for centuries. However, the existing ritual artifacts of the bahal in the open court may prove to be important clues to trace the historical development of Bubahal. The present inconsistency in the layout order of some of the artifacts and the constituting spaces of Bubahal within the court makes it clear that the present form was a transformation dictated by expediencies other than the requirements of monastery architecture.

The assumption that the original structure of Bubahal reflects the classical order, like most of the other primary bahal, may be cautiously used to reconstruct a part of its history and the evolutionary sequence of large bahal courts. Thus, in this study, a typical plan form of a classical bahal was superimposed on the open court maintaining the present north-south axis passing through the main shrine and the central caitya (5 in Fig. 4-4). If the present location of the main shrine is to remain unaltered, the central caitya would lie within the northern wing of the bahal and there would not be any caitya within the open court itself. In all the primary bahal, however, one caitya is located either at the center of the court or towards the other half of the open court in the axis near the main shrine. Thus, considering that a caitya is a necessary votive ritual artifact of a bahal and that in all the cases such caitya are enshrined in the open court (constituting the central element in the organization of the ritual artifacts), a reconstruction that keeps the present location of the main shrine unaltered would not be congruent with tradition.

An inscription on a bell installed on the east side of the central caitya records the date of its donation as 1657.

The caitya itself then is a much earlier structure. Its central location in the court in relation to the other ritual artifacts certainly indicates that it was the earliest structure installed. Thus, it can be safely assumed that the central caitya, which is presently at the center of the north-south axis of the court, was also at the center of the original structure. In this instance, the location of the main shrine is to be shifted by approximately 11 m towards the north from the present position. As the image is not a permanent artifact in the shrine structure, shifting the image would involve no physical alterations. It is to be noted that the existing votive artifacts around the central caitya then lie within four blocks of the wings of the bahal. However, the available records on the installation dates of some of these artifacts and their styles show that they were built later, that is, after the reorganization of the bahal. The oldest of these artifacts is the shrine (9 in Fig. 4-4). It was built in the sikhara style, an atypical form for a Buddhist artifact. The date of its installation, that is, its construction and official dedication, was 1672, which is later than the installation of the Krishna temple (1637) in the palace square. It is possible that these votive artifacts were built in such a way as to mark and retain the sacredness of the boundaries of the earlier bahal structure. The fact that the central caitya faces east indicates the possibility that the early bahal structure was entered from the east. This axial relationship between the entrance and the main shrine can be found in other bahal, such as Daubahal. The present entry gate to the quadrangle must have existed from the beginning as an access to the bahal community complex.

The above reconstruction of the early form of Bubahal closely resembles a number of other extant bahal complexes in Patan. In particular, Nakabahil and the two primary bahal—Subahal and Bhinche bahal (see Fig. 3-3)—indicate a possibility of the formation of large bahal quadrangles once the core court of the bahal was reorganized. In the case of Bubahal, the location of the shrine (9 in Fig. 4-4) indicates that Bubahal underwent reorganization prior to the end of the seventeenth century. This reorganization consisted of dismantling the four wings of the court, shifting the main shrine towards the south, and aligning the shrine building with the existing building line of the residential court. In this process an important spatial element of bahal constituting space—the dalan—was moved to an awkward location (C in Fig. 4-4), which shows a departure from the usual organizational plan of bahal courts. The phalaca to the right of the main entry gate (B in Fig. 4-4) replaced the phalaca of the earlier bahal court's entrance hall. In a number of primary bahal and in most of the branch bahal (which have undergone changes due to the building of private residential dwellings replacing the wings of bahal court), the votive artifacts of the bahal court, the main shrine, and dalan have been kept in their original positions thus maintaining the classical order. The reorganized Bubahal thus retained the basic constituting bahal artifacts although in a changed configuration. The new arrangement maintains the original north-south axis with no change in the spatial relationship between the ritual artifacts in the court and the orientation to the main shrine. However, the sacred ritual space of the classical bahal court has merged with the open court of the secular residential space.

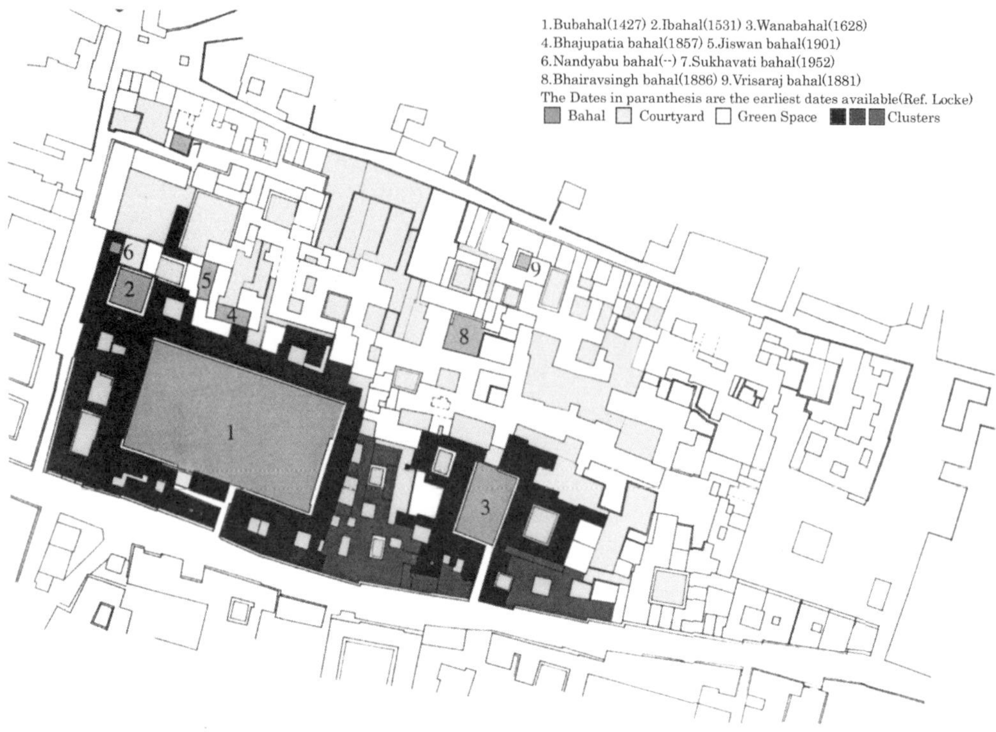

Fig. 4-5. The Bubahal quarter

The bahal architecture thus underwent a historical transformation.

The Bubahal Cluster

The entire Bubahal settlement clusters around Bubahal proper that is located in the southwestern corner of the quarter. The settlement quarter is a honeycomb structure with open spaces formed by bahal and family courtyards (Fig. 4-5). The houses in a cluster are usually built with a common party wall, which gradually leads to the formation of a contiguous cluster block. The quarter has many access ways leading to the interior courts. These access ways rise to about 45–60 cm high from the street level and they pass through the ground floor of the houses above. With their width of about 1 m and a height of less than 2 m, these access ways link a series of courtyards and bahal, thus making the settlement quarter like a maze which is difficult for an outsider to navigate.

An analysis of the settlement cluster was done using a 1 : 500 scale cadastral map that delineates the built-up area and the property boundaries of the locality. It is found that the settlement is made up of clusters with three different alignments indicating three origin centers of the clusters. The hierarchical order of bahal suggests that Bubahal proper is the primary nucleus which generated the entire Bubahal settlement and that it is the center of alignment in the building of the first group of clusters. On the other hand, the association of the branch bahal with the respective clan community tells us that the settlement cluster is made up of two blocks—one in the east comprising two clusters with Wanabahal as its center and the other in the west with Ibahal as the center. The corresponding agnatic communities of these two cluster groups are Bapijol and Nanicaya. The earliest inscriptions with dates found at these two branch bahal are 1531 and 1628, indicating that the area had a substantial population by the beginning of sixteenth century.

That the bahal were the centers guiding residential development is evident from the examination of the housing blocks. As a morphogenetic unit, a typical traditional urban dwelling of the Newar community has a depth of about 5.8–6.3 m. There is a considerable variation lengthwise.[6] This depth is divided into two halves by a meridian wall. Thus, with three rows of load bearing walls of 50–60 cm thick, the dimension of two bays becomes almost a minimum requirement for the interior layout to be lived in. The dwelling blocks around the Bubahal court show a uniform depth of 5.8–6.4 m confirming to the traditional standard. Houses fronting the main road have a depth of less than 5 m. In fact, the width left between the Bubahal court and the road is, on average, less than 14 m. This does not leave enough space for two rows of housing blocks of 6 m in depth when the necessary space for the light wells is considered. Because of the difficulty to achieve the standard depth of the dwellings facing the main street, the building lines formed by the rows of dwellings parallel to the street is discontinuous. This is in contrast with the regularity that is observed in the rows immediately around the Bubahal court.

The analysis of the cluster alignment also reveals that there is an orthogonal relationship between the building lines and the bahal courts, while there is no such definite alignment relationship between the building lines and the streets. This pattern of development is found throughout the section from Daubahal to the west end of Bubahal, which borders the street. Only the segment between Wanabahal and Bubahal shows an opposite development pattern. This is a development beginning from the street towards the interior. The east and west wings of this cluster are narrower than the standard depth, which is found in the north and south wings. This can be attributed to the earlier development of the adjoining clusters of Bubahal and Wanabahal.

Taking into consideration the ritual hierarchy of the bahal and the dates of available inscriptions, a spatial pattern in the sequence of development of the Bubahal quarter can be drawn. The first stage of development was the ring around the Bubahal quadrangle, similar to the pattern seen in Nakabahil, when there was an original classical court of Bubahal, as shown in its reconstructed form (Fig. 4-4). The regularity of the quadrangle plus the smooth alignment of the buildings around the court and their regular depth confirm that the ring was not a fringe development filled later from the expansion of dwellings surrounding it. The next stage was marked by the establishment of Ibahal and Wanabahal, which then became the secondary centers of the settlement expansion. The chain of the contiguous development of the dwelling blocks around the Bubahal court is broken by the establishment of these two bahal. The association of the two agnatic communities with these two bahal and the bipartition of the quarter into two areas indicate a possibility that Wanabahal and Ibahal are contemporary. The available inscriptional records of these two bahal do not give the date of their foundation, but they indicate the donation of artifacts. It appears that this expansion had already occurred by the fifteenth or sixteenth century. The formal pattern of the shrine and the regular pattern of the two bahal's courts indicate that they were built at the beginning of the development of the dwelling clusters. Thus, these bahal were probably the nuclei of the settlements around them. The remaining bahal were probably private branches associated with one of these two bahal.

All the private branch bahal indicate the third stage of expansion, which is towards the north of the quarter. Unlike Wanabahal and Ibahal, these branch bahal have neither the form of a classical bahal nor any extant shrine building elaborate enough to be reminiscent of a classical bahal's wings. More simple shrines are built in the courtyard and evidence tracing these bahal to earlier than 1881 is yet to be found. The style of the shrine of Jiswanbahal, definitely known to have been established in 1901, is similar to all the branch bahal except the Bhairavsingh bahal, where the caitya and *dharmadhatumandala*[7] were built earlier than the shrine itself. The form of the court as well as the location and form of the branch bahal's shrine indicate that the designation of the precinct as bahal followed the building of the main shrine when the residential clusters were already in existence around the court. Whether the pattern of development in this area is a continuation of the second stage or it marks another phase in the morphological

development of the quarter is difficult to resolve. However, the fringe areas between the clusters marked by a change in alignment, irregularities in the dwelling blocks, and the vacant spaces in between them provide some clues. From the pattern of the dwelling clusters in the north, it is apparent that it is not a concentric development with Wanabahal or Ibahal as the center. Nor is there another center comparable to these two bahal. In these areas, houses were built in an incremental way. They later joined together to form a courtyard. Unlike the bahal, there is no definite hierarchy within the courtyards. The cluster is a simple expansion of dwellings with the multiplication of the courtyards developed on the individual property rather than governed by the frame of the bahal quadrangle. Thus, this pattern of development may be considered as the phase of consolidation, a development at the back areas of the centers. The private branch bahal of this part of the quarter are fundamentally different from the secondary bahal. Developed in later periods, these private branch bahal are not the nucleus or the structure of the morphological history of the settlement quarter. They are not recognized as the official branches of Bubahal and initiation rituals are not performed here. The guardian of the main shrine of Bubahal does not render daily worship in the private bahal, but he does so in the secondary bahal. Ritual traditions and morphological structure converge in telling the development history of the quarter. The historical period of this development cannot be ascertained. Based on the dates of available inscriptions, however, it could have been between the seventeenth and nineteenth centuries, when the existing traditionally built clusters would have been completed.

Conclusion

The morphological analysis of the Bubahal quarter shows that bahal are pivotal in the organization of the settlement clusters. The current classification of bahal into primary, secondary (or the official branch) bahal, and private branch bahal according to ritual hierarchy is important because it can be used to understand the development of both the settlement's temporal and spatial dimensions. The analysis of the cluster group shows that Bubahal is the central axis of the whole settlement quarter and its two official branches, Wanabahal and Ibahal. These two branches comprise the secondary axis generating a concentric and hierarchic pattern in the settlement clusters. In contrast, the private branch bahal are not the embedded structures of the settlement morphology. The evolutionary sequence of the housing clusters in the quarter indicates that the street is not an important factor in determining the form of the settlement and that the developments along the street occurred at a later phase than those at the centers of the interior. The settlement cluster can be distinctly divided into two blocks, which coincides with the two agnatic communities of Bubahal. This form of development indicates that street markets were not strong enough to influence the urban development pattern governed by the religious institution and the clan relationship.

The analysis of the Bubahal quadrangle reveals that the value of the classical bahal type underwent a change sometime before or during the seventeenth century. This resulted in the merging of the ritual space of the classical bahal court with the secular residential court. This reorganization of the bahal, however, maintained the basic bahal artifacts, namely the shrine, dalan, and open court. This transformation is a significant stage in the development of the bahal typology. The existence of such types of large bahal quadrangles without an identifiable building, such as the form of classical bahal or bahil in Patan and Kathmandu, indicates that these structures constitute a third type in the evolution of the vihara or monastery architecture of Nepal. The present analysis assumes the existence of the classical bahal court prior to the development of the present large quadrangle of Bubahal. The process of this transformation may be further substantiated with the availability of new evidence. In Chapter 6 we will further analyze the planning principles of such bahal residential quadrangles, which represent a unique planning theory and methodology of the Buddhist community settlements.

5

Neighborhood Quarters II: Jyapu Community Quarters

The study of the Buddhist monastery quarter, Bubahal tole, shows that the neighborhood residential quarter developed with the Buddhist monastery as the primary axis both in terms of its physical and social dimensions. The neighborhoods are primarily inhabited by communities of both Vajracharya and Sakya Buddhist clergy while the forms of residential clusters are directly related to the hierarchical structure of the bahal. The bahal courtyards are the centers of the community's main social and religious activities. They are located in the interior section of the neighborhoods. This structure is different from other neighborhoods like those of the Jyapu community where street squares are the settings for community activities. The Jyapu constitute almost half of Patan's population. As such, they are the dominant community in the Newar population of the Kathmandu Valley and of Patan in particular. In this chapter, we focus on one Jyapu settlement area in Patan and argue that it is the earliest settlement form of an indigenous community in the settlement history of the city.

Historical Background

In Patan, the settlements in the northern and eastern quarters of the city—from Lunkhusi and Tyagal in the southeast to the Mikhubaha tole in the northwest—contain the major concentration of Jyapu communities (Fig. 3-1 in Chap. 3). It is here that more Licchavi inscriptions can be found.[1] During the Licchavi period, royal promulgations concerning the administration of a locality and the records of religious donations, such as shrines and images and the establishment of trusts for their maintenance, were posted in the form of inscriptions on steles and erected in the locality. More than 200

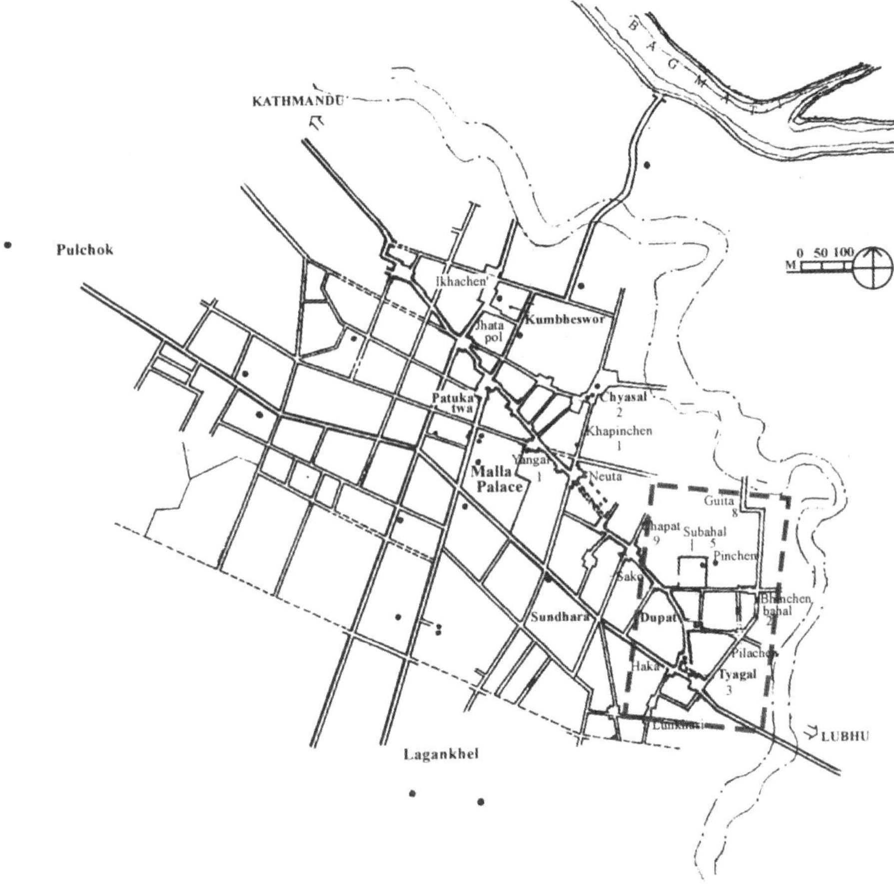

Fig. 5-1. Location of Licchavi inscriptions

such inscriptions have been discovered within and outside the Kathmandu Valley, with the biggest concentration of 32 found within the old city limits of Patan (Fig. 5-1). These inscriptions are the only evidence that indicates the existence of the settlements and the architectural structures of that period.

Religious artifacts identified as belonging to the Licchavi period are also found in larger numbers in Jyapu settlement areas compared to other localities. Bangadel, an eminent artist and art historian, identified an image of Gajalaxmi installed in a fountain at the northeastern quarter of the town, to be of first century BCE (Bangadel 1982).[2] He also identified an image of Vaisnavi (one of the mother goddesses) that was installed in the fountain of Subahal quarter which belong to the third–fourth C. All the images in Patan, which were identified by Bangadel as belonging to the prehistoric period prior to the fifth century, are located in quarters that lie northeast of the major street cross at the palace square. The location of the Licchavi period caitya also shows similar distributions. In Gutschow and Basukala's survey (1997) of 105 such caitya within Patan, 60 are located in the quarters that border this street or lie further north or east of it. The rest are in the quarters that lie southeast of the palace square with a few in the west. No other street in Patan has such an abundance of prehistoric and ancient artifacts.

All our sources of information suggest that the northeastern part of Patan developed earlier compared to the other sectors of the city. The location of the Jyapu community quarters and the fact that these areas contain records of Patan's earliest history reinforce the argument that among the Newar of the valley, the Jyapu are most closely related to the early settlers such as the Kirata. Thus, it is in the Jyapu quarter that one should seek the early forms of settlements in Patan. The study of these quarters is of crucial importance in discovering the history of Patan.

The Morphology of Patan

The degree of formal planning of the Patan's streets is not so obvious to a casual observer. However, it can be observed from the existing morphology of Patan that the streets and lanes forming the urban settlement blocks at the south and the west of the palace square exhibit orthogonality at the street crossings. Two major streets—one running north to south and the other east to west—pass through the palace square and comprise the primary axes of this network of streets. In addition to this regular pattern, a network of streets with a different alignment and different forms of street blocks can be found in the northeastern sector of the city. These blocks are structured along a diagonal street that connects the southeast and northwest ends of the city. This street runs near the edge of the town plateau that gradually slopes down towards the

Bagmati River basin in the north and Manohara in the east, winding along with the river's tributary toward the south. Places of antiquity such as Kumbheswor, Chyasal, and Guita[3] are found along this street, which also connects Kathmandu to the west of Patan and Bhaktapur to the east. A large number of inscriptions and Buddhist caitya from the Licchavi period are found in the neighborhoods along this street.

Worthy of note is the Lalitasatah, a community house, which stands as a memorial in Jhatapol, one of the squares at the crossing point of the north-south axial street and the diagonal street. It is a monument to Lalita, the Jyapu man who, according to a legend, was entrusted for the planning and building of the city (Chap. 3). The area where the Lalitasatah is located belongs to the Tandukar, a group in the Jyapu community who also offer annual worship to Lalita (Tandukar 1994 (2051 VS), 3–4).

The Jyapu Community Quarter

Settlements of Jyapu communities are found in all the quarters towards the northeastern section of this street, particularly in its eastern segment. The Maharjan, the largest group in the Jyapu community, is spread throughout all the quarters of the city with primary concentrations in the east and northwest. There is another cluster of Maharjan at the northern end of the city. Other communities of Jyapu—Awale and Vyanjankar—are in the northeast. All Jyapu tole have their community centers either in one of the squares that lie along the diagonal street or in an area directly connected to it by a street or a lane. No other street is as important as this diagonal street in terms of linking the quarters of Jyapu communities. Therefore, it is on this street and the neighborhoods along it that we have to search for the earliest traces of Jyapu settlement structures.

Organization of Space in the Neighborhood

To understand how space is organized in a Jyapu community settlement quarter, a detailed analysis of the Dupat tole was conducted. This tole is located in the eastern part of Patan and in particular at the southeastern section of the diagonal street (Figs. 5-2 and 5-3).[4] All Dupat inhabitants are Maharjan, but Dupat abuts five tole, that are all overwhelmingly inhabited by Jyapu. The other five tole are Haka, Tyagal, Pinchen, Pilachen, and Subahal. Altogether the six tole are known as "the group of six tole that lie to the east of Sundhara." Sundhara is a major urban square at the eastern section of the east-west street that crosses the center of the city. The Dupat tole is considered the centre of this group since the Dupat residents hold major responsibilities and decision-making powers in community activities involving the six tole. For example, in the *rathayatra* 'chariot procession' festival of the paramount deity Rato Machhendranatha, an elderly resident of Dupat fells a tree in the forest, cuts it into beams which are carried to a place where a *ratha* 'chariot' is built for the deity.[5] This "group of six" participates in the festival of Machhendranatha by building and pulling chariot around the streets of the town. Since ancient traditions like these are observed in Dupat, it is likely that this tole already existed when such traditions, which according to a chronicle, Gopalrajavamabali, began in

Patan during the time of Narendradeva in the seventh century (Vjracharya and Malla 1985, 79).

The section of the diagonal street that leads through the Dupat tole constitutes the spine of the settlement quarter. A street from the center of this spine leads to the agricultural fields outside the settlement by cutting through the Pilachen tole. The confluence of the diagonal street and the one leading to the fields expands into a square known as Dupa-lachi. A *lachi* is an open space in the tole which serves as a communal space in the neighborhood. It is a feature in Jyapu community settlements that medieval documents mention as early as 1507 [NS 628] (Kolver and Sakya 1985).

A series of parallel lanes branches out from the spine towards the interior of the quarter with each lane leading to a housing cluster. The lanes form cul-de-sacs while opening to areas behind the cluster through a maze of access ways passing through the ground floor of the houses. This pattern resembles other settlement quarters such as Bubahal in that the bahal and residential courtyards are connected by similar access ways. The lane, the end quadrangle, and the individual houses served by these accesses constitute a second level of the tole's community structure collectively known as *nani*. There are ten nani comprising the Dupat tole settlement cluster. These nani usually have their own names which they derive from their topographical relationships or they carry the identity of the clan inhabiting the nani. The boundaries of the tole are made of the minor lanes that serve only the tole bordering each other or the property boundary lines, occasionally in the form of drainage gutters. Through streets connecting different tole of the

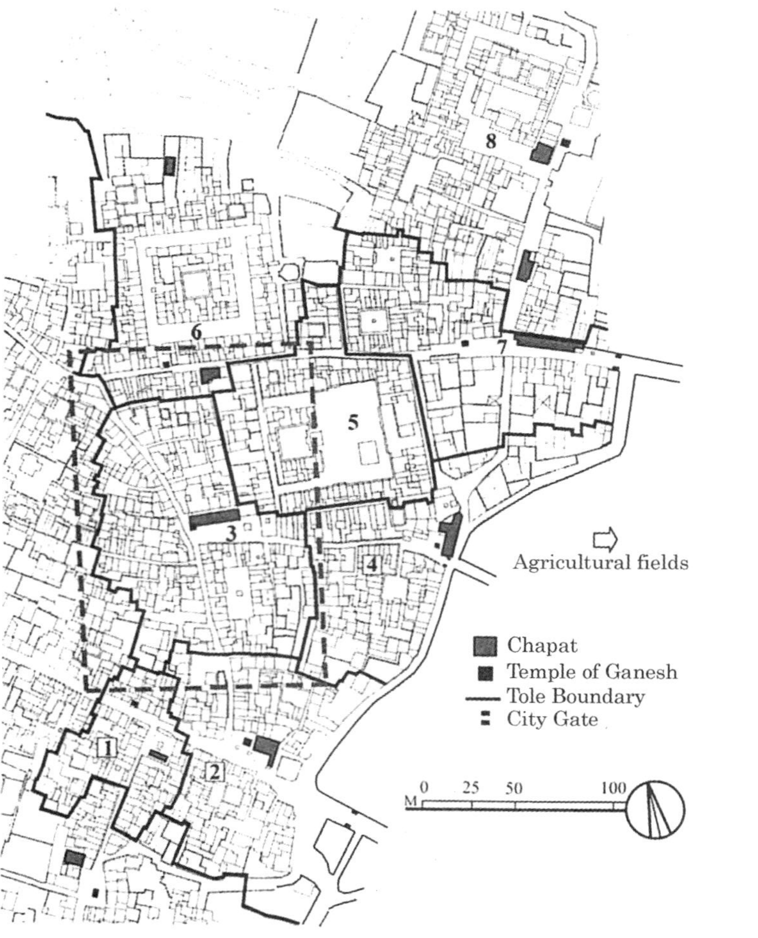

Fig. 5-2. Dupat tole and its neighboring quarters

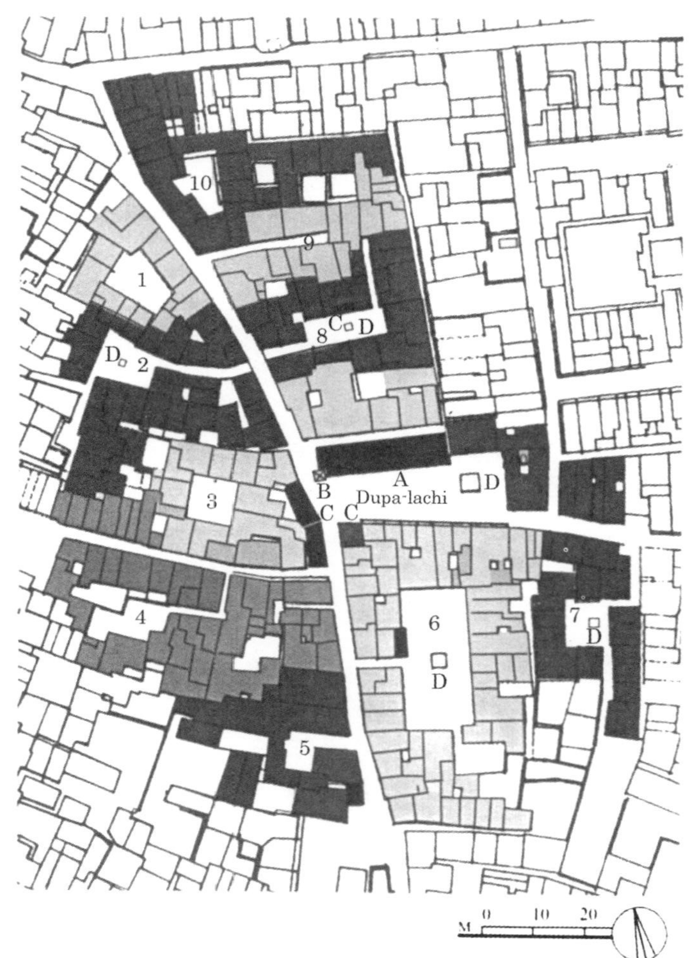

Fig. 5-3. Dupat tole settlement cluster

town usually do not constitute the tole's boundaries.

Early medieval documents from NS 224 (1103 CE) give addresses of vendors or sellers belonging to the house of a *livi*, a term denoting the back court of the house.[6] They also frequently refer to houses with a common gate as *griha-mandala* (Sanskrit for 'a cluster of dwellings'),[7] a concept akin to nani both socially and spatially. The organization of nani clusters is decidedly influenced by the orientation of the two major streets, the spine, and the street leading to the fields. The analysis of the orthogonality of the building forms and their relationship with the nani lanes and the main streets shows that the houses were first built along the courts at the end of the lane, before they were put up along the sides of the lanes and finally next to the main streets. This can be seen in the contrast between the non-orthogonal corners of the housing blocks facing the streets and the regular pattern found around the houses of the court. Likewise the nani lanes were originally accesses for the courts at the interior of the cluster rather than for the rows of the houses aligning it. This kind of structure indicates that each nani developed from a nucleus in its interior and a contiguous development occurred from this interior towards the street at a later stage. The structure of the clan cluster or nani, which branches from the main street rather than aligning with it, also suggests that such clusters evolved in the same manner. As the Jyapu community is traditionally not engaged in commodity or service trades, the diagonal street does not function as a market street. Thus, the characteristic form of the tole's early settlement can be visualized as a hamlet with farmers' homesteads rather

than a growing neighborhood of street row houses or a perimeter cluster around the square.

The Neighborhood Square: Dupa-lachi

The central open space or dupa-lachi is the community square of the Dupat tole. It constitutes the physical and social center of the neighborhood. Facilities serving the neighborhood community are built around this area. The four facilities that characterize Jyapu community quarters comprise a community house or *chapat*, a temple of Ganesa, a *pati* (Newari: *phalacha*), 'public rest house,' and a well. As a Buddhist community, a votive *caitya* is also enshrined in this square.

The temple of Ganesa and the chapat constitute the primary symbolic structures of the Dupat tole as a community (Fig. 5-4). A temple of Ganesa is found in every tole in Kathmandu Valley towns.

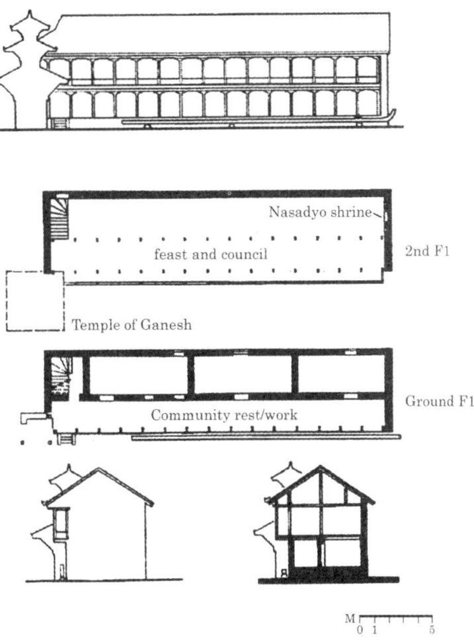

Fig. 5-4. Chapat of Dupa-lachi (Korn, 1979)

Ganesa is a deity of the Hindu Saivite pantheon who is honored for his protection of the tole. He is one of the two guardian deities in Buddhist monasteries. Everyone visits this shrine as part of their daily ritual offerings. In medieval documents Ganesa is addressed as *tole-devata*, the deity of the neighborhood. There is an inscription in the temple dated NS 771 (1651). It notes the brick pavement of the dupa-lachi by the members of a *gunila* trust, that is, a group of devotees who offered alms to Buddhist monks when they took shelter in monasteries during gunila, the name for the July-August rainy season in the Newari calendar. The resident members were not called Maharjan but "Bhavo," a practice that was prevalent until late in the medieval period. The place names noted are Dupat and Kothu nani (of Dupat).

At the right side of the temple facing east, there are two pati joined to each other. The one nearer the temple is an adjunct of the shrine itself. It serves as a place for the regular weekly recitation of songs in honor of Ganesa. The adjoining pati provides shelter for the *kusle*, a man who plays music during the ritual ceremonies of the community and cleans the dupa-lachi facilities. The structure at the southwest corner of the dupa-lachi in front of the temple was also originally a pati, but it has been converted into a modern four-storey building made of reinforced concrete which houses the municipality's ward office.

The next important artifact which identifies a Jyapu community is the chapat or community house. This structure is not found in other communities. The architectural form of the Dupat tole's chapat is an extended form of pati architecture, which is a ubiquitous urban community architecture found in all types of communities in the Kathmandu Valley. The Dupat tole's chapat is a two-storey colonnade which opens towards the lachi. The frontal colonnaded space on the ground floor is used for informal community gatherings as well as a place to rest and even do household chores. The chambers behind this space are used to store farm implements and for community feasts. Ritual implements for funeral ceremonies are also stored in one of the chambers. The upper storey is an open hall which serves as a space for the regular functions of various community organizations. A shrine for Nasadyo (Sanskrit: Nrityanatha), the god of dance, is installed in a niche on one of the walls. Ritual music and plays are learned and performed in this hall.

In some tole, there are more than one chapat and a number of households are attached to each of them. For instance, there are three chapat in the Subahal tole with 130, 110, and 27 households, respectively. Population growth and divisions in the clan community cause the building of new chapat. Until these are built by the community, provisional accommodations are provided by individual houses. Alternatively, an individual house might be donated for use as the community chapat, as is done in the Haka tole. Moreover, the local government might build such a chapat and take responsibility for its maintenance. The chapat in front of the Ganesa temple of Subahal has an inscription dated NS 746 (1625) that describes its repair work under a chief who was a Patravamsa Rabut Sivaram. Rabut comes from a noble family, but the members of the chapat trust are common people. It suggests the building of a chapat and its maintenance was also a responsibility of the local government. The social functions of a chapat thus make it the most important community artifact in the tole. In addition, since the chapat is not found in other communities, it may be seen as the symbol of the cohesive social structure of a Jyapu community.

The Maharjan of the Dupat tole have traditionally been a farming community and they utilize open spaces within the settlement for farming-related activities. For instance, during the harvest season the courtyard of the nani is used for drying and stacking farm produce. Traditionally, families have shared the space in front of their houses with others for these purposes. People in houses adjoining the dupa-lachi also used this area this way, but this practice has ceased with the increasing traffic within the settlement. However, the open courts of the nani continue to be used in this traditional fashion.

The dupa-lachi along with the temple of Ganesa, chapat, pati, and the open space crystallize the Dupat tole as a community. Here the community expresses its religious and social values through physical artifacts and socio-cultural activities. The lachi is also an extension of the private dwelling space of the individual households. The dupa-lachi is thus an indispensable space for the residents, and it constitutes the central feature of the Dupat community.

Jyapu Settlement Structure

The traditional farming activities of the community appear to have a direct bearing on the location of the Jyapu settlement quarters. All the neighborhoods of Patan's Jyapu community border open fields found at the lower level of the river basin. The Dupat tole and all its bordering neighborhoods each have one major street leading to the fields. These streets are generally wider than those inside the settlement which link the various neighborhoods to each other. They are even wider than the diagonal street, that is, the spine linking the settlements of the Jyapu community quarters from the southeast to the northeast corner of the town. This suggests that the connection between the Jyapu community and the fields is considered more important than the connection of the community to the city and its center.

The structure of the individual neighborhood and its link with other communities and zones of activities suggests a four-level hierarchy in the street network of the Jyapu community settlements. The first level comprises the street that serves the individual clan cluster of the tole. It is usually in the form of a cul-de-sac, and it serves as the communication link among the households of the nani. The second level consists of streets linking the individual tole to the neighborhood squares. But, the links between the Haka tole, the dupa-lachi, and Subahal or the links between Pinchen and Pilachen are not as direct indicating their secondary importance in the organization of these quarters. Another example of this second level is the link from Guita to Tyagal which, although relatively distinct, tortuously follows the topography gradually sloping towards east. The third level comprises the street connecting the neighborhood to the fields outside the settlement. This is the most significant level because of its important to the farming community. It is also the street linking the individual tole. Finally, the fourth level consists of the diagonal street, which is the spine connecting the clusters of the

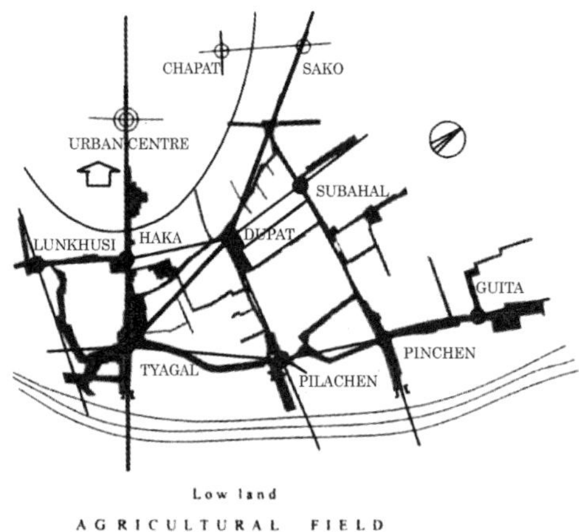

Fig. 5-5. Polygonal approximation of the Jyapu community settlement of Dupat neighborhood

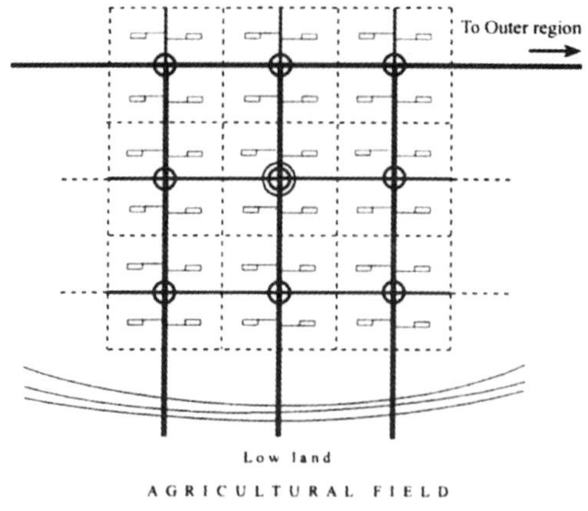

Fig. 5-6. Conceptual model of street patterns of the Jyapu community settlement

settlement quarters to the farther regions. It is through this street that the Jyapu community settlements are linked to the urban center. This form of settlement structure becomes clear when the neighborhood quarters around the Dupat tole are linked together (Figs. 5-5 and 5-6). This settlement structure is formed by connecting the community squares of each tole to the hierarchical network of streets to complete the settlement's grid. It should be noted that in this pattern of Jyapu community settlements, the clusters of Bhinche bahal and Subahal tole are formed with the Buddhist monasteries at the center, in a manner discussed in Chapter 4. While the community of Bhinche bahal consists of Vajracharya, the inhabitants of the Subahal community are Maharjan with a few Sakya living at the interior. Unlike the community halls (*digi*) of the Sakya and Vajracharya that are located in the internal residential court or the bahal, the Maharjan's community centers in Subahal tole are built along the main street of the quarter. While the available records of the Bhinche bahal and Subahal monasteries indicate their existence prior to the twelfth century, the historical connection between the Jyapu community quarters in the Dupat tole and these Buddhist monasteries is yet unclear. However, a morphological analysis of this area (discussed in Chapter 6) shows that the two bahal and their residential clusters are laid on a grid that is later than Pilacchen and Dupat tole. Despite this difference, the physical and social structure of the Jyapu communities in Dupat tole and their neighboring quarters clearly identify them as exhibiting the settlement pattern of a Jyapu community.

The Earliest Settlement Pattern

The analysis of the Dupat tole and its neighboring quarters inhabited by the Jyapu community reveals a settlement form that is distinct from those in other areas of the town. As mentioned earlier, these Jyapu settlements border agricultural fields outside the city and the hierarchy of their street patterns shows a closer relationship with the fields than with the city center. Furthermore, the diagonal street acts as a border zone between the city and the quarters inhabited by Jyapu communities.

The above analysis shows that the typical Jyapu settlement quarter began as hamlets of homesteads at the interior of the quarter, developed into a cluster of clans or nani, and then matured into a neighborhood with a square as the community center. This square, with its temple of Ganesa and chapat (community house), is the symbol of a matured Jyapu community settlement. This pattern is distinct from those communities which have a Buddhist monastery as the community center. In these neighborhoods of Buddhist monasteries, the streets and square are not crucial to the settlement cluster's organization. Instead, dwellings are built in a pattern of concentric circles with the monastery at the center. The digi (a hall which forms part of the monastery) functions partly as a chapat. Alternatively, it is a structure built separately in the interior court of the quarter but never in the street square. Despite these differences, there are also similarities in the organization of the two settlement forms that need to be pointed out. First, both forms of settlements developed from a nucleus at the interior of the quarter. Second, the court or the lane is the primary axis for both communities but not the main street in the organization of the individual clan clusters.

The paucity of dated materials makes it difficult to determine precisely when the settlement form of Jyapu communities evolved. Available historical records show that the Tyagal and Guita tole existed during the Licchavi period while the Bhinche and Subahal tole were in existence by the early medieval period. The Dupat tole was probably settled by the Licchavi period prior to eighth century. This is suggested by the fact that the Dupat has traditionally carried out the Machhendranatha rituals that go back this early period. The legends of Guita tole take us to the prehistoric past when it was the palace court of the legendary King Sarvananda (Wright 1972, 88). When artifacts such as Buddhist caitya and images are considered, the history of the area goes back to the Licchavi period and further even to the Kirata period.

In the Kathmandu Valley, the cult of Ganesa is known to have existed before the seventh century. By the ninth century, Ganesa had become the patron deity of some artisans. One of the most popular forms of Ganesa in the valley is Nrityanatha, the patron of dance. For example, Ganesa is depicted in a dancing posture in an image of Uma-maheswora found in Tyagal, south of Dupat, and dated 1012. It is not certain when Ganesa became the central symbol of the tole settlement, but a 1642 inscription in Bhaktapur records Ganesa as tole-devata 'the deity of the tole.' A chronicle about the establishment of a town in Deupatan, east of Kathmandu, by Sivadeva, a Licchavi king, provides some clues on the settlement form during the ancient period. The chronicle presents the following account:

> In his reign the Durbar [palace] near Baneswara was abandoned, and one of nine stories in height was built in Devapattana, where the Raja established his court. After removing to Devapattana, he brought Nrityanatha, known as Bhukuns, from the Satarudra mountain, and established him on the western side of Pashupatinatha. This Nrityanatha is possessed of great gifts.

The Raja built nine new tole, or divisions of the city and erected nine Ganesa... (After performing all the requisite ceremonies) he founded and peopled the place known as Navatol ... and named the town Suvarnapuri (Wright 1972, 124–5).

The chronicle also shows that in the foundation ritual of a town, the king constructed four squares oriented to the four points of the compass and enshrined Ganesa and other deities in each square.

The historical accuracy of this legend is partly substantiated by an edict by Narendradeva dated 647. It describes the locality of Navagriha as an area where the local administration had been given some autonomy. Sivadeva is known to have ruled it sometime between 535 and 590. This is verified by two other inscriptions of the same period found on the pedestal of the images of the deities mentioned in the legend. The locality at the western part of Deupatan is presently known as Navali-tole.

The same chronicle describes the marking and construction of nine centers to constitute the town's nine tole. Two possible street patterns of this settlement may be hypothesized. The first pattern is one where the individual quarters are bounded by the main streets and the community square is located at the center of the quarter's interior. In this pattern, minor streets connecting the internal squares might be considered in the hierarchy of the street network. This form of a street network is not characteristic of the Kathmandu Valley towns, except in parts of the urban quarters inhabited by the Buddhist Sakya and Vajracharya communities, where the center of the community is the Buddhist monastery or

a residential quadrangle (Chap. 4). The second pattern is the location of the community squares at the crossing of the main streets and the tole boundaries cutting through the settlement blocks bounded by these streets. The pattern closely mirrors the settlements of the Jyapu community (Fig. 5-6). Therefore, according to the chronicle, the tole of Suvarnapuri is defined by the location of its community center and not by the streets bounding a quarter. In essence, the town's network of streets is a result of linking the neighborhood's central nodes. Further hierarchy in the street networks can be visualized in the case of the Dupat tole neighborhoods. The chronicle does not indicate the types of communities inhabiting the new town though it shows that generally the form of this settlement is similar to that of the Jyapu community. Perhaps this planning principle that centers on the community nodes probably inherits and encapsulates the indigenous mode of the individual community settlement forms and suggests an attempt to bring together the separate hamlets within the defined limits of the town's boundaries.

The two settlement forms—the street-square pattern of the Jyapu communities and the bahal pattern of the Vajracharya and the Sakya Buddhist clergy—are the historic urban forms of Patan. The rootedness of the Jyapu community in the Dupat tole indicate that the street-square pattern is more indicative of the earliest forms of the community settlement structure in Kathmandu Valley towns. The bahal pattern, on the other hand, is associated with the advent of Vajrayana in Buddhism, which is considered to be later than the seventh century.

PART III

Spatial Order: The Ancient System of Measure and Planning Modules

6

The Layout of Courtyard Settlement Quarters

The ancient cities and towns of the Kathmandu Valley exhibit clusters of settlements organized in the form of courtyard structures. In particular, there are extensive residential dwelling clusters around Buddhist monasteries in cities such as Patan, which has the largest number of Buddhist monasteries in the valley. This development is thought to have coincided with the coming of Vajrayana which, unlike the Mahayana Principle, allowed the Buddhist clergy to marry. A series of courtyards were subsequently formed around the monastery quadrangle, some of which functioned both as extensions of the main monastery as well as residential courts. The extensive distribution of bahal in the city, the regularity in their physical configuration, and the dwelling clusters around them suggest that they had a significant influence on the development pattern of the city. In many cases, the classical vihara architecture was transformed by merging the bahal court with the residential courts around it as illustrated by our description of Bubahal in Chapter 4. However, whether or not there were underlying planning concepts and models that guided the development of such settlement quarters remains unexplored. If such planning concepts and models on bahal quadrangles and settlements around them did exist and if evidence of their planning features could be found in other quarters and buildings such as palaces, it would help explain the planning features of the city as well.

This chapter demonstrates that the layout of the bahal settlement quarters, particularly the monastery residential quadrangles, was built following a planning grid that employed a standard modular measure and planning method. In this respect, Watanabe's study of I baha-bahi (1998b, 100–2) and Kurotsu's studies of Patan palace courts (1991a and 1991b) suggest planning grids in the layouts of these two structures. They also suggest that the structural sections of these courtyard buildings were determined by certain standard measures of a cubit (Sanskrit: *hasta*) and its multiples. However, Watanabe and Kurotsu's above studies focus on the individual monastery structure or the palace quadrangle proper. They do not analyze the layout and planning relationship of the monastery courts with respect to the residential courtyards, the dwelling clusters, the quarter block, and the planning modules used for the quarters of residential settlements. Pant's study (2002) of Thimi, a town between Patan and Bhaktapur which existed by the Licchavi period, demonstrates that Thimi was planned in regular blocks that employed a standard dimension, which in metric measure is close to 38.40 m. This study of Patan began with the hypothesis that settlement quarters of Patan might have been planned using a grid similar to that used in Thimi.

Method of Analysis

Our study utilized cadastral survey maps of Patan that were drawn on a scale of 1 : 500 by the Department of Land Survey, Government of Nepal in 1979. These maps delineate the individual buildings, including public utilities and land parcels. We verified the accuracy of these maps through our field measurements[1] and with the measured drawings of the Patan Palace produced by the Nippon Institute of Technology (1981). Consequently, we found the maps to be sufficiently accurate for the purposes of our analysis.[2] To create a complete map on a single sheet, however, the cadastral maps were scanned and joined together. The resulting map was then traced using a computer-aided design drawing. In the entire process, care was taken that no detail was distorted or omitted.

Once our map was completed, we used the standard module discovered in Thimi as the reference measurement to search for settlement blocks with regular dimensions. Measurements were taken of areas between streets, plot boundaries, and boundaries of dwelling clusters in areas that showed more regular geometric patterns. A cursory observation of Patan city map shows that such areas are more apparent in Buddhist monastery settlement clusters. These quarters are marked by the presence of large open residential courts with dwelling clusters around them. Through measurement trials, four such settlement areas in different sectors of the city were selected (Fig. 6-1).

Within each of the selected quarters, an orthogonal grid of 19.2 m and its half—9.6 m—was superimposed in both the longitudinal and transverse directions. The measurement module of 19.2 m was derived from Pant's 2002 study of Thimi, which revealed that the town blocks were laid out in a grid composed of standard units of blocks of 38.40 m wide. This figure corresponds to the *paridesha* measure in the system of measurements described by Kautilya in his Arthasastra (Chap. 1: Table 1-1).

In laying out the grid for this study, reference lines were checked repeatedly to determine the best fit of the grid-net with existing building lines, boundaries of clusters and plots, and streets. Major boundaries defined by streets, open courts, and cluster or plot boundaries were used as the basis for choosing the reference lines for the layout of the grid. Plinth

Notes: 1. The numbers in the figure are referred to Table 5-2.
2. The shaded areas represent selected quarters for the case study.

Fig. 6-1.   Location of settlement quarters surveyed in Patan

lines were also taken into consideration. Generally, buildings fronting streets, lanes, or courtyards have a raised plinth with a width of about 80 cm to 1 m. These plinth lines, which are considered to mark private property, are usually shown in the cadastral maps. All the measurements and grid take the plinth line as reference when dimensions are measured. In cases when the lines are not shown in a map, a width of two cubits (96 cm) is assumed for the measurement analysis.[3]

The value of the grid-size was initially open to some degree of adjustment from the base reference value of 9.6 m. The possibility of variable grid values for the different quarters was also taken into consideration to account for possible changes in the measuring standards due to practical requirements as well as time gaps in their historical development.

The four settlement quarters selected for the present study include the quarters of Bhinche bahal, Subahal, and Guita bahil in the east, and the Nakhachuk-Kwabahal in the northwestern sector of the city (Fig. 6-1). Dates in records for all these bahal show that they existed before the twelfth century (Chap. 4).[4] However, chronicles and legends suggest that they have existed since at least Licchavi period. The settlements in these areas could well be from the pre-Licchavi period, according to iconographic evidence from art historians.[5] Bhinche bahal, Subahal and Kwabahal are among the 16 primary bahal of Patan (Wright 1972, 234-5).[6] Guita bahil is among the 25 bahil of Patan, most of which are located at the periphery of the city. In each of these quarters are located a number of branch bahal belonging to each of the three primary bahal. Figures 6-2 to 6-4 show that the physical configurations of most of these settlement clusters have a primary bahal at the core. The regularity in the arrangement of the dwelling clusters around large quadrangular open courts is readily apparent. The individuality and uniformity of these quarters' planning principles will be analyzed separately. Although there is a possibility that their layout planning is linked to the quarters abutting and the settlement at large, the present analysis will be limited to the physical boundaries of their quarter blocks, which are mostly defined by streets. The shaded areas in Figures 6-2 to 6-4 show the present boundaries of the neighborhood quarters. The dimensions in the figures are given in metric measures; their corresponding danda measurements can be checked in Table 6-1.

Bhinche Bahal and Subahal Clusters

The Bhinche bahal and Subahal are two neighboring tole which are separated by a street that leads to a town gate to the east (Fig. 6-2). Unlike the layout of other bahal, the corners of these tole's open quadrangles are aligned with the four cardinal directions while their main shrines face west. Upon observing the

Table 6-1. Danda and metric measures.

danda (d)	metric (m)
1 (0.1r)	**1.92**
2	3.84
3	5.76
4	7.68
5 (0.5r)	**9.60**
6	11.52
7	13.44
8	15.36
9	17.28
10 (1r)	**19.20**
11	21.50
12	23.04
13	24.96
14	26.88
15 (1.5r)	**28.80**
16	30.72
17	32.64
18	34.56
19	36.48
20 (2r)	**38.40**
21	40.32
22	42.24
23	44.16
24	46.08
25 (2.5r)	**48.00**
26	49.92
27	51.84
28	53.76
29	55.68
30 (3r)	**57.60**
35 (3.5r)	**67.20**
40 (4r)	**76.80**
50 (5r)	**96.00**

regularity in the layout of the Bhinche bahal and Subahal clusters, a question arises about "whether [or not] they constitute a planned insertion in the earlier organic form of the towns" (Nippon Institute of Technology 1986, 40).[7] The Bhinche bahal has a northern entry gate

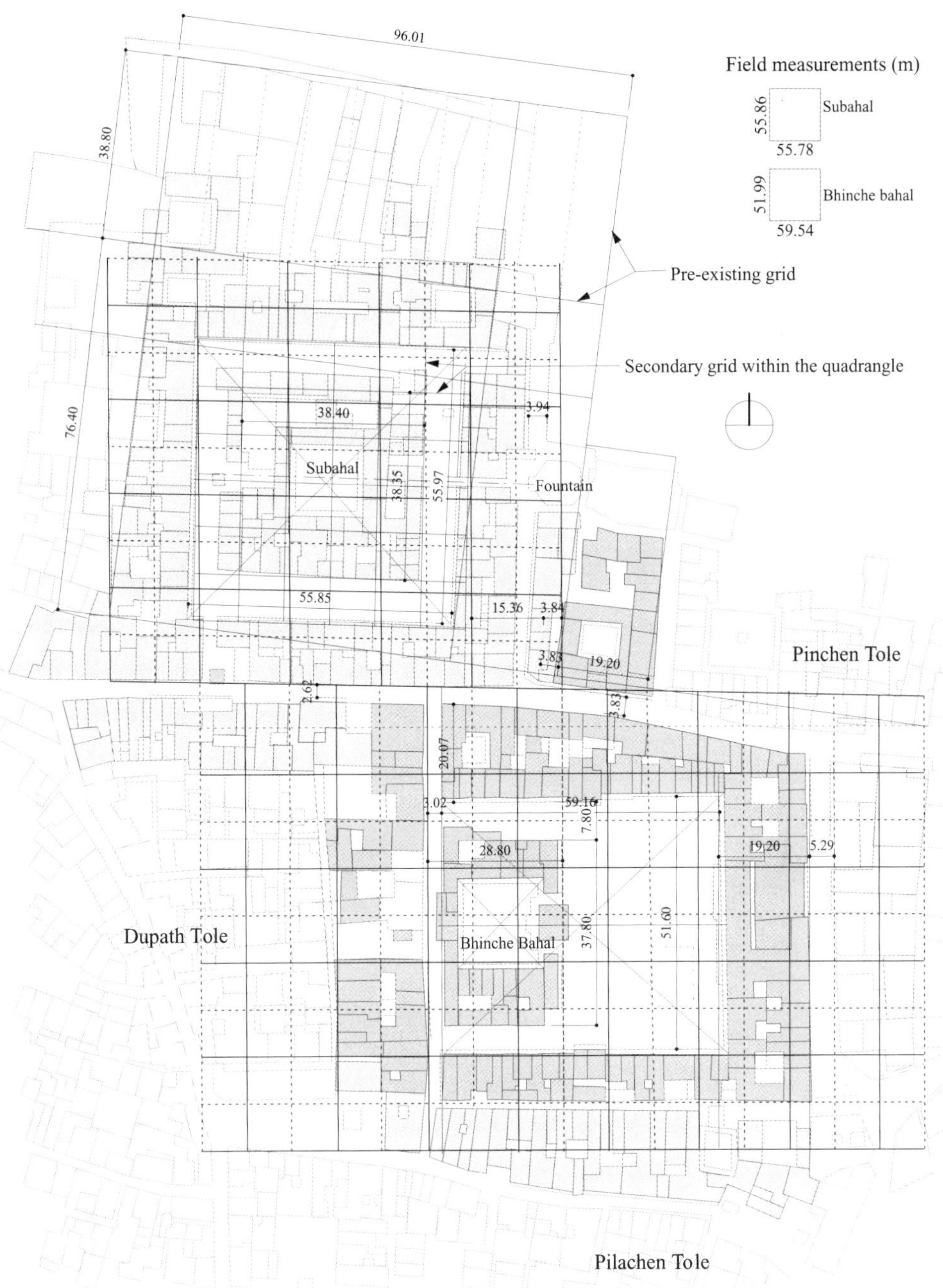

Note: The spacing of grid lines is 19.2 m, i. e., 1 rajju (1r).
All the dimensions are measured from the cadastral map of Patan (1:500)
made by Department of Land Surey, HMG of Nepal in 1979.

Fig. 6-2.   The quarters of Bhinche bahal and Subahal

while Subahal has such a southern gate on the main street. In Subahal, the monastery court is laid out exactly at the center of the larger residential court, while in Bhinche bahal it is offset towards the west on the central east-west axis of the larger court. Moreover, the court of Subahal is a square of approximately 55.85 m × 55.97 m while the one in the Bhinche bahal is 51.60 m × 59.16 m in the direction of north-south and east-west respectively. The superimposed grids are laid in a manner described in the previous section. Note that the grid-net does not always coincide with the four sides of the open quadrangles (Fig. 6-2). However, the use of standardized modular units to layout these quadrangles is evident. For instance, all the four wings around the open quadrangle of the Bhinche bahal have a width of 19.2 m or 1 rajju (r). The layout of its open court follows this division of the site allowing space for the lanes and the streets. The inner block of the monastery, including the dwelling clusters around it, measures 37.8 m (~2 r) north-south and 28.8 m (1.5 r) east-west (including the width of the north-south lane).

Unlike the Bhinche bahal, the layout of Subahal has a more complex relationship with its boundary quarters. While the layouts of the Bhinche bahal and Subahal are found in one grid-net, the alignment of the street in the east, the boundary line in the west, and the plots in the north of Subahal have a common orientation which deviates from the Subahal monastery court by 13 degrees east. Such is also the case at the quarter south of the Bhinche bahal. The fact that all the three adjacent zones of Subahal and the one south of Bhinche bahal, belong to one orientation suggests that the layout of Subahal as well as the Bhinche bahal was planted in a pre-existing system of alignment. This is probably the reason why the open quadrangle of Subahal is slightly rotated towards those existing boundary alignments. The superimposed grid in the Subahal quarter has been drawn in conformity to the general orthogonality of the bahal court and the dwelling clusters surrounding it.[8]

The juxtaposition of the Subahal grid and the grid alignment of its neighborhoods clarify some aspects related to its planning layout. With respect to the "neighborhood grid" (noted as a preexisting grid in the Figure 6-2), it is to be noted that the distance between the western oblique boundary of the Subahal block and the east side of a lane that forms the boundary between the Bhinche bahal and Subahal tole is 5 r, while it is 6 r between the southern end of the oblique boundary to the southern edge of a track in the north. The existing settlement cluster is formed within a block whose size corresponds to 4.5 r × 4.5 r. However, if we consider the boundary of the Subahal and Bhinche bahal tole in the east, which also coincides with the oblique grid, it becomes apparent that the east-west width of the Subahal quarter is 5 r. In this block of the grid, if we include a lane which is 2 danda (d) wide (3.84 m) in the east, the width of the eastern wing becomes 1 r. Furthermore, the bahal court will then be located at the center between these two east-west boundaries. This relationship between the two sets of grids shows that the existing lane east of the Subahal block was the result of an adjustment due to the presence of a fountain there prior to the planning of the quarter. The existence of the fountain also appears to have helped determine the east-west axis of the monastery, which is the same as that of the fountain itself.

The existing deviations in the layout alignments of the cluster blocks of the quarter as seen from the superimposed grid and the layout axis are neatly explained by a pre-existing grid layout. It is to be noted that the larger residential court, which is in the shape of parallelogram, and the bahal court at the core have the same center while that defined by the square grid is 2 m offset to the east. Yet, the consistency of the use of the grid is particularly clear from the block size and the residential court and its subdivisions with a circumambulatory path around the monastery, as shown by the secondary grid. The widths of these surrounding paths at the south, east, and west are close to 0.5 r, that is, 5 d or 9.6 m when we consider the alignments of the grid and the lines of building clusters. This suggests a uniform plan regulating the development of the settlement in a manner similar to the Bhinche bahal but with a more pronounced concentric order.

The Guita Bahil Cluster

Guita bahil, lying on the eastern border of the city, is thought to be one of the oldest settlements of Patan. It is one of those quarters where the arrangement of the dwelling clusters shows a neat orthogonal pattern (Fig. 6-3). In this quarter, one also finds the grid-net in close conformity with the court quadrangles, major cluster boundaries, and plot boundaries. The layout shows the three square quadrangles arranged in one longitudinal axis (shown by the diagonals and dotted

lines in the figure). The largest outer quadrangle, which includes the street on the east, measures 3.5 r × 3.5 r. The innermost ring which consists of three bahil is 2 r × 2 r, while the middle ring is 3 r × 3 r. Surrounding the open courts are blocks of dwelling clusters with widths of 5 d or 0.5 r, 1 r, and 1.5 r. The width of the lane surrounding the middle ring is 4 d in the north and 2.5 d in the east and west. The settlement quarter shows this regular layout within a grid of 5 r × 7 r. A secondary axis of symmetry runs north-south. It is defined by the inner ring of bahil clusters close to the centre line of the clear width of the outer court and shown by the access leading towards a stupa located at the northern boundary of the quarter. Likewise another stupa in the east is located at the east-west axis of Guita bahil and Mul Guita bahil. The grid-net, like those in the Bhinche bahal and Subahal, closely coincides with the existing boundaries of Guita bahil's neighborhood quarter.

Nakhachuk-Kwabahal Cluster

The area defined by the Nakhachuk-Kwabahal axis has the largest monastery settlement cluster in Patan (Fig. 6-4). In the east, it borders one of the two major north-south streets of the city (Fig. 6-1), while in the west there is a lane, which appears to have been closed recently, as shown by the remnant sections at its north and south ends. The street in the south links the town settlement with the city's northwest gate. The settlement quarters are developed along three large open quadrangular courts, which are linked both in terms of their physical configuration as well as religious affiliation. Kwabahal, situated to the east of the

Fig. 6-3. The quarter of Guita bahil

clusters, is one of the primary bahal of Patan. Its branch bahal are located in the various quarters within this group of clusters. Each of the larger courts—Elanani, Nagbahal, and Nakhachuk—is also a bahal or, according to legend, contains the remains of a past bahal (Locke 1985, 52; 56; 58). No historical records describing the chronology of their foundation have yet been found. Nevertheless, the earliest dated record found in a colophon of a palm leaf manuscript indicates that Kwabahal had existed by the eleventh century.

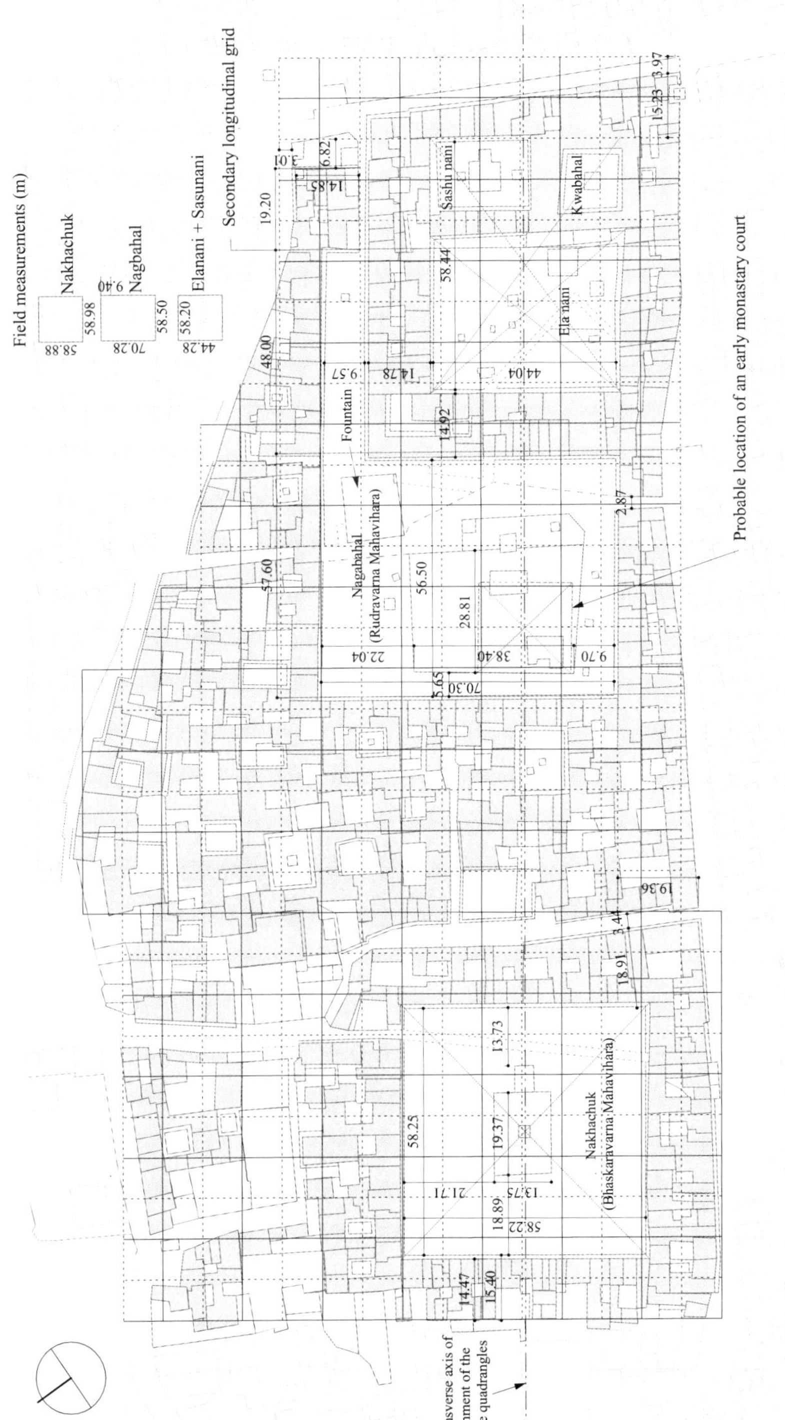

Fig. 6-4. The quarters of Nakhachuk, Nagbahal, and Kwabahal

The open quadrangle of Nakhachuk at the west end of the cluster is a square with sides measuring close to 3 r, while the next quadrangle, Nagbahal, has north and south sides of the same width. The sides of Elanani are 35.80 m × 44 m. However, the quadrangle formed by Elanani and Sasu nani (Fig. 6-4) taken together gives the east-west a width of 3 r. The analysis of the grid-net with respect to the major boundary lines of the cluster further sheds light both in their planning features and a relative temporal sequence in their development.

As in the Bhinche bahal and Subahal, we find that the superimposed grids in Nakhachuk do not always coincide with the quadrangles for the same reason given for Bhinche Bahal. The layout of Nakhachuk has allowance for the width of the street in the east and a width of 1 r for the courtyard wing. Nakhachuk also resembles Subahal in that despite the firmly orthogonal structure of the layout in these quadrangular clusters, the street east of Nakhachuk enters obliquely from its southeast corner. This alignment of the street deviates seven degrees towards the west from the alignment of the quadrangles. Additionally, the plots in the north and the settlement clusters in the northwest, south, and southwest of this Nakhachuk-Kwabahal block as well as the main street in the east of Kwabahal conform to the alignment of the street that is oblique to Nakhachuk. This juxtaposition bears striking similarity to Bhinche bahal and Subahal, suggesting that Nakhachuk and the other quadrangles in this quarter also represent a realigned layout in the existing alignment structure of streets and field boundaries.

The relationship of Nakhachuk and Nagbahal is apparent from the coincidence of the traverse grid line on the north side of the open quadrangle. The south side of the Nagbahal quadrangle appears to have been determined by allowing 1 r for the cluster width measured at the southwest corner in a manner similar to the layout of Nakhachuk. The longitudinal alignment of the quadrangle is most likely explained by the remnant structure, which is presently found 45 cm above the general ground level of the courtyard. The structure shown by the dotted lines in Figure 6-4 is a space of 2 r × 1.5 r. The longitudinal grid coincides with the eastern and western sides of this structure, while the grid is offset at the northern and southern sides. It is notable that the space left between the south side of the quadrangle and the edge of the ruins is 0.5 r. Although no historical documents are available to shed light on the early form of these remains, both the quadrangles of Nakhachuk and Nagbahal are said to have had core structures with bahal courts in earlier times (Locke 1985, 58).

The horizontal relationship among the three quadrangles is also emphasized by the central transverse axis that is common to both Nakhachuk and Elanani (with an offset of 50 cm). We can see from the coincidence of the superimposed grids with the east side of the open court of Sashu nani and the axial relationship with Nakhachuk and Nagbahal the determination of the size of the Elanani quadrangle by following the modular grid of 19.2 m. The fact that there exists such a central axis to link Elanani and Nakhachuk suggests the possibility that there once existed a monastery court at the core of the Nagbahal quadrangle in this axis. If laid in this axis, a typical monastic court the size of Nakabahil, which lies to the southwest across the street, would fit exactly over the space of the remnant structure. In determining the exact location of the Nagbahal open quadrangle along the transverse axis, it is found that there exists another longitudinal grid system, whose reference point is probably the northeast corner of the quarter block used in our study. At the border of the northeast corner, there is a terrace in high plinth with a monument associated with the legendary Lalita Jyapu, the man who is said to have planned the city (Wright 1972, 134–5). Longitudinal grid lines drawn from this border as a reference give the exact width of the block (1 r) adjoining this border, the position of a lane going north, the western boundary of the west wing of the Elanani court, and the western side of the Nagbahal quadrangle. We consider this grid to be of secondary importance as its control, unlike the general grid, is found to be limited to the quadrangle of the Nagbahal clusters.

A Classical Monastery Residential Block and the Nivartana Court

The preceding analysis of the four residential quarters shows the repetitive use of the dimension 3 r for the open quadrangle. The Bubahal quadrangle studied in Chapter 4 also employs this measure. Table 6-2 lists the sizes of those bahal open courts where one side is longer

Table 6-2. Measured dimensions of residential quadrangular open courts with one of the sides larger than 1.5r = 15d (28.80m), Patan. (location indicated by s. no., cf. Fig. 6-1)

	Monastery-resident quadrangle courts	measured value (m)	theoretical measure by danda multiple (m)	danda multiple	margin of error with respect to 10d (1 rajju) multiples
1	Bhinche bahal	59.16 × 51.60	57.60 × 51.84	30d × 27d	+8.1%
2	Su bahal	55.85 × 55.97	57.60 × 57.60	30d × 30d	−9.1%, −8.5%
3	Guita bahil	57.60 × 67.20	57.60 × 67.20	30d × 35d	0%, 0%
4	Elanani + Sasunani + Kwabahal	58.44 × 44.04	57.60 × 44.16	30d × 23d	+4.4%
5	Nag bahal	55.83 × 70.30	57.60 × 71.04	30d × 37d	−9.3%
6	Nakhachuk	58.25 × 58.22	57.60 × 57.60	30d × 30d	+3.4%, +3.4%
7	Naka bahil	41.65 × 37.60	42.24 × 38.4	22d × 20d	−4.2%
8	Bubahal	57.80 × 32.00	57.60 × 32.64	30d × 17d	+1%
9	Daubaha-nani	32.92 × 33.49	32.64 × 32.64	17d × 17d	
10	Na bahal	32.82 × 32.30	32.64 × 32.64	17d × 17d	
11	Daubahal-south	31.00 × 31.90	32.64 × 32.64	17d × 17d	
12	Machhindra bahal	51.45 × 77.40	51.84 × 76.80	27d × 40d	+3.1%
13	Cakra bahil	37.94 × 39.08	38.40 × 38.40	20d × 20d	−2.4%, +3.5%
14	Jyabahal	29.40 × 23.90	28.80 × 23.04	15d × 12d	+3.1%
15	Oku bahal nani	36.80 × 29.20	38.40 × 28.80	20d × 15d	−8.3%, +2.1%
16	Jyapu nani	28.64 × 15.64	28.80 × 15.36	15d × 8d	−0.8%
	Average margin of error				−0.64%

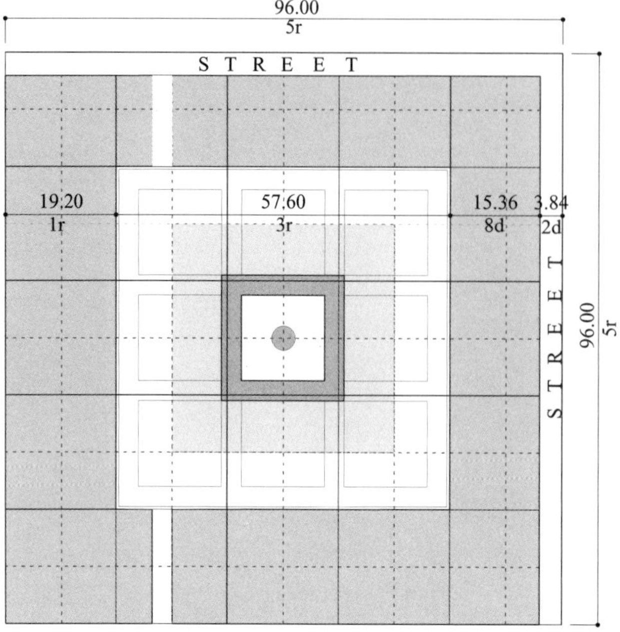

The open quadrangle accommodates exactly nine typical Buddhist monastery courts, or, four courts leaving an ambulatory path of half a *rajju* width.

Fig. 6-5. A standard Nivartana court residential block layout in a classical grid of 1 rajju width.

than 28.8 m or 1.5 r. It can be seen from the table that while other bahal courts also show a close correspondence to the size which is a multiple of 1 r, it is the 3 r size which is most conspicuous and closely related in giving the minimum size of the quarter block as 5 r × 5 r, if the layout of the block is to conform to the grid of 1 r width. This is illustrated by the Bhinche bahal, Subahal, Nakhachuk, and Elanani-Kwabahal quadrangles. Why is this particular dimension more popular than others? Is it a functional requirement or a symbolic form? At present, it is unclear exactly what system of land units were employed in ancient Nepal. This system may be one factor which influenced the decision regarding court size. Nevertheless, three possible reasons

are posited to explain the pattern in the layout of courts, land measure, and symbolism. These may have been the considerations in the planning of the block, and they will be explained with the use of an ideal model illustrated by Figure 6-5.

Figure 6-5 illustrates a quarter block measuring 5 r × 5 r with a square open quadrangle measuring 3 r × 3 r. The plan of this block makes an allowance for streets which are 2 d wide. This is derived from the lanes in the east of Subahal and Nakhachuk which correspond to this theoretical dimension while giving values for dwelling block widths similar to those found in the quarters studied. The size of the quadrangle is big enough to accommodate four monastic courts of a typical size at the center, which are exemplified by Chusya bahal or Khunbahal (see Chap. 7)[9] leaving an ambulatory path of 0.5 r around the monastery cluster, a feature seen in Guita bahil. A variation of this pattern is the residential cluster ring around the central monastery court such as those found in the settlement quarters of Patan. In a similar manner, the quadrangle of 3 r accommodates nine courts, each one of which is the size of a typical monastery court. However, since this form does not leave space for the ambulatory path, it is not considered in the planning of the court, although the symbolic meaning of a nine-court quadrangle might be of significance.

Another reason, which is related to the unit of land measure, again comes from the Arthasastra of Kautilya. According to him, 2 r make 1 paridesha and 3 r make a *nivartana*. Nivartana is a Sanskrit word meaning 'causing to turn back, returning or retreating.' The corresponding Pali word is *nivattana* (Rhys-Davids and Stede 1972) whose meaning is similarly attributed to certain Buddhist artifacts.[10] The use of such a measure in ancient Nepal is yet unverified. However, there are fifth to eighth century copper plate inscriptions from central and western India which mention donations of land by the rulers in units of nivartana.[11] Nivartana is also said to represent a day's plowing by a team of six or eight oxen, or an area measured from the point where they started to the point where they stopped after a day's work (Kane 1973, 145).

When coupled with its literal meaning, the land measure nivartana symbolizes completeness. Furthermore, a Buddhist Jataka mentions a nivartana movement. This pertains to how Siddhartha wins his bride, Yasodhara, by archery:

Siddhartha set up four banana trunks at the four corners of the courtyard and fastening a thread at the feathered end of the arrow, he shot at one of the trunks; the arrow penetrated it and then the second, the third, the fourth and finally the first again returning the arrow to his hand, while the trees stood encircled by the thread (Lalitavistara (1902) cited in Snodgrass [1982, 40]).

The Nivartana court is essentially a practical choice consequential to the adopted grid system and the tradition of a concentric layout system with the Buddhist monastic court at the center. It may as well have been simultaneously associated with the Buddhist symbolism and the concept of completeness. A significant variation of this model found in Patan is the open court which is 17 d wide. This court size results in a quarter block of 4 r × 4 r. The layout gives 1 r for the width of the wings and 3 d for the street width (17 d + 10 d + 10 d + 3 d = 40 d = 4 r). If a monastery court of typical size (12 d × 12 d) is laid at the core of this quadrangle, there will be ambulatory paths measuring 2.5 d in width. This is illustrated in the case of Nabahal, where there is a stupa at the centre (Figs. 6-6). These forms of courtyard quadrangles, therefore, may be said to represent a planning concept of Buddhist community settlements.

Conclusion

The analysis of four Buddhist monastery residential clusters shows that all of them were planned settlement quarters and that there was a pre-existing grid order in Patan over which the new settlement grid was laid out. The concurrence of the grid in the layout of the quarter block, the

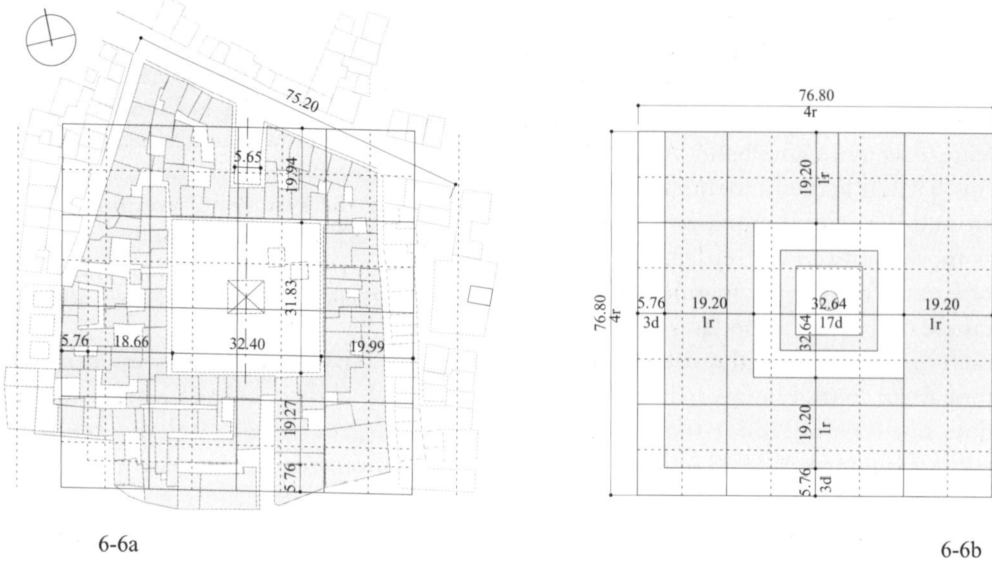

6-6a   6-6b

Fig. 6-6. Nabahal: The quarter block of 4 rajju with a 17 d square courtyard

existence of the central axis, and the modular dimensions in both the larger and lesser multiples confirm that the open bahal quadrangle was planned and it was central in determining the layout of the dwelling clusters. The standard module conforms to an earlier finding in Thimi. The main features of the planning of bahal courtyard settlement quarters may be summarized as follows:

1. The planning follows an orthogonal grid system that controls the division of the whole settlement quarter. The orthogonality is maintained even when the neighboring boundaries follow different alignments.

2. An open quadrangle in the layout of the settlement is a central concept. It defines the central axis of the settlement quarter. Monastery courts are laid in this central axis. Furthermore, there is a greater occurrence of open court quadrangles with sides of 3 r, which results in a theoretical model of a quarter block of 5 r wide. The basis of this size is the use of a classical grid system with standard measures that are described by Kautilya. Likewise, the ideal width for the wing of the bahal is 1 r, but which in general depends upon the total size of the quarter block and the central open quadrangle.

3. The size of a standard module that measures 1 r or 19.2 m as well as its multiples is applied uniformly to control the layout dimensions. The lanes, pathways, and streets within the court-yard and around the neighborhood show clear widths close to 5 d, 4 d, 3.5 d, and 2 d.

4. The quarter blocks planned in the grid coincide with the existing boundaries of neighborhoods indicating a convergence of the social and the physical orders.

This chapter has analyzed some of the physical planning principles used in the city's quarter blocks characterized by Buddhist monastery quadrangles. In the next chapter we study in detail the planning principles in the layout of dwelling plots around the open quadrangle of these courtyard settlement quarters.

7

Patterns of Plot Divisions

The courtyard form of residential settlements and the formation of contiguous clusters in Patan as well as in other Newar town settlements together make the urban fabric of the valley towns a honeycomb-like structure. In Patan, the width of these courtyards range from a few meters to more than 75 m, with dwelling blocks belonging to families of various clans built adjoining each other. The larger types of courtyards are generally known as nani or in some instances, as *chok*.[1] As mentioned earlier, a greater part of the Patan population is made up of Buddhist communities. Of these the Sakya, Vajracharya, and Maharjan communities make up the majority. In general, the settlement quarters of these communities are organized around large quadrangular courtyards where facilities such as fountains, wells, caitya, temples, community houses, and various other artifacts serve the religious, social, and functional needs of the residents. Among the religious establishments Buddhist monasteries, the bahal, often constitute the central core of the settlement quarters.

In previous chapters, we analyzed the spatial and community structure of such settlement quarters with the Buddhist monastery courtyard at the center, and demonstrated the primacy of this courtyard in its organization. Further studies (Chap. 6) demonstrated that such residential quarters are laid out in a larger grid system. This chapter investigates the planning principles related to the division of dwelling plots around such open courtyards. To do this, four large courtyards were selected for a detailed analysis. Results show that the dwelling plots around the open courtyards had been planned following a principle that is specific to the courtyard form related to the tradition of Buddhist monastery architecture in the Kathmandu Valley. For instance, the size of the plots and frontages is determined by the size of the open courtyards, and their layout follows the swastika pattern. This ancient symbol, sacred to both Buddhist and Hindu traditions, is one of the rational ways of dividing the area to get a uniform distribution of plots within a courtyard system of settlement. Furthermore, the analysis shows the relationship of this pattern of division and plot planning to the layout of Buddhist monastery architecture, indicating that the form of the monastery could have been the model that inspired the planning idea of the larger residential courtyard settlements of Patan.

To the best of our knowledge, no research has been carried out to explore concepts in the planning of residential plots in the settlement quarters of traditional cities in the Kathmandu Valley. Moreover, there are no available historical records that indicate such planning works. However, there are nineteenth century manuscripts stored in the archives of the Nepal Department of Archeology with drawings that show various patterns in the layout of plots or buildings around an open courtyard. It is possible that these are copies of earlier works. Without the earlier works to refer to, however, it is difficult to use the copies for examining the planning of residential quarters in Patan, as the settlements existed more than a millennium earlier.

During our fieldwork in Patan, the planning of dwelling frontages was suggested to us by the residents of Nabahal, one of the quarters of the city (1 in Fig. 7-1 and Pl. 7-1).[2] This information was subsequently verified, and similar instances were sought in other courtyards.

Fig. 7-1. Location of quarters surveyed

Pl. 7-1.　The courtyard of Nabahal facing west

A preliminary observation of the arrangement of dwelling frontages in a number of courtyards in other settlement quarters was then conducted. This led to the selection of three more such courtyards—Elanani, Nag bahal, and Nakhachuk—for further studies. They were selected because Elanani showed apparent similarity to the first courtyard, while Nagbahal and Nakhachuk formed parts of the same settlement cluster. Furthermore, these open courtyards belonged to the same quarters which we had studied earlier to examine the employment of planning modules and grids in their layout (Chap. 6).

The courtyards of Nabahal and Elanani were then surveyed to obtain detailed ground plan measurements of dwellings around the four sides of the courtyard while only the frontages of Nag bahal and Nakhachuk were measured.[3] The survey works were facilitated by cadastral survey maps made by the Nepal Department of Land Survey in 1979 and drawn on a scale of 1 : 500. These maps showed property boundaries, built-up and open areas, and community artifacts. Particular attention was given to the presence of a party wall between adjoining dwellings that had a bearing in the identification of partition or merger of dwelling plots. The analysis primarily focused on the frontage of dwellings facing the open court and the depth of plots. The frontage width of every dwelling was noted to the nearest centimeter. It should be noted that while the traditional system of measure is in the hasta system, all measurements in this study are stated in the metric system for the sake of convenience. Further, metric values will be related to traditional units of measure whenever necessary. This study also makes use of measured drawings of Buddhist monasteries made by the

Nippon Institute of Technology (1986) and Watanabe (1998a) for a comparative analysis of the various forms of courtyard structures.

Planning of Courtyard Dwelling Plots

The analytical method to determine patterns of plot division was developed from a detailed analysis of the first courtyard, Nabahal. The method was then applied and further extended to the three other courtyards of Elanani, Nag bahal, and Nakhachuk that form one of the largest courtyard settlement clusters in Patan. Finally, the study compared the existing division pattern with a particular model courtyard to show that this model was the standard adapted for residential courtyard planning.

Nabahal nani Court

The Nabahal nani quarter located at the city's western end (1 in Fig. 7-1 and Fig. 7-2) belongs to the Na-tole neighborhood. Fig. 7-2a gives detail ground floor plan of this quarter. Nabahal is a branch of Bubahal, one of the 16 main monasteries in Patan. The residents of Nabahal nani are Sakya, while those of Bubahal are Vajracharya. It is believed that the ancestors of the present resident Sakya of Nabahal came from the Lagan tole neighborhood of Kathmandu to build the Taleju Bell (1737) in the Patan Palace square. Consequently, they were given the place where they now live (which had belonged to Bubahal) for their settlement (Sakya 1995). Another resident group of the Nabahal nani, who are also Sakya, trace their lineage to Sribahal, another main bahal located across the main street, north of the courtyard. The ancestral ties of

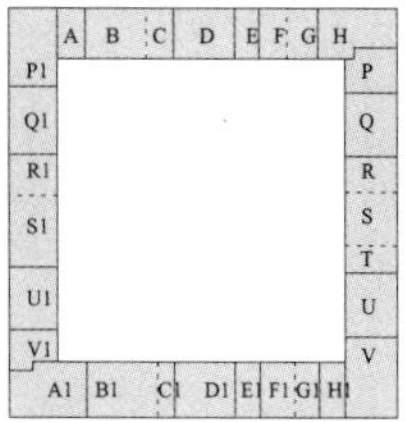

7-2b. Diagramatic representation of frontage divisions (frontages A, A1,.., P, P1,..., are referred to Table 1). The arrangement of corner plots show a rotation similar to a *swastika*.

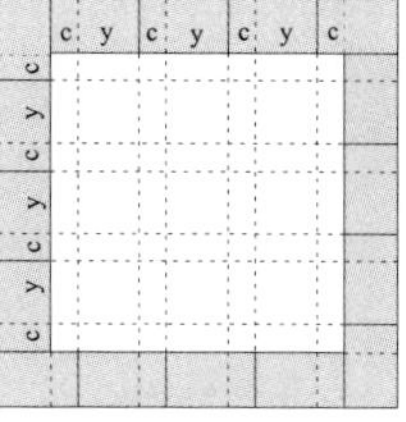

7-2c. The Pattern of sequence in the division of plots. The theoretical values for c and y are 320 cm and 726 cm respectively.

7-2d. *Swastika*--symbol and patterns.

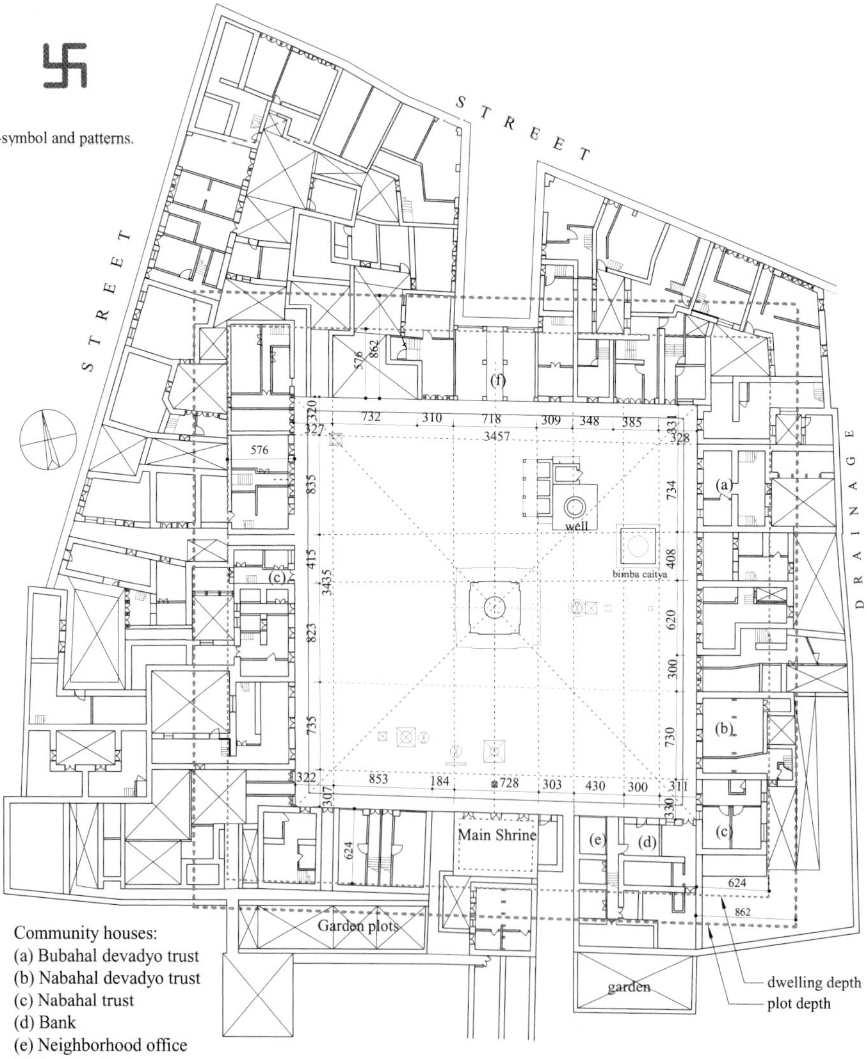

Community houses:
(a) Bubahal devadyo trust
(b) Nabahal devadyo trust
(c) Nabahal trust
(d) Bank
(e) Neighborhood office
(f) funerary trust

7-2a. Building frontages (cm) of Nabahal nani court.

Fig. 7-2. Nabahal nani quarter

Nabahal residents with the two main bahal mentioned above continue to exist in a number of religious rituals (Sakya 1995).

The Nabahal nani has a square open courtyard with four sides that have similar measurements (~18 d = 34.56 m). Oriented approximately towards the north, the courtyard is entered through the main east-west street of the city. The entrance lane is exactly at the center of the square courtyard. The location of a caitya at the center and the main shrine of the bahal to the south, exactly opposite to the entrance, show the strictly symmetrical and axial disposition of the courtyard. The earliest record of the Nabahal nani, dated 1453, comes from one of the inscriptions installed within this shrine. It describes the renovation of the shrine building. The dates for the central caitya and the bimba caitya at the east[4] (Fig. 7-2a) are yet unknown.

Planning Features of the Nabahal nani

In addition to the existence of a central axis in the layout of courtyard elements, Nabahal has several other planning features, which are indicated by physical dimensions and the layout of the dwelling blocks. One of the peculiar features of the latter is that the eight corner blocks, two in each direction, have the same width. This feature is common to the three other courtyards that will be analyzed in the following sections. This width ranges from 310–330 cm, with an average of 320 cm. The corner blocks are narrow when compared to the usual widths at the central sections. In many instances, the dwelling blocks of the wing alternately recess by about 10 cm. Beginning with the corner block, this recess arrangement displays striking similarity with the facade of a Buddhist monastery (Fig. 4-1). However, the recesses and protrusions are gradually disappearing with repeated reconstructions.

The frontage dimensions of all dwelling blocks facing the courtyard are shown in Table 7-1, which compares the frontages of respective dwellings of opposite wings facing each other (Fig. 7-2b). The relationship is also seen in Figure 7-2a. There are three features, which are clearly seen in this layout. First, the dwelling blocks

Table 7-1. Dwelling Frontages (cm) of Nabahal nani courtyard.

North		*South*		*East*		*West*	
A	327	A1	322	P	331	P1	320
B	732	B1	853	Q	734	Q1	835 (731)
C	310	C1	184	R	408	R1	415 (519)
B+C	1042	B1+C1	1037				
D	718	D1	728	S	622	S1	823
E	309	E1	303	T	304		
F	348	F1	430	R+S+T	1334	R1+S1	1342
G	385	G1	300				
F+G	733	F1+G1	730	U	737	U1	735
H	328	H1	311	V	334	V1	307
Total	3457		3431		3470		3435

facing each other have equal frontages. Second, there are two frontage types, the values of which are close to 3.20 m and 7.30 m. These are laid out alternatively. Finally, some of the plots are formed by the merger of the first two types of frontages.

The relative clarity of the sequence followed in the layout of Nabahal nani plots allows us to derive an equation governing the division pattern of the quadrangle (Fig. 7-2c). This equation is $n(y + c) + c = w$, where w is the width of the open courtyard, c is the corner frontage (320 cm), and y is the width of the plot with a longer frontage towards the courtyard. Based on this equation, given the width of the open court (= 34.57 m), the value of y comes to 7.26 m. Consequently, the frontages of the plots are 3.20 m and 7.26 m, in addition to one of 10.46 m, when a merger of adjoining blocks is considered. Furthermore, differences in various frontage widths that are related to the party walls, which could belong to one of the house owners, are the result of the partitions from parent plots. The different frontages at northeast and southeast corners of the courtyard exemplify this situation. These resulted from dividing 7.3 m into two, thus giving the width for two dwellings. Thus, it can be seen that two basic frontages could generate a series of dwelling frontages between 3 to 10 m, which may suggest randomness if the above relationships are not known. It is only through the merger of these varying dimensions and the close scrutiny of the party wall that one can see certain patterns in the layout. It is fortunate that the Nabahal nani still preserves the original frontages in the majority of its plots, making the feature familiar to the residents themselves.

Following the usual division pattern of courtyard wings where the central segment is a longer one, and considering the tradition of symmetry, an odd number of divisions is to be expected. Probably the numbers of divisions were also adjusted according to practical requirements and limitations due to different lengths of the open courtyard. However, the fixed corner frontage (c) of 3.20 m is one significant feature in this division pattern, the meaning of which will be discussed in a later section.

It is significant to note that when the form of corner plots is considered, the division pattern gives equal plot sizes when the depth is equal to frontage y. However, when the depth is smaller than y, the corner plot is smaller than the plots at the central segment and vice versa. It is to be noted that the courtyard is an important feature of the settlement, and the need for and desirability of frontage to each plot is apparent. To a certain extent, the area of the corner plot could be larger to compensate for its narrow frontage towards the courtyard. This consideration in the division pattern that requires access frontage to the corner plots creates a plan in the form of a swastika, which is probably one of the most rational ways of dividing the plots that surround a courtyard. This manner of planning of courtyard plots finds an exact parallel in the layout pattern of the courtyard wings of Buddhist monasteries. That the plots of Nabahal were planned in a swastika pattern is shown by corner blocks where the exterior walls from the corner end of the courtyard continue inward like that of swastika's arms[5] (Figs. 7-2b and 7-2c).

The alternating of plot frontages of 320 cm and 726 cm in the layout forms a sequence that can be represented by the simple expression c-y-c-y-...-c. There are other frontage widths deviating from this regular pattern, but as seen from Table 7-1 these larger frontages are also the sum of the components c and y, such as y + c or c + y + c, a combination of adjacent plots of widths c or y.

Noteworthy is the fact that important community buildings, such as the main shrine and the three buildings that serve various needs of the community, are close to 7.26 m wide. Among these structures, the earliest renovation date noted is 1453 for the main shrine. This enables us to date the existence of the planned court earlier than the fifteenth century.

The Courtyards of Elanani, Nakhachuk, and Nagbahal

The courtyards Elanani and Nakhachuk belong to one neighborhood, the Nagbahal tole. The settlement cluster of Nakhachuk is separated from Nagbahal by a lane (Fig. 7-3). However the three courtyards and their settlement clusters belong to one larger settlement block. The Sakya are the major community of this neighborhood followed by Vajracharya. Kwabahal, one of the primary monasteries of Patan, is situated at the southeast corner of this settlement block and is the religious centre of the neighborhood community. In all of these courtyards, community facilities such as wells or fountains, shrines and

temples, community houses can be found either in the open court or as one of the structures along side the residential dwellings around the courtyards. Further a number of secondary bahal associated with Kwabahal can be found at the interior of the quarters. The earliest date available for Kwabahal is 1082. In contrast, there are Licchavi period (fifth to ninth century) artifacts in Nakhachuk and Nagbahal.[6]

Elanani Courtyard

The courtyard of Elanani is connected to Nagbahal to the west, and Saraswati nani and Kwabahal to the east (Fig. 7-4 and Pl. 7-2). The size of the Elanani open courtyard is close to 24 danda (d) [= 46.08 m] north-south and 19.5 d (= 37.44 m) east-west. Unlike the Nabahal nani court, the main entry approaches to Elanani—from the street to the south and from the Nagbahal court to the west—are not laid through the central axis of the courtyard. However, the layout of dwelling plots and dimensions of the dwelling frontage of Elanani show a manner of planning similar to that of the Nabahal nani. A comparison of frontage dimensions of the four wings given in Table 7-2 shows various plot sizes (also see Fig. 7-4b). However, when adjacent plots are merged, a consistent use of certain frontage widths becomes apparent. These frontages approach the values derived by the method described in the case of Nabahal nani. The common denominators in this case are the corner constant of 3.2 m and the standard frontage of 8.6 m on the eastern and western sides (w = 46.18 m), and 8.55 m on the northern and southern sides of the courtyard (w = 37.41 m). The working equation for the eastern and western sides is

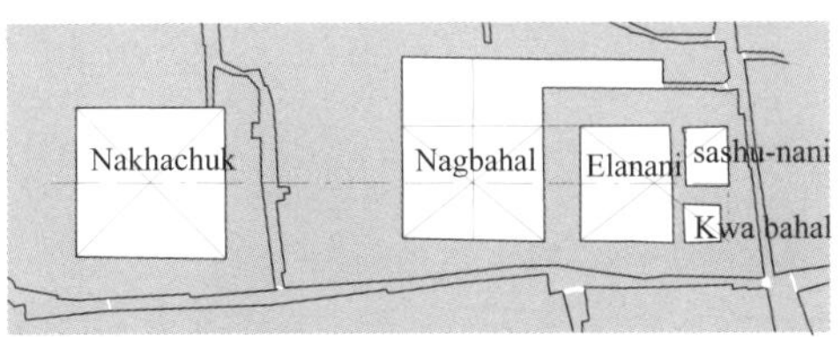

Fig. 7-3. Spatial relationship of Elanani, Nagbahal, and Nakhachuk

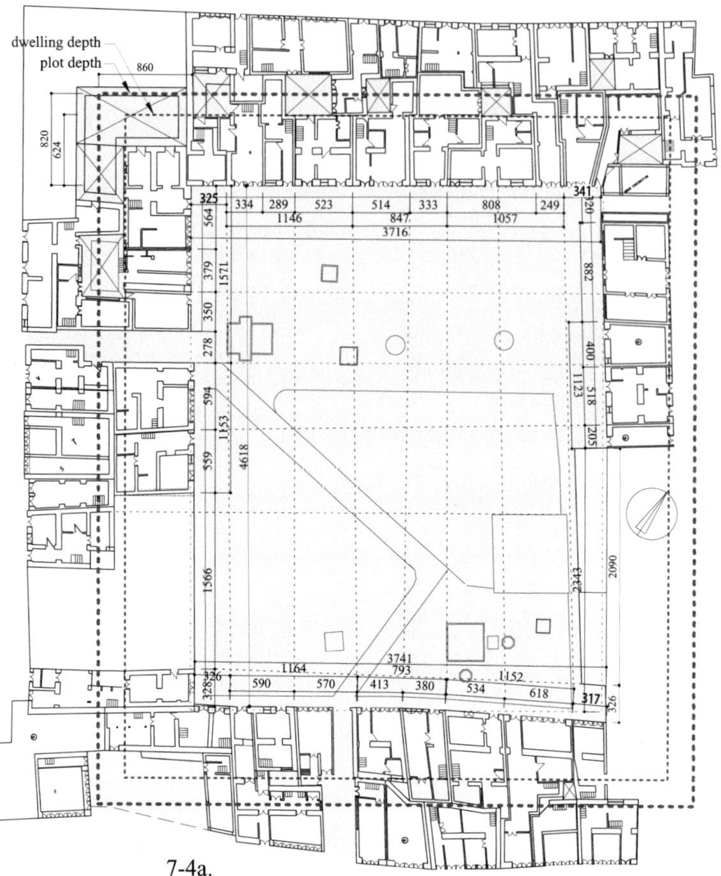

Fig. 7-4a. Dimensions of dwelling frontages (cm).

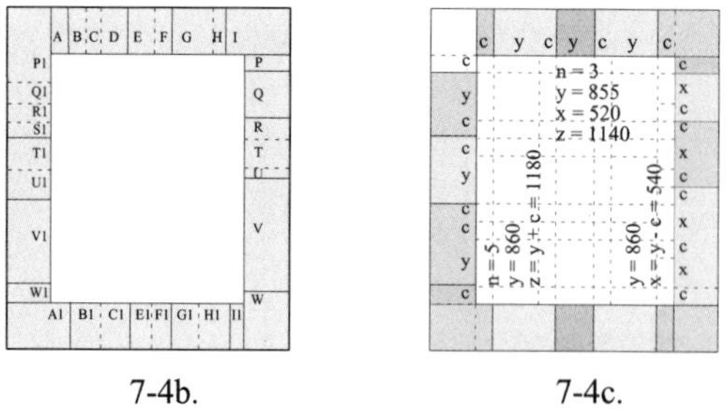

7-4b.   7-4c.

Fig. 7-4b. Diagramatic representation of frontage
division.
(frontages A, B,.., A1, B1,..., are referred to Table 7-2)

Fig. 7-4c. Pattern of sequence in the division of plots.

Fig. 7-4. Elanani courtyard

Table 7-2. Dwelling frontages (cm) of Elanani courtyard.

North		*South*		*East*		*West*	
A	325	A1	326	P	320	P1	564
B	334	B1	590	Q	882	Q1	379
C	289	C1	570			R1	350
D	523			R	400	S1	278
B+C+D	1146	B1+C1	1160	P+Q+R	1602	P1+Q1+R1+S1	1571
E	514	E1	413	T	518	T1	594
F	333	F1	380				
E+F	847	E1+F1	793	U	205	U1	559
		V	2090	V1	1566		
G	808	G1	534	U+V	2295	U1+V1	2125
H	249	H1	618				
G+H	1057	G1+H1	1152				
I	341	I1	317	W	326	W1	328
Total	3716		3748		4741		4618

n (x + c) + c = w, where x + c = y. When merged, the most frequent frontages are close to 3.2 m (c), 8.6 m (y), and 11.5 m (y + c). The frontages on the east and west show about a three per cent deviation from the standard values given above. The dwelling frontages reveal sequences indicated in Figure 7-4c that correspond to the values obtained from field measurements, including mergers and divisions. This shows the hidden structure behind the pattern of plot division, that is, the structure of sequences given in Figure 7-4c. The east side of the courtyard further shows a division in the standard frontage y into x + c (x = 8.6 – 3.2 = 5.4 m). The logic of this manner of division with c as an operator will be explained in later sections.

The frontage of y + c appears to be the most common. It is followed by that of y and x. A greater occurrence of frontage that is close to x is also related to the fact that the division of y + c into two halves may give one of them the width of x. The other half that includes the party wall becomes larger. Presently in Elanani, there is not a single dwelling with the frontage y + c. The two dwellings with frontages longer than this value are community religious structures (Pl. 7-2 and Pl. 7-3). It seems, therefore, that the plot divisions made with the y + c frontage were not meant to be occupied by a single dwelling block. Rather, they were meant to be occupied by later generations, most probably by descendants of the same family. Some of the frontage dimensions that deviate from the standard denominators are beside the entrance lanes, which probably affected the regular planning layout of the plots.

The existing structural pattern of the layout of dwelling blocks also sheds light on the general uniformity of dwelling and plot depths in this system of courtyard planning. In the Nabahal nani, the depth of a dwelling block is close to 5.76 m (= 12 hasta [H], north and west) and 6.24 m (= 13 H, south and east). Most

Pl. 7-2.　The courtyard of Elanani facing east

Pl. 7-3. The west wing of Elanani

dwellings have partial extensions at the back with small light wells or backyards. When we take into account these features and wall boundary alignments, the depth of plots on all four sides comes close to 8.64 m (= 4.5 d). Similar analytical observations in Elanani show the general depth of dwelling blocks to be 6.24 m, while the depth of plots (8.20 m north and south, 8.60 m east and west) is close to the standard frontage y in the respective sides of the courtyard. Thus, one may assume that 6.24 m (= 13 H) is a commonly employed depth for dwelling blocks while it is 8.64 m (4.5 d = 18 H) for the depth of plots in the above two courts.

Nakhachuk and Nagbahal Courtyards

The open courtyard of Nakhachuk is approximately a square with its sides measuring $31\frac{2}{3}$ d (60.80 m), while Nagbahal is a rectangular court of 72.20 m × 58.62 m. The divisions of the courtyard wings that give dwelling frontages are shown in Figures 7-5a and 7-5b. For Nakhachuk, the standard average as calculated using the Nabahal method gives a frontage of 8.32 m. Figure 7-5a clearly shows that, when merged, existing dwelling frontages agree with the values of y and y + c (8.32 + 3.2 = 11.52 m). The existing frontages can be ordered to make sequences of c-yc-yc-y-cy-cy-c on the west, and cy-cy-c-yc-y-cyc on the north side. A similar sequential order is noted on the other two sides of the courtyard. The corresponding measures and sequence of order in the division of plots are also to be found in Nagbahal, which lies to the east of Nakhachuk. The northern side of Nagbahal shows certain changes in its pattern, probably due to its extended loop in the northeast. Nonetheless, regularity in the frontages is observed and the values can be derived following the Nabahal method.

Meaning of the Division Pattern

The division pattern described in the case studies on the planning of four courtyards raises a question about the meaning of such a pattern. The most simple division would have been to divide the remaining central segment of the wing with a single denominator, that is, creating plots of frontage y and its multiples at the central segment, and c or y + c at the four corners. However, it is clear that in all of these courtyards, this straightforward manner of plot division was not applied. There must have been a reason for using a fixed frontage for the eight corner blocks of the courtyard. The arrangement of plots around the courtyard that forms the swastika pattern is an important feature of this system of planning. At the moment, it is not known whether any ritual or metaphysical concepts of the age when they were built influenced the layout and division patterns of the courtyard dwelling plots. However, certain functional and preexisting traditions can be cited as reasons for this system of courtyard planning.

First, the width of the corner block is related to the ancient standard of measure mentioned in the preceding section. This width is exactly one sixth of a rajju (19.2/6 = 3.2 m). The use of this dimension for the width of the bay of a monastery and as one division in the wing facades is shown in Kathmandu's Khun bahal and Chusya bahal which were built in 1591 and 1649, respectively (Figs. 7-7a and 7-7b).[7] The proportion of the width of the sections of the interior

Pl. 7-4. The courtyard of Nakhachuk facing north

Pl. 7-5. The courtyard of Nagbahal facing east

7-5b.

Fig. 7-5a

7-5a. Width of dwelling frontages (cm);
7-5b. Pattern of sequence in the divison of plots.

Fig. 7-5. Nakachuk

7-6b

Fig. 7-6a

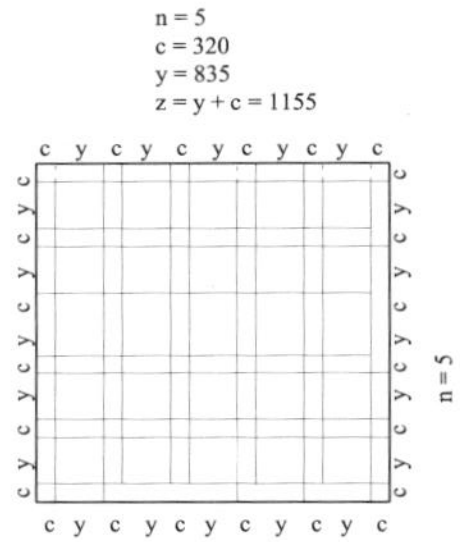

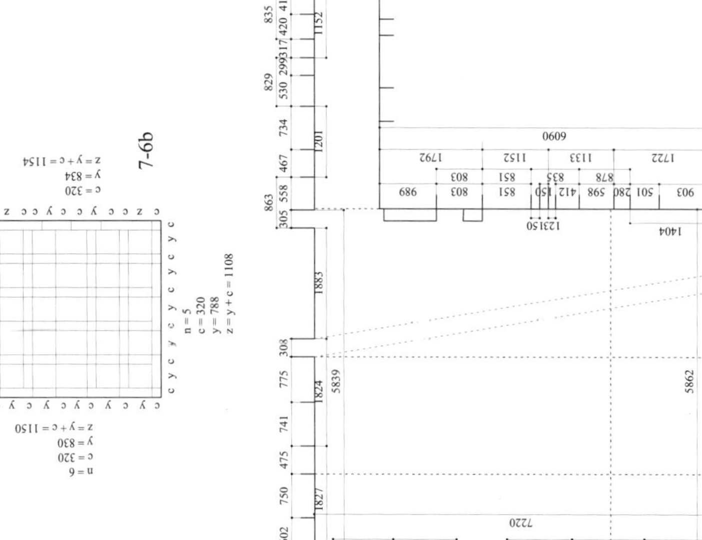

7-6a. Width of dwelling frontages (cm);
7-6b. Pattern of sequence in the division of plots.

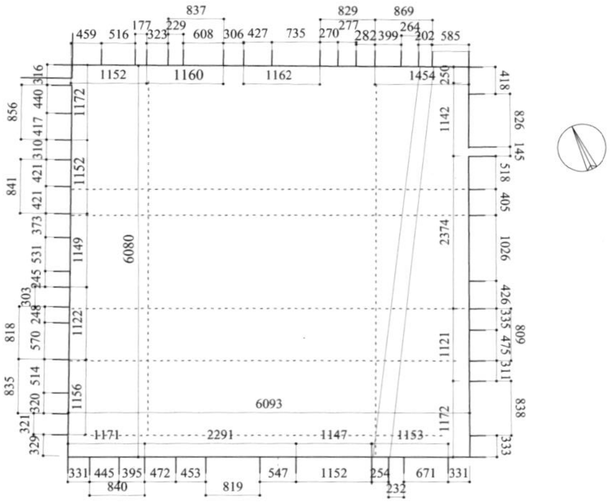

Fig. 7-6. Nagbahal courtyard

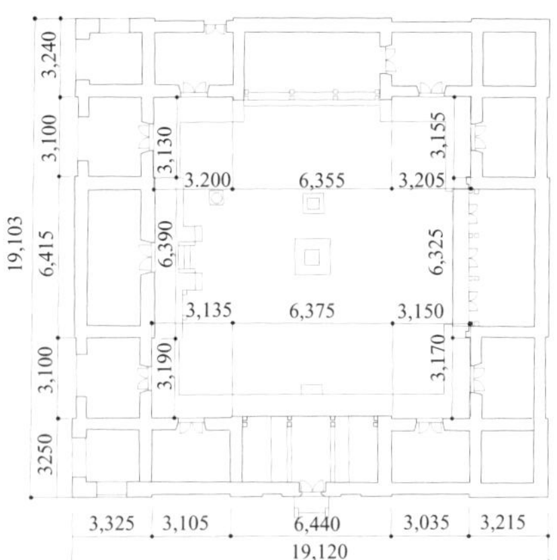

Fig. 7-7a. Khun bahal, Kathmandu (redrawn from Nippon Institute of Technology 1986)

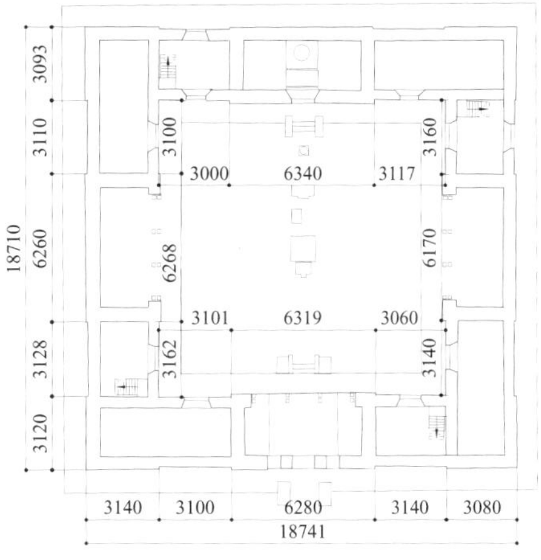

Fig. 7-7b. Chusya bahal, Kathmandu (redrawn from Korn 1978)

facades in the open courtyard of Khun bahal are $1:2:1$, that is, $c:y:c$; the corresponding proportion at the external facades is $1:1:2:1:1$ or $c:c:y:c:c$. Thus, the fraction 6 is the result of the overall proportional division in the planning of a bahal whose one side is 1 r wide. We consider these divisions and dimensions to be of special significance because

the proportions are wholesome, and the dimensions of these two monastery courtyard blocks, which are close to the square of 1 r (19.2 m), are also a standard modular grid in the planning of settlement blocks (Pant 2003). While the width of the bay might have served a practical purpose, the width as a division in the internal and external facades emphasizes

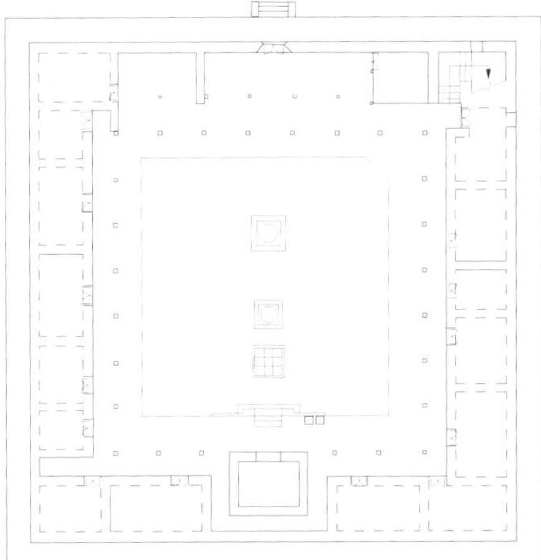

Fig. 7-8a. Cha bahil, Kathmandu (redrawn from Watanabe 1998)

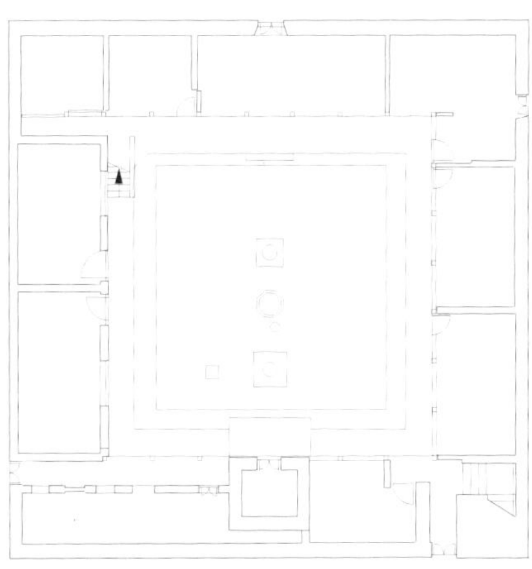

Fig. 7-8b. Jya baha bahi, Patan (redrawn from Watanabe 1998)

the symmetric treatment of the facade and the rhythm created by the alternating sequence of recessed and protruding walls. This kind of facade treatment and bay width is a common feature of bahal architecture not found in bahil, which are considered to be earlier forms of monasteries in the Kathmandu Valley. This leads to the hypothesis that the form of planning with the standard corner block developed after the seventh century when Vajrayana Buddhism began to take the place of Mahayana Buddhism in Nepal (Bhattacharya 1927). The bahal is thought to be the product of this change, the representative institutional form of Vajrayana Buddhism. Thus, it also appears that the generation of sequence in the plot division and dwelling frontages is a parallelism between the bahal courtyard architecture and the residential courtyard dwellings.

The logic behind the development of such a sequence can be explained from the requirements for symmetry and a corner block as an access to the plot located at the corner. Figure 7-9c illustrates the process of development of the sequence proceeding from uniform plot divisions of the courtyard wings to a pattern creating a swastika arm with symmetrical divisions. The side that may give uniform divisions of width (a) is divided into components of c, the corner width, and y, the standard frontage, showing the corner width as a key operator to the generation of symmetry. This first order of symmetry is further elaborated by dividing y into components c and x. The first sequence with width (a) that is without symmetry thus leads to a symmetrical sequence of c-y-c-y-...-c and then to c-x-c-c-x-c-...-x-c. The formation of the second order of symmetry might have been the result of the need to guide the

inevitable division of original plots; that is, when a plot of width y was to be built, divided, or partitioned to sell, the corner width was again used as one of the components to bring the whole division into harmony. The use of this constant thus acts like an operator to generate symmetric sequences. When the neighboring plots are merged in a variety of combinations and then partitioned into equal divisions, the above sequences give numerous dwelling frontages. In the case of courtyards which were analyzed, the ratio of such a division, however, did not necessarily lead to the proportion of $1:2:1$, but it varied according to the width of the courtyard.

In Nabahal nani and Elanani, the corner plots (not the frontage) alternate in a sequence of standard plot size and minimum size. In other words, one of the two adjacent plots at the corner is of a standard size while the other one is 3.2 m. What particular function was allocated to the smaller corner plot? A plausible explanation is that the four plots at the four corners served as accesses to the interior courtyards which were also arranged in a similar manner of courtyard planning or that they were small family courtyards. Such corner access links are seen at the southwest and northwest corners of the Nabahal nani courtyard and the northeast and southeast corners of Elanani. Other access links from plots at the central segments of the courtyard are also seen. However, the corner links, in addition to the main central entrance, could have been a planned feature, while the other links might have been formed over a period of time in a more organic pattern. The possibility of these corner plots of being such access ways is again suggested by Buddhist monastery courts

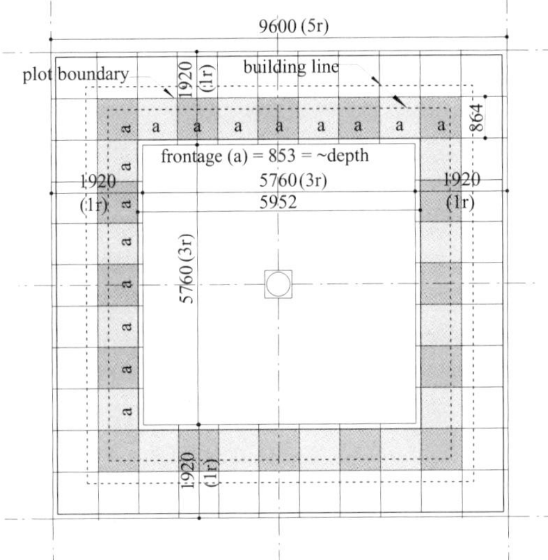

Fig. 7-9a. Schematic diagram of a model: *Nivartana* courtyard.
The court whose sides are 57.6 m (3 *rajju*) gives 32 units when the interior ring is divided into square plots. The outer ring may belong to adjacent quadrangles when courts are built in continuity. (dimensions are in cm)

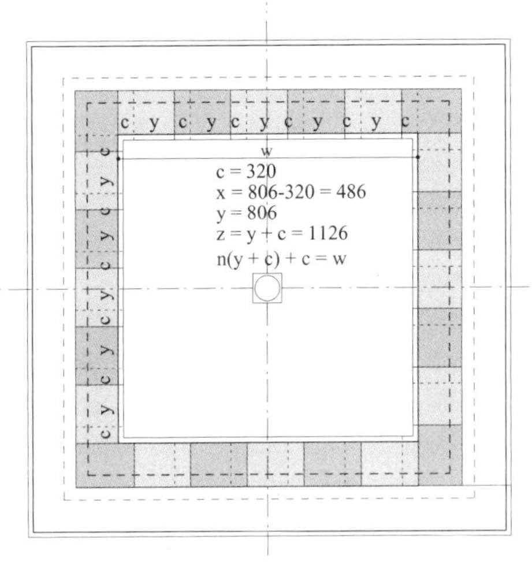

$$c = 320$$
$$x = 806\text{-}320 = 486$$
$$y = 806$$
$$z = y + c = 1126$$
$$n(y + c) + c = w$$

Fig. 7-9b. The division pattern in practice as exemplified by Nabahal, Elanani, Nagbahal and Nakhachuk courtyards.
This division gives 24 units, which are arranged in a *swastika* pattern.

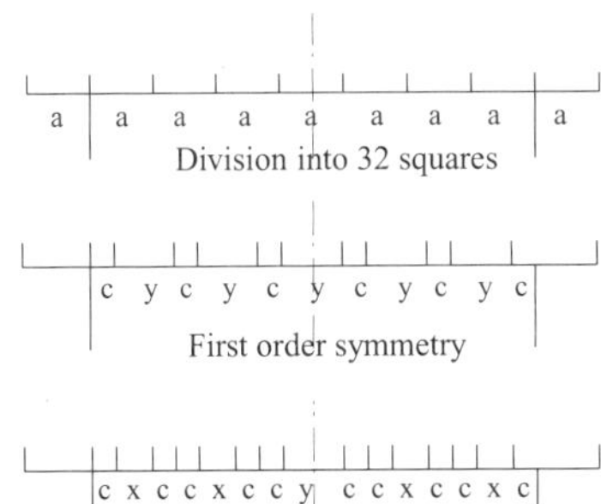

Fig. 7-9c. The symmetry and rhythm.
This diagram shows the procedure to make symmetrical layout divisions of the plots, and, to regulate further divisions by the employment of a constant frontage c.

Fig. 7-9. The Nivartana courtyard

(Figs. 7-8a and 7b). Chabahi, which is considered to be one of the oldest monasteries in Nepal, has passageways reminiscent of a swastika pattern. Likewise, Jya baha-bahi, also thought to be a Licchavi structure has doors on the exterior walls exactly in positions that are directly reached from the four corners of the courtyard, and which are laid out to create the swastika pattern. The room arrangement of Chusya baha (Fig. 7-7b) with its opening on the exterior walls in south and west is an example of such a layout. This organizational pattern is also seen in other monasteries. In residential courtyards, changes due to particular location requirements and reconstructions through the centuries have changed the standard pattern somewhat, but the general preference to have such access links from the corners of the courtyard can still be discerned.

Plot Divisions: The Existence of a Model Residential Courtyard

Based on the analysis of the four courtyards, theoretical planning dimensions have been worked out through the use of a "model courtyard block." This will explain how the above planning division may relate to a settlement grid. The measurements of this model follow the system of ancient standard measures. This system of measure consists of hasta (H), danda (d), and rajju (r) (Chap. 1). There is also a unit known as nivartana, a measure of 3 r. In Patan, the measurements of the seven largest open courtyards show the use of 3 r (57.6 m), the nivartana unit, as the most commonly used measure.[8] Among the case studies discussed above, Nakhachuk represents such a standard courtyard. Nagbahal has

one side consisting of one nivartana. The Elanani court, when combined with Sasunani to its east, is also one nivartana wide (Fig. 7-3). This measure of open courtyard excludes the plinth, which is private property. Figure 7-9 illustrates such a model settlement block in a grid of standard module and the process of plot division described in the four case studies.

The uniform division of the courtyard's surrounding plots, without using the concept of the kind of corner plot discussed above, produces eight plots which are 8.53 m wide and 8.64 m deep in one wing, making 32 squares altogether (Fig. 7-9a). Whether or not this manner of division is related to the Mandala construct of the residential block is not known at the moment. However, this basic division of 32 squares is subsequently transformed to a pattern of divisions creating sequences and a swastika pattern in the manner described above in the cases of the four courtyards. This division of plots laid in a swastika pattern gives a standard frontage of 8.06 m with the corner block being 3.2 m wide and 8.64 m deep (Fig. 7-9b).[9] Thus, when the plots are uniformly divided, the result is five standard plots of 11.26 m (8.06 m + 3.2 m) frontage towards the courtyard, while the corner plots are slightly larger (11.84 m × 8.64 m). In this model courtyard, if the dwelling width is taken to be 6.24 m (13 H), as found in the case studies of Nabahal and Elanani, the width of the backyard between the dwellings (the space between the dotted lines in Figures 7-9a and 7-9b) will be 4.8 m (2.5 d).

One of the remarkable features of this division pattern is that the division of plot frontages does not follow the principle that results in multiples of hasta and danda, although the depth of the dwelling and the plot conforms to standard multiples. However, it can be observed that in Nakhachuk and Nagbahal, the most common frontage is close to 6 d or 24 H (11.52 m). In Figures 7-5 and 7-6, we see that the total dimensions of the two courtyards closely reflect this manner of plot division (Nakhachuk is 5 m × 11.52 m + 3.2 m = 60.80 m; Nagbahal is 6 m × 11.52 m + 3.2 m = 72.32 m). Thus, we may conclude that the size of the two open courtyards was first determined by plot planning rather than the other way round, that is, where the plot divisions were determined by the size of a courtyard. Elanani also approximates this type of division. It is probable that, in the above cases, standard multiples for plot width were preferred, making slight adjustments for the size of the open courtyards which are given in multiples of danda or rajju. However, when the sizes of open courts are in multiples of standard modules of danda or rajju, the plot divisions are consequently not in multiples of danda. As can be seen from above, the corresponding frontage is 11.26 m (~23.5 hasta = 11.28 m) for a standard nivartana court. Further divisions of this measure similarly lead to fractions of hasta. The divisions of the Nabahal nani are examples of this. Such a division that has to take into account añgula (1 hasta = 27 añgula) divisions is certainly strenuous to maintain accuracy in the surveyor's work than in the case where divisions are made in units of hasta multiples. However, with a fixed size for a court, this manner of division produces plots of equal size. This suggests that uniformity in the distribution of plot size was given first priority. Thus, the case of Elanani, Nagbahal and Nakhachuk and the case of Nabahal show that there existed two methods of planning in the plot divisions of courtyard wings. One was determined by the larger grid and the other, a more preferable method, was determined by the convenient frontage of the plots, which resulted in a slight adjustment in the size of the open court.

To summarize, the close concordance of the existing dimensions, such as frontages and the plot depth of the four courts, with those of the model court (which may be called a Nivartana court) suggests that, along with the Buddhist monastery courts, such a model existed to guide the planning of these residential courtyards.

Conclusions

This analysis of Buddhist monastery residential quarters demonstrates that the dwelling plots of large residential courts were planned, and the planning principle had its roots in Buddhist monastery traditions. The planning of plot divisions may be summarized as follows:

1. The courtyard plots were planned by giving a uniform plot size and frontage to dwellings around the courtyard. The narrowness of the corner plot was a result of a predetermined plan; it was a functional requirement as well as a planning feature related to the structure of the courtyard system of the settlement block. The fixed corner width is related to an ancient standard of measure. The swastika pattern of layout division is a rational layout in this manner of courtyard settlement planning.

2. Apparently there existed two traditions in the divisions of courtyard plots: the first one used convenient multiples of hasta and danda for the

plot width, while the other maintained the width of open courts to conform to multiples of the above measure. In the latter case, the width of plots deviated from the hasta multiples (dhanurgraha hasta) due to the use of a fixed width for the corner plot, which was 3.2 m (1 r/6) or 6⅔ h.

3. The planning suggests the existence of a model—the Nivartana court—of three raiju wide. The 32 divisions of the Nivartana court suggest a possibility of the Mandala construct in the planning of such residential courts. Further research is needed to examine any ritual and metaphysical underpinnings of this system on planning.

4. The evident correspondence of the courtyard plan with the bahal court suggests that such a planning principle evolved following the introduction of Vajrayana in the history of Buddhism, which is thought to have happened during the seventh or eighth centuries. Results of the case studies conducted in this study suggest that such planning existed in Patan at least by the twelfth century. This planning principle of settlements is probably unique to the Kathmandu Valley as it shows a direct relationship to the Buddhist culture.

8

Palace Courtyards and the Palace Squares

The early history of Patan Palace is notoriously obscure. It remains to be seen if the city served as a capital during the Licchavi period and if there was ever a Licchavi ruling court at the site where the Malla rulers in the late medieval period built their palace and from which they ruled Lalitpur. This question remains unsolved partly because there is no other site in Kathmandu or Bhaktapur which has been confirmed as the location of the palace court before the beginning of the Malla period in the twelfth century. Palace names such as Managriha, Kailasakuta-bhavan, and Bhadradivas are known from Licchavi period inscriptions, but their locations are still a matter of controversy among historians. According to Baburan Acharya, Manadeva, the celebrated Licchavi king of the fifth century, moved his capital from Daksinakoligrama (the southern part of the Kathmandu) to

Patan and built Managriha (Acharya 1997, 30; 35–7).[1] The palace continued to function as a court for the later ruler, Narendradeva.[2] Acharya, however, does not explain the reasons for his opinion about the site of Managriha in Patan. Despite such legends like the one told in Chapter 2 about the building of Patan and the palace for King Varadev and claims made by historians with regard to the Licchavi palace site, the matter still remains to be proven.

Manigvala is the term which was used for the palace and its vicinity from early medieval times down to the late Malla period. The place was central, and its importance to Patan is evident from the palm leaf documents where the locations of Buddhist monasteries are described with Manigval as the center. As mentioned earlier, *gvala* is a Kirata name. "Mani" is interpreted by some scholars as 'central'

Pl. 8-1. Patan Palace Square

Pl. 8-2. Patan Palace, Keshavnarayan chok west façade (Nippon Institute of Technology, 1981)

(Slusser 1982), and even today "mani" implies an 'axis.' It is not a Sanskrit word. In any case, Manigval was of central importance to Patan at least by the end of the Licchavi period. The reason could not be other than the location of a palace, as there is no source indicating that Manigval was a site of religious importance.

When Bhaktapur was the capital during the early medieval period, Patan was ruled by feudal lords and they used epithets such as *manigvaladhipati* 'the lord of Manigvala.' In the late medieval period, the palace was known as Chaukwatha 'palace fortified in four corners' (Vajracharya 1964b).

The existing structures of Patan Palace and the Palace Square (Pls. 8-1 and 8-2) are the remains of the later medieval period following the division of the Bhaktapur court into three city-states—Bhaktapur, Kathmandu, and Patan—in the fifteenth century.[3] However, the present study demonstrates that the palace was built upon earlier foundations. This is evident from the fact that the layout of the palace precinct and the square are laid in one continuous grid and that the grid conforms to modular dimensions that were applied in the planning of settlement quarters. In this chapter we will analyze the site layout and the planning dimensions of the quadrangular courtyards of Patan Palace and the Manihiti Fountain to the north of the square, which was built in 560 (Figs. 8-1 and 8-2). Our study adds a new dimension to the ongoing debate about the age of Patan Palace. Furthermore, the existing palace courtyards of the three cities are similar in their form and planning with one of the monastery types in the Kathmandu Valley, the bahal.[4] The uniform pattern in the types and forms of monastery and

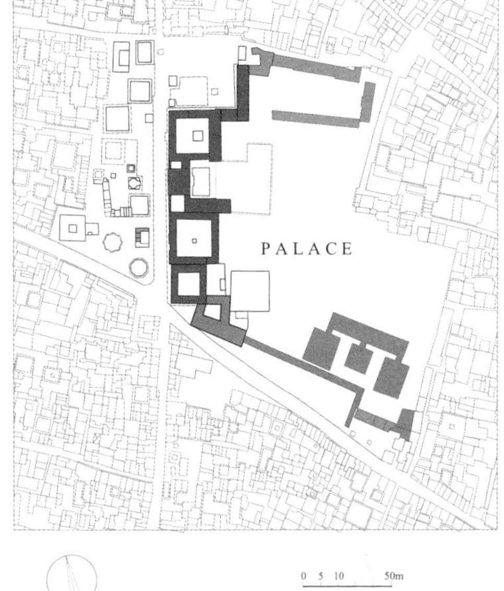

Fig. 8-1. Palace Square and the existing palace precinct in Patan

palace architecture throughout the valley demonstrates a firmly established tradition, the study of which is pertinent to the understanding of modular measures in the traditional building construction and planning of the valley towns.

The earliest studies on the royal palaces of the Kathmandu Valley consist of Gautamvajra Vajracharya's work (1976) on the Hanuman Dhoka Royal Palace of Kathmandu and a research paper by Dhanavajra Vajracharya on Patan (Vajracharya 1964b). Though both works are introductions to the historical aspects of the palace, they were written from the perspective of cultural historians. They do not dwell on the architecture and planning aspects of the building structures. However, the Nippon Institute of Technology (NIT) has published its results on the palace architecture, the results of which were published by (Nippon Institute of Technology 1981 and 1986). In addition,

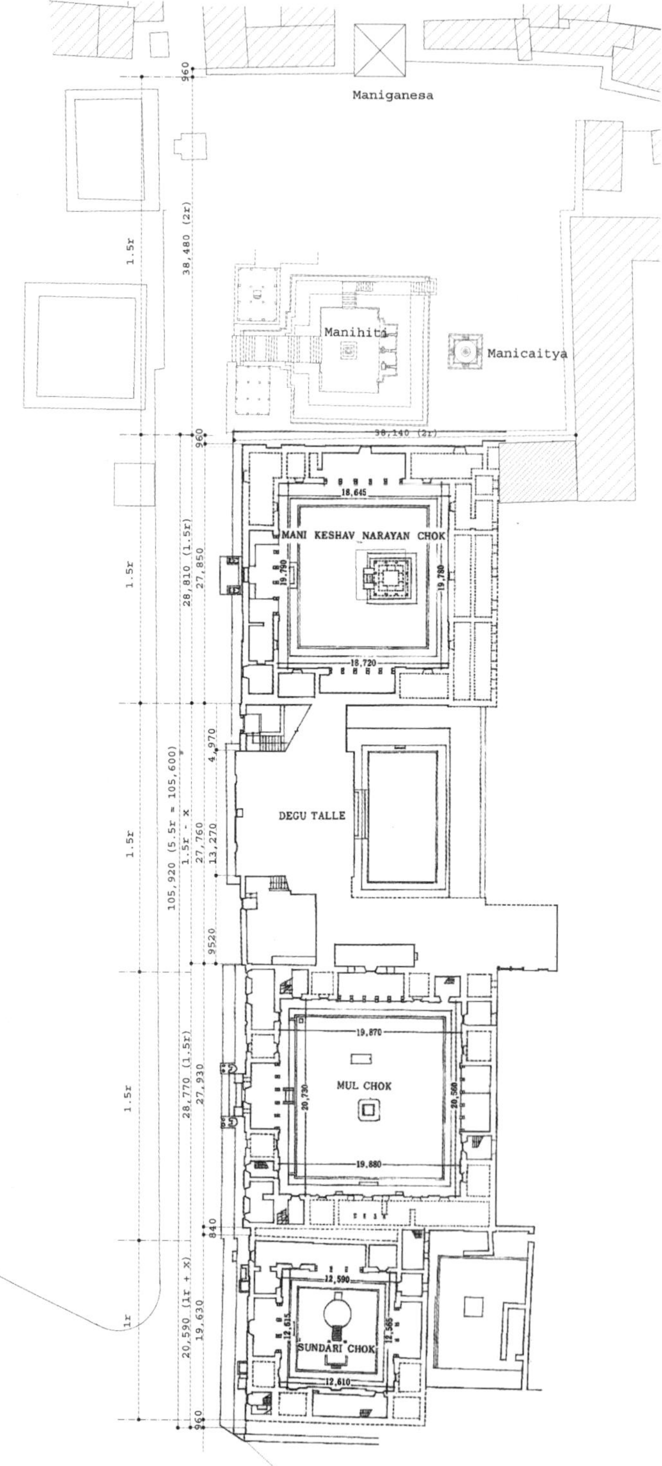

Fig. 8-2. Modular dimensional relationship in the layout of the Patan Palace courtyards

a series of research papers in Japanese were published by several members of the NIT research team on the functions of palace temples, towers, and courtyard buildings of the palaces of Kathmandu and Patan.[5] The studies, complemented with excellent drawings, are valuable documents for the understanding of the palace architecture of Nepal. In addition, a special report, "The Study on Quadrangle Architecture of Old Royal Palaces of Nepal," authored by Kurotsu was published by NIT in 1991 (Kurotsu 1991b).

Proportions of façades and plans were also analyzed by Gutschow in his study of a palace quadrangle in Gorkha, the seat of the present ruling dynasty (Gutschow 1985). Valuable findings are also expected from the completed restoration work of one of the courtyards of Patan Palace which was done by the Austrian Government from 1983 to 1992. The documentation report of this work is important to future research; however, it is not yet available.[6]

The materials for the present study consisted primarily of the measured drawings made by the NIT (Nippon Institute of Technology 1981). The cadastral survey map done by the Department of Land Survey of Nepal (Scale 1 : 500) in 1979 was also used for the analysis of the site layout of palace quadrangles. In addition, the drawings of Becker-Ritterspach on the plan of the Manihiti Fountain were used in conjunction with our field measurements (Becker-Ritterspach 1987). The ground plans of one of the palace courtyards of Kathmandu, as well as those of Bhaktapur and Gorkha which were produced by Gutschow, supplied additional data on the analysis of palace courtyard buildings (Gutschow 1985). The NIT drawings use the scale 1 : 100

and 1 : 200, while the scale of Becker-Ritterspach's drawings is 1 : 50. The latter do not provide specific dimensions and, therefore, are supplemented by our field measurements. The above data have been verified and supplemented by our fieldwork.[7]

In the present study, we have limited the investigation of the palace to the dimensions of its layout, leaving the detailed analysis of the floor plans and their functions for another time.[8] The modular measures have also been one of the central concerns in the research of the NIT and Gutschow. It should be noted, however, that the subjects of the aforementioned studies are not the same building structures. Moreover, their methodological approaches as well as their findings do not converge. Gutschow analyzed the plan of the Gorkha courtyard, which was built in 1838, into 81 or 64 square grids. He compared it to models described in the classical Vastusastras. On the other hand, the analytical method used by Kurotsu (1991b) in his study of the floor plan of two palace quadrangles takes a functional approach. He proposed that the thickness of the wall was the basis for the governing module on the planning of the courtyard buildings, one of such modules was subsequently found to be related to the scale supposedly decreed by Jayasthiti Malla, the ruling king of Bhaktapur in the fourteenth century (Kurotsu 1991a, 64–5). However, the grid layout for the two courtyards is different and the dimensions obtained for one of them do not conform to the standard measuring rod of the other. Likewise, I baha bahi, a Buddhist monastery to the southwest of the palace, which Kurotsu and Watanabe studied in detail, was found to have been laid out using a different principle (Kurotsu 1998a and Watanabe 1998b).

The present study employs a uniform standard of measure in analyzing the palace quadrangles. Moreover, comparisons were made with monastery courtyards since these are similar to palace courtyards in structure and layouts. The dimensions of the plans were checked against multiples of three different hasta measures. Two of them were derived from our earlier studies, that is, the dhanurgraha hasta (H = 480 mm) and the sishu hasta (h = 426 mm). Another hasta of 457.2 mm, suggested by Kurotsu, was also used for comparative purposes.

Layout of the Palace Quadrangles: The Site Layout

From descriptions in the chronicles of Nepalese history, it appears that some kind of palatial structures existed within the present palace precinct during the Licchavi period (fifth to ninth century).[9] However, the structures that still exist today are known to be comparatively late constructions belonging to the later Malla period, following the division of the kingdom into three city-states in 1565. Among these structures within the palace compound are three quadrangular courtyards, a temple structure dedicated to the tutelary deity of the Malla kings, and a water tank (Fig. 8-2). These structures were built about 100 years apart from the early seventeenth century to the early eighteenth century. The earliest construction is the southernmost courtyard known as Sundari chok. It was built by Siddhinarasingha Malla in 1646 or 1647 (Pl. E).[10] He is also said to have rebuilt the temple of the tutelary deity, known as Degutale, in 1641. The courtyard between

Sundari chok and Degutale, known as Mulchok (Pl. 8-3), and Keshavnarayan chok, the courtyard to the north of Degutale, were built or reconstructed by his son, Srinivasa Malla in 1666 and 1680 respectively.[11] The tradition of building Mulchok, an important place for the palace ritual, can be traced back to the Mulchok of Bhaktapur. It is thought to have been built in the fifteenth century by Yaksya Malla[12] who reportedly divided his kingdoms among his three sons. The fact that these structures were built by successive members of the same dynasty gives us reason to believe that similar measuring standards were used for their construction. Besides these palatial courtyards, the stone fountain at the square north of the palace, which existed by the sixth century during the Licchavi period (Vajracharya 1973), is relevant to the siting and dimensional study of the palace quadrangles.

Figure 8-2 shows that the outer dimensions of the courtyard blocks of the palace are not very different from the standard modules that are the multiples of rajju (r) and danda (d). The outer dimensions of the three courtyard blocks are close to 10 d (1 r = 19.2 m) and 15 d (1.5 r = 28.8 m). Yet, the difference of about 1 m in each of the three courtyards, excluding that of Sundari chok, is such that it needs to be explained. A closer examination of the dimensions in the figure shows that this is a variance related to the width of the plinth, a raised structure extending approximately 2H (96 cm) from the exterior wall. If this allowance, along with the 80-cm gap that exists between Sundari chok and Mulchok is considered, the dimensions of each courtyard structure when the plinth width is included almost coincide with the standard module

Pl. 8-3. Mulchok, Patan Palace

Table 8-1. Measured Dimensions (cm) of Manihiti Fountain

	North-south	hasta	East-west	hasta
width of inner openings	1442	30 (1440)	1437	30 (1440)
	1176	24½ (1176)	1149	24 (1152)
	915	19 (912)	871	18 (864)
stair widths	144	3 (144)	293	6 (288)
			112	2⅓ (112)
			98	2 (96)
stepped plinths	133	2¾ (132)	144	3 (144)
	136		150	
	133	2¾ (132)	136	
	126	2⅔ (128)	144	3 (144)

multiples of 10 d and 15 d. The comparatively earlier structure of the ground floor wall of the Degutale temple beside Sundari chok also shows a coincidence with the modular dimension of 7 d × 7 d (13.27 m = 6.91 d).

The possible use of the standard module in the division and measurement of the palace site is also indicated by the length and breadth of the palace square that incorporates a fountain in the north of Keshavnarayan chok. The width of the square is 38.48 m north-south (NS) and 38.14 m east-west (EW), values close to 20 d or 2 r (38.40 m), respectively. Therefore, the total length at the west side of the palace precinct is 105.92 m, which is close to 5.5 r (105.60 m). The unit of half a rajju (0.5 r = 5 d) as a modular unit was demonstrated earlier in the study on the planning of the settlement quarters of Patan (Chap. 6).

The multiple of danda is also manifested in the dimensions of the Manihiti Fountain, which is fed by an underground channel (Figs. 8-3a and 8-3b). The fountain is built below ground level with a stepped terrace descending to the floor, where three fountainheads are installed.

The measured dimensions of the enclosure openings are given in Table 8-1.

Table 8-1 shows that the fountain is designed as a square, and except on the third lowest level, the dimensions of each side are close to each other. On the lowest level, if we measure the distance between the two ends of the frieze of the east wall, we find that the NS width is longer only by about 1 dhanurgraha hasta (H) than the EW width. It can be seen that all the measurements of the openings in both directions closely fit the hasta module of 48 cm. Furthermore, the EW width of the three openings each differ by 6 H. In the NS direction it is adjusted to 5.5 H because of the longer width of the lowest terrace in this direction. Thus, it appears that the standard width of each terraced plinth is designed to be 3 H (144 cm) wide. The standard hasta as a module also appears in the width of the stair's steps laid in each direction. Thus, the dimensions of the square to the north of the palace and the fountain structure clearly demonstrate the use of the standard hasta measure of 48 cm in this sixth century fountain. The dimensions of the fountain structure are of crucial importance for

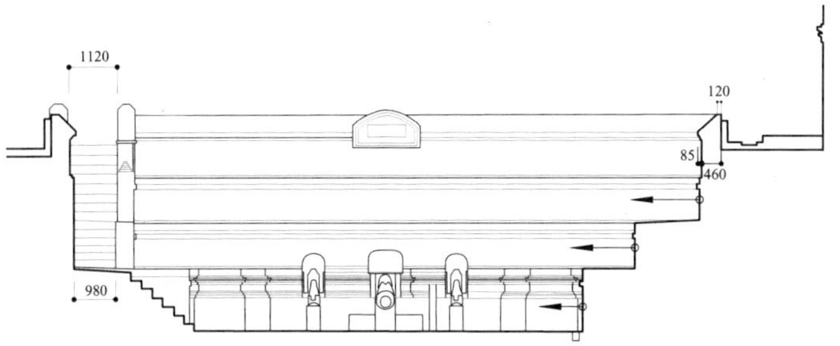

Fig. 8-3b. Manihiti: Section A-A: points of measurements.

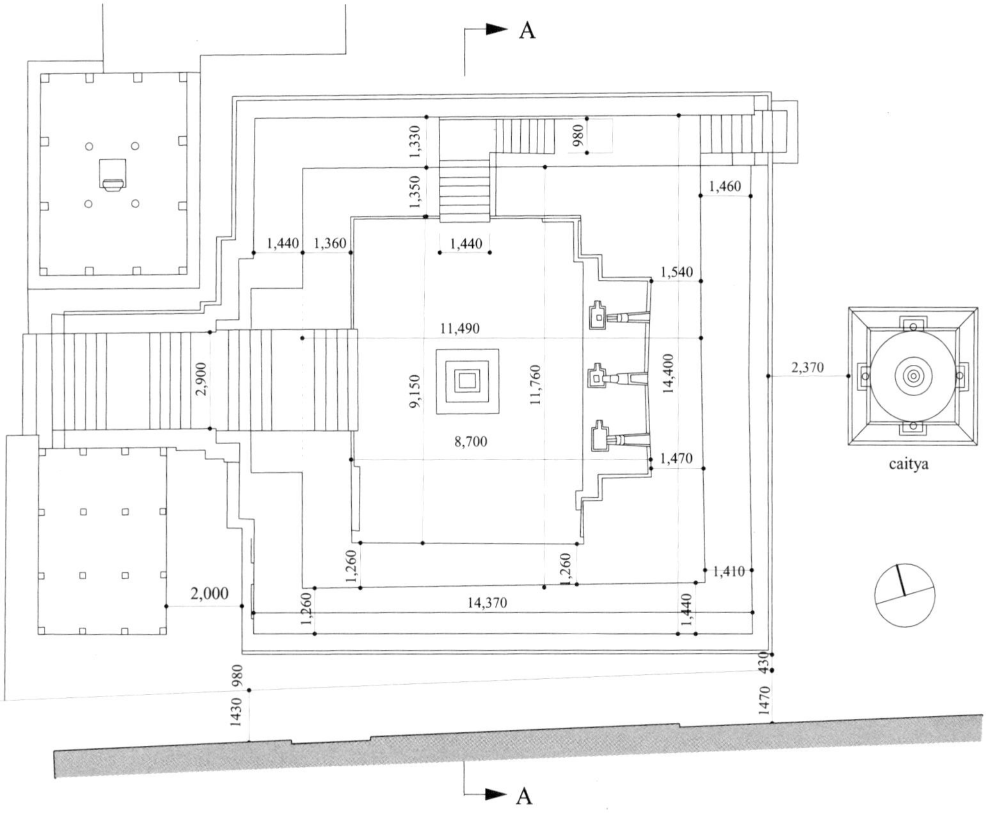

Fig. 8-3a. Manihiti: Plan

Fig. 8-3. Manihiti: Measured dimensions (redrawn from Becker-Ritterspach, 1987)

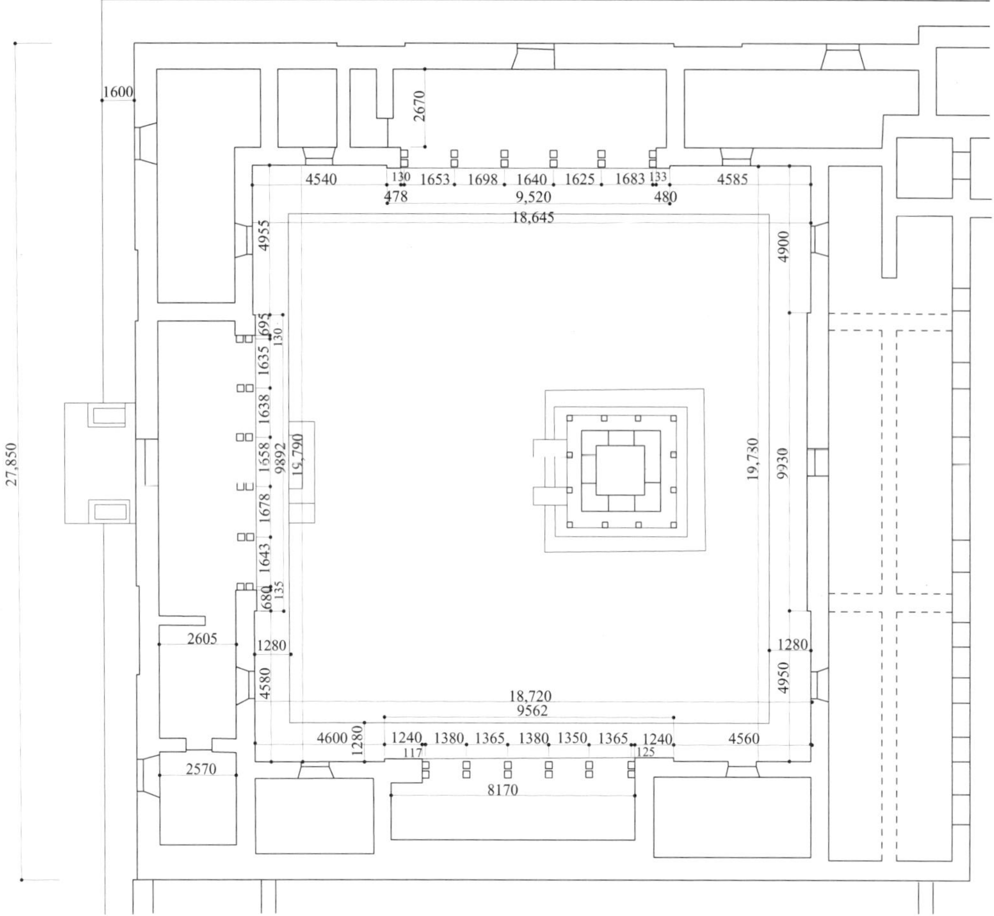

Fig. 8-4. Keshavnarayan chok (redrawn from Nippon Institute of Technology, 1981)

they provide a very accurate measure for the hasta, and a chronological reference for the use of this ancient standard in the planning of Kathmandu Valley towns and building artifacts.

Dimensional Layout of Palace Courts

The examination of the layout of palace courtyards further suggests that the planning of palace quadrangles also used a standard that relates to the hasta and danda modules of the ancient period (Figs. 8-4 and 8-5). The spatial arrangement of palace quadrangles shows a pattern similar to those of Buddhist monasteries of the bahal type. The central sections of all four wings on the ground floor, like the bahal, are open to the courtyard. It is a symmetrical layout along the central axis. The central open area of the wings, called *dalan*, has a row of twin posts at the front to support the second floor. The posts are intricately carved with floral patterns and images of deities, making them a deco-

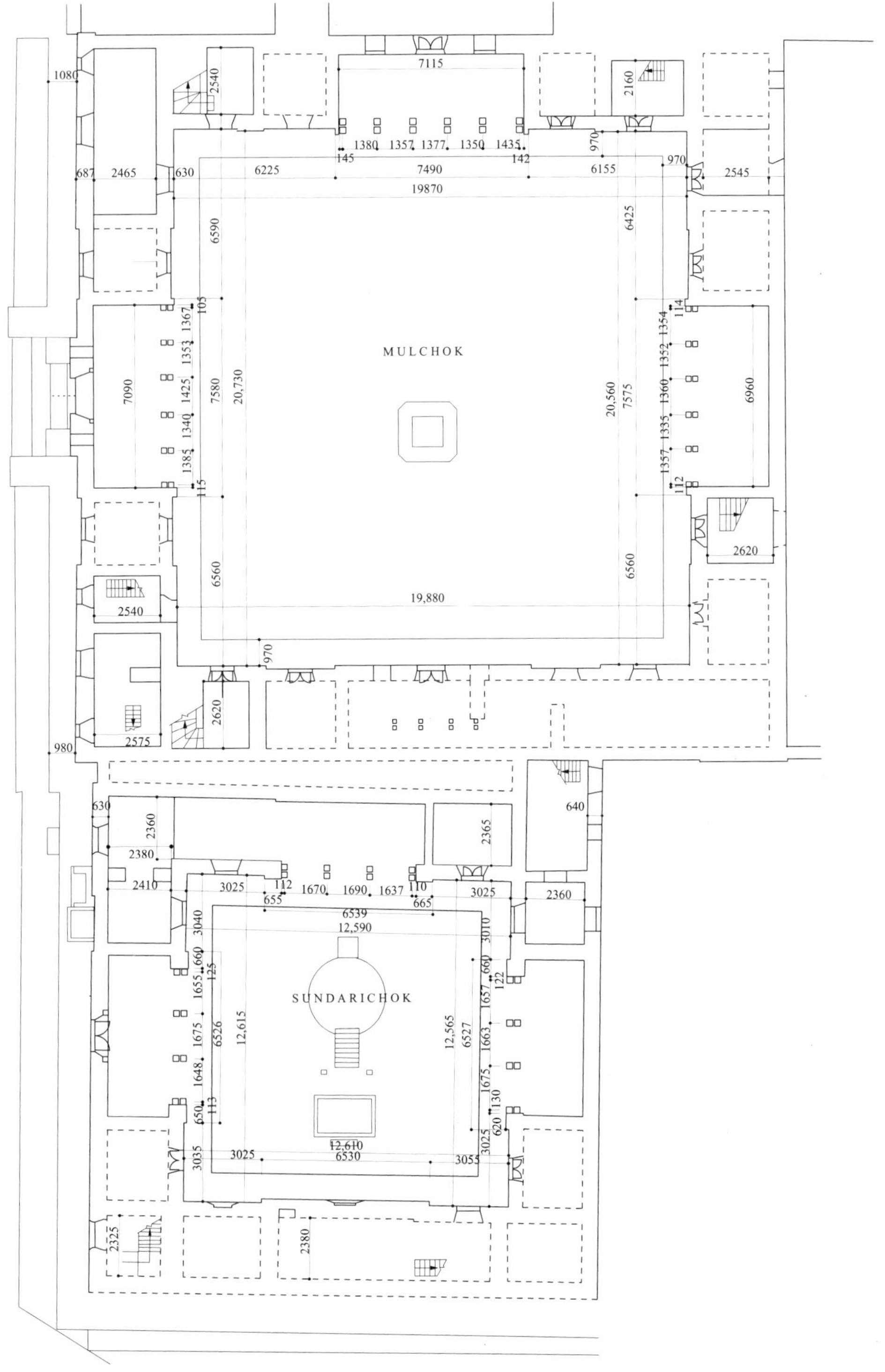

Fig. 8-5. Mulchok and Sundarichok (redrawn from Nippon Institute of Technology, 1981)

Table 8-2. Column spacing in dalans of Keshavnarayan chok, Mul chok and Sundari chok of Patan Palace (mm)

Palace court		measured dimension					average
Keshavnarayan chok	north	1656	1688	1640	1630	1683	1659
	south	1380	1365	1380	1355	1370	1370
	west	1645	1680	1660	1640	1640	1653
Mul chok	north	1380	1358	1378	1350	1438	1381
	east	1356	1370	1360	1355	1355	1359
	west	1385	1340	1425	1355	1370	1375
Sundari chok	north	1670	1690	1635			1665
	east	1680	1660	1660			1666
	west	1665	1675	1655			1665

rative frame for the courtyard buildings. In Sundari chok and Keshavnarayan chok, the center-to-center spacing of the timber posts is about 1666 mm and 1656 mm, respectively (Table 8-2). These spans correspond to 3.5 H (1680 mm) of the standard hasta measure mentioned above. However, the corresponding span in the dalan of Mulchok is 1375 mm. It should be noted that the dalan spans of this courtyard are unusually narrow. (In fact, they are even narrower than those of individual residential houses, as shown by studies done elsewhere (Pant 2002, 82; 84). However, despite similar outer dimensions, the size of the open court-yard of Mulchok is larger than that of Keshavnarayan chok. The narrower span was due to certain changes in Mulchok's room layout, interior courtyard façade, and pattern of fenestration. In particular, compared to Keshavnarayan chok and Sundari chok, Mulchok has two more rooms added symmetrically in each wing of the court. Further, the windows of the rooms with the usual traditional pattern that extends its decorative lintels to a

considerable length and the recessed wall design make the dalan narrower to the extent of omitting the bracket wall at its two ends, which is a common feature of the dalan structural layout. Nevertheless, it works out that the average width of the dalan, if divided into 4 spans, comes to 1710 mm to a span, a value close to the dalan of other courtyards. However, the division into even numbers is not permissible as it is inauspicious. In other words, it does not accord with the tradi-tional symmetry.

In studying the application of module measures, the most obvious parts to scrutinize are the dalan of the courtyards with the post and lintel constructions. The spacing of the posts of the palace quadrangles can be closely approximated with two other alternate values of 418 mm, a dimension closer to sishu hasta (h = 426 mm, h_1 in Table 8-3) Keshavnarayan chok, Sundari chok: 4 h; Mulchok: 3.25 h) and 457 mm (h_2) (Keshavnarayan chok, Sundari chok: 3.66 h_2; Mulchok: 3 h_2), if one takes multiples of one-half or one-third of a hasta, with the hasta measure being anywhere between 400 to 500 mm. The two values corroborate the earlier findings of Watanabe and Kurotsu. In their detailed analysis of the plan and section of a fifteenth century Buddhist monastery, I baha bahi, they demonstrated that a standard measure of 420.6 mm corresponded to one 'cubit' (Kurotsu 1998a and Watanabe 1998b) while 457.2 mm is suggested for Mulchok in the palace (Kurotsu 1998a). It should be noted that 420.6 mm is close to the classical standard where a sishu hasta (h) is 24 digits (426 mm) and where a dhanurgraha hasta (H) is 27 digits (480 mm) (Chap. 1). In this respect, it may also be noted that in his study of the lower palace courtyard of Gorkha, Gutschow found modules of 4260 mm (10 h) in the spacing of windows placed at equal intervals, and its one-third 1420 mm (~3H) in its further divisions (Gutschow 1985b).

While the modular dimensions calculated from the spans of the dalan thus suggest 480, 457, and 426 mm, Kurotsu in his analysis of Mulchok suggests 457.2 mm as the standard for the hasta measure used in the planning layout of this courtyard building. Certainly this value fits the dalan spans in Mulchok ($3 h_2$); however, for Keshavnarayan chok and Sundari chok, the multiple is $3.66 h_2$. It can be assumed that multiples of one-third of a hasta may have been used. However, before the planning method of palace courtyards can be explained, other problems need to be resolved. For instance, Kurotsu does not find the grid system suggested for Mulchok applicable to Sundari chok while, even for Mulchok, the grids do not accord consistently with the reference lines of the walls (Kurotsu 1991a). Furthermore, the hasta unit of

457.2 mm is not found in the grid of Sundari chok. Therefore, in this study an attempt was made to determine whether or not there is a standard applicable to the planning layout of all of these courtyard structures by comparing three hasta standards (480 mm, 457.2 mm, and 426 mm) with the specific dimensions of these courtyard wings (Table 8-3). The comparison was carried out by taking dimensions in two different ways. In the first method, the width of the wings were measured from the external wall line to the wall line at the courtyard side, while the length of the dalan block was considered to be the outer dimension of the section that juts out from the recessed section on its two sides. In the second method, the dimensions were taken from the center line to the center line of the walls, and for the dalan section the central line being through the center of the wall that juts out from the recessed wall. The thickness of all the relevant walls was assumed to be 630 mm. This is close to the measurement obtained from the drawings, except that for the outer walls of Keshavnarayan chok and Mulchok, which measured 680 mm. For the other dimensions, such as the sides of the open courtyard, the average measure of the opposite sides were taken, while for the internal clear width of the wings all known measures of the west wings were averaged with respect to each courtyard structure. Five different sets of dimensions, namely the width of the wing, the dalan, the recessed wall section, the open courtyard, and the outer dimension of the structures measured in the west were then compared. Table 8-3 shows that the value of 480 mm applied in the first method gives comparatively less error and more wholesome multiples for the wing block as well as the

Table 8–3. Block measures of three palace courts and comparison with multiples of three hasta measures (mm).

Outer wall line measures

Palace quadrangle	Block		measured width	H = 480			h₁ = 426			h₂ = 457.2		
				hasta multiple	theoretical value	margin of error	hasta multiple	theoretical value	margin of error	hasta multiple	theoretical value	margin of error
Sundari chok		wing block	3600	7.5	3600	0.0%	8.5	3620	+16.6%	7.75	3658	+12.7%
	west {	dalan block	6530	13.66	6557	+16.9%	15.33	6530	0.0%	14.25	6515	−13.1%
		recess block	3025	6.33	3038	+8.1%	7	2982	−8.9%	6.66	3045	+13.1%
		court width (E–W)	12600	26.25	12600	0.0%	29.66	12635	24.6%	27.5	12573	+23.6%
		courtyard block width (W)	19670	**41**	19680	+2.1%	46.25	19702	30.2%	**43**	19660	−2.2%
Mul chok		wing block	3800	**8**	3840	+8.3%	**9**	3834	+8.0%	8.33	3808	+5.3%
	north {	dalan block	7490	15.66	7517	+16.9%	17.5	7455	−33.0%	16.33	7466	−15.8%
		recess block	6190	**13**	6240	+10.4%	14.5	6177	−12.3%	13.5	6195	+4.4%
		court width (E–W)	19875	41.33	19838	−23.1%	46.66	19880	+3.5%	43.5	19888	+11.4%
	west {	dalan block	7580	15.75	7560	−16.7%	**18**	7561	−17.9%	16.5	7544	+31.5%
		recess block	6560	13.66	6560	0.0%	15.33	6530	−21.1%	14.33	6552	−5.3%
		court width(N–S)	20640	**43**	20640	0.0%	48.5	20661	+20.0%	45.25	20688	+42.0%
		courtyard block width (W)	27985	58.33	27998	+8.1%	65.66	27971	−9.7%	61.25	28004	+16.6%
Keshavnarayan chok		wing block	3890(w)	**8**	3840	−10.4%	9.25	3940	+47.0%	8.5	3886	−3.5%
	north {	dalan block	9520	19.75	9480	−33.3%	22.33	9513	−4.8%	20.75	9489	−27.1%
		recess block	4560	9.5	4560	0.0%	10.66	4541	−13.1%	**10**	4572	+2.6%
		court width (E–W)	18680	**39**	18720	+8.3%	43.75	18637	−40.6%	**41**	18631	−42.8%
	west {	dalan block	9910	20.66	9917	+4.1%	23.25	9904	−5.7%	21.66	9903	−4.60%
		recess block	4930	10.25	4920	−8.3%	11.5	4899	−29.2%	10.75	4915	−9.8%
		court width (N–S)	19790	41.25	19800	+8.3%	46.5	19809	+17.9%	43.33	19810	+13.1%
		courtyard block width (W)	27850	**58**	27840	−2.1%	65.33	27830	−13.8%	**61**	27889	+8.5%
Average margin of error (absolute)					185.4% = 8.8%			377.9%/21 = 18%			350.4%/21 = 16.7%	
Average margin of error in symmetry					−2.4%/21 = −0.1%			−42.3%/21 = −2.0%			+37.0%/21 = +1.8%	

Table 8–3. *continued*

Centre line measures

Sundari chok		wing block	2980	6.25	3000	+16.7%	7	2982	0.0%	6.5	2972	−6.7%
		dalan block	5875	12.25	5880	+4.1%	13.75	5857	−17.0%	12.75	5829	−40.2%
		recess block	3677	7.66	3677	+0.0%	8.66	3689	+8.5%	8	3658	−4.2%
		court width (E–W)	13230	27.5	13200	−25.0%	31	13206	−5.6%	29	13258	+1.7%
		courtyard block width (W)	19040	39.66	19040	0.0%	44.66	19025	−10.6%	41.66	19046	+3.9%
Mul chok		wing block	3170	6.66	3197	+16.8%	7.5	3195	+23.65	7	3200	+6.6%
	north	dalan block	7770	16.25	7800	+25.0%	18.25	7775	+4.7%	17	7772	+0.4%
		recess block	6370	13.25	6360	−8.3%	15	6390	+4.7%	14	6401	+6.8%
		court width (E–W)	20510	42.75	20520	+8.3%	48.25	20554	+41.5%	45	20574	+14%
	west	dalan block	7640	16	7680	+8.3%	18	7668	+6.6%	16.75	7658	+15.7%
		recess block	6840	14.25	6840	0.0%	16.25	6816	−22.6%	15	6858	+3.9%
		court width(N–S)	21270	44.33	21280	+6.2%	50	21300	+7.0%	46.5	21260	−8.7%
		courtyard block width (W)	27305	57	27360	+11.45%	64	27264	−9.6%	59.75	27318	+11.4%
Keshavnarayan chok		wing block	3220	6.75	3240	+16.7%	7.5	3195	−23.6%	7	3200	−4.4%
	north	dalan block	9730	20.25	9720	−8.3%	22.75	9691	−36.8%	21.25	9716	−12.2%
		recess block	4790	10	480	+2.1%	11.25	4792	+1.9%	10.5	4801	+9.6%
		court width (E–W)	19310	40.25	19320	+8.3%	45.33	19310	0.0%	42.25	19317	+6.1%
	west	dalan block	10140	21	1008	−12.5%	23.75	10118	−20.75%	22.25	10173	+28.9%
		recess block	5140	10.66	512	+12.5%	12	5112	−6.6%	11.25	5144	+3.5%
		court width (N–S)	20420	42.5	20400	−16.7%	48	20448	+6.6%	44.66	20419	0.0%
		courtyard block width (W)	27110	56.5	27120	+8.2%	63.66	27119	+6.3%	59.33	27126	+10.5%
		Average margin of error (absolute)			215.5%/21 = 10.3%			264.6%/21 = 11.7%			199.6%/21 = 9.5%	
		Average margin of error in symmetry			+73.8%/21 =+3.5%			−41.7%/21 = −2.0%			+46.8%/2 = +2.2%	

Note: *Hasta* multiples are assigned to give nearest value to the measured dimension. One *hasta* of 480 mm is divided into 27 digits while the other two *hastas* are divided into 24 digits each. Margin of error is then calculated with respect to 1/4, 1/3 or 1 unit of respective *hasta* measure depending to which fraction the value is equated.

building block. In 15 of the 21 measurement data, the average margin of error is less than 1 cm with a maximum of 2.7 cm. Furthermore, in comparison with other hasta multiples, the distribution of error is symmetrical (–0.1%). The validity of the first method, where the outer dimensions for the wing block and dalan are controlled separately rather than by a continuous grid system, is also suggested by the central position in the layout of dalan and their similar widths in each wing, despite the fact that the NS width of the open court is longer by about 1 m in both the Keshavnarayan chok and Mulchok.[13] Another set of data showing comparable closeness is the value of 457.2 mm by center-line measures. However, the distribution of error in the former instance of outer wall-line measures is much more symmetrical as well as smaller. The relationship of the standard measure of this hasta may also be checked from the widths of the recessed and jutted sections of the façades of the three courtyard quadrangles. Generally, the façades show a symmetrical form, although there is a certain degree of variation in the dimensional layouts in the existing west and north façades of Keshavnarayan chok. In both Mulchok and Sundari chok, the width between the center lines of windows is 5.5 H, just like the width of the recessed sections. The central section reflects the width of the central dalan block. Likewise, the recessed sections on the courtyard side are reflected

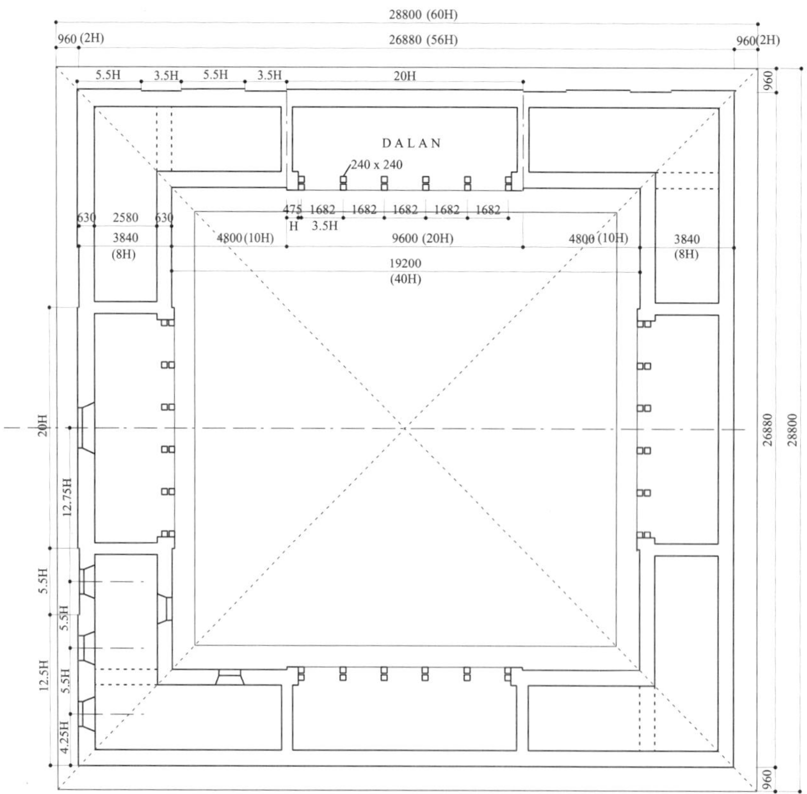

Fig. 8-6. Layout of a theoretical model of palace courtyard quadrangle

in the outer façades. Based on the above analysis of measurement data and the layout pattern, we can say that there is a greater likelihood of the use of a hasta of 48 cm length in the planning of the palatial courtyards.

Palace Quadrangles: A Dimensional Layout Model of the Ground Plan

The extent of the application of the ancient hasta standard in the planning the layout of palace quadrangles becomes clearer when we compare the existing dimensions of Keshavnarayan chok and the theoretical layout plan illustrated by the model in Figure 8-6. In this model, the width of the dalan, wing block, and the open courtyard are laid in multiples of a standard hasta of 48 cm. It can be seen that the existing width of the wing block, the length of the central dalan block, and the recessed walls as well as the span between the columns of Keshavnarayan chok almost coincide with the theoretical model. In the model, the site for the courtyard structure is a square of 28.80 m (15 danda). Within this site, a plinth width of half a danda is left around the building. In this layout, the quadrangle structure has a clear width of 10 d (19.2 m) for the central open courtyard, while the block itself that excludes the plinth is 14 d wide (26.88 m). The three quadrangles are longer in the NS direction because of the inclusion of the plinth width between them into the building block. This can be seen from the NS width of Keshavnarayan chok, which is 14.5 d (58 H). In this respect, the dimensions of the Kathmandu Mulchok (Fig. 8-7a) accords even more closely with the theoretical model, where the width of the block is 26.96 m (~14 d = 26.88 m)

and the open courtyard is 19.25 m × 19.35 m (~10 d = 19.20 m) with the clear width of the wing block being 2.60 m.[14] A comparison of the three Mulchok of Bhaktapur (Fig. 8-7b), Kathmandu, and Patan with the model plan shows that the external width of the wing blocks is given a standard dimension of 8 H (3.84 m), while the size of the open courtyard varies with the size of the quadrangular block. We presume that this similarity in the dimensions of all the Mulchok's layouts mentioned above suggests the possible existence of a courtyard structure like that of the model even earlier than the construction of the Mulchok of Bhaktapur. In this respect, it may be worth recalling an account in the Bhasavamsabali, one of the chronicles of Nepali history. The chronicle states that King Gunakamaadeva (tenth century) built the Mulachhen agam and a courtyard for his palace in the shape of a *vrisha-varga* on one karsha of land (Lamsal 1966, 19–20).[15] Vrisha-varga is a Sanskrit term where *vrisha* means "a potent man, a bull, the chief of a class or anything, the most excellent and pre-eminent of its kind," while *varga* is "a square (area) or a class" (Williams 1899). Another lexicographer, Halayudha (prior to the thirteenth century) defines vrisha as virtue and justice, while according to Varahamihira, a fifth century astronomer, vrisha also signifies a piece of ground suitable for the foundation of a house, and the feminine form, *vrishi,* means "a woman's apartment." In all, the meaning of a courtyard in relation to vrisha-varga could well be "a courtyard of excellent virtue." The chronicler does not give the reigning period of King Gunakamadeva, although there are two kings with such a name between the tenth and twelfth centuries (Vajracharya and Malla 1985).

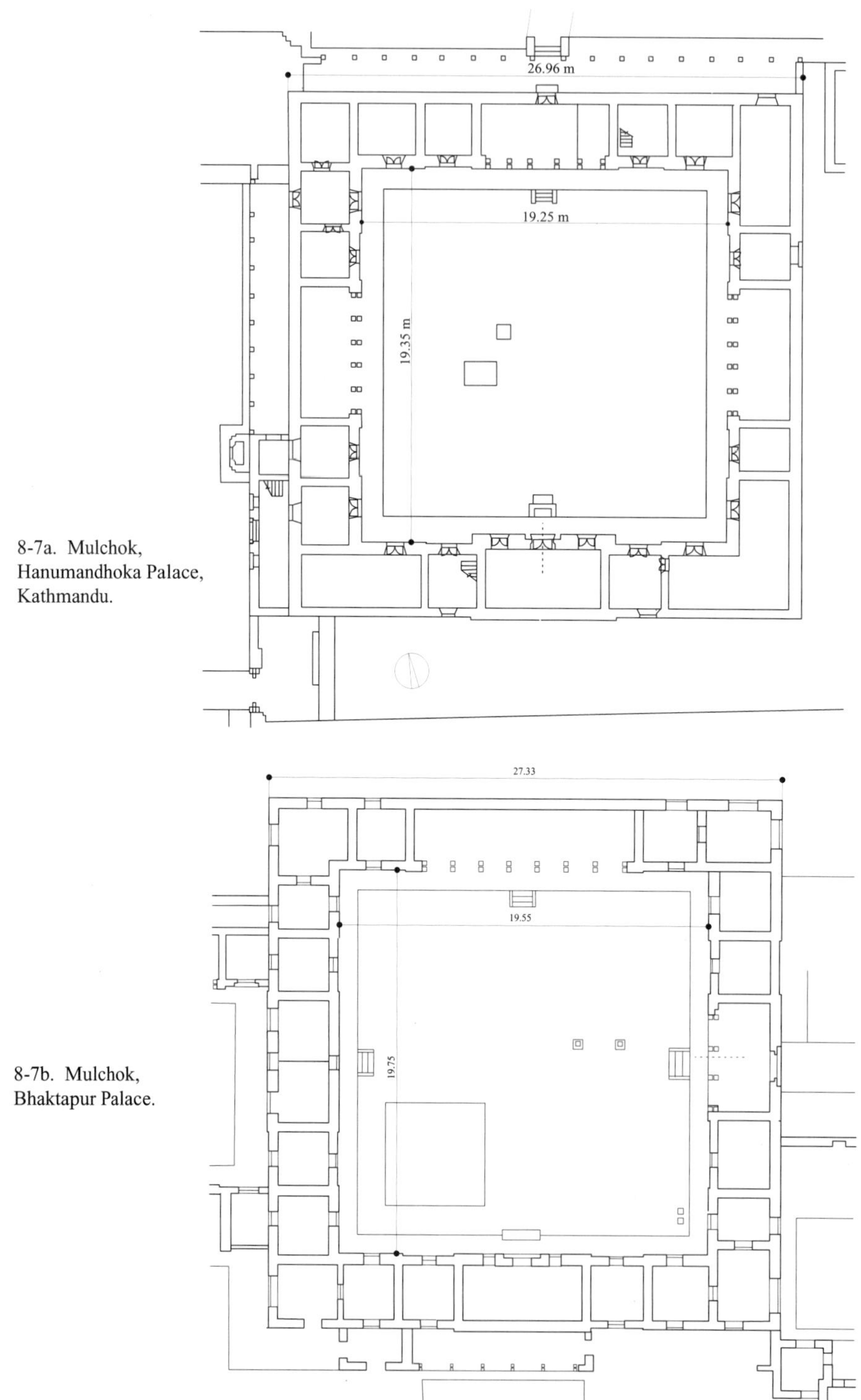

8-7a. Mulchok,
Hanumandhoka Palace,
Kathmandu.

8-7b. Mulchok,
Bhaktapur Palace.

Fig. 8-7. Mulchok of Kathmandu and Bhaktapur (redrawn from Gutschow, 1985a)

The *mula-chhen* (Newari: chhen = house) mentioned by the same chronicle is equivalent in meaning to Mulchok, the main court. Considering the extensive use of the Mulchok type quadrangle where the inner open courtyard is exactly 1 r square, the use of a standard module in the planning of settlement quarters, and the relative antiquity of Keshavnarayan chok, we presume that the structure mentioned by the chronicle is the kind of courtyard illustrated by this model.

There is an illustration of Khum bahal (Fig. 7-7a), a Buddhist monastery in Kathmandu built in 1590 [NS 711] (Locke 1985, 354), which proves that the planning method shown by the theoretical model of Keshavnarayan chok was truly applied. The dimension of the Khum bahal block quadrangle is 19.10 m × 19.12 m, a value close to a square of 1 r width (19.20 m). Its wing width is 7.5 h and the dalan block is 15 h long. The recessed part is also 7.5 h wide. However, the standard hasta measure in this instance is the sishu hasta (426 mm) that, as mentioned earlier, belongs to the same system of measurement. The correspondence of the measured dimensions with the theoretical values demonstrates that this is an established planning practice with regard to courtyard buildings. Tadhuchhen bahal of Bhaktapur also shows a similar practice.[16] It has two bay wings and a square open courtyard with sides measuring 0.5 r. Thus, it can be seen that Keshavnarayan chok and Mulchok illustrate a classic layout planning of a courtyard quadrangle building using the ancient system of measure of hasta, danda, and rajju. This was also an established tradition in the planning of Buddhist monastery courtyards as is clearly shown by Khum bahal (Chap. 7).

Khum bahal and the palace quadrangles were structures built between late sixteenth and early eighteenth centuries. Although we do not have the measurement data on the buildings belonging to the period between the construction of the Manihiti Fountain and the palaces, the extensive use of the ancient measure in the planning of settlement quarters illustrated in the Chapters 6 and 7 shows that the standard was used from the ancient period to the end of the medieval period. A recent survey of residential courtyard buildings has provided evidence that shows the standard was used at least until the beginning of the nineteenth century. This evidence is seen in a courtyard dwelling located in the northern section of a Buddhist community quarter of Nagbahal to the northwest of the palace. The two-way dimensions of its open courtyard, the width of the plinth, and the depth of each wing are multiples of the ancient hasta measure (Fig. 8-8). The closeness of the measurement values with the ancient standard displays a degree of coincidence not explainable by mere chance. This example further shows that the planning layout, which takes external wall lines of the courtyard wings in multiples of hasta, was used from palace and monastery courtyards to common residential dwellings.

Conclusions

The study on the layout dimensions of the palace structures of Patan shows that the dimension of the palace site accords with the modular measure of the hasta and its multiples, the danda and the rajju, an ancient standard of measure first discovered in the town plan of Thimi and then found widely applied in the planning

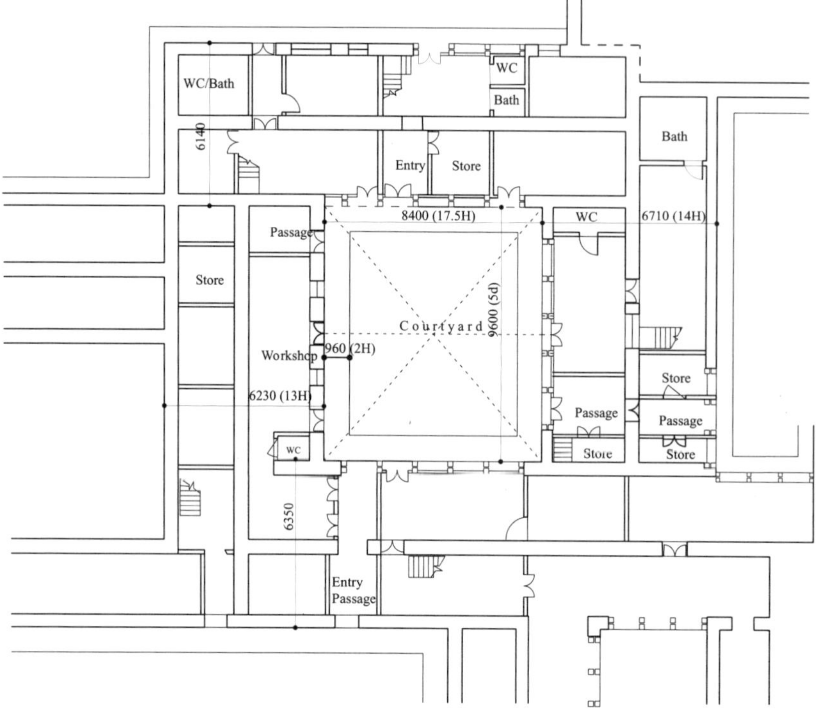

Fig. 8-8. A residential courtyard of Akibahal

of courtyard settlements in Patan. In particular, the findings on the planning of Patan Palace may be summarized as follows:

1. The existing palace precinct and the fountain square to the north are laid in a continuous grid layout as shown by the use of the same modular measure of rajju.

2. The courtyard quadrangle structures use the same standard of measure in determining the size and layout of the courtyard wings. A theoretical model of a 1.5 r wide courtyard block has been shown to fit the planning layout of such palatial courts, such as Mulchok and Keshavnarayan chok.

3. The application of the ancient standard measure extends to Buddhist monasteries and to the planning of residential courts.

4. The layout dimensions of the fountain of the palace square, the palace courts, and the residential court that date from the sixth, sixteenth, and nineteenth centuries indicate that the ancient standard was adopted in the Kathmandu Valley from the ancient period to early modern times.

We believe that the continuity of the grid from the northern border of the square to the southern border of the palace is an important clue that indicates the palace area was planned on a grid at an early stage prior to the building of the Manihiti Fountain or prior to 560 CE. The grid continues to the north and extends to the west when measured from the western wall of the palace, which is seen in the analysis of the settlement grid of the city (Chap. 11). We cannot expect such exact alignments of the general grid with the palace if it had been constructed centuries later, that is, in medieval times.

Whether or not the seat of the ruling court was in Patan during the Licchavi period is debatable, but it is most probable that the site was marked for a palace by the time of or prior to the construction of the Manihiti Fountain.

9

The Buddhist Monastery Architecture

The preceding chapters have demonstrated the use of ancient standard measures, referred in Kautilya's *Arthāsastra*, both in the planning of settlement quarters of Buddhist communities and palace quadrangles in Patan. In this chapter, we look more closely at the application of these measures in the planning of Buddhist monastery courts. In particular, we analyze the layout and planning dimensions of the monastery courtyard and dimensions of its columns. Our detailed analysis of these dimensions and their proportional divisions into various sections indicate the use of the same system of measure down to the scale of the *angula* unit that constitutes the *hasta* measure. It then derives the corresponding value of the *angula* unit in metric terms to a degree of precision that differs from our earlier reckoning of the *hasta* measure by only a few micrometers. The study thus independently derives and verifies the value of the ancient measure used in building construction and town planning in the Kathmandu Valley.

For our case studies we focus on the medieval and ancient monastery courts of Patan including those in Kathmandu and Bhaktapur, some of which have dated records of their foundation. Although we do not know the extent to which the extant structures of the monasteries have preserved their early forms, it is apparent that the monastery architecture of the Kathmandu Valley shows similarities with the ancient monastery court structures of India, such as those indicated by the remains of Sanchi and Gandhara as well as the cave sites of southwest India.[1] Our case studies include those structures, which have available measured drawings. In particular, the measured drawings made by the NIT during its study and

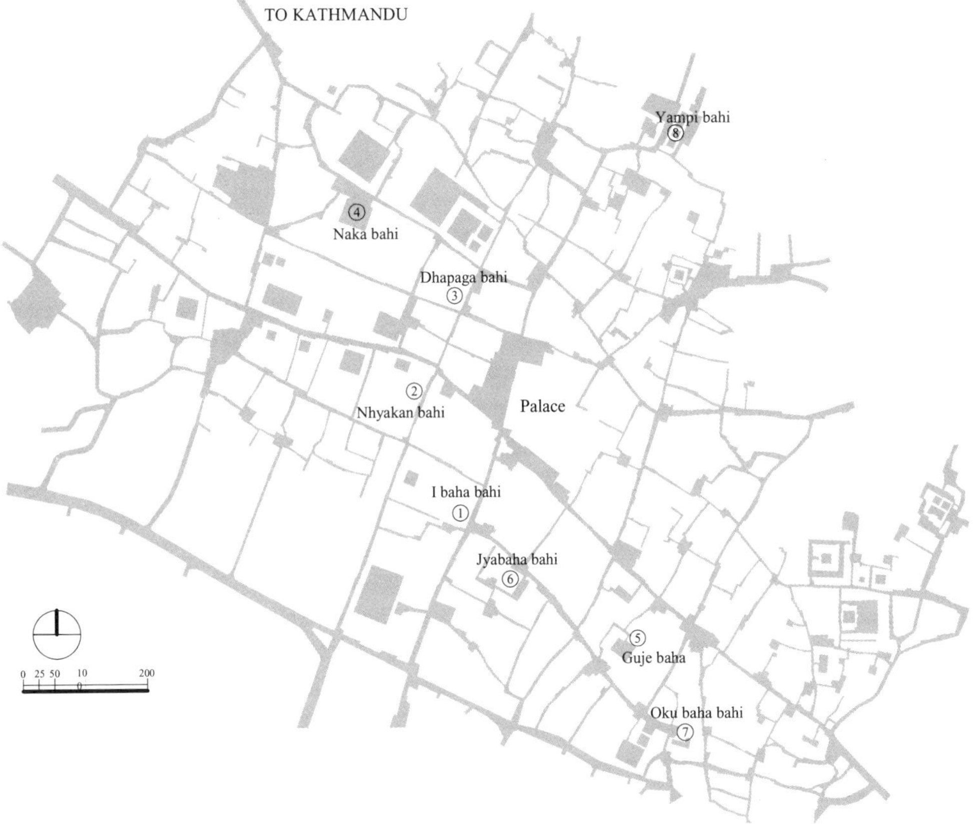

Fig. 9-1. Location of bahil surveyed in Patan

restoration of one of Patan's Buddhist monasteries are an important source of data for this study. In addition to these materials, we conducted a survey of other monasteries in Patan and obtained measurements to analyze the dimensions of columns of the monastery courtyard structures (Fig. 9-1).[2]

Buddhist Monastery Courts

As mentioned in the earlier chapters, the Buddhist monastery architecture of Nepal is classified primarily into two types—bahal and bahil. There is also another type called baha-bahi which, in some instances, shows a composite form of the above two types.[3] Figures 9-2a to 9-2f give the layouts of the ground floors of six bahil, four from Patan and one each from Kathmandu and Bhaktapur, with measurement dimensions. Figure 9-2a shows Chabahil, a bahil located in the east of Kathmandu which, according to Nepalese chronicles, is one of the oldest extant Buddhist monasteries in the Kathmandu Valley. Figure 9-2b shows the layout of the ground floor of Yampi bahi in Patan, which is also thought to be an ancient monastery going back to the early Licchavi period (Wright 1972). The remains of Buddhist monasteries in India such as the

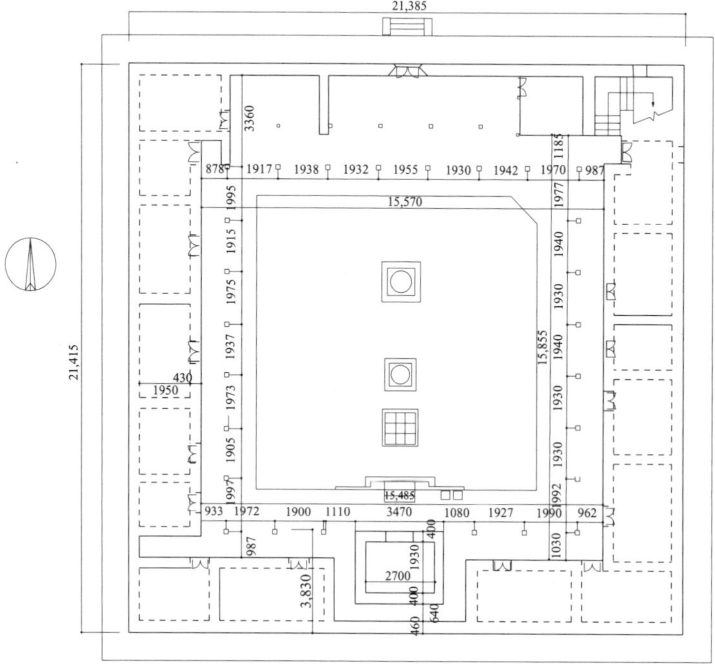

Fig. 9-2a. Ground floor plans of Buddhist monasteries: Chabahil, Kathmandu (redrawn from Nippon Institute of Technology, 1986)

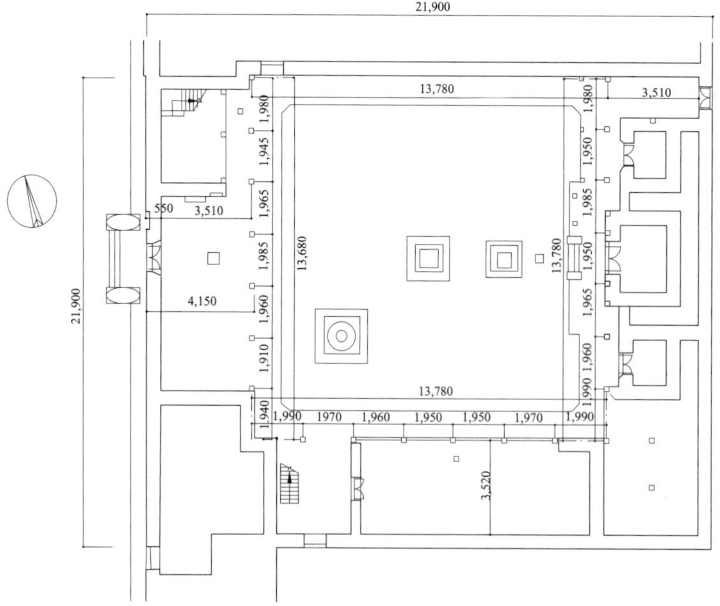

Fig. 9-2b. Ground floor plans of Buddhist monasteries: Yampi bahi, Patan (redrawn from Nippon Institute of Technology, 1986)

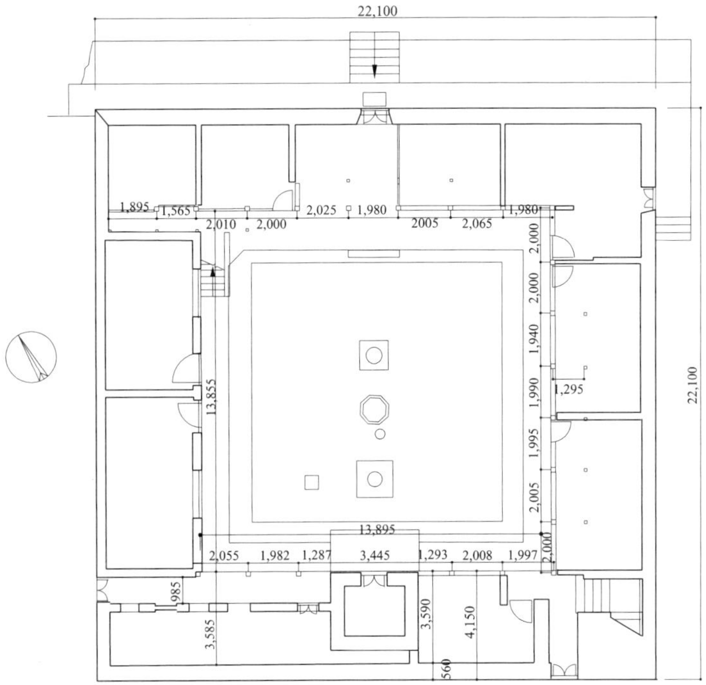

Fig. 9-2c. Ground floor plans of Buddhist monasteries: Jya baha bahi (Cakra bahil), Patan (redrawn from Nippon Institute of Technology, 1986)

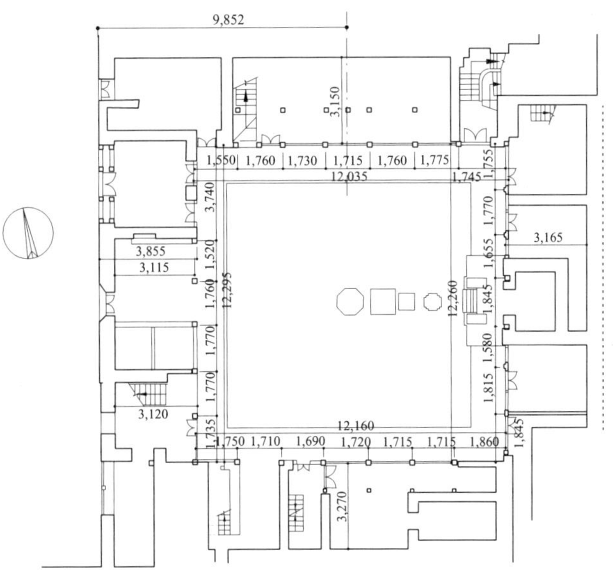

Fig. 9-2d. Ground floor plans of Buddhist monasteries: U baha bahi, Patan (redrawn from Nippon Institute of Technology, 1986)

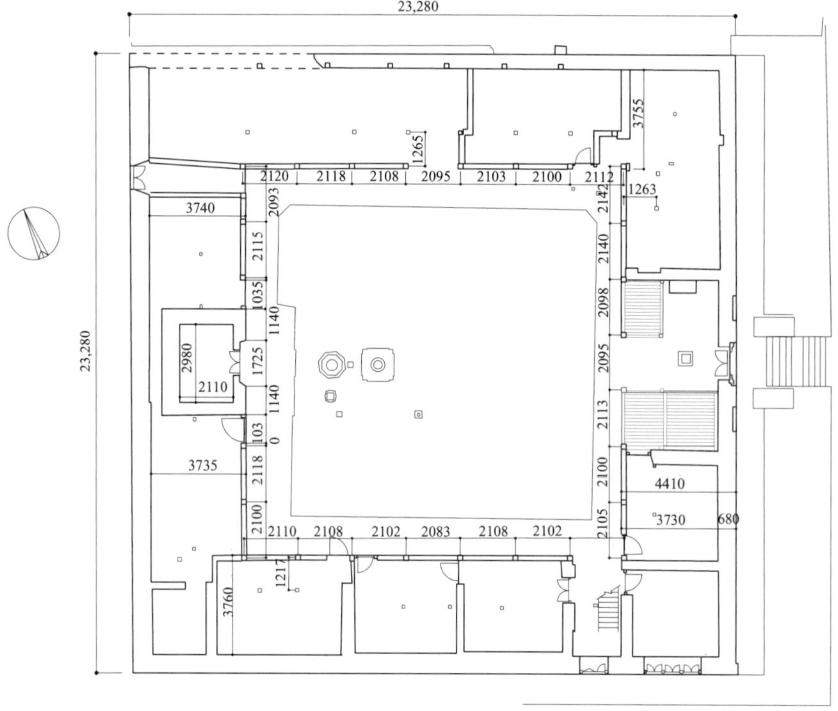

Fig. 9-2e. Ground floor plans of Buddhist monasteries: I baha bahi, Patan (redrawn from Watanabe, 1998)

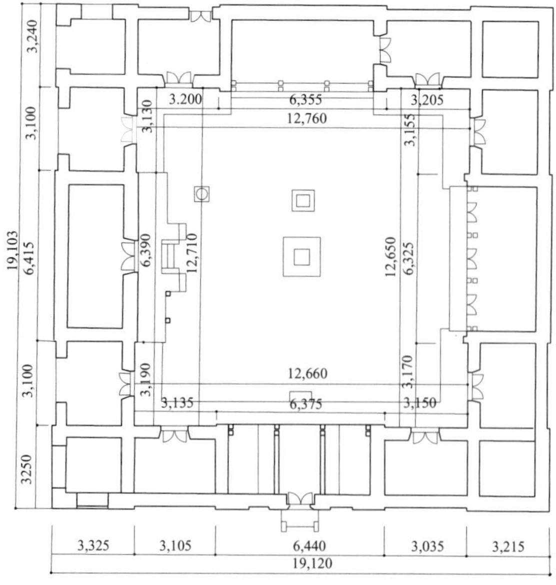

Fig. 9-2f. Ground floor plans of Buddhist monasteries: Khun bahal, Bhaktapur (redrawn from Nippon Institute of Technology, 1986)

Ajanta caves and Sanchi, or the Gandhara region of Pakistan including those built in Taxila, show a striking resemblance to the plan of Chabahil, where monastic cells are arranged around an open quadrangular courtyard (Hatano, 1998, 12). In the layout of monastery cells around this courtyard, other bahil use light partitions and wooden posts, whereas Chabahil has brick masonry walls. Bahal, on the other hand, which followed the development of *Vajrayana*, has a different layout of rooms as illustrated in Figure 4-1 (Chap. 4).

While the differences in architectural forms between the two types of monasteries have been described by various researchers,[4] here we are primarily concerned with the modular measures used in one particular type—the bahil—and their relationship with the standard measure employed in the larger context of settlement planning. Although the number of bahil included in the case study is limited, the data when taken together with those obtained from the palace courtyards and the residential quadrangles are significant enough to help us understand and demonstrate certain planning principles of Buddhist monasteries in the Kathmandu Valley.

Planning Dimensions of the Monastery Court

The dimensions of the selected monasteries given in Figure 9-2 are arranged in Table 9-1. These are compared with the multiples of *hasta* measures. The two *hasta* measures employed are assumed to be 426 mm and 480 mm and correspond to *sishu hasta* (h) and *dhanurgraha hasta* (H) in the system of measure given by Kautilya. Our earlier studies have shown

the use of the larger *dhanurgraha hasta* in the planning of settlement blocks and in the division of dwelling plots. This *hasta* is also the standard module in the planning of palace courtyards. The *sishu hasta* belongs to the same system of measure, where the larger *hasta* (H) is divided into 27 digits and the smaller one into 24 digits. The multiples of *sishu hasta* and *dhanurgraha hasta* are related. For instance, 4.5 h is equal to 4 H, which is one *danda*. In smaller fractions, 3h/4 is equal to 2H/3. Furthermore, Watanabe and Kurotsu in their study of one of the monasteries, I baha bahi of Patan, have shown the use of a cubit measure of 420.6 mm, which approximates a *sishu hasta* by our reckoning. It should be noted that among the four kinds of *hasta*—*sishu hasta*, *prajapatya hasta*, *dhanurmuhsti*, and *dhanurgraha hasta*—it is only *sishu hasta* which has a common denominator with *dhanurgraha hasta*. The possible use of *sishu-hasta*, on the other hand, is suggested by the Khun bahal of Kathmandu (Fig. 9-2f), where the sections of the elevation in the interior and exterior façades are divided into multiples of 7½ h (= 6⅔ H). The unit of 7½ h itself is mentioned in the chronicles of Nepalese history, further indicating the use of this *hasta* as well.[5]

It is noteworthy that despite the different historical periods of the monasteries' foundations, the manner and size of their layouts are strikingly similar. The outer dimensions of these monastery blocks are between 40 to 48 H. Bahil are much closer to each other in size and comparatively larger than bahal. The open courtyards of all bahil are seven spans wide. U baha bahi (Fig. 9-2d), with a size close to 1 rajju (19.2 m) square, is smaller in size than other bahil, but the number of spans is maintained by making the span

Table 9-1. Comparison of layout dimensions of selected Buddhist monasteries (dimensions in paranthesis are in mm)

monastery	block size						wing width					average span (dalan)			X : W
	X	Y	hasta (h)	error	hasta (H)	error	W	hasta (h)	error	hasta (H)	error	L	h	H	
Chabahil	21,385	21,415	50.25 (21,406)	+5.63%	44.66 (21,437)	+23.12%*	3,830	9 (3,834)	+0.94%	8 (3,840)	+2.00%	1,942	4.5 (1,920)	4 (1,920)	5.59
Yampi bahi	21,900	21,900	51.5 (21,939)	+36.60%*	45.66 (21,917)	+10.60%	4,150	9.75 (4,153)	+2.80%	8.66 (4,157)	+4.37%	1,963	4.5 (1,920)	4 (1,920)	5.29
Jya baha bahi	22,110	22,100	52 (22,152)	+11.03%	46 (22,080)	−5.20%	4,150	9.75 (4,153)	+2.80%	8.66 (4,157)	+4.37%	2,005	4.75 (2,023)	4.25 (2,040)	5.32
U baha bahi	19,705	——	46.25 (19,703)	−1.89%	41 (19,680)	−5.20%	3,855	9 (3,834)	−4.92%	8 (3,840)	−3.81%	1,727	4 (1,704)	3.5 (1,680)	5.10
I baha bahi	23,280	23,280	54.66 (23,285)	+3.50%	48.5 (23,280)	0.00%	4,410	10.33 (4,400)	−7.04%	9.25 (4,400)	−8.33%	2,107	5 (2,130)	4.33 (2,080)	5.29
	absolute average			5.74%		5.25%			3.70%		4.57%				5.32
	asymmetrical error			+4.57%		+0.05%			−1.08%		−0.32%				

Notes:

1. h (*sishu hasta*) = 426 mm, H (*dhanurgraha hasta*) = 480 mm

1. The error is calculated against the margin of 1 *hasta* or 1/4 or 1/3 of *hasta* depending upon which multiple the theoretical value corresponds. The average error excludes deviant values marked in asterisk (*).

2. The error on the block size is calculated against the average of X and Y, the breadth and length of the Monastery, when the values are close to each other, while otherwise, it is calculated against X.

narrow. An even number of spans is avoided, and U baha bahi would have a comparable span width with that of other bahil if the number of its spans were six. One of the significant features seen in the layout dimension of all bahil is the proportional relationship between the size of the block, given by its outer dimension, and the wing width, which on average is 5.3 : 1 (X : W, Table 9-1). Consequently, a proportional relationship also exists between the size of the monastery block and the width of the spans.

Table 9-1 shows that the overall dimensions of the courtyard buildings, as shown by margin of error, are not always the exact multiples of these two types of *hasta*. However, the width of wings in all the monastery buildings accord with *hasta* multiples with considerable accuracy. This conformity is especially significant compared to the other dimensions when we see a consistent application of particular dimensions—3830 mm (8 H) and 4150 mm (8.66 H)—for the wings of Chabahil and U baha bahi which differ in size. Table 9-1 also shows that the two kinds of *hasta* measures are in comparable conformity to the layout dimensions of these monasteries. This is because, as mentioned earlier, there exists a common denominator of 18 digit (*aṅgula*) between them, that is, $\frac{2}{3}$ H equals $\frac{3}{4}$ h. The conformity of *hasta* with the width of the wing, at the same time, shows that the assigned values for the two *hasta* are fairly accurate.

Unlike the width of the wing blocks, the deviations in the spans of the peristyle are larger, although the values may still be considered close to *hasta* multiples. This indicates that the widths of the courtyard wings were first marked by giving them convenient multiples of the basic *hasta*

module. The width of the spans of the peristyle colonnade was consequently adjusted and distributed among the customarily fixed number of seven spans. This is evident particularly in Chabahil and U baha bahi. Their outer dimensions differ significantly but the widths of their courtyard wings are the same.

Between the two *hasta*, the value of the *dhanurgraha hasta* shows greater symmetry in error, while the average error is comparable to the *sishu hasta*. Therefore, if the statistical indicator is to be taken into account, within the limitation of the above data, the module of the larger *hasta* appears to have been employed in the layout planning of bahil.

The Columns of the Peristyle

As stated earlier, the specific values for H and h were found applicable in the layout dimensions of monastery courts. Moreover, the measure for a *danda* could be calculated from either *dhanurgraha hasta* or *sishu hasta*, thereby giving the value as 4 H or 4.5 h for 1 *danda* (d). In this section, we will see that these standard *hasta* measures are used to determine the height of a column and its proportional divisions, which allows us to obtain more accuracy in the value of this measure. This will be illustrated through case studies of Patan's bahil monastery courts, with columns whose heights measure close to 1 d (d = 1920 mm) (Pl. 9-1 and Fig. 9-3).

Of the 16 bahil in Patan, eight were included in our survey. The other eight bahil were not surveyed because they either have not preserved the original courtyard structures or they are in such a state of disrepair that the required survey work would not have been possible. The

Pl. 9-1. A column of Guita bahil, Patan

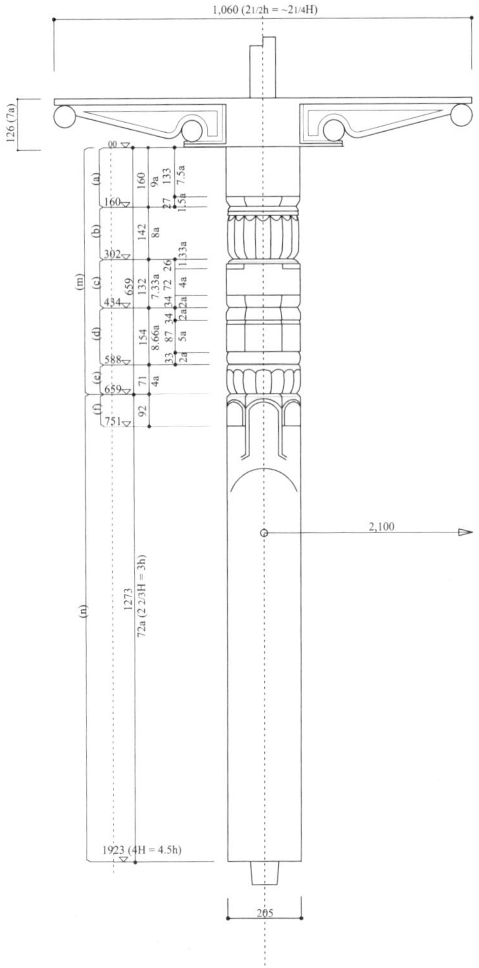

Fig. 9-3. The typical column style of bahil

plans of four among the eight bahil surveyed are given in Figure 9-2 (9-2b–9-2e). It is to be noted that all the surveyed bahil show exactly the same iconographic detail in the design of their respective columns.[6]

The Height of the Column and the Measures—Danda, Hasta, and Añgula

In his analysis of I baha bahi, a monastery built in the fifteenth century, Kurotsu (1998c, 88) illustrates a sequence of pillars and provides their measured heights. Their average value is 1925 mm, with the tallest being 1930 mm and the shortest being 1918 mm. The columns in the second story of the monastery are also of similar heights. Different lengths of tenons to receive the capital brackets and socles at the bottom protrude from the top and bottom of these posts. In his analysis of the unit of measurement of the pillar, Kurotsu (1998a) defines the height of the pillar as including the bracket capital, thus making its total height 2055 mm. This measure is then equated with 108 *añgula*s or 4.5 h. In this equation, the measure for 1 h is 458.4 mm. This is in close concordance with the *hasta* measure Kurotsu suggests for *Mulchok* in the Patan Palace, which is 457.2 mm. However, he finds it difficult to reconcile this value with the standard "cubit" measure of 420.6 mm, which he and Watanabe find to have been used in the plan and sections of the same building. This incongruence leads Kurotsu to suggest two different standard measures—one for planning the layout and structure of the building and the other for detailed measures for the column and its internal proportions and ornamental carving. This hypothesis is difficult to postulate until more data on the use of the above standard measures in the construction of the monastery are obtained.[7]

Our analysis of the column measure is, therefore, given here in the light of the preceding studies. The typical column of a bahil is illustrated by Figure 9-3, which shows a column with two sections, the upper part carved in floral patterns and the lower part with the plane shaft.[8] The height of the column, in this instance, is taken to be between the top of the base stone and the bottom of the capital bracket, both of which are separate elements connected to the column by tenon and mortise joinery. This measure is in accordance with the carpentry and structural considerations.[9] Figure 9-3 also gives measured dimensions of one such column from I baha-bahi, while the dimensions corresponding to this diagram for the columns of other bahil are given in Table 9-2.[10]

This analysis may also be taken as a corollary to our previous findings on *danda* and *hasta* units of measures. But more importantly, this analysis is of fundamental value as it independently gives a precise value for the *angula* unit, which is not possible to obtain from an analysis of larger measures. The measure of *angula* then gives precise measures of *hasta* and *danda*.

Division of Column Segments and the Measure of Angula

The line of division of the column segments needs some explanation before proceeding to the analysis of their dimensional relationships. During the survey, some carpenters were queried about this matter but no definite answers were obtained from them. Thus, the measurement of the column sections was done by considering the differences in the iconography of the sections and the distinctive neckline between them. Finer divisions, that is, those smaller than 10 mm, were not measured separately. The data obtained could be combined with the measurements of the upper or lower consecutive sections for the purpose of analysis. With the assumption that any meaningful division of the segments would be related to a fixed basic unit of measure, a

preliminary examination of the data was conducted with a number of possible combinations. The division pattern shown in Figure 9-3 is based on the findings of this analysis. It should be pointed out that the manner of division used in this analysis differs from that given by Kurotsu (1998a, 107) with respect to certain segments.[11]

The measurements obtained following the above criteria were then checked against the multiple of *angula*. The value of the *angula* was assumed to be the unit that constitutes the *dhanurgraha hasta* measure derived from our previous studies. This *hasta*, according to *Manasara* and *Mayamata*, consists of 27 digits. This accords with the *danda* (d) measure of Kautilya, where 108 *angula* makes 1 d. Based on our preceding studies (Chaps. 6, 7 and 8) this relationship gives 17.78 mm in metric measure for 1 *angula*. The heights of the bahil columns given in Table 9-2 are close to 1920 mm. This is exactly 1 d in the above system of measure giving the above value for 1 *angula*. This *angula* is taken as a reference when the divisions of the column segments are examined. It is referred to as *angula*$_{ref}$.

An analysis of the measurements of column sections given in Table 9-2 shows consistency in the dimensions and divisions of columns in all the bahil. In the table, the measures of segments, which are close to the multiple of *angula*$_{ref}$ (within a deviation of 10 per cent, that is, 1.8 mm), are noted in bold letters. This gives 23 of the 48 measures in the multiples of *angula*$_{ref}$. The divisions which are not the integer multiple of this *angula* are checked by adding them together to make 'sum of the segments.' It can be seen that this sum is in the multiple of *angula*$_{ref}$. Thus, in a set of measurements that includes the sum of the segments

Table 9-2. Metric dimensions and angula multiples of columns of peristyle colonnade of selected Patan bahils

For each monastery the sub-columns are: measurement value of segment | angula multiple | value of angula (17.xx) | measure of division (a1/a2, c1/c2/c3, d1/d2/d3).

Monastery: column location[1]	I baha bahi: x-x				Nhyakan bahi: 1-C				Dhapaga bahi: 4-A				Naka-bahi: 6-A			
Height	1932 (109a)				1920 (108a)				1795 (101a)*				1940 (109a)			
span	2120				2005				2010				1914			
bracket	1060				1025				1090				1070			
capital	126				116				120				152			
column width	205				195				205				180			
(a)	160	9.00	17.78	133/27	144	8.10	18	120/24	143	8.05	17.87	114/29	161	9.06	17.89	126/35
(b)	142	7.99	17.75		135	7.60			144	8.10	18		123	6.92	17.57	
(c)	132	7.43		26/72/34	117	6.58		23/69/25	137	7.71		18/81/38	148	8.33		27/80/41
(d)	154	8.67		34/88/33	145	8.16		28/90/27	156	8.78		40/81/35	161	9.06	17.87	38/90/33
(e)	71	3.99	17.75		86	4.84			70	3.94	17.50		82	4.61		
(f)	92	5.18			105	5.91	17.50		95	5.35			81	4.56		
sum of segments	c+d =286	16.09	17.87		b+c+e =338	19.02	17.79		c+f =232	13.05	17.84		c+e =230	12.94	17.69	
(m)	659	37.08			627	35.28			650	36.56			675	37.96		
(n)	1273	71.63			1293	72.76			1145	64.40			1265	71.15		
(m)/(n)	1.92				2.06				1.76				1.87			

Monastery: column location[1]	Gujebaha: 5-A				Jyababahi: 5-A				Okubaha bahi: 4-A				Yampi bahi: 4-A				average	angula ratio
Height	1916 (108)				1910 (107a)				1842 (104a)*				1850 (104a)*				1923 (108a)	108a
span	1700				2000				1955				1955					
bracket	930*				1060				1075				1080				1073	60a
capital	110				130				125				133				123	7a
column width	165				177				180				182				189	10.66a
(a)	137	7.71		110/27	143	8.05	17.87	113/30	143	8.05	17.87	110/33	144	8.10	18	117/27		8a
(b)	123	6.92	17.57		143	8.05	17.87		127	7.15			121	6.81				8a
(c)	125	7.03	17.86	22/69/34	119	6.70		74	126	7.09	18	21/70/35	134	7.54		26/73/35		7.33a
(d)	143	8.05	17.87	30/75/38	145	8.16		34/79/32	138	7.77		33/76/29	155	8.72		35/88/33		8.67a
(e)	137	7.71			69	3.88	17.25		70	3.94	17.5		73	4.11	18.25			4a
(f)	72	4.05	18		94	5.29			93	5.23			86	4.84				5a
sum of segments	a+e =274	15.42			c+f =213	11.98	17.75		d+f =231	13.00	17.77		b+c+d+f =496	27.91	17.71			
(m)	665	37.40			619	34.81			604	33.97			627	35.28			642	36a
(n)	1251	70.35			1291	72.60			1238	69.62			1223	68.82			1273	72a
(m)/(n)	1.88				2.09				2.05				1.95				1.98	

1. Index to column location:

2. Index to the measure of column sections [illust: Naka bahil segment (a)]

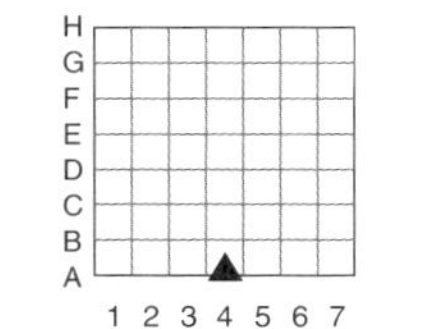

Notes:
(1) All measurements are in mm.
(2) Average measures exclude values marked in asterisk (*).

and excludes the individual data incorporated in the sum of segments, 30 out of 39 measurements (77 per cent) are the multiples of $angula_{ref}$. It is noteworthy that among 20 measures of column divisions that do not conform to the integer multiple of the above $angula_{ref}$, 11 are multiples of $\frac{1}{3}$ or $\frac{2}{3}$ of this $angula_{ref}$, suggesting that this fraction of $\frac{1}{3}$ of the $angula_{ref}$ was employed for finer divisions. This degree of agreement satisfactorily demonstrates the validity of the hypothetical value of $angula_{ref}$ used to analyze the dimensions of column segments.

Following this agreement with the hypothetical value of $angula_{ref}$, it was possible to calculate the mean value of $angula$ to get the smallest deviation in the measurement of the column segments. The data that are close to integer multiples of $angula_{ref}$ are first rounded off to make integer multiples. This gives $angula$ measures to each segment that differ slightly from the $angula_{ref}$ itself. The mean value of all these $angula$ measures accordingly comes to 17.79 mm with a standard deviation of 0.2 mm. The largest deviation from this mean is 3.0 per cent (0.53 mm). Calculated against this mean value, the margin of error for 30 of the 39 measured dimensions of the column segments are below 10 per cent, that is, 1.7 mm to the segment. When the error due to survey measurements is considered, such as a tape calibrated in millimeters, there is a possibility of a maximum error of 2.2 mm (1.7 + 0.5) to the column segments. This range of deviation should be unavoidable in the carpentry works of ancient and medieval times.[12] This degree of accuracy is not possible from any other values of the $angula$ unit which may be applicable to segment divisions of all the bahil columns.

The fact that the standard of this $angula$ (a) existed in the order of columns is also shown by other features as well. The average of the most frequent column height is 1923 mm, which is 108 a (a = 17.80 mm), the length defined as 1 d in Kautilya's Arthasastra. Furthermore, the lengths of the upper section (m in Fig. 9-3) and the lower section of the column (n in Fig. 9-3) are in a constant ratio of close to 1 : 2. Table 9-2 shows that the average length of the upper section is 36 a or 1.5 h ($1\frac{1}{3}$ H) while the average length of the lower section is 72 a or 3 h ($2\frac{2}{3}$ H). Further, when we take into account the most frequent measures of the segments of the upper section from (a) to (e) their average measurements are 8 a, 8 a, 7.33 a, 8.67 a, and 4 a, respectively, which add to make 36 a. The value for the upper section does not change substantially even when the height of the column is shorter than 108 a as shown by the columns of Dhapaga bahi. Likewise, the width of the columns, and the height and length of the brackets of all bahil are close to each other, indicating the use of standard dimensions to these members. We can therefore conclude that the divisions and the total height of the standard column follow, in principle, the above proportional relationships.

In practice, however, the proportional detail has to take into account the width of the columns, which in the cases studied range from 165 mm to 205 mm. Such differences are likely to necessitate adjustments in the proportional measures. A close examination of these measurements shows that there exist two kinds of order in the proportional divisions, where the upper and lower sections of the column are divided into ratios of 37 : 71 or 35 : 73 a, that is, into 1 : 1.92 or 1 : 2.08.

Corresponding proportions of the segments are represented by I baha bahi (9 a, 8 a, 7.33 a, 8.66 a, and 4 a), and Jya baha bahi (8 a, 8a, 7 a, 8 a, and 4 a). The above proportional relationships in a column are based on the height of 108 *añgula* divisions and the width as 1/10 of the height. Considering the detail measures in the division of the columns, it should be noted that the divisions of columns of I baha bahi and Jya baha bahi conform best to the standard when compared to other bahil.

The total length of the column, which is exactly 108 units, corresponds to 4.5 h or 4 H. This is the measure of 1 standard *danda* described by Kautilya. Therefore, the *añgula* unit (a), which measures 17.79 mm and gives wholesome multiples to the divisions of column segments, is concluded to be the standard value of 1 a. Since 24 a make 1 h and 27 a make 1 H, their respective lengths in this measurement system are 426.96 mm and 480.33 mm. In metric terms, the values can be rounded off to 427 mm and 480 mm. The exact coincidence of the values derived from this analysis of the columns to the values derived from the study of planning modules of settlement blocks is surprising.

As mentioned earlier, the span between the columns of the wings around the open courtyard of I baha bahi is 2100 mm, which is close to 5 h (2135 mm) or $4\frac{1}{3}$ H (2080 mm) conforming to the above value without significant deviation. We note that this measure of 1 h is longer by 6.4 mm than that derived by Kurotsu (1998a) and Watanabe (1998b) in their analysis of column spans and sections. However, the present value is close enough to suggest that the builders of I baha bahi employed the same standard measure for both the layout of the plan and height of the building and for the detailed ornamental carvings of the column and its internal proportions. If we accept this value as the standard measurement, the difference of 30 mm in the span is due to the manner of layout planning that we described in the previous section; that is, the wings are first marked with convenient modules and then the span of the peristyle colonnade is adjusted. While 420 mm for the *hasta* module accords perfectly with the column grid layout of I baha bahi, the value of 427 mm and the manner of layout described above provides a consistent explanation for all the aspects described in this study.[13]

The perfect coincidence of the multiples of *hasta* measure derived from the column dimension with that found in the settlement planning works is undeniable evidence of the authority of this standard.[14] We, therefore, conclude that the columns of I baha bahi and Jya baha bahi represent the ancient *danda* itself par excellence.[15] Such a degree of consistency in the employment of classical modular measures endorses Kurotsu's findings on I baha bahi when he writes, "The I baha bahi in Patan is a superbly designed structure and a classic example of one architectural style to be found in Buddhist Monasteries of Nepal" (Kurotsu 1998a, 103).

Conclusions

The analysis of the plan of the Buddhist monasteries has shown that the classical measures of *hasta* and *danda* were widely used in the Kathmandu Valley from ancient times. The planning of bahil and the dimensions of their columns, as well as the proportions and lengths of the various sections, correspond to the ancient standard measure. These findings come independently of previous studies on grids and module measures, and prove the existence of a classical measurement system in Nepal during the Malla period of the fifteenth century. They also provide the exact value, to the precision of a few micrometers in *aṅgula* measures of the *hasta* scale hitherto unknown in the traditional measurement system of Nepal. At the same time, the findings verify the relationship of *dhanurgraha hasta* and *sishu hasta*, which is based on the same standard measure of *aṅgula* given in *Arthasastra* and other *Vastusastras*. Other major findings of this study are as follows:

1. The columns of the bahil type Buddhist monasteries bear the standard length of 1 d, and their internal proportions and divisions are governed by *aṅgula* measures. The precise measure of 1 a is 17.79 mm, which gives dimensions for *dhanurgraha hasta* and *sishu hasta* as 480 mm and 427 mm, respectively. These conform to the measurements of palace and monastery quadrangles and the earlier findings on the standard modules of settlement planning.
2. I baha bahi and Jya baha bahi in Patan display the rigorous application of the standard measurement system as well as the proportional divisions of the segments of the columns.
3. In the planning of the ground plan's layout, the width of the wings was first determined according to the standard multiples of *hasta*; the size of the open courtyard was then the result of the remaining width of the courtyard building block.

Further studies are anticipated on the iconography of the columns of bahil of other settlements, in addition to those of bahal, which differ from bahil in the detailing of both the layout plan and columns.

The previous chapters have demonstrated that the towns and settlement quarters of the Buddhist community were planned according to a grid system that employed the ancient measuring system described by Kautilya in his Arthasastra. In this chapter, we have demonstrated further the use of the same measuring system in the scale of courtyard buildings and building elements, such as the columns and their divisions. The study of Buddhist monasteries and settlements, in particular, provides a key to understanding the measurement systems and the planning principles of individual buildings and settlements of ancient and medieval Kathmandu Valley towns.

PART IV

The Four Stupas and the Planning Grid of Patan

10

The Four Stupas

Patan has four large stupas located at different points on the periphery of the town. These stupas are known as the Asoka Stupas (see Pls. 10-1; 10-2; 10-3), based on a legend that a Mauryan king, Asoka, of the third century BCE built them as a memorial of his visit to the valley (Wright 1972, 116).[1] However, this legend is historically questionable. Buddhist communities believe that the position of the four stupas outline the shape of the *dharmacakra*, the Buddhist Wheel of Law, on which the city is thought to have been planned. Until now the historicity of the stupas and their relationship with the order of the city have not been studied, and our knowledge of the purpose of these stupas remains as vague as the legend itself. This chapter will examine the relationship between the four stupas of Patan and the physical order of the city.

The four stupas present an intriguing problem about the origin of Patan. While historical records allow us to study most of Patan's monasteries, there are as yet no available documents related to the stupas.

Nevertheless, a number of scholars have attempted to understand the historicity and significance of these stupas. Allchin (1980) thinks that the mounds may pre-date Asoka. Snellgrove suggests that the monuments could have been established to commemorate the foundation of Patan towards the end of the fourth century while other scholars think that they are funerary monuments (Slusser 1982, vol. 1, 96).

Herdick's excellent research (1993) on the orientation of a number of large stupas in the valley shows that these stupas have particular orientations and form a system of axes that point to particular celestial positions which are related to the sunrise and moonrise in seasonal oscillations during the year. His study deserves serious attention as it throws light upon ancient astronomy and survey technology. However, due to the lack of archaeological excavations and detailed study, the four stupas continue to be shrouded in the mystery of legends.

Our study investigates the significance of the four stupas with respect to the city

Pl. 10-1.   The Northern Stupa (Gutschow and Basukala, 1997)

Pl. 10-2.   The Southern Stupa (Lagan Stupa) (Gutschow and Basukala, 1997)

Pl. 10-3.   The Southern Stupa, nineteenth century (Wright, 1972)

as a whole through the analysis of site topography and geography of the city and the location of these stupas. It shows that the four stupas are planned foundations which are configured to the valley's geography and which served as pivotal structures for the foundation of Patan.

Method of Analysis

The study is limited to a physical analysis of the topography of the terrain, using the 1979 cadastral map of the city made by Department of Land Survey, Ministry of Land Reform and Management, Government of Nepal. Our field verification showed that the range of error for the map's measurements of structures, dwelling plots, etc. was less than 1.5 per cent, which provided the accuracy needed for our analysis. The map shows the area of the historic city on a scale of 1/500 and the peripheral area on a scale of 1/1200. However, we used a map on a scale of 1/2000[2] that allowed us to study the topographical features of a wider peripheral area than the cadastral map would have permitted. The measurement values from the 1/2000 scale map were found to be around 1.5 per cent larger than that from the cadastral map, which our field survey proved to be reliable. The 1/2000 scale map was consequently reduced to conform to the cadastral map, which then fit well in its entire configuration.

We then made a location analysis of the four stupas with respect to the topography of the town plateau and examined their configuration in the terrain of the plateau and its relationship with the larger geography of the valley.

The perimeter formed by the four stupas encircles the traditional settlement area of Patan (Fig. 10-1a). The diagonal lines drawn between the stupas do not point towards the cardinal directions, and they do not intersect at the present central square of the city. However, they cross roughly at the central section of the town. Herdick worked out the orientation of the four stupas based on the orientation of the *harmika*, the square structure on top of the stupa's mound and on which the spires of the stupa rest (Herdick 1993). His work shows that the north face of the *harmika* of the stupas are oriented 20–22 degrees to the east except the northern one, which is oriented 14 degrees to the east. Interestingly, the line joining the South Stupa and North Stupa is 16 degrees to the east. The four stupas are arranged in such a way that they form a diamond-shaped parallelogram. Our field survey shows that the length of the line joining the East Stupa and North Stupa (1540.95 m) is very close to the opposite line joining the South Stupa and West Stupa (1534.55 m). The line connecting the North Stupa and West Stupa is 1137.94 m, which is shorter by about 102 m than the line connecting the South Stupa and East Stupa (1240.34 m). If an exact parallelogram with the north side equal to the south side of the present measure is formed, then the line joining the North and South Stupas makes an angle of 71 degrees (19 degrees to the east measured from the north, the angle of azimuth), approximately the angle of orientation of the *harmika* of the stupas.[3] This orientation is also the alignment of a major road at the west of the city that runs close to the West Stupa and other roads further west.

Another significant feature of the configuration of the four stupas is that it approximates a 120/60 degree parallelogram, with the diagonals bisecting the

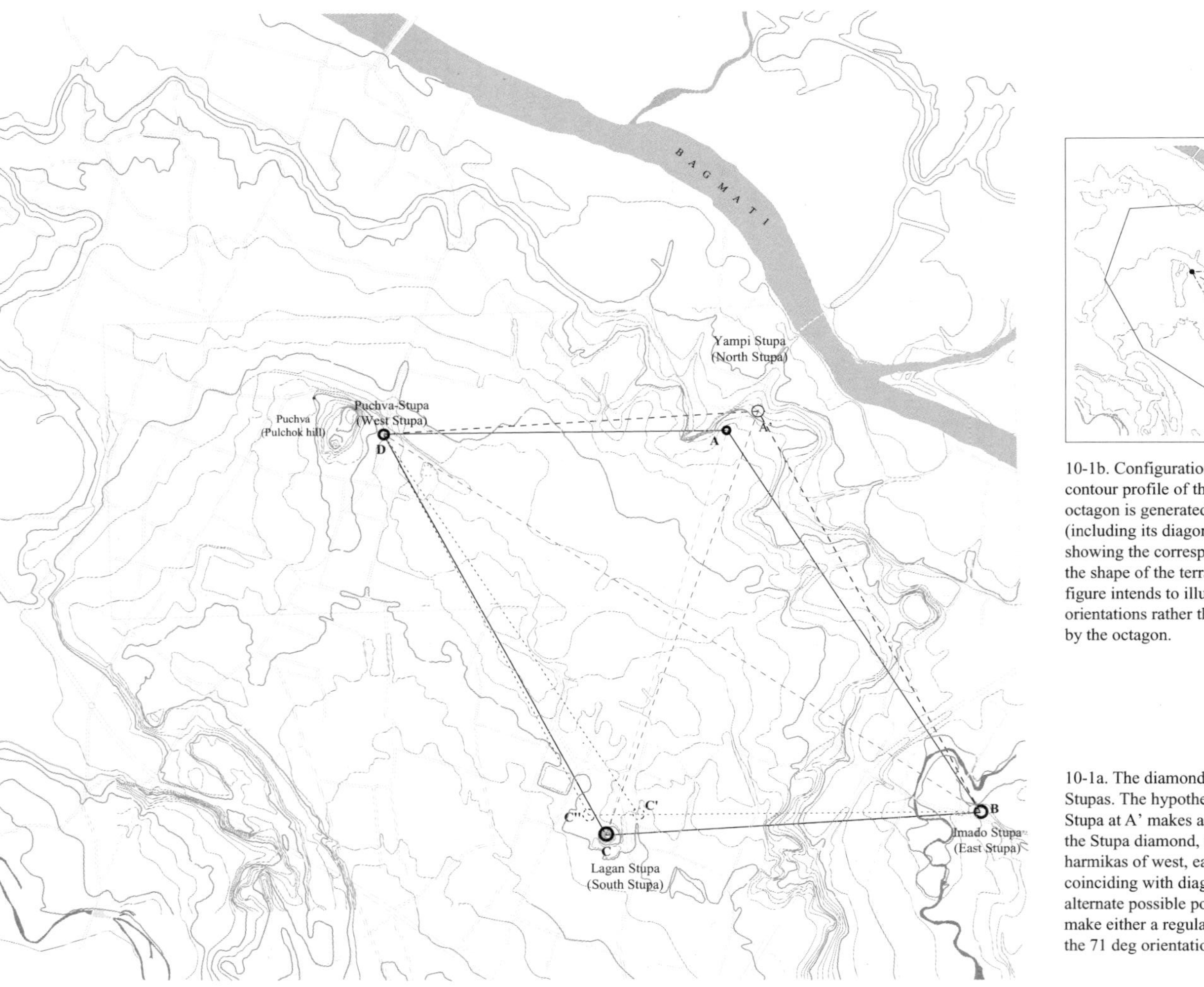

10-1b. Configuration of Four Stupas and the contour profile of the terrain. The regular octagon is generated from the parallelogram (including its diagonals) of the four Stupas showing the correspondence of the shape with the shape of the terrain of the spur head. The figure intends to illustrate the possible grid orientations rather than the enclosure formed by the octagon.

10-1a. The diamond shape formed by the four Stupas. The hypothetical position of north Stupa at A' makes a perfect parallelogram to the Stupa diamond, with the orientation of harmikas of west, east and south Stupas coinciding with diagonal CA'. C' and C" are alternate possible positions of south Stupa C to make either a regular parallelogram or to get the 71 deg orientation (parallel to CA') for CA.

Fig. 10-1. The location of the four stupas of Patan

opposite angles. The existing shape makes a 116-degree angle at the South Stupa and a 118-degree angle at the North Stupa. The angle would be 122 degrees if the north and south sides were to be oriented at zero degree east. The irregular shape of the parallelogram can be explained in terms of topographical features around each stupa. Depressions and valleys around the neighborhood of the northern, eastern, and western stupas do not permit a perfectly aligned parallelogram. The site constraints on the North Stupa and the East Stupa are particularly severe.

The North Stupa is in the route connecting Patan to Chabahil, one of the ancient sites known in the history of the valley towns, which is also the ancient route to Tibet from the valley. The route links the two spurs on either side of the river with the shortest vantage point from the Patan plateau to the north of the river.

The East Stupa is located on the route to Lubhu. The route passes through the southern edge of elevated terrain and gives a shorter course, which is a natural choice for building the track. The stupa is located on a small spur overlooking a stream flowing between the town and the stupa. These features almost fix the location of the two stupas to standout as landmark constructions.

Compared to the North Stupa and East Stupa, the location of the West Stupa is not as constrained by topographical features. However, the strategic importance of the hillock immediately at the west of this stupa as a vantage point to look over the valley and the route linking the hillock to the east makes the existing location a preferable choice.

The South Stupa is not constrained topographically like the other stupas and could be located anywhere if the planning so dictated. However, the intriguing factor in the consideration of the precise location of the stupas is their orientation and the orientation of the field tracks west of the city. As mentioned earlier, the tracks and the *harmika* of the three stupas show the same orientation. Thus, it can be presumed that the matter of orientation figured into the planning of the stupas' locations. If we assume that the positions of the northern, eastern, and western stupas were fixed first, the position of the South Stupa would then be located at point C' as shown in Figure 10-1a to create a perfect parallelogram. However, the North-South diagonal C'A would then have deviated significantly from the planned orientation which the *harmika* of the stupas suggest.

Another possible correction is to maintain the axis of AC aligned with the planned orientation by positioning the location of the South Stupa at C". However, this creates a difference of around 100 m between the southwest and northeast sides and 150 m between the north and south sides. It is possible that the surveyors adopted the midway position C although the axis AC would deviate by about 5 degrees from the planned orientation. A perfect parallelogram with exact planned orientation of the diagonal CA would have been possible if the northern stupa could be located at point A'. But, the land at this point is on a downward slope, and the stupa's level would be lower by about 12 m from the present position. The hypothetical axis A'C passes through the central axis of the little spur at the north and aligns with the route leading towards the north of the Bagmati River. Therefore, if we consider orientation as the major factor in positioning the stupas and the topographical limitations on the positioning of the East Stupa and the West Stupa, a hypothetical position of the North Stupa at A' would create a perfect parallelogram. However, if the location of the North Stupa was determined first due to topographical constraints, the present location of the South Stupa gives the ideally mediated geometry of configuration. Given the consistency in the orientation of the *harmika* of the eastern, western, and southern stupas and the alignment of the above mentioned roads in this particular direction, the hypothetical position, Point A', for the North Stupa would be most convincing if the terrain was favorable. It seems, therefore, that the location of the North Stupa was changed entirely due to the topographical considerations. The shift was made to a location that measures 4 r (76.8 m) (Fig. 11-3 in Chap. 11) from the hypothetical north-south diagonal without changing the length of the northeast side. These three sets of measurements (that is, the alignment of the hypothetical north-south diagonal and the *harmika* of the eastern, western, and southern stupas; the equal length of the northeast and south-west sides; and the shift from Point C' to Point C by a distance that is the multiple of a *rajju* measure) confirm that the positioning of the four stupas was indeed a planned and precisely measured configuration.

The four stupas of the north, east, south, and west—known as Satya, Treta, Dvapar, and Kali, respectively, and ordered in clockwise direction—are said to have been founded on the anniversary of the beginning of the four eons. The sites are visited following the aforementioned order on the occasions of ritual visits to Buddhist shrines. If this reflects the order of their construction, then the West Stupa was the last to be built. However, from a planning perspective, it seems logical that the South Stupa was the last among the four stupas to be positioned in the present site.

Configuration of the Four Stupas and the Terrain of Patan Plateau

It may be judicious to assume that the choice for the location of the settlement in the context of the plateau was the first consideration in determining the location of the stupas. In this case, the route linking the plateau with the northeast region across the Bagmati River in the early period of settlement activity appears to be one of the determining factors. This route then suggests the location of the settlement at the eastern part of the plateau. On the other hand, the topography of the Patan plateau is such that the tail in the south is narrower than the head of the plateau in the north. A settlement located further south would have not only have less space, it would also have increased the distance to the river basin, which would have been undesirable for farming or communication with the region to the north.

The northern part of the plateau is again divided by the Pulchok hill, leaving the eastern part much wider than the area in the west. Thus, if a hill at the central part is to be avoided, the northeastern part of the plateau becomes the preferable choice for the location of the settlement in terms of the topographical features of the terrain and this reinforces the rationale for the stupas' location.

The configuration of the stupas, which is not a rectangle or a square but a parallelogram, is an odd feature in the concept of regular planning. But this form, as will be seen later, better fits the contour profile of the site defined by the area enclosed by the stupas as well as the plateau in general. From Figure 10-1a, it can be seen that the sides AB (and CD) of the stupa diamond are parallel to the northeast and southwest edges of the settlement. The diagonal BD is parallel to the profile of the terrain that is within the area enclosed by the stupas and the northwest edge of the plateau, while CA is parallel to the edges of the plateau to the east and west. Thus, the diagonals and sides of the four stupas follow the land profile of the plateau. As will be seen in Chapter 11 (Fig. 11-5), the tracks in the peripheral farmland of the town and the streets within the settlement are just parallel to the sides AB (CD) or the two diagonals of the stupas. There are no tracks parallel to the northern and southern sides, which do not align with the contour of the plateau. In this respect, it can be said that the orientation of the plateau is determined by its northeast profile.

As a matter of fact, there exists a geometrical relationship between a terrain of complex topography with changing directions of the contour profile and the shape of a parallelogram. The different sides of a parallelogram allows eight differing orientations when diagonals and their perpendiculars are included, which can be smoothly fitted to almost any contour shape of the land. Figure 10-1b illustrates this relationship between the terrain of the Patan plateau and the grids that could be developed through the employment of this diamond-shaped "grid generator." Compared to this diamond shape, a rectangle can generate only four orientations. Therefore, the diamond shape naturally suits a complex terrain with changing contour profiles, although the resulting grid network is a mosaic and it is complex at adjoining and overlapping zones. Compared with alternative forms derived from a square or rectangular shape the present diamond shape is a better solution with respect to the contour profiles of the plateau.

The Four Stupas and the Context of the Valley Region

The orientation of the four stupas and the streets is not a feature unique to these monuments in Patan. According to Herdick (1993), the location of the East and West Stupas are part of an observatory system. His analysis of the configuration of Patan's four stupas in the Kathmandu Valley context is illustrated by Figure 10-2. He notes that the diagonal BD (Fig. 10-1a) passes through the center point joining the Swayambhu Stupa and Chilancho Stupa of Kirtipur, and the CA diagonal (Fig. 10-1a) makes the central third section when projected to the Swayambhu-Chilancho axis. The center point is like an observatory station which is related to the Chabahil Stupa. The two axes one linking to the West Stupa and East Stupa in Patan and the other to Chabahil Stupa and Bauddha Stupa at northeast of Kathmandu City are oriented to positions of moonrise at the time of maximum summer turning and minimum winter turning, respectively. Since the location and axial positioning of the stupas also have an important bearing on the planning of settlements, Herdick's findings deserve further study in the light of the valley topography with the astronomical considerations involved.

Thus, following Herdick's findings on axial relationships of the stupas of the

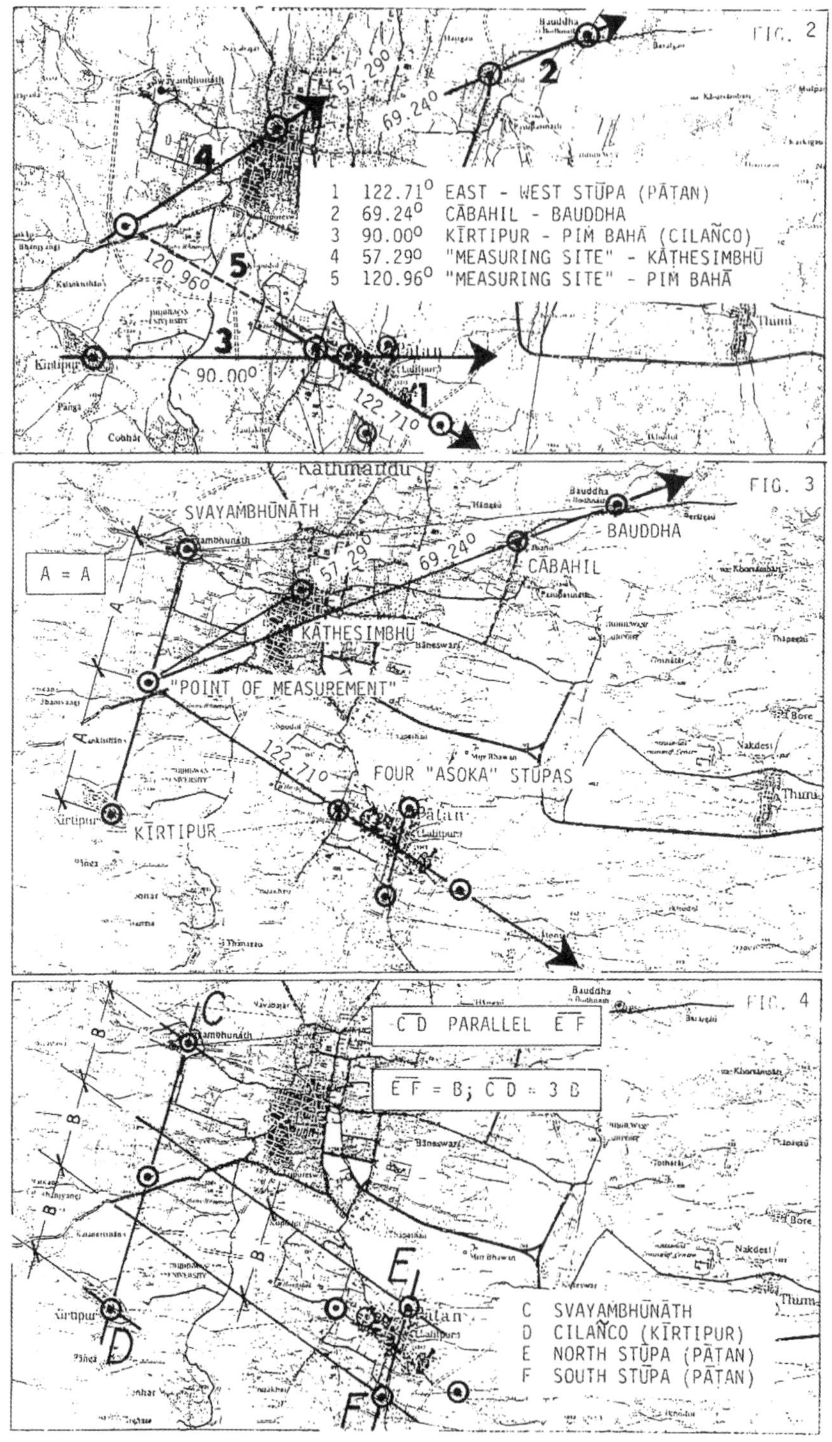

Fig. 10-2. Relationships in the configuration of large stupas in the Kathmandu Valley
(Herdick 1993)

Fig. 10-3. The location of the four stupas and the five mountain summits in the Kathmandu Valley

valley, it can be seen that the Swayambhu-Chilancho axis also has the same orientation as the axis made by the North Stupa and South Stupa of Patan. Besides the configuration of these stupas, the general orientation of ancient settlements to the north of Patan, such as Hadigaon and Kathmandu, is also close to the orientation of this axis. The longitudinal north-south streets are also the trunk roads in both of these towns and follow the shape of the terrain as well.

The next conjunction of the location and configuration of the four stupas of Patan is with the natural geography of the Kathmandu Valley. The valley has five summits at the four directions in the mountain ranges that surround the valley floor (Fig. 10-3). According to the legend, the four summits were the meditation sites of the four Buddhas who visited the valley at the four ages of the world as described in Chapter 2. Thus, Buddhists of the Kathmandu Valley venerate these summits as sites of religious significance. The reconstructed diagonal CA' in Figure 10-1a formed by the North Stupa and South Stupa is exactly oriented to Shivapuri (2732 m), the summit to the north. The east-west diagonal does not have such an orientation, but the side CD is oriented to the summit to the west, the Jama-chva (Nagarjun, 2096 m). The side DA is oriented towards Mahadeva hill (2164 m) to the east. Although Mahadeva hill is not mentioned in the legend, it is the highest peak in the mountain range in this direction. Likewise, the side AB is oriented to Phu-chva (Phulchoki, 2762 m) to the south and the side BC is oriented to Bhasmesvar (2545 m) to the southwest, near Dhila-chva, (Champadevi, 2278 m). The orientations of the respective axis to Shivapuri in the north and Phulcho in the south have no significant deviations, while the other three have slight deviations up to 1 degree. The alignment of these axes falls closer to these summits rather than any other lesser peaks of the valley mountains.

Conclusions

The legend about the summits could allude to early surveys of the valley plain from these mountains. If the summits served as preliminary survey stations of the valley plain, it is entirely possible that the surveyors of later times related their survey work for the settlement plan again back to these summits, while at the same time sanctifying their work and the settlement. It is to be noted that four stupas placed anywhere in the valley plain could be related to the above summits in a manner that the four stupas of Patan show, but to do this one should bring changes in their configurations. The special feature of Patan is that the shape of the configuration is a parallelogram. The orientation of all the sides of the parallelogram and one of its diagonals to the summits of the valley mountain ranges is, however, difficult to imagine in other areas; the present location as well as the configuration of stupas is a mysterious coincidence. Given the four summits in the valley geography, when the location for any one of the four stupas is fixed, location of the other three stupas, if the configuration is to be a parallelogram, is then fixed in the valley space. The orientation of one of its diagonals to the fifth mountain summit—Shivapuri—is possible for only one specific site in the valley. An exact orientation to all the summits from a location, which must also be desirable for a town settlement, is impossible without a planning concept and sophisticated survey technology.

Thus, the four stupas of Patan are uniquely situated with respect to the symbolism of the valley geography. Furthermore, the orientations to the summits of the sides of the four stupas move in a clockwise relationship that can be related to the *swastika*, or the *dharmacakra* of Buddhism, a notable feature of this geometry.

Two additional features of this stupa configuration must be noted here. One is the local topography where the stupas are sited and the terrain of the Patan plateau, which in our analysis are found to be appropriately related to both the stupa monuments and the settlements. The second is the relationship of the stupa axes in the larger context of the other stupas of the valley. All these features taken together make the stupa configuration a Grand Conjunction.[4] This conjunction will remain a mystery until we come to know the survey technology of the ancients who planned and built the four stupas of Patan and the other stupas of the valley.

11

The Four Stupas and Settlement Grid

In Chapter 2 we mentioned a number of legends that describe the planning and founding of the settlement in Patan. Licchavi period inscriptions demonstrate that the settlement within the present city area was established before the fifth century, but the social and spatial structure that exists today took its form much later in medieval times. The preceding chapters on Patan's neighborhood quarters and Buddhist monasteries show that the city quadrants did not develop in a uniform manner as they show a time lag spanning several centuries to a millennium. Within this long period of development, the chronicles have suggested that there were a number of large-scale planning projects. Two were carried out during the Licchavi period—one by Varadev in the second century and another by Amsuvarma in the seventh century. A third was carried out by Gunakamadev during the early medieval times in the eleventh century. According to the same chronicles, prior to the above-mentioned planning events, there were already a number of settlement areas such as Matilinagar and Yupagrama. Indeed, Patan is said to have been the capital of the prehistoric Kirata.

Related to these legends, there exist artifacts, such as monuments and shrines that identify the man whom the chronicles consider to be the planner of Patan during the reign of Varadev.[1] The five earth mounds, on which Patan's five stupas are built, are also notable monuments which the chronicles in the above legend identify as one of the main features of this planned city at this time.

It is the existence of four large stupas at the periphery of the settlement that gives Patan a unique character among the towns of the Kathmandu Valley. According to Buddhist communities, the

  Stupa and Swastika

position of these stupas suggests that Patan was planned in the shape of the *dharmacakra*, the Buddhist Wheel of Law. The four stupas pose one of the intriguing problems related to the origin of Patan. In Chapter 10, we demonstrated that the stupas are planned foundations. Their configuration embodies the natural terrain of the Patan plateau. This configuration is also symbolically linked to the natural geography of the valley and its creation myth. We now focus on this particular feature of Patan and present an analysis of its street patterns and settlement blocks to discern the planning features and the significance of the four stupas with respect to the physical order of the city.

The Data

This chapter presents a detailed examination of the morphology of street patterns and the modules employed in the divisions of settlement blocks and farmlands. For this part of the study we utilized the same maps which we used to study the configurations of the stupas. Since the measure of the minimum module multiple used in this analysis required more accuracy with respect to the alignments such as streets and building blocks, further explanation about the 1/500 scale 1979 cadastral map is necessary. This map, which constitutes our primary analytical data, delineates all the dwellings, property boundaries, and community artifacts, such as fountains, wells, and temples. For the individual structures such as dwellings, it gives the buildings' external wall lines and plinth lines.

The minimum measure used in this study is the 0.5 r (9.6 m). On further verification of the maps with respect to this analytical work, it was found that the maximum error in the dimension measured from the survey map is within 2 per cent for measures lower than 10 m, with the error diminishing as the length of the measure increases. This range of error was considered to be within the limit for the accuracy needed for the present analysis. Another 1/2000 scale map, used for the peripheral area, needed a slight reduction by 1.5 per cent to fit to the cadastral map and the field measure. The accuracy of this map was also verified by independent field measurements in the area around the four stupas.

We then analyzed the dimensional and configurational relationship of the four stupas with the layout planning of the city. Modular measures confirmed from preceding studies on the settlement quarters of Patan were then employed to check the spacing of the tracks in the peripheral farmland as well as the streets of the settlement areas. We primarily used the physical data embedded in the ground plan of the town settlement and its surroundings to discern the relative temporal order of various structural layers that constitute the fabric of the town. Chronological studies were pertinent in determining the periods of development in this city that has had more than two thousand years of history. For this, dated inscriptional records and results derived from previous studies do, to a certain extent, help to form a temporal framework in the developmental changes of the city.

The Street Pattern and Analytical Framework

The street pattern of the city area presents a specific class of problems as a settlement area which is unlike the surrounding farmland. The network of streets is more complex with overlapping streets having differing orientations within a range of few settlement blocks (Figs. 1-8 in Chap. 1). In this chapter we analyze each large and small settlement block in a frame of grid nets and relate these blocks to the larger pattern that was presumably guided by certain physical and historical factors, including the configuration of the four stupas. In the course of this study, a concept, which is referred as 'grid topography' was developed. Briefly, a grid topography is a network of streets determined by a nexus of predetermined factors such as natural terrain, pre-existing tracks or roads, and historical artifacts. The grid topography encompasses the whole settlement as far as all the parts of the street network are related to that predetermined nexus. All the individual grid nets of the settlement can then be explained by the structure of such a grid topography.

By definition, the construction of the grid topography of a settlement first required the construction of grid networks that could fit to each settlement block. Once the individual grid networks were constructed, we could determine if there was any relationship among them and, if so, whether or not this relationship indicated a larger pattern in the town settlement. It was then possible to analyze the morphological properties of the individual grid sectors as well as the larger pattern— the grid topography which they formed.

Construction of the Grid Networks

The existing street pattern of the town is a complex network with streets and lanes crisscrossing at different alignment orientations. The streets are punctuated by squares at the crossings and they make slight shifts or bends from the initial alignment. Regularity in the width of the street is also not apparent unless revealed by analysis. Therefore, no single grid network can be used to describe the street structure of the town. At most, a grid may cover one or a few blocks, thus making it necessary to constantly shift the grid alignment from one sector to another. The basic problem in laying out such a grid is the choice of the module to be employed in the grid interval and their alignments. There is also the problem of the line of reference along which the measurement proceeds. These problems have been dealt with in Chapter 5 where the planning of courtyard settlement quarters of the town is analyzed. In this part of the study, we follow the same principle in the choice of the module, the alignments, and the line of reference to construct the grid networks in the scale of the town settlement, that is, the grid module is 1 r (19.2 m) and its multiples. The alignment of the grid follows the building line along the streets. This is partly because it was difficult to decide the centerline of the street due to bends and building lines at the two sides of a street, which are not always parallel to each other. Further, internal boundaries of the plots and building clusters were also considered so that the grid lines in most of the situations coincided with the building lines of the streets or the internal boundaries. The coincidence of the grid network not only in one individual interval but also in the next several consecutive intervals was required to demonstrate the validity of the selected module measure and alignment. It was also required that, in general, the grid lines coincide with the building lines that were on the same side of the two opposite streets of a block or within neighboring blocks if the grids were in continuity.

The orientation of the grid net of a block primarily follows the orientation of the building clusters and plot boundaries. Often, the orientation of building clusters and the streets around it differ significantly. In such cases, however, it is usual that the deviant orientation of the street agrees with the orientation of the building clusters at the adjoining block or the next block across the street. In any event, the orientations of building clusters and the plot boundaries determine the construction of the grid networks within a settlement block. The grid networks constructed in this manner are shown in Figure 11-1. The settlement blocks are generally covered by grids of 1 r module. The degree of coincidence with the boundaries of the settlement blocks is significant with almost all the streets and lanes coinciding with the grid network. The coincidence with the boundary lines formed by plots or building clusters is also significant. The construction of the grid network showing coincidences with streets, plot boundaries, and other important nodes of the city reveal certain morphological features that highlight certain planning principles and the development pattern of the city.

Morphological Properties

A number of special features identified through the grid network highlight the physical planning features and the layers of the street networks that show a temporal and spatial relationship with each other as well as their relationship with the topography of the terrain and the four stupas. Some of the features such as grid orientation, grid sector, grid belt, and the base reference line of the survey measure-ment works, possibly represent general morphological properties of historic cities that have either been rebuilt and expanded through different historical periods or built where land features were important considerations. The terms grid sector, grid belt, base line, and grid topography comprise both the conceptual and analytical tools in the present study. Each term is explained in the relevant section below.

Grid Orientation and the Grid Sectors

The orientation of the streets including the grids of the town settlement, measured from the east, ranges from 139° to 159° for those aligning in the east-west direction and from 51° to 72° for those aligning in the north-south direction (Fig. 11-2). The grids are not always orthogonal, but the deviation from orthogonality is within a range of 2°. Depending upon the situation, the grid networks are adapted to individual settlement blocks and continue across neighborhood blocks. The area, which is formed by the blocks in contiguity and covered by one grid network, forms one grid sector. According to their orientations, the grid sectors of Patan's city area can be broadly divided into three groups. Characterizing each of these sectors by their north-south orientation measured from the east, the three groups have average orientations of 70° (Group A), 60° (Group B), and 53° (Group C). The orientation of 70° aligns Group A to the diagonal line CA between the North Stupa and the South Stupa in Figure 11-1; Group B's orientation of 60° aligns it perpendicularly to the diagonal line BD between the East Stupa and the West Stupa; and Group C's orientation of 53° aligns it perpendicularly to direction of the town's central east-west street. If we

Fig. 11-2. Grid sectors

consider that the central east-west street is an adjustment to the stupa diagonal BD due to local topography and pre-existing tracks (see the later sections), the orientation of the grid sectors are the orientation of the two diagonals formed by the four stupas.

Figure 11-2 shows that the sectors with a similar orientation are, in general, connected, thus forming grid belts. Conceptually, the grid belt is a specific form of Conzen's morphological region (1988). These belts are occasionally intercepted by one of the other two sectors. It is also noticeable that the sectors of Group B show more contiguity with that of Group C than of Group A. Another important feature in the distribution pattern of the grid sectors is the orientation of the belts formed by each group of grid sectors. It is notable that all the three grid belts extend from the northwest to southeast and are not parallel to the grid orientation. The differences in orientation and distribution between sectors of Group A and the B-C groups is probably related to the different periods of their respective development, which will be discussed in later sections.

Base Line and Division of Blocks

The base line is a hypotetical line along which the survey measurement is presumed to have been done when the block divisions or the divisions of plot boundaries were planned. This is the line along which dimensions, measured consecutively, are observed to be in the multiples of the standard module (Fig. 11-3). For each grid block, the base line may be assumed to be one of the sides of the street it borders. But the grid sectors, formed by numerous grid blocks, have

irregular boundaries. Consequently, the base line of an entire grid sector is not a single line. In fact, it may not even be always along the boundary of the street. The bold black lines in Figure 11-3 show the assumed base lines for the grid sectors. From the present construction of the grid that covers the core area of the city, six base lines are identified, three of which are in an east-west direction (EW-L1 to EW-L3) while another three are in a north-south direction (NS-L1 to NS-L3). Five of them follow five primary streets that cross from one end of the town to another. The alignments of these base lines are of two types. The first type follows the grid alignments of the blocks, while the second follows entirely the idiosyncrasies of the streets (see NS-L2 and NS-L3). Both of these types are important features which help explain the planning of streets and lanes of the settlements.

The dimensions given in between the intervals along the base lines refer to those between the streets, covering almost all major streets that cross the blocks of the settlement quarters. The minimum module in these dimensions except for NS-L3 is 48 m; that is, the dimensions are multiples of 48.0 m (2.5 r). It is equal to 100 hasta units and is represented by the unit "s" in the figure ("s" stands for *sata* which is Sanskrit for 100). The extent of modular measure makes any discrepancy readily apparent in the given scale of the drawing. A set of commonly employed multiples from the dimensions noted in the base line becomes apparent, thus giving the preferred widths for quarter blocks. Among them, the most frequent is 96 m (5 r = 2 s), followed by 144 m (7.5 r = 3 s). Divisions of 240 m (12.5 r = 5 s) are also significant as they may be considered the super blocks of the settlement. For example, along the base line EW-L2, along the central east-west strip, there is a series of super blocks from east to west including the palace area at the centre. The measurement along the base line also reveals important nodes of the town settlement. In line NS-L1, Point A1, at the central east-west street, is exactly at the center of A2 and A3, two crossings at the edge of the settlement. Likewise, measured in the east-west direction along the base line EW-L1, Point B1 (that is, the southwest corner of the palace) lies at the exact center of Points B2 and B3, the other two boundaries of the town.

Blocks of 5 r (2 s) are found at all quadrants, but most frequently in the northern and eastern parts of the city. The blocks in the west of the palace are also of this size. Intervals of 2 s are also employed all the way from the East Stupa for the spacing of tracks that are perpendicular to the stupa diagonal BD along the main east-west street. The basic module of 1 s is also apparent in the distance (5 s) from the West Stupa to a street at the west end of the city, thus giving a continuous module measure from the East Stupa to the West Stupa along the base line EW-L1.

The measure of 2 s may be considered as the standard block size in the planning of Patan. A finding reported in Chapter 6, which suggested a size for a typical residential block on the planning of settlement quarters of the Buddhist community, is found to be one of the standard patterns in the block division of the town. The module of 1 s common to all block dimensions as shown in the figure is significant. It is a 100 hasta measure. Thus, the blocks of Patan are multiples of 100 hasta—that is, of 200, 300, and 500 hasta (96 m, 144 m, and 240 m).

Our measurements from the 1979 aerial photographs of valley settlements made by Department of Land Survey and Management, Government of Nepal show that 500 hasta is also the standard block size in Hadigaon as well as in the old city areas of Kathmandu. The additional significance of this measure, if any, is not yet known. However, it may be noted that we have discovered the modules of 48 m (1 s) including that of 240 m (5 s) in cities of the Indus Valley civilization such as Mohenjodaro and Kalibangan (Appendix 2).

Temporal Sequence of the Grid Sectors

The central east-west street generally follows the base line EW-L1, which in turn runs parallel to the east-west diagonal axis, BD. However, the street departs from its course making an unexpected arc-like bend to the north at its central section. This bend cannot be explained by either topography or alignment to neighboring grid blocks or streets. The block of the palace, tapered at southwest due to the bend of the street, appears to be the result of external contingencies rather than a determining factor to the generation of grid. It is an important proposition as to the nature of this present palace site at this early stage of planning layout.

The eastern section of the central east-west street is in alignment with its western section. But, the central third section of the street conspicuously bends towards the north, shaping the southern boundary of the palace block. The use of standardized street intervals and the block sizes in the planning of Patan would lead one to anticipate a standardized block for the palace, assuming the palace and road were constructed at the very beginning of the settlement on the plateau. The shape of the existing palace block is difficult to explain unless we assume that the existing street alignment south of the palace existed prior to the planning of the town settlement including the palace. This hypothesis is strengthened by the streets in the north and south running parallel to this section of the main street south of the palace. The street NE-L1 in the north (Fig. 11-4), although not wide, is conspicuous as it crosses almost diagonally all the quarters it passes through in a straight line. Such a street is difficult to imagine as a late development of a town not known to have been deserted in any period of its history. This street runs parallel to the contour line at the northeast edge of the settlement. The street also crosses the northeast corner of the palace block. Likewise, south of the main street, NE-L3 runs obliquely to the grid orientation of the respective quarter blocks. All these streets do not accord with the grid blocks they border. The juxtaposition with the general grid pattern in the blocks adjacent to this group of streets is evident (Fig. 11-1). However, the intervals between these streets again follow the module of 1 r and show agreement with the prevailing multiples of 3 s or 4 s. Another reason to believe that this group of streets existed prior to the planning of the town settlement is that along the northeast street NE-L1, there exists a base line where the street intervals crossing it show a spacing that are in multiples of 1 r. The significance of this base line is not the same as that of NS-L1, where streets orthogonal to it are laid at modular intervals. As in NS-L3, there appears a planning feature where lanes branching from a street, not necessarily orthogonal, are spaced according to the principle of modular measures taken along the idiosyncratic bend of the street whose alignment may not accord with the grids of the adjacent blocks. The measure along NE-L2 and NE-L3 south of the palace, which is 5 s (= 240 m) (Fig 11-3) is such an example. The presence of modular intervals between these streets and between the lanes crossing them, as well as their juxtaposition with other regular streets, suggests that this group of streets belongs to a planning stage earlier than the one that encompasses the city area and the four stupas.

The orientation of this NE set of streets coincides with the formation of belts of the grid sectors mentioned in the preceding sections, a strong argument for their existence prior to the planning of other networks of streets. The northeastern set of streets (NE-L1–NE-L4) thus guided the development of a settlement that was planned in a new network of street grids.

The development of the grid network, as can be seen from the grid sectors, is determined by the temporal and spatial relationship of these tracks. The north-south streets are parallel to the NS diagonal axis CA', and they are part of the planned network of tracks on the Patan plateau. These tracks are the basis of the north-south traffic network on the plateau including that of the town. However, because the B-C sector and A sector interlace it is a complex task to make a neat separation between the two both in temporal and in spatial dimensions. In this respect, certain specific morphological features of the grid net help to identify both the spatial and temporal relationship of the two grid sectors.

Chapter 6 points out that the grid sectors of C, particularly in the Nagbahal quarters, are surrounded by A type grid blocks (Pant and Funo 2003). Such blocks also enclose the Subahal area which, unlike

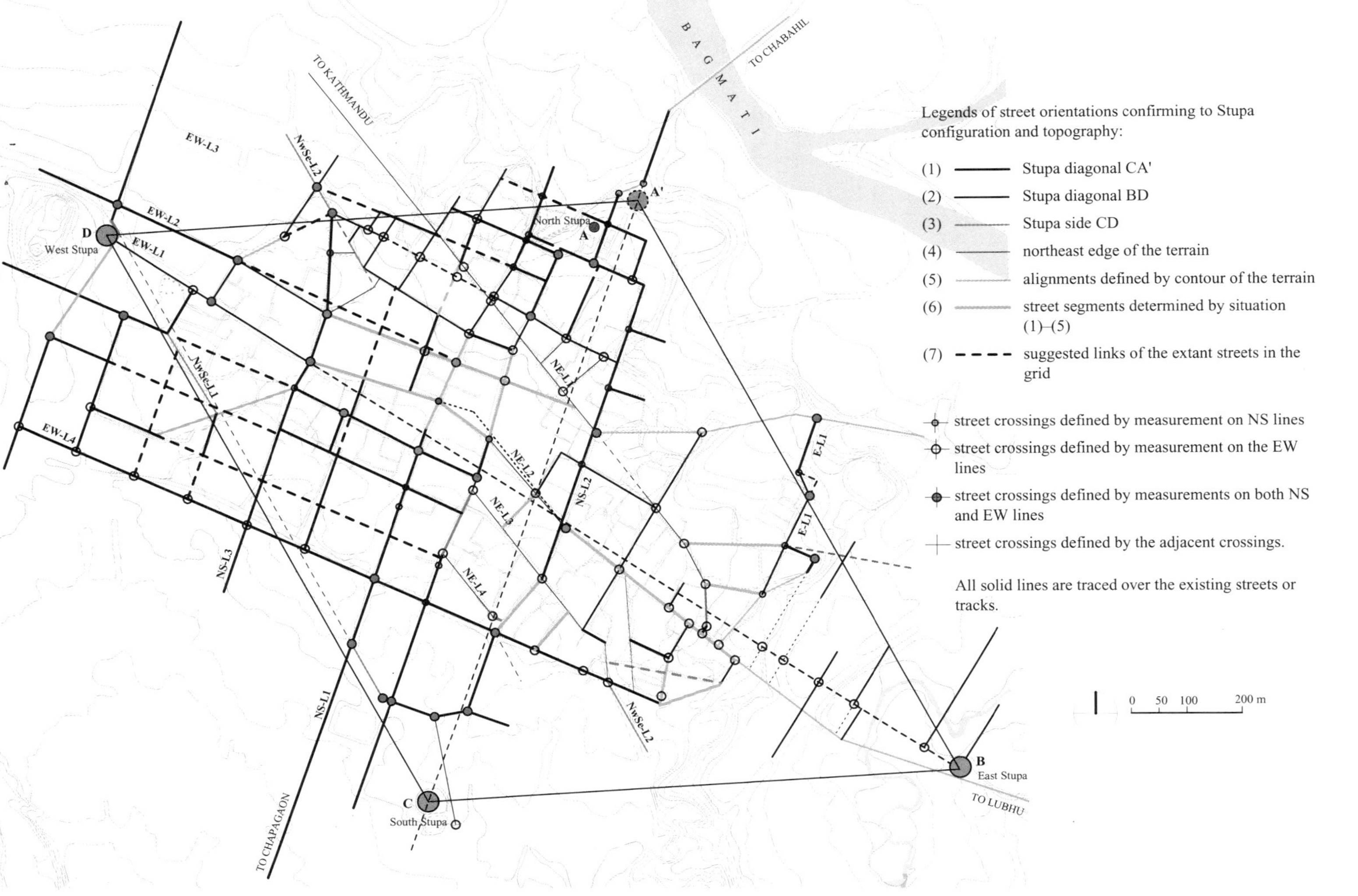

Fig. 11-4. Grid Topography of the city

other grid sectors of the town, is aligned in a north-south direction. An examination of the distribution of the grid sectors in the town as a whole shows that the B-C sectors are more often than not enclosed by A type sectors suggesting that the A types are earlier than the B-C types. Further, it will be clear from the following section that the north-south tracks were planned as the primary road system for the plateau as a whole, and the east-west tracks were planned as branches from the north-south tracks. We suggest that the grid network in the town also followed a similar structural pattern at the initial stage of planning. However, particularly in the EW direction, the existing northeast tracks and the terrain fitted better with the orientation of the east-west diagonal BD. Presumably, this was the factor that was taken into account in developing the grid sectors along this alignment for the settlement, rather than the orthogonal grid line that followed the north-south diagonal CA'. This appears to be a revision that was made later. From Figure 11-2, it can be seen that while the B-C sectors expand along the northeast street group, the blocks of the A sector are found in the southwest section of the town.

This morphological feature of the grid sectors and the street alignments is in astonishing agreement with our historical records and the distribution of communities when viewed in conjunction with our hypothesis regarding the Jyapu and the early history of Patan. Firstly, Plate F shows a map detailing the distribution of the various communities of Patan. The major communities of the city consist of Jyapu who have settled along the northeast diagonal street. It is also along this street that the earliest inscriptions and artifacts are concentrated in greater num-

bers than elsewhere (Fig. 5-1 in Chap. 5).

Secondly, from our study of the distribution of Buddhist monasteries, we have seen that the settlements at the southwestern quarters of Patan developed later compared to the areas in the north and east.

Thus, the morphological analysis of grid sectors shows that the northeast group of streets are the remains from the first planning of settlements in Patan and the arc-like bend of the main east-west street at the central section, along with the southern boundary of the palace, followed the earlier street structure.

The Grid Topography

It is evident both from the preceding analysis that the streets of Patan were not laid in one simple grid network. Yet, the existing street pattern is not simply a result of organic growth, which is seen from the use of modular measures in the spacing of streets and in the regular sizes of settlement blocks. All the major streets that make up the settlement blocks of the town can be grouped into three distinct categories, in a manner that corresponds to the grid sectors: (1) the first category consists of streets oriented to the stupa configuration; (2) the second category consists of streets oriented to local terrain of the land; and (3) the third category consists of streets determined by the configuration of the first and second group of streets. As previously discussed, the configuration of the stupas was determined by the general topographic feature of the plateau. The streets that deviate from this configuration are finer adjustments to local contours. Figure 11-4 shows the street pattern of Patan that identifies the different groups of streets thus classified. The streets that are determined by the configuration of the stupas are further divided into three groups: (1) streets aligning with the CA' diagonal; (2) streets aligning with the BD diagonal; and (3) streets oriented to the side CD. In all these groups, including those determined by the local terrain, the streets aligning with the CA' diagonal are the most numerous in the settlement. The next most numerous is the group that follows the east-west BD diagonal of the stupas.

The streets that follow the terrain are of two groups—the streets that run parallel to the northeast edge of the plateau (see [4] in Fig. 11-4) and which are within the town settlement, and those at the edge of the town (see [5] in Fig. 11-4). The northeast group of streets is important in shaping the street patterns of the town, while those at the edge are isolated instances.

The street structure of the town is thus assumed to have been built upon by taking one of the existing streets from each of the first two categories, namely streets aligning to stupa diagonals CA' and BD mentioned above, as base lines for the survey measurements. Other streets were then laid by using the principle of modular measures along these base lines. When the two streets of differing grid orientations meet at a point that does not give the modular measure in the street interval, a mediating point was found at the neighborhood of that point. There appears to be a kind of "pulling effect" between the grids of different orientations which resembles the process of triangulation in survey works. Figure 11-4 shows the street sections joining the two consecutive street crossings as they exist in the field and which are, as shown in Figure 11-3, at a distance of modular measure in their respective base line. It can be seen from Figure 11-4 that the existing bend and the deviation in the street sections from the orientations described above are a result of the "pulling effect" due to the alignment differences of the adjacent streets towards a node that is at a point of modular spacing from both sides. This makes the third category of streets, which are at the central part of the city, including the eastern section of the central east-west street (see [6] in Fig. 11-4).

As our analysis in the previous section shows, the three categories of Patan's streets appear to have a chronological hierarchy where streets determined by the northeast edge of the plateau and by the orientations of the north-south and east-west diagonals show a temporal sequence, with the streets determined by the terrain at the northeast edge being earlier in the sequence and those following the BD diagonal being the revision of some sectors of the town from the grid orientation of diagonal CA'. The time period of this sequence requires a detailed study using additional historical evidence.

The street network as shown in Figure 11-4 forms the base structure for the development of the grid networks of the individual quarters. There are grid networks in contiguity between the adjoining blocks, as well as those of differing grid orientations, depending upon which street around the quarter block is chosen as the base line for the planning of plots. Just as the land topography is a primary consideration in planning the grid network of streets, the existing street pattern is an important consideration in the formation of grid of the settlement quarters; that is, the street pattern constitutes the grid topography for the plot planning of settlement blocks. On the other hand, the base lines and the modular measure constitute the base for the development of street networks of the settlement. We have seen that, in Patan, these base lines are again determined by the configuration of the four stupas. Thus, the configuration of the stupas in Patan constitutes the primary hierarchy in the grid topography of the settlement. On the other hand, there is a set of streets determined by the terrain, some of them belonging to the earlier period and influencing the development direction of the settlement belts. The stupa, the terrain of the land, and the pre-existing tracks thus form a set of factors, which constitute the grid topography of Patan that governs the planning of the settlement as well as its development in time.

It should be noted that for a settlement planned in one simple regular grid that lacks idiosyncratic details, identification of features such as the base line is considerably difficult. On the other hand, for a settlement with a complex grid topography it is easier to identify those features of grid topography, which can then be related to the spatial and chronological hierarchy, location of monuments, and other important nodes of the settlement.

The Four Stupas and Planning of the Field Tracks

As noted in the preceding section, the land topography of the plateau, an aspect that influenced the planning of field tracks, is in concordance with the configuration of the four stupas. The east-west diagonal of the stupa diamond is parallel to the contour in the north, which is the general declination of the plateau, while the north-south diagonal is parallel to the contour in the east and west. The

relationship between the terrain and geometrical shape of the stupas is, therefore, clearly an aspect that was considered in the planning of streets and tracks in the plateau.

The siting of the town settlement leaves a considerable farm area towards south and west of the plateau. The area in the present analysis of field tracks lies within the Ring Road, a construction in the recent decades. Within this area, the land westward of the city is more extensive (Fig. 11-5). Most of the tracks in the peripheral farmland, as they exist at present, are not so straight as to lead from one end to another. Thus, the application of a single grid presents similar difficulties as in the town settlement area. However, the network of tracks is relatively simple due to the smaller number of tracks compared to the settlement area.

In several instances, the tracks are not straight but bend at some points or sections. This is a general feature of the tracks both in the settlement area and the fields. Such bends are due to topographical features such as contour lines, depressions, or the existence of a hillock. For the purpose of the present analysis, street crossings are considered as the key nodes for measuring the dimensions. Solid lines are drawn where the streets exist and drawn in such a way as to reflect the general orientations of the track. Spacing between the tracks was checked to determine if there are any common modules. Figure 11-5 shows the alignment and the spacing of the tracks which were found through this method.

At the peripheral farmland, there exist four groups of track networks that follow different orientations. The largest among them is in the west followed by the one in the south. To the west, there are two major tracks running north-south that align with the north-south diagonal of the four stupas. In general, the alignments of the tracks conform to the configuration of the four stupas, in particular with the CA' diagonal, which is also the case in the layout of streets within the town settlement. There are also tracks in the peripheral farmland in the south that run parallel to the southwest side CD of the stupa diamond. These tracks, however, are not so extensive compared to the grid of the north-south diagonal. It is to be noted that the southwest side is parallel to the edge of the plateau towards that direction. There are no tracks parallel to the northern and southern sides, and the contour of the plateau also does not follow this direction.

Furthermore, like the town settlement, the tracks in the peripheral farmland were measured and laid out on a grid with the four stupas as reference points. The tracks are also laid in intervals that confirm the raiju as the basic unit of measure for these intervals. The east-west tracks that cross the two major north-south tracks are laid right from the existing Ring Road in the south to the Bagmati River to the north. To the west, they are laid at an interval of 12 r, and the orientation is orthogonal to the north-south axis of the stupas. The group of tracks running parallel to the southwest diagonal CD shows a peculiar juxtaposition with the grid of the tracks that follow the north-south diagonal CA'.

The axial importance of the West Stupa to the tracks in the west is apparent from the road that aligns both with the orientation of its harmika and its center. The tracks that branch from this road are laid at an interval of 8 r towards the north. This interval is different southward where most intervals are in multiples of 2.5 r

(1 s). The first track towards the north is a continuation of the east-west street of the town settlement in the east. It is at a distance of 4 r from the center of the West Stupa, again indicating the stupa as a point of reference for the planning of the tracks. This grid in the area between the west of the town and the West Stupa is also found to exist all the way from Ring Road to the Bagmati River in the north. The measurement shows that the spacing of all tracks is fairly consistent; the maximum deviation from the standard grid intervals is within the limit of the width of the track, while the cumulative error is negligible. The intervals between the major north-south tracks vary, but they are in the multiples of 1 r or 2 s.

It can be seen from Figure 11-5 that the centers of each of the four stupas are the reference points for the layout of tracks in their respective neighborhood farmlands. They are references not only for one grid network of the tracks but for two or more networks of tracks. For instance, the West Stupa is the reference of four separate networks of tracks. All the four network of tracks with reference to the West Stupa are generated from the diagonals CA' and BD of the stupa diamond. This demonstrates that the four stupas were the original reference points in planning the track layouts in both the farmlands and the town settlement. The configuration of the stupas represents the landform of the Patan plateau and thus guided the layout planning of tracks both in the peripheral farmland as well as the streets of the city settlement.

Conclusions

We have explained the specific patterns of the street network of Patan as planned in terms of the terrain of the land, the configuration of the four stupas, the pre-existing field tracks, and the modular measures employed in the survey planning. These are the primary factors that define the grid topography of the town on which the complex net of settlement grids were developed. The grid topography is a conceptual tool to analyze the settlement forms of historic cities where complex landforms and layers from different historical periods are knitted together. The construction of the grid network in the settlement of Patan following this concept has brought to light findings that have an important bearing on understanding the physical planning principle of the city.

This study demonstrates that the city of Patan is a planned development. All its streets and lanes are governed by the principle of modular intervals. A standard size for the settlement block is 5 r wide. Super blocks of 12.5 r are also significant in the block division. The standard module measure of this division is 1 s (2.5 r = 48 m) or 100 hasta. Likewise, the standard basic module measure of the finer grid network within the settlement blocks is 1 r or 0.5 r.

The existing settlement grid shows a continuity outward coinciding with the center of the four stupas, and the networks of tracks of the surrounding farmland also refer to the centers of these stupas and the shape of their configuration. The planning of the tracks extends all the way from the existing Ring Road at the south of the city to the banks of the Bagmati River to the north and to the western edge of the plateau. Our study of the configuration of the stupas and the dimensions of the block divisions shows the grid was planned with a great degree of accuracy.

The tapered forms of the blocks are not the result of organic growth but a mediated consequence of the grid topography. This has to do with the earliest phase of settlement planning in Patan, when the streets were planned following the northeast terrain of the plateau. It appears that the abiding principle was to follow the rules of grid topography that encapsulates the historic and physical context of the land. With respect to the planning within the town settlement area, two different principles and stages are identified: one that followed the natural terrain guided by the northeast edge of the town plateau and the other a comprehensive plan of which the four stupas were the pivots. Because Patan was already inhabited in the Kirata period, it is likely that the first planning dates at least from this period.

In the second and final planning of Patan, the pivotal importance of the stupas in the planning of the settlement is re-inforced by the alignment of streets to the configuration of the four stupas and the survey measures taken with the center of the four stupas as the reference origin.

By analyzing the terrain of the plateau and special topographical features in the neighborhood of the existing location of the four stupas, the preceding chapter has established the rationale for their configuration. The configuration of the stupas is a conjunction of a number of features that are of symbolic, geographic, geometric, and functional import. It is an excellent example of the knowledge of the planning and survey technology of the past. The sides and diagonals formed by the stupas and the stupas themselves represent the terrain of the plateau and the geography of the valley. In other

words, the diamond configuration of the four stupas is the genius loci par excellence.

The planning of the city and its surrounding land further demonstrates the four stupas as the pivots for planning in the plateau. In this sense, the settlement is a veritable dharmacakra, the Wheel of Law, represented by the configuration of the four stupas.

12
Conclusion

This study of Patan has demonstrated that Patan is a planned city. The city is planned from the choice of its location to the layout of its streets and settlement quarters. The pivot of its planning are the four stupas located at the periphery of the city. The location of the four stupas is determined by the natural geography of the Kathmandu Valley and the terrain of the Patan plateau. The valley is surrounded by mountain ranges with five main mountain summits—Sivapuri, Nagarjun, Champadevi, Phulchoki and Mahadev *danda*—that are located respectively to the north, northwest, west, south and east of the valley. The four stupas form a diamond shape parallelogram; each of its four sides is oriented to one of these summits. The four arms pointing to the four summits in a clockwise manner resemble the shape of the clockwise swastika. The positions of the South and North Stupas form an axis that is oriented to the fifth summit—Sivapuri to the north. The faces of the four stupas' *harmika*, the cube atop the hemispherical dome of Nepalese stupas painted with Buddha's eyes, have the same northward orientation towards the summit Sivapuri, as is also the axis that connects South and North Stupa. This axis towards Sivapuri is the orientation of north-south streets of Patan. The streets with a north-south orientation are primary roads in the street network of the city as well as in the plateau as a whole.

The four stupas, thus, define the location as well as the geometry of Patan and determine the boundary and configuration of the city. This is a unique relationship between the stupas, city, and valley geography that fits the terrain features of Patan plateau.

The Buddhist creation myth of the valley states that four early Buddhas meditated on the four mountain summits overlooking the valley. And one of the Bodhisattva, Manjusri, drained the valley lake making it fit for habitation. Oral tradition holds that Patan is a city originally planned in the shape of the *dharmacakra*, the Buddhist Wheel of Law. The configuration of the four stupas and the geometry of Patan defined by the five mountain summits demonstrates that there is a factual link between the planning of Patan with the creation myth and oral tradition.

The stupas, therefore, have paramount symbolic value to Patan. It is through these four stupas that the city is linked to the topography of the place, to the nature and geography of the valley, and to the culture of its prehistoric past.

The stupas have another function in the planning of the city. They originally served as reference stations in the survey and layout of streets and tracks in the town settlement and in the fields surrounding it. This is known from the street grids that pass through the center of the stupas.

The physical plan of Patan displays an ancient system of measurement. In literature, this system is first mentioned in the Arthasastra of Kautilya who lived in the fourth century BCE. This system of measure consists of *angula* (digit), *hasta* (cubit), *danda* (4 hasta), and *rajju* (10 danda). Their corresponding metric values were discovered in Thimi, a small town east of Patan. The streets and lanes of Patan are laid out in a grid that follows this ancient system of measure. Certain specific module measures are employed in the division of settlement blocks. These measures are multiples of 100 *hasta* (48 m)—100, 200, 300, 400 and 500 *hasta*. Among these module multiples, 200 *hasta* is more common. The study of Patan demonstrates the extensive application of this ancient system of measure in the planning of the Kathmandu Valley towns.

The grid of Patan is not a unitary or gridiron plan. It exhibits a terrain of grid networks that we call "grid topography" which takes into account pre-existing tracks and settlements, terrain slopes, and other natural features in the planning of new street networks that were defined by the stupa axes. From this grid topography, one can see three distinct layers in the street networks and plot divisions of Patan. These layers might be likened to periods or phases in Patan's development. The first two phases employ a similar measurement system and modules. The area covered by the development of the first phase is at the northeast sector of the city and is represented by the street running parallel to the northeast edge of the city, and by the main streets at the southeast quarter of the town. The second phase is the planned foundation of Patan with the four stupas as pivots. The third layer is the planning of individual settlement quarters. This planning rests on the grid topography of the second phase.

The plan of the settlement quarters has two distinct patterns. The first is the pattern that centers on the community square. The settlement clusters are developed around courtyards with access from the main street. The second pattern exhibits a courtyard planning system which shows a parallelism with the planning of bahal, that is, Buddhist monasteries. It is concentric and axial; the center and axis is emphasized by caitya or stupa and monastery courts. The division of plots and their layout organization in the planning of such a residential quarter follow a standard model called the Nivartana courtyard block, which is a square with 200 *hasta* sides (5 rajju). It permits an open courtyard of 120 *hasta* (3 rajju) and 24 plots around it. This open court can accommodate a typical monastery courtyard building of 1 square *rajju* at the centre of the open courtyard. The standard planning principle is based on the swastika pattern of plot layout and is applied to all sizes of courtyard planning.

The Nivartana courtyard also exhibits a mandala-like diagram. The model, which is so profoundly based on the age-old planning tradition, could well be the seed of the varieties of mandalas mentioned in the Vastusastras, of which swastika is one, for the planning of cities and buildings. While the mandala in the Vastusastras is a sacred ground to enshrine Hindu deities in each of its quarter blocks, it is also a sacred concept of the Buddhist world so profusely expressed in the mandala genre of Buddhist arts.

The swastika is also a standard principle in the planning of individual courtyard buildings. This includes the Buddhist monasteries, palace courtyards as well as the courtyards of a family clan. This planning principle is evident in Chabahil, one of the earliest monasteries of Nepal, and in residential courtyards built as late as the nineteenth century. The plan of these individual structures is governed by the modules of the same system of measure used in Patan's layout. The study of the bahil (an ancient type of monastery) in Patan demonstrates this application in detail and gives the accurate measures for *angula, hasta* and *danda*. The *angula* is 17.79 mm, the *hasta* of 27 *angula* is 480.3 mm and the *danda* is 1921 mm. The iconographic divisions of the columns of these monasteries are based on this *angula* measure, where the height of the column is one *danda*.

Thus, the physical planning principle of Patan is the organization of space through a system of axes and centers emphasizing a concentric order articulated through an ancient system of measure mentioned in Kautilya's Arthasastra. It has standard models to follow for the planning of settlement blocks, the layout of residential quarters, the courtyard buildings, and the architectural elements such as the column. The center and axes are symbolized by caitya, stupa, and mountain summits. The concentric order is expressed by the swastika pattern.

This study does not present a chronological analysis that settles the historical time frame of Patan's planned foundation. However, it discovers the earliest layers that still exist on the surface and over which there still are some of the settlement quarters of the city. The greater part of the city and all the monasteries, with probable exception of the cluster of Guita bahil at the east end of the city, was built only after the second phase (the planned foundation of the city based on the four stupas). Dated artifacts and structures analyzed in this study show that the planned frame of the second phase with four stupas that characterize the feature of Patan existed earlier than the sixth century CE. More study of ancient Saiva-Hindu shrines is also necessary to shed further light on matters of chronology as well as their relationship to the historic development of the city.

On the existence of this planning tradition in ancient and prehistoric times in the wider region of South Asia, our studies have demonstrated that the system of measure and the layout principle employed in Patan and other Kathmandu Valley towns were also common in the cities of the Indus civilization. The layout of settlement blocks of Indus cities such as Mohenjodaro and Kalibangan employ exactly the same measures. The modules in the planning of these cities are also the multiples of 100 *hasta*. The width of the streets and the division of blocks by lanes into smaller blocks follow same modular standards. A continuous tradition of this planning system is traceable to the cities of Taxila—the Bhir Mound and Sirkap—in Gandhara in present-day Pakistan. The Bhir Mound is a settlement that existed prior to the sixth century and Sirkap existed until early centuries of the Christian Era. Kautilya, who described the system of measure that is now known to have existed by Indus period, is known to have lived in Taxila.

On the other hand, the stupa and swastika, the two symbolic icons of Patan's planning, are prehistoric monuments and symbols. The stupa originates from funeral tumuli. Likewise the swastika is a sacred symbol in the Indus civilization. The planning of Patan embodies these two symbols as the guiding principle to articulate the structure of the city, at the same time encapsulating the creation myth of the Kathmandu Valley. The four mounds, known in later periods as the four stupas of Patan, are the monuments required for a city plan and not funerary tumuli. Their status as stupas—the Buddhist religious monuments—at the time of their first construction, cannot yet be demonstrated since the advent of Buddhism in the valley is a later event than the beginning of settlement in Patan. Thus it is also possible that these mounds were constructed before Buddhism began to take hold in the valley.

In the course of history, the stupa and swastika were absorbed into Buddhist religious tradition, and their symbolism took on a cosmological significance in the Buddhist world. Yet these icons should not be interpreted only in terms of their symbolic dimensions; they are also the planning principles of Patan. Nevertheless, when we realize that the city is inhabited by Buddhist communities and that these icons structure the city space at its different hierarchic levels, the plan of the city itself can be recognized as a Buddhist artifact. The city is built upon the swastika with stupas as the pivots. Patan displays a special way of settlement planning that can be stated as a Buddhist city planning principle. This is a planning tradition that has much in common with the Indus urban civilization.

Historians of Nepal on etymological grounds, Puranic literature, legends and fragments of historic evidence have suggested the migratory links between the prehistoric communities of the Kathmandu Valley and the regions of the Indus Valley. The tradition of settlement planning that exists in Patan is the material evidence that demonstrates at the same time a Buddhist city and an unbroken link between the urban civilization of the Indus and the Kathmandu Valley.

APPENDICES

Appendix 1

The Town of Thimi, Kathmandu Valley

The planning module of Patan, discussed in the previous chapters, was first discovered in Thimi, a town situated about five kilometers east of Patan. Inhabited by the Newar, the social structure and physical form of the town represents one of the traditional settlement types in the Kathmandu Valley. Earliest records indicating the existence of settlements in Thimi are two Licchavi period inscriptions found in the town and a third one in Deupatan, east of Kathmandu.[1]

In this appendix, we study the plan of the town and the use of planning modules in Thimi. We then continue this investigation in the regions of the Indus Valley in the Appendix 2. Results of our study show that the planning principle used in Thimi spans a wide geographic region from the Kathmandu Valley to the Indus Valley and millennia of time.

Thimi exhibits a relatively simple structure in its street pattern compared to larger towns such as Patan, Kathmandu, and Bhaktapur. The town has one major street running from north to south almost through the central part of the settlement (Fig. A1-1). Minor lanes branch towards the east and west from the main street, which provides access to the interior part of the residential quarters. The scale and simplicity of the physical form of Thimi allows us to discern the social and spatial features of the settlement, which in large historic cities are often intertwined in complex layers due to geographical, historical, and social factors. The study on the planning dimensions of Thimi was facilitated by our discovery of Lavadol, a site east of the town plateau which is divided into sectors of equal width. The dimensions of these sectors are related to

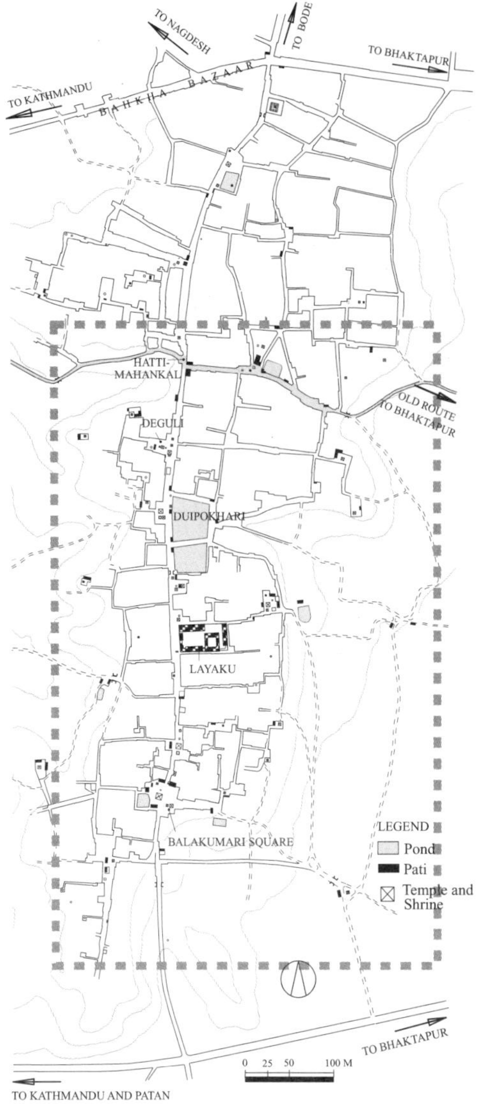

Fig. A1-1. The town of Thimi

the division of blocks of the town settlement in the plateau. These findings on the measurement module and the system of measure on Thimi were used as the primary reference in our study of Patan and is found to have been applied in the ancient city of Taxila in Gandhara and Mohenjodaro in the Indus Valley.

Layout Dimensions of Thimi— The Lavadol Plan

The low, flat Lavadol Basin lies between two spurs—the town of Thimi to the west and the fields of Warcho to the east (Pl. A1-1).[2] The basin is about 30 m below the edge of the town plateau and around 400 m wide. At present the land is used to grow rice and vegetables. The old route connecting Bhaktapur and Kathmandu marks the northern end of the basin, while the road that passes through the southern end of the town marks the southern end of the basin, which extends down to the Hanumante, a stream in the south. A road running north to south divides the basin into a western and eastern sector. The narrower western strip abuts the town plateau and is about one meter higher than the wider eastern sector. This strip of the Lavadol Basin is further divided into two halves by an east-west track. This track leads to Layaku (a medieval palace and administrative precinct) located at the centre of the town to the west.

Planned divisions of a field 80 m wide by 350 m long were discovered in the southwestern part of the basin. For convenience, the field is referred as Lavadol and the planned divisions as the Lavadol Plan (Fig. A1-2). The field is longer from north to south than east to west and rises towards the north. A narrow strip of leveled land about two meters high with a road at its edge constitutes the western boundary of Lavadol. The field is divided into nine sectors (L1 to L9). Several of the northern sectors on the higher level are terraced. While certain sections of the dividing strips have yielded to erosion and encroachment, their basic features are still clearly apparent. Because of possible encroachment from bordering

Pl. A1-1. Location of the Lavadol basin (Dept. of Land Survey, 1978)

Fig. A1-2. The Plan of Lavadol and the streets and blocks of Thimi on the town plateau

plots in the past, it was thought that measuring the width between the center-lines of the dividing strips could more accurately reflect the original dimensions than measuring the internal widths of the individual sectors. The measurement was done along the western boundary of the field where all the dividing strips can be clearly identified. If allowances are given for the erosion of the dividing strips, the sectors show equal and consistent widths, the average of which, according to this measurement, is 38.48 m. However, one of the sectors, L7, is 48.82 m wide and therefore deviates from the average. Sectors L8 and L9 are also close to the width of the average block module. It is important to note that the first dividing strip between L1 and L2 is at a distance of one block from the cross-section in the south where a Sivalinga is enshrined. Similarly, the central east-west road dividing the Lavadol Basin is at a two-block distance from the dividing strip between L6 and L7. The larger size of L7 might be due to the fact that it is a terraced field that is lower than the northern sector of the field (L8) by about three meters and higher than the southern sector of the field (L6) by about two meters. Furthermore, there is a short strip at the east of L7 that divides this block into sections following the regular division pattern. This gives nine sectors of equal width marked along the eastern road. This pattern of division suggests that the eastern road was taken the base line for the division of the field, while the street crossing at the south of this road at the Bapa shrine was the starting point.

The width of the strips between the measured sectors range from 3.70 m to 4.50 m. When the scarps are included, the widths in the terraced sectors are wider by as much as 6.7 m. However, the standard width of the sector measured from center to center of the strip is the same even in the terraced sectors. This suggests that the divisions of the sectors were made by marking either the center line or the consequent boundaries of the strips by excluding the scarp width. The eastern north-south road is 4.40 m wide with about 1.30 m of additional scarp width on either side. When the inevitable erosion of the scarp on both sides during the past centuries is taken into account, it can be said that the initial width of the road could have been much wider than what remains today. The exact original form of the alignment orientation of this road, however, cannot be ascertained.

The existing patterns of division of the individual plots within the sectors are an additional feature that distinguishes the Lavadol field from other neighboring fields of the basin. All the planned sectors are longitudinally divided into two halves. Furthermore, there is a continuous border traversing north to south, approximately at the center of L3, L4, and L5, which continues to the northern sectors as the boundary of the terraced plots. This kind of continuity does not exist with plot boundaries in other neighboring fields. Nor there are plots so regularly divided as those within the sectors of Lavadol. This suggests that each sector was divided longitudinally into eastern and western halves and then traversely divided to make four plots per sector. If we assume that these were the original plots, each of which possibly belonged to one individual house-hold, this resulted in plots for 36 families. The pattern of plot divisions discovered in Lavadol is not traceable in the neighboring fields immediately next to it. It is most likely that this particular form of division was made for residential settlement. However, one cannot entirely disregard their use as plots to grow vegetables for families living elsewhere.

Within the planned area of Lavadol today, there are two open shrines both without roofs. The one at the southern corner is a Sivalinga, known as Bapa Mahadeva. The other one is in the north, just west of the north-south road crossing the central east-west road. It is dedicated to a deity known as *Chulanchhi-dyo*. During the dry season farmers offer worship at the Bapa shrine because there is a belief that the deity has a special power to make rain. The shrine of *Chulachhi-dyo* has several boulders that serve as aniconic images. Annual rituals of worship performed by certain communities and by the officiants of Layaku, the medieval administrative court, shows that the shrine was of some importance in the settlement even in medieval times.[3] Other structures present in Lavadol are two pati 'rest houses,' and a fountain to the north near the shrine of *Chulachhi-dyo*. There is one more pati to the west and a fountain east of the shrine of Bapa Mahadeva. The two pati in the north bear inscriptions dated 1706 (NS 826) and 1732 (NS 852) respectively. A town gate is situated slightly to the west of Bapa Mahadeva, which is south of the Lavadol field. This is located on the road that leads to Balakumari Square, the southern end of the town settlement on the plateau.

Street Grid of the Town

The average modular dimension of 38.48 m found in the Lavadol sectors provides a standard reference rod to check the widths of the quarter blocks of the town. The dimensions of these blocks (Fig. A1-2) are derived from measurements of the width of the lanes and frontage of dwellings facing the main street. The measurement was done from Balakumari Square in the south to Hattimahankal in the north. Two sets of dimensions are noted in Figure A1-2: the first set is the clear width of the blocks and the second set is the width of the lanes in both the eastern and western sections of the main street measured center to center. Because the width of the lane varies considerably in different sections, the dimension given is measured at the entry point of the lane between building facades.

The street blocks are divided into four groups according to their widths, namely A, B, C, and D. Among these groups, the average width of the blocks of Group A is 38.42 m. However, this excludes block A9 which is much larger than the blocks in the three groups. The individual width of the blocks is fairly consistent and without much deviation from the average. In particular, the blocks in the eastern section of the main street show a regular division pattern from Balakumari Square in the south to Deguli square in the north. It should be noted that in developing this grid, some reconstructions have been worked out. These are the four grid lines drawn between A1 and A2, A2 and A3, A6 and A7, and between B4 and B5. The basis of the reconstruction takes into consideration the standard block width, the coinciding of the grid with sections of the currently existing lanes, and the alignment of boundaries formed by building clusters. The reconstruction was necessitated by the smaller size of Layaku in A3 and the complexity of A2. This reconstruction has brought to light some important aspects of the plan.

The northern boundary of A1 and the southern boundary of A7 coincide with the route of *de-bahu*, a ritual performed on the day of pisacha-chaturdasi[4] to propitiate the malevolent spirits for the protection of the town. The southern boundary of the A3 block (Layaku) is taken as the reference base line to divide the total width formed by blocks A1, A2, and A3. The boundary was the dividing line between the upper and the lower neighborhoods (Thatu and Kothu tole) in earlier times, a fact that is still reflected in a ritual known as ghasya-puja.[5] To this day, the lane is the border of the Inaya and Dathu tole neighborhoods in the north and south, respectively. At this border, there is an open shrine on the main street to the deity, *Sweta-Bhairava*, facing north. Instances of Bhairava being enshrined as the protecting deity of the settlements are mentioned in the chronicles.[6] Given these coincidences, the southern border of the Layaku block was considered as the base line of reference from which measurements towards the north and south were taken.[7]

It can be seen from the street pattern of the town that the lanes leading to the east and west from the main street are staggered. The pattern is not generated by the simple longitudinal shift of the western blocks. This is evident from the coincidence of the northern border of A1 and A11 in the north, and southern borders of A7 and D2 in the south. Furthermore, A8 and A10 in the vicinity of Layaku measure close to the standard width used in the eastern blocks showing a preference for the consistent use of the same module. Therefore, it appears that the staggering of the lanes is a result of the extra width of A9. Whether or not this extra block width was a planned

consequence is uncertain, but there is a possibility that Layaku and a settlement in A9 already existed before the development of the enlarged planned settlement of the town.[8] Without ruling out the possibility of such early settlement, A9 nevertheless serves as a security barrier for Layaku. A8 and A10 are consequently measured with A9 as the reference, while A11 is the remainder delimited by the northern boundary of A1.

The size of the blocks further north of A1 and A11 and the street patterns are not as regular as they are in the south. Blocks B1, B3, and B5 are of similar width, yielding an average of 36.46 m with a standard size block in between them. C1 and C2 are apparently partitioned from a single block. The Deguli temple in this area is one of the ancient foundations related to the ancestral worship of one of Thimi's major communities (Pant and Funo 2001a).[9] Its location as well as the old route to Bhaktapur might be the factors related to the planning of the quarter blocks. The convergence of the standard modular measure with the distance from Balakumari to Deguli strengthens this suggestion (Table A1-1).

Unlike the standard modules of the A and B blocks, the D blocks southwest of the main street are much wider with an average width of 49 m. Blocks further south of D3 lie out of our survey area. However, the measurements in the aerial map (Pl. A1-1) show two blocks south of D3 with widths close to those of the northern blocks of this group. The accuracy of the measurements derived from the aerial map is verified from other known field measurements in the north. Therefore, it can be concluded that the blocks south of A10 were measured using its southern border as the reference line, and proceeding southward from this border. The southernmost division is a minor track leading to the western fields. The eastern part of this southern section falls steeply to the southward route that extends from the main street of the town.

The above analysis of the dimensions of the street grid and the groups of the quarter blocks derived from them shows that the planning of the town was not done in a symmetrical manner along the main north-south street. The development of the eastern sector was a primary consideration. In this sector a uniform division was obtained by producing seven blocks of similar widths. The end blocks of this sector define the northern and southern limits of the town. The divisions in the western sector follow this limit which was set by the planning of the blocks in the east. Another important feature of this planning is that the measurement for the division of the blocks does not begin from one end to the other end of the sector. Rather, it first assumes a centre, which is Layaku, from which measurement work proceeds outward. Undoubtedly, the first planned area is the one now enclosed by the de-bahu ritual route. As mentioned above, the town is circumambulated during this ritual and offerings are made to protect the town from evil spirits. This area is within the cross-section in the north (the northern border of A1 and A11), where there is an aniconic shrine of Sapalan-dyo, and Balakumari Square in the south. It is not certain when this ritual was instituted, but it may well indicate the first phase of the town plan.

It should be noted that the division between the eastern and western sectors of the town follows the division of community groups. These are known as the dewali community and identified on the basis of their ancestral deities. An analysis of the distribution of various *dewali* communities has shown that a community inhabiting the eastern sector is older than those communities in the western sector (Pant and Funo 2001a). Similarly, the differences in the type of clan clusters between the two sectors (*nani*) show the northern and southern sectors to be a later development than the central area enclosed by the circuit route. This consistency and correspondence with the community structure and the type of dwelling clusters supports the above analysis on the manner of planning of the town of the old core of Thimi.

The Standard Module of the Planning dimension

The dimensions obtained from the Lavadol field and the town settlement needs to be interpreted in terms of the measurement standards that were possibly used in ancient Nepal. The only historical documents of the Licchavi period discovered so far consist of stone inscriptions, which are not known to have mentioned any particular measuring rods. However, it is safe to assume that *hasta* ('cubit'; Nepali: *hat*), which is found in the records from the medieval period, was a common measuring unit for buildings, towns, and fields from ancient times. The earliest of these relevant records are to be found in Kautilya's *Arthasastra*. In the Arthasastra, 108 digits, that is, 4 *dhanurgraha* or 4.5 *sishu-hasta*, make up a *danda* measure, which is recommended for the planning of villages and towns. Furthermore, it notes that 10 *danda* makes one *rajju*, 2 *rajju* make one *paridesha*, and 3 *rajju*, one *nivartana*. Moreover, according to the Buddhist *Jataka*, the *rajju* was also used in field measures, which is suggested by the use of the term *rajjugahaka* for field surveyors.[10] The conversion of these ancient units to the present-day metric system depends upon the value given to the standard of *hasta*. Different authors have suggested different values for the *hasta* that range from 42 cm to 60 cm, depending upon the context (Dutta 1995, 40; Nakagawa and Tsuchiya 2000, 179; Tiwari 2002, 203). In this study, the value used is 48 cm to one *dhanurgraha hasta*. This value is close to that found by Nakagawa and Tsuchiya in their study of Angkor Wat.[11] This measure gives 1.92 m for one *danda* and 19.2 m for one *rajju*, following the relationships in Kautilya's *Arthasastra*. Thus, it can be seen that the width of the Lavadol blocks is close to 2 *rajju* (38.40 m), or a *paridesha* unit, according to the system of measure given by Kautilya. Furthermore, given the above standard for dhanurgraha *hasta*, the *sishu-hasta* will be 42.6 cm. This is again close to the value of 42.06 cm which was derived by Watanabe and Kurotsu in their study of a Buddhist monastery— I baha bahi, which was built in Patan during the fifteenth century (Watanabe 1998a, 16–17). Therefore, considering that the history of Thimi precedes the medieval periods, and since definite standard measures of any size for the ancient period have not yet been discovered, we assume the value of 48 cm is a workable hypothesis to explain the dimension modules both of Lavadol and Thimi.

Table A1-1 shows the correspondence of the measured dimensions of the town blocks and their theoretical values in the multiples of *danda* measures. The margin of error is calculated with respect to the base multiple r (*rajju*) or d (*danda*) depending upon which the value is equated.

It can be seen that those blocks, which are not the integer multiples of *rajju*, coincide with the multiples of *danda*, proving the finer accuracy of the value assumed for one *hasta*. Likewise, the blocks of Group D and one of the sectors of Lavadol, L7, are the multiples of 5 d or 0.5 r. Further, the convergence of the widths of blocks A11, B1, and B3 with the *danda* multiples suggests that the divisions of these blocks, along with those of Group D, used the standard of the same *danda*. The variations in their width from the standard multiple might have been due to topographical factors and already existing field tracks. In this context, it is important to note that the total length measured from A7 (Balakumari Square) in the south to B3–B5 (Deguli Square) in the north is 20 r, which shows a control in deviations in the widths of certain blocks from the standard measure. Notably, the centerline of this segment at 10 r runs close to the crossroad that is at the northeast of Lavadol. The coincidence of the total length from Balkumari Square to Deguli Square with remarkable accuracy (which is 20 r) against the deviations in individual blocks suggests the pre-existence of field tracks passing through these points at Balkumari Square and Deguli Square, which were laid following the same standard measure of field division. The deviation of the widths of A5, B1, and B3 can be explained by considering the limitations set by the pre-existing location of Layaku and the two borders of Balakumari Square and Deguli Square.

While the blocks show the *danda* as the minimum module, the use of the *hasta* multiple is apparent in the street widths. Table A1-2 shows the widths of the lanes as varying from 4 *hasta* or

Table A1-1.   Dimensions of the block width in metric measure and Kautilya's danda standard.

Block no.	measured width (m)	metric value of danda multiple (m)	danda multiple	margin of error*
A1	38.63	38.40	2r	0.50%
A2	38.57	38.40	2r	0.44%
A3	38.57	38.40	2r	0.44%
A4	37.22	38.40	2r	3.07%
A5	42.21			
A6	38.03	38.40	2r	0.96%
A7	38.80	38.40	2r	1.04%
A8	39.57	38.40	2r	3.04%
A9	61.50	61.44	32d	5.20%
A10	38.14	38.40	2r	0.67%
A11	24.82	24.96	13d	7.29%
B1	36.79			
(B1+B3)/2	36.46	36.48	19d	1.04%
B2	38.47	38.40	2r	0.18%
B3	36.13	36.48		
(B1+B3)/2	36.46	36.48	19d	1.04%
B4	—	—	—	—
B5	36.13	36.48	19d	
C1	43.86	42.24		
C2	41.03			
D1	48.88	48.00	2.5r	9.16%
D2	48.50	48.00	2.5r	5.20%
(D2')	32.69	32.64	17d	2.60%
D3	50.88	50.88	26.5d	0.00%
Total length from A7 to B5 = 383.43			20r	1.43%

* Margin of error are calculated with respect to the theoretical value of the corresponding base module of the block width, i. e., r (*rajju*), 0.5r and d (*danda*).

1 *danda* to 2 *danda*. The width of the north-south main street varies in different sections. It is significant to note, however, that the width of the street measured between the building facades at major sections where buildings at the two sides run parallel is close to 0.5 r [9.60 m] Fig. A1-2). It appears that this was the standard width set at the planning stage of the town.

Temporal order of the Lavadol Plan and the Town Core

No dated records have been found either in Thimi or Lavadol that explicitly mention the planning of the old core of Thimi and the Lavadol field. Furthermore, the lack of built structures on the surface within the planned sectors of Lavadol does not allow us to compare built forms

Table A1-2. A comparison of hasta multiples and measured width of the streets

measured width (m)	metric value of hasta multiple (m)	hasta multiple
1.17	1.20	2.5
2.57	2.64	5.5
3.75	3.84	8.0
1.83	1.92	4.0
2.22	2.16	4.5
2.93	2.88	6.0
2.10	2.16	4.5
2.35	2.40	5.0
2.60	2.64	5.5
1.90	1.92	4.0
2.90	2.88	6.0
2.28	2.16	4.5
3.80	3.84	8.0
3.20	3.12	6.5
2.42	2.40	5.0

in the two sites. All the existing structures in Lavadol are situated on the periphery of the planned area. Nevertheless, based on the available information, we have compared the Lavadol Plan and the plan for the Thimi town core and suggest that there are three points of comparison to note regarding the temporal relationship between the two settlements.

First, the clear difference in the manner of division and the dividing strips of the sectors of Lavadol with other neighboring fields suggests that Lavadol was planned to be a residential settlement. There are similarities between the Lavadol Plan and the plan of Thimi. The most evident among them is the block module. Moreover, this common module accords more with the blocks of the central core, which was the first planned area of the town,

rather than with those of other sectors to the north and south of this core.

The second important feature of comparison is the manner of physical planning of the street of the upper town and its social planning. As indicated by the community distribution, the planning of the town did not proceed symmetrically from the main north-south street; rather planning proceeded from the eastern sector of the town (Pant and Funo 2001a). This shows its affinity with the structure of Lavadol Plan that is also an asymmetrical linear structure. However, unlike the development of the town towards both sides of the main street and neighborhoods spanning across this street, the Lavadol Plan does not indicate such a structure in its remains (Pant and Funo 2002).[12] The form of the Lavadol plan envisages uniformity in social structure, and even possibly a community structure resembling the peripheral neighborhoods of the town (Pant 2002). Such simple structures, as shown by Lavadol, are more akin to the features of early settlement forms.

Both within and without its planned area Lavadol lacks the typical community religious structures, in particular a shrine of Ganesa (one of the symbolic aspects of a neighborhood) and the temple squares (ubiquitous features of the town settlement of the valley by the later medieval period). This suggests that the settlement is either ancient, or that it was not settled for a period of time long enough to lead to the formation of a community similar to the neighborhood quarters of the town. However, the oral and ritual traditions of Thimi suggest that there previously existed a nucleus of a settlement on the plateau, though the planning of this area could have been later than the Lavadol plan.[13]

Conclusions

The discovery of the Lavadol Plan has been of central importance in the analysis of the street plans of Thimi as it establishes a direct relationship between the classical measurement standards described by Kautilya and its use for town planning in the Kathmandu Valley. The simplicity of Thimi's settlement structure demonstrates without ambiguity an example of settlement planning in the Kathmandu Valley. More historical studies are required to firmly anchor the time frame for the planning of Thimi, and to establish chronological order between Thimi and Patan or other towns of the valley.

Nevertheless, we outline here some of the important features of planning in Thimi that have also been demonstrated in Patan.

1. The planning of Thimi employed a module that accords with the standard units given by Kautilya. The theoretical measure for the width of the settlement block is 2 *rajju* wide or 20 *danda*. The corresponding value of this measure in our present-day metric standard is 38.40 m. The module of 48 m (1 s = 2.5 *rajju*), most common in the planning of Patan, was also applied in the later phase of planning in Thimi.

2. The distribution of the block widths and their layout pattern shows that the area described by the de-bahu ritual is the core area of the town and represents the first phase of town planning. This coincides with earlier studies on the spatial structure of Thimi. Further, the grouping of the settlement blocks suggests that the blocks to the north and south of the central core are later extensions.

3. Existing artifacts at Lavadol, oral traditions, and rituals suggest that planning for Lavadol occurred prior to the planning of the town plateau. It also suggests that a core settlement existed around Layaku before the planned development of the town.

Appendix 2

From Indus Valley to Kathmandu Valley: The Journey of the Indus Grid in Town Planning

Mohenjodaro is a city in the Indus Valley plain that flourished around 2500 BCE (Fig. A2-1 and Pl. A2-1). The site of the city was first discovered in 1922 by R. D. Banerjee,[1] and excavation works followed under John Marshall who published the results of the work in 1931.[2] The city is a planned settlement with a regular layout unlike those found in the settlements of Mesopotamia.[3] Marshall had earlier begun excavation works on Taxila, an early historic city located about 500 km northwest of Mohenjodaro. Taxila incorporates several settlements. Among these, Marshall excavated a lower settlement known as Sirkap and another nearby site known as Bhir Mound. The excavated strata of Sirkap clearly revealed that the town was a planned settlement. Marshall (1921) ascribed the planned settlement, including the building of the city wall, to the Saka who followed the Indo-Greek Bactrean to rule the region of Gandhara. In his later work, however, Marshall (1951) ascribes the building of the planned city to Bactrean.[4] Although similar assumptions made by Marshall with respect to other artifacts found in

Fig. A2-1. The Indus region and Kathmandu Valley

this city have been refuted by other researchers, his suggestion that Sirkap was built on Hellenistic principles was often uncritically accepted by subsequent writers (Ghosh 1948).

Our interest in Taxila and Mohenjo-daro began in the course of our study of Patan and Thimi. We saw the possibility that the planning features we discovered in Patan and Thimi also existed in the ancient cities of the Indus region. It was by chance that we discovered that Sirkap, like Thimi, had used similar measurements in the division of its urban blocks. Our review of research literature into ancient settlements led to Mohenjodaro and then to other excavated settlements of the Indus civilization where, surprisingly, the modular dimensions and module multiples found in Patan were found to be similarly used in the division of settlement blocks.

In the past seventy years, many settlements and sites that belonged to the Indus culture have been discovered in the Sindhu and Punjab plains. Settlements such as Kalibangan and Lothal further demonstrate that the Indus people did have planned town settlements (Rao 1979).[5] Metrological studies of Mainkar (1984) and Vij (1984) have also shown the use of a standard system of measure and weights throughout the Indus region.[6]

Studies of pottery and other artifacts have now extended the zone of the Indus civilization to the area from the middle Ganges in the east to Afghanistan in the west, and Maharastra in the south to the

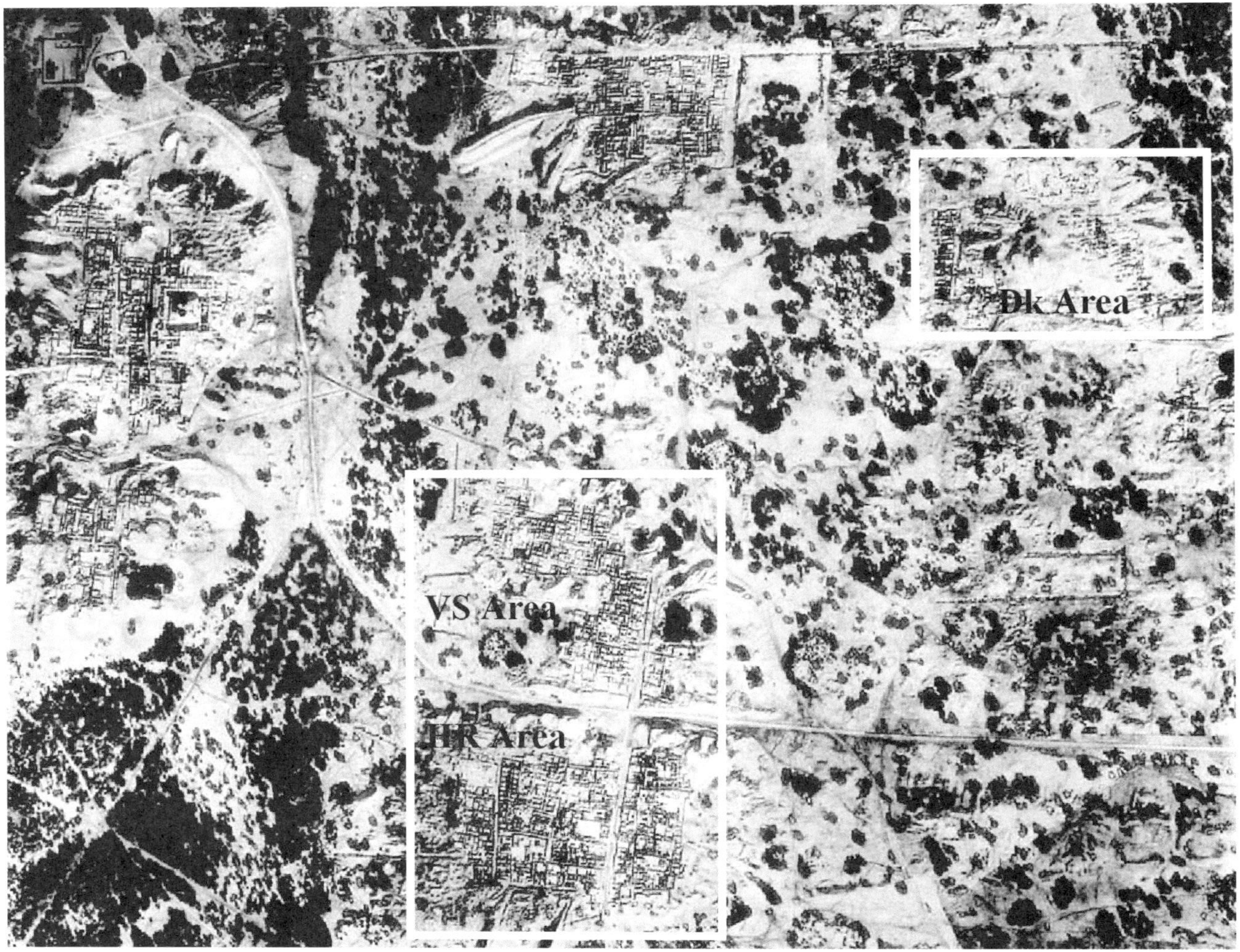

Pl. A2-1.　Aerial photograph of Mohendaro (Ghosh 1948)

Himalayan belt in the north. These studies also show the Indus culture spanned a time of more than two millennia. In spite of the extensiveness of the Indus urban culture that includes the Taxila region, the available literature does not relate the town settlement of Sirkap to the culture of the Indus people. Marshall's three volumes on Sirkap and his other works on Taxila make no mention of Mohenjodaro or Harappa.[7] However, later excavation works within the Taxila region and in localities close to Sirkap have shown that these areas were settled from almost the beginning of the Indus civilization to as late as the first centuries of the first millennium. This suggests a probable continuity in the patterns of settlements in Taxila and the Indus Valley.[8] On the other hand, Nepalese historians such as Gyanamani Nepal and Baburam Acharya consider that early settlers in the Kathmandu Valley came from the Indus Valley region. In his *Nepal nirukta* (1983) Nepal writes that the name "Nepal" owes its origin to the Nipa tribe which migrated from the Indus region.[9] There are also place names in Nepal that echo its ancient connections with the Indus Valley.[10] However, these connections between the Kathmandu Valley and the Indus region in prehistoric times must be substantiated by evidence in the form of continuity of cultural traditions. With its analysis of the town plans of the three cities, the present study demonstrates for the first time a close cultural affinity between the Indus region and Kathmandu Valley.

Method of Analysis

The study analyzes the layout of the streets, particularly the dimensions of blocks defined by building clusters and quarter blocks revealed through the excavations in Mohenjodaro and Sirkap. In these two former settlements, it is possible to discern cluster blocks, which are formed by exterior walls or the boundary walls of a group of adjoined dwellings. These cluster blocks have well defined boundary lines, which either coincide with a street or lane or are separated from the adjoining cluster block by a narrow gap. In many instances, the boundary lines show continuity through several cluster blocks, emphasizing even more their functions as boundaries of plots. The next measurement is along the settlement blocks defined by an interval of lanes or streets. Thus, the side of the lane or the boundaries of the blocks define the terminal for the measurement and dimensional analysis of the settlements.

The maps used in this analysis were obtained from Marshall for Mohenjodaro (1931, scales: 1/250 and 1/732) and for Sirkap (1951, scales: 1/1000 and 1/380). They provide enough accuracy for the purpose of our analysis. The dimensions of Thimi come from field measurements conducted by the authors in 1996 (Pant and Funo, 2003).

A preliminary study of the drawings showed that the layout of settlement blocks was related to a modular dimension of 19.2 m, a length equivalent to one rajju (r) in ancient times. This was found to have been extensively used in Patan and Thimi. Hence, the grid of 19.2 m (1 r) was superimposed on all areas of Mohenjodaro and Sirkap to examine the extent of planned regularity in these settlements. Thus, although the three cities are widely separated in terms of space and time, the same analytical approach has been used for all of them.

Mohenjodaro

The excavated areas of Mohenjodaro are distributed over different locations as seen in the aerial photograph in Plate A2-1. These areas have been named as in the original drawings. The HR Area is defined by two streets running north to south. Within the region of the excavated area, this part lies in the southern end. The wider street to the east, Street 1, is considered to be the main street of the city. Until now, this HR sector includes the biggest area, and it has the highest density of built clusters among the excavated areas. The VS Area to the north is connected to the HR Area by the main street. The HR, VS, and DK areas were selected for the purposes of this study since detailed drawing plans are available for them and they constitute large clusters.

The Main Street and Axis of Alignment

Except for slight deviations in their layout, the settlement blocks and dwelling clusters of Mohenjodaro generally follow the orthogonal pattern (Figs. A2-2a, A2-2b and A2-2c). For instance, the HR Area (Fig. A2-2a) shows three different alignments in the building clusters although alignment of the main street within the range of this area does not change. The lanes are found to be occasionally staggered. The building clusters at the interior that follow the alignment of lanes thus present an obvious difficulty to assuming that the planners used a single reference axis for superimposing the grid. However, in this instance, the main street, which runs straight from the south to the north of the city, is taken as a reference to proceed for the measurement of the quarters. The dimensional measures obtained

between the boundaries of the clusters, between the lanes, and between the boundaries of the blocks are shown in Figures A2-2a, 2b, and 2c. It can be seen that all the lanes, including the main street, closely coincide and align with the grid network. Furthermore, minor cul-de-sacs and cluster boundaries are aligned with 9.6 m grids. The cluster blocks with a 19.20 m width are most evident in the DK and VS areas.

It is important to note that despite four different cluster alignments in the HR Area, boundaries in all cluster groups basically follow one reference grid that aligns with the main street. The differing alignments are only a slight rotation from the reference grid and show continuity in the grid lines. The conjunction of the grid lines of various cluster alignments with the main reference axis, therefore, suggests their single reference origin. Minor bends from the reference alignment forming clusters of the local grid are similarly found in other sectors. Aligning with the reference axis of the main street, the grids are continuous between the HR and VS Areas which are separated by a distance of about 90 m. The measurement of the aerial photograph shows that the two areas follow one reference axis along the east-west direction as well.

Pattern of Plots and Block Division

Among the east-west and north-south boundaries of cluster blocks, the latter is comparatively more pronounced in its continuity. The longitudinal divisions, in general, define the depth of cluster blocks, which is most evident in HR and VS Areas. The transverse divisions that give the width of the blocks show some degree of variation. Figures A2-2a, 2b, and 2c do

Note: The superimposed grid lines are at 19.20 m (1r) interval. The dimensions measured are of the cluster blocks not coinciding with the superimposed grid net. The measurements marked by circle are close to the multiples of danda. The measures close to 9.60 m (r/2) and its multiple are not marked. The values may be checked to the following scale:

danda	1d	2d	3d	4d	5d (r/2)	6d	7d	8d	9d	10d (r)	11d	12d	13d	14d	15d
meter	1.92	3.84	5.76	7.68	9.60	11.52	13.44	15.36	17.28	19.20	21.12	23.04	24.96	26.88	28.8

Fig. A2-2a. Grid Patterns of Mohenjodaro: HR Area (Excavation plan: Marshall, 1933)

danda	1d	2d	3d	4d	5d (r/2)	6d	7d	8d	9d	10d (r)	11d	12d	13d	14d	15d
meter	1.92	3.84	5.76	7.68	9.60	11.52	13.44	15.36	17.28	19.20	21.12	23.04	24.96	26.88	28.8

Fig. A2-2b. Grid Patterns of Mohenjodaro: VS Area (Excavation plan: Marshall, 1933)

danda	1d	2d	3d	4d	5d (r/2)	6d	7d	8d	9d	10d (r)	11d	12d	13d	14d	15d
meter	1.92	3.84	5.76	7.68	9.60	11.52	13.44	15.36	17.28	19.20	21.12	23.04	24.96	26.88	28.8

Note: Cf. Fig. 12-3a.

Fig. A2-2c.   Grid Patterns of Mohenjodaro: DK Area (Excavation plan: Marshall, 1933)

not note the width of the blocks whose boundaries closely coincide with the superimposed grid. Instead, measurement values are noted only for those blocks whose boundaries do not coincide with the grid. It can be seen that most of the cluster blocks have a width of 9.6 m to 19.20 m, while quarter blocks with a depth of 38.40 m are not uncommon in all the three areas. The coincidence of the 9.6 m grid is an indication that the measurement of 9.6 m × 9.6 m is one of the standard plot sizes.

The reference grid, which is aligned with the western boundary of the main street, has revealed a vital feature of the layout of streets, lanes, and plots. The alignment of lane and plot boundaries with this reference grid shows that the survey measurement was not done by measuring from the center of one street or the lane to the other. The continuity of boundaries in the longitudinal directions and the orientation of major streets suggest that these divisions were primary considerations in the settlement layout. The conjunction of modular measures with the layout of streets and the close alignment of boundaries of the blocks suggest that the area was first divided regularly into longitudinal sectors of 19.20 m wide. It is not certain whether this division preceded the beginning of the settlement or if it was needed as the first step for the foundation of the settlement. The layout of the streets and lanes of the city might have complied with the existing field boundaries without obliterating them. This is suggested by the fact that the blocks east of the main street in the HR Area are of a 9.6 m depth that is not of the usual depth formed by the 19.2 m grid due to the width of the main street which is half a grid wide. Thus, it

appears that the depth of the plots were defined by the existing net of field divisions and by lanes drawn within this grid, not by laying out the blocks in uniform size.

Modular Dimension

In the three areas of Mohenjodaro, the dimension which frequently occurs in major cluster blocks is 19.20 m. Likewise, the most common dimension of minor individual blocks is 9.60 m, which is also the width of the main streets. The coincidence of lanes with the grid of 19.20 m shows that this measure is a determinant in the layout of the settlement blocks as well as street planning. Interestingly, this grid measure is verified from street plans and survey measurements of Indus cities by other researchers.

Piggot's reconstructed street plan of Mohenjodaro (1945) suggests that the town is formed by a grid net of three longitudinal streets and two traverse streets within the settlement area (Fig. A2-3).

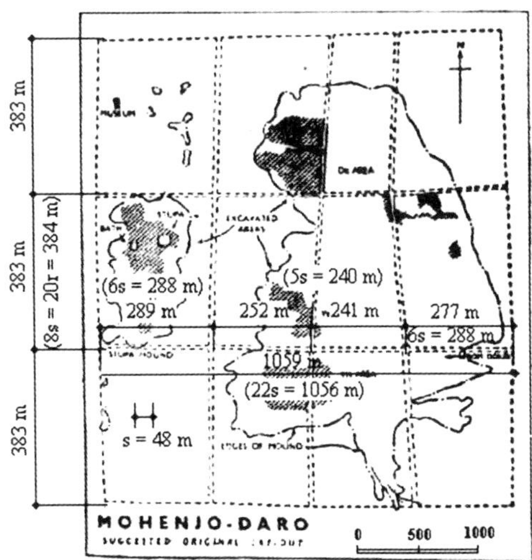

Fig. A2-3. Street layout of Mohendaro
(Piggot 1945)

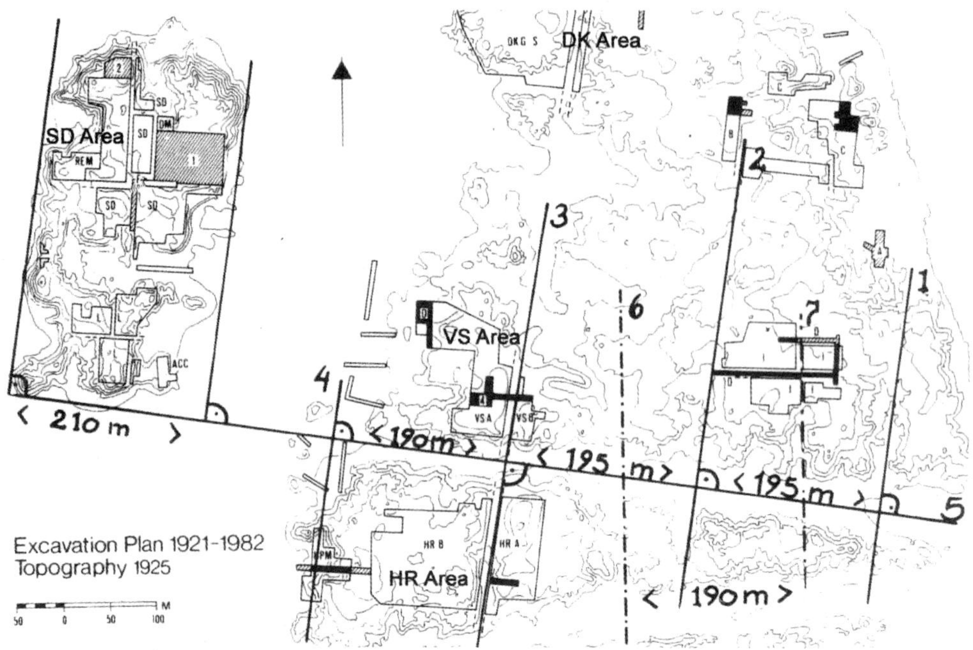

Fig. A2-4.　Grid interval in the access axes of Mohendaro (Wantze 1983-4)

Although his reconstructed street plan does not note the measurement dimensions, our measurements on his scaled drawing shows a consistent use of the basic module of 48 m (1 s)[11] with street grids at intervals of 383 m, 288 m, and 240 m. These measurement values show modular correspondence with Wantzke (1983–84) whose data (Fig. A2-4) show that the street axes of the town, which include the streets, are at an interval that is the multiple of 1 rajju with a repetitive use of a larger module of 192 m (10 r = 48 × 4).[12]

Similar modular multiples are found when measured using the street plan of Kalibangan (Fig. A2-5). These data from independent studies of widely separated places in the Indus Valley attest to the use of the 1 rajju module in the planning of Indus cities.

In addition to these modular multiples defining the grid of the city, various other dimensions are noted in the width of the cluster blocks of Mohenjodaro.

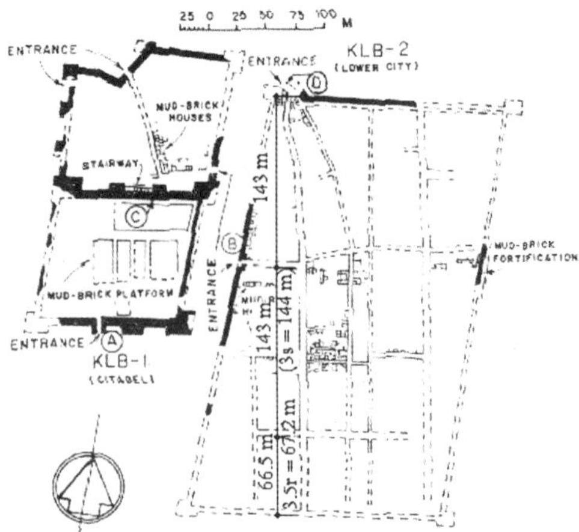

Fig. A2-5.　Street layout of Kalibangagan
(Thapar: cf. Jansen 1984)

These values are multiples of a standard unit measure which is close to the danda, a measure which is known only from Kautilya in the fourth century BCE (Chap. 1). The studies of Thimi and Patan show that this danda is 1.92 m. Most of the dimensions of Mahenjodaro's cluster blocks (the encircled numbers in the Figures A2-2a, 2b, and 2c) are close to the multiples of this value.[13] In particular, it must be emphasized that 9.60 m and 19.20 m are five and ten times the value of one danda (5 d and 10 d), respectively. According to Kautilya, 10 danda is a unit called rajju, while 2 rajju equal one paridesha. In Mohenjodaro, more detailed and accurate measurement studies are required to identify the lower units that make up a danda than the scale of currently available maps will allow. But it is clear from available data that the unit measures of danda and rajju, as described by Kautilya, were already used by the peoples of Mohenjodaro in their town planning.[14] To this must be added a recent report on the excavation of Rakhigarhi that describes the settlement as a well-planned town with streets 1.92 m wide.[15]

Sirkap (Taxila)

Sirkap is one of the three separate settlement areas discovered within the Taxila Valley (Fig. A2-6a). Bhir Mound, which lies southwest of Sirkap, is thought to be older than Sirkap, while Sirsukh, a town to the northeast, was built later in the second century CE (Marshall, 1960). The excavated area of Sirkap reveals a settlement enclosed by ramparts within which there is a town on the lower plain and an elevated hill terrace. The hill terrace has a few monastery complexes and an area thought to be a citadel.

The town has one main street almost at the center of the settlement area that runs straight in a north-south direction (Fig. A2-6b). The town is then divided into blocks of equal width by lanes that run orthogonally in an east-west direction to the main street. The sizes of the quarter blocks differ in the central sector of the settlement and in the southern part of the town. The width of the blocks in the northern section where there is a consistent pattern of division is close to 38.4 m (2 r). These regularly patterned quarter blocks were analyzed to determine how they were divided into plots and what standard measures were employed in the planning of Sirkap. The quarters, marked according to Marshall, are A to C in the east and A' to G' to the west of the main street.

The continuity of the boundaries of building clusters within the blocks shows a longitudinal division of the quarters into two halves with additional divisions within them. A series of divisions that are 9.6 m in width can be seen in the A and B blocks. There are a number of instances where the boundaries of the cluster blocks have a width of 9.6 m and 19.2 m suggesting a uniform plot division in the settlement. Blocks larger than 19.2 m are not common. The three measures of 9.6 m, 19.2 m, and 38.4 m are thus hierarchical divisions of plots and quarter blocks of the town. Interestingly, the measure of 9.6 m, as in Mohenjodaro, is also the width of the main street of Sirkap. The unit of danda also appears when checked in particular blocks (Block H in Fig. A2-7) of 1/380 scale map. The dimensions of quarter blocks in the south that differ from the standard width of 38.4 m, also give us a modular unit close to 1.92 m, the equivalent of a danda.

An analysis of Ghosh's aerial map (1948) of the neighboring fields both inside and outside the walled area of the city shows a division pattern similar to the layout of the town settlement's lanes. In other words, the fields are parceled into plots of 19.2 m wide which are further subdivided in many instances. However, it is not certain whether the land division preceded the town layout or followed it along the same line. Given that Taxila was an inhabited area many centuries prior to the building of Sirkap and that it was the capital of the richest Satrapy of the Achemedian Empire as well as a center of learning during the sixth to the fourth century BC, it is certain that the valley basin was intensely cultivated.[16] As mentioned earlier, the measuring system used in Sirkap was already known during the Maurya period (324–189 BCE), long before the Bactreans arrived in Taxila.

Another even more important evidence supporting the earlier existence of this system of planning in Taxila comes from the settlement of Bhir Mound, which has been described as a settlement that existed by the sixth century BCE (Marshall 1960). Marshall described this settlement as irregular and haphazard. His opinion is based on the limited area of excavation and the pattern of streets revealed from the upper stratum. Fortunately, however, wall lines of the building clusters in the lower stratum are also shown in the drawings (Fig. A2-8). From these drawings it can be seen that the earlier structures shown by dotted lines have more regularity in their layout. This is particularly apparent in blocks between the first and third streets. The superimposed grid shows a number of blocks in contiguity with a width of 19.2 m. The blocks that follow the grid cover a greater part of the exca-

vated area lying between the second and fourth streets. Furthermore, the width between the first and second street also measure 19.2 m. The divisions of the 19.2 m-wide blocks into half are apparent in the blocks between the first and fourth streets. The regularity of the block size within this small area establishes a definite relationship between the settlement of Bhir Mound and the pattern of field divisions in Sirkap neighborhoods, as well as the planning of the settlement there.

From Mohenjodaro to Sirkap and Kathmandu Valley Towns

The preceding analysis of the settlements of Mohenjodaro and Sirkap demonstrates that the units of rajju and its half as standard modular measures are common to both of the towns. Moreover, these towns share this particular feature with Patan and Thimi in the Kathmandu Valley. We know from the other standards of measure of the Indus culture that they employed a decimal as well as a binary system. If the decimal system is adopted, a danda is one tenth of a rajju. The unit of danda is demonstrated in Patan as well as Thimi. The larger modules of 1 r, 2 r, 2.5 r (1 s), and 10 r (4 s) in the divisions of settlement blocks found in the Indus cities and the Kathmandu Valley prove that Mohenjodaro, Sirkap, and the Kathmandu Valley towns used the same measuring systems and followed the same planning tradition. The plot division of Sirkap shows similarity with Thimi. It is, therefore, not a simple coincidence that the main street of all the three cities has the same width of 5 danda (9.6 m). In the Patan study, the same width was also noted in the eastern quarter of Guita and Pinchen neighborhoods (Chap. 5).

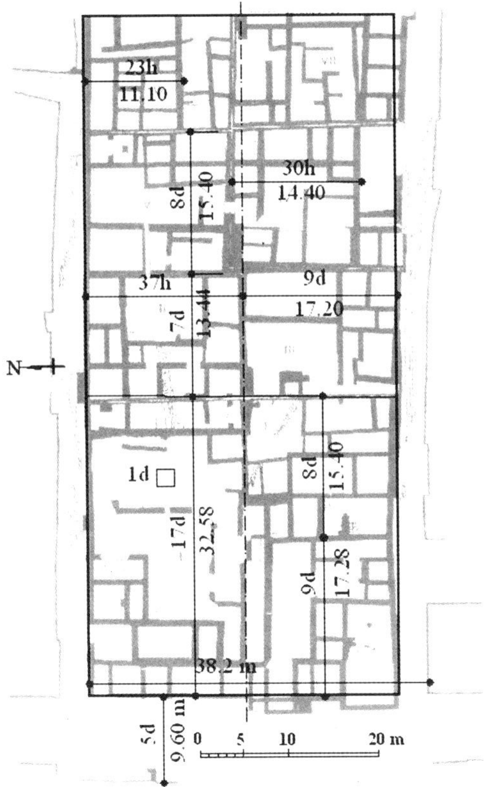

Fig. A2-7. Block H, Sirkap (Marshall, 1951)

If we set aside the fundamental convergence that exists among the three settlements, the differences in the manner of the division of the plot between the two settlements of Sirkap and Mohenjodaro are apparent. In Mohenjodaro, the excavated areas have not revealed equal-sized quarter blocks in between the lanes, although the more important lanes are invariably at a grid of 1 rajju (19.2 m). The lanes are often not straight, but doglegged. Short cul-de-sacs are often found leading to the interior from the main street. The lanes are narrower, almost half the width of the lanes in Sirkap.

Thimi has affinities with both Sirkap and Mohenjodaro. While the grid of 38.4 m is common to Sirkap, the lanes of

Thimi (including other towns in the Kathmandu Valley) when not straight, show a dogleg pattern similar to that in Mohenjodaro. In all these towns, the access lanes to the plots of the quarter blocks are from the lane and not from the main street. However, the layout of Patan has grown more complex in the course of its development with Buddhist monasteries later becoming the determining factor in the organization of its settlement quarters.

Marshall assumed that Sirkap was planned by the Indo-Greeks when they ruled the region in 189–90 BCE. Although Mohenjodaro clearly exhibited a grid system of planning, Marshall nevertheless thought that the planning principle of Sirkap followed the Greek tradition. However, there was no evidence to unequivocally support this argument and his reports written at different times contradict each other.[17]

Conclusions

The present study has revealed for the first time the planning modules that guided the division of settlement quarters and dwelling plots in Mohenjodaro. These modules used a measurement system that conforms to the system described by Kautilya in the fourth century BCE. The study has also demonstrated that the planning modules used in the Indus city of Mohenjodaro, Sirkap in Gandhara, and Patan and Thimi in the Kathmandu Valley are exactly the same. One of the documented links in the history of these widely separated settlements is found in Kautilya himself who lived in Taxila and Pataliputra (Patna), the capital of the Maurya Empire (321–185 BCE), and who describes this system of measurement in his economic

Notes: Cf. Fig. 12-3.

Fig. A2-8.   Grid patterns of Bhir Mound, Taxila (Excavation plan: Marshall, 1951)

treatise, Arthasastra. According to this treatise, Nepal was already in communication with the Maurya Empire.[18]

On the other hand, later archaeological works have indicated links between the settlements of Taxila and Indus period settlements. While excavation reports on the remains of Sirkap and Bhir Mound have not yet found evidence that can establish the definite foundation dates of these settlements, later archaeological works in the region of Taxila, Saraikhola for instance, have shown the evidence of settlement in Taxila contemporary to Indus period (Halim 1972a, 1972b). Allchin (1980) reports the finding of pottery shards that belonged to the early Indus period as well as those of later periods in the Hathial Mound area located a few hundred meters away from Sirkap, thus suggesting continuity of settlement in Taxila from as far back as the beginning of the Indus period. Our analysis of the structural remains of Sirkap shows its link with Bhir Mound and the Mohenjodaro tradition of town planning. Thus, if evidence shows that town planning ideas of Indus civilization continued to Sirkap and on to the Kathmandu Valley, it can be said that there was also continuity in the people who built their settlement upon this tradition.

Notes

Chapter 1

1   Swastika vihara, a seventh century monastery in Madhya Pradesh, is so named because it was in the shape of a swastika (Huntington 1985, 418). An inscription from western Nepal dated 1356 CE mentions swastika and *nandyavarta* (curvilinear swastika) patterns as the features of its palace courts (Naraharinath n.d., 49; Gutschow 1985a).

    Many other towns in the valley are also said to have been planned using sacred forms that are the symbols of certain deities. For instance, Kathmandu is said to have been planned in the shape of the sword of its protecting goddess, Kali (Poudel 1963, 23).

2   This work is published in Japanese. It analyses the structure of Madurai and Jaipur in India, Cakranegara in Indonesia, and other capital cities of Southeast Asia. For his contribution on Cakranegara in English, see Funo et al (2002).

3   Nepal discusses at length the problem of historiography in the Indian context when learned Sanskrit scholars were more concerned with describing the world of deities than the material world. He contrasts this tradition to that of China where the historian's task was always to record in their annals the events of the empire. He considers Kashmir as an exception in this matter. Levi (2005, 2) similarly notes the difficulties one encounters in writing the history of the region permeated by Hindu culture.

4   For example, see Sakya (1994) and Locke (1985), which gives a bibliographic list of Sakya's publications since 1956.

5   Vajrayana is one of three principal Buddhist sects, the other two being Theravada and Mahayana.

6   According to the Manasara, one of the ancient texts on architecture and town planning, prastara is one of the eight model plans for towns. Such a town is oblong or square in shape. It has two major streets crossing at right angles from the centre and one internal circumambulatory road. Other minor streets further divide the quarter blocks of the town. Further details on the layout of shrines and community distribution are described, and the town is said to be fit for Kshyatriya and Vaisya. See Acharya (1984).

7   The three are Mangahiti north of the Patan Palace, Chyasa-hiti to the northeast of the palace, and Subaha hiti to the east. There certainly could be more that are not yet known from inscriptions or other historic records (D. Vajracharya 1973).

8   The Jyapu make up 42 percent of the population according to Rosser (1966), which is a household survey of 31 towns including Bhaktapur and estimates from other sources for Kathmandu and Patan. Specifically for Patan, see Chapter 3.

9   These maps resulted from the UNDP (SF) Project 0025 (Nepal), Kathmandu Water Supply and Sewerage Project and are available from the Department of Land Survey and Management, Government of Nepal.

10   This journal publishes articles on archival records stored in the Department of Archaeology as well as those historic documents available from other sources including those privately held. Another regular journal publication of the Department is *Ancient Nepal* with articles both in Nepali and English.

11   *Documents of Rudravarna Mahavihara, Patan* (Kolver and Sakya 1985b) is a corpus of palm-leaf land deed documents stored in the monastery Uku Bahal of Patan that date from 982–1765 (NS 103-886). One of these documents, dated 1003 CE (NS 224), mentions a *hasta* unit for measuring dwellings (Kolver and Sakya 1985b, 112) while most of the sales concerned with farm fields use the areal unit, ropanika. But the relationship between the ropanika and *hasta* measures is not yet known. Licchavi period inscriptions mention *bhumi* instead of ropanika. Vajracharaya (1973, 54) thinks that the later unit ropanika of the same area replaced the earlier term bhumi.

     In the later medieval period when the Newari language was used, *ku,* the Newari term for *hasta,* was in use. Official documents from 1768 onwards use *hat,* a Nepali term, for *hasta,* and then its division añgul (See B. L. Shrestha 1999, 32–3). According to the Bhasavamsabali, King Jayasthiti Malla (1381–1395) is said to have revised the then existing *hasta* standard and system of taxes levied on houses and land. The basis of the *hasta* is said to have been 24 *añgula,* the width of his thumb (Lamsal 1966, 38).

Chapter 2

1   The only available historical records of ancient Nepal are official records inscribed on stone slabs. The language is Sanskrit and most of the documents are government charters on land and temple management. One of the notable inscriptions is about King Manadeva dated 468 CE that gives a list of his ancestors and describes his victorious march and subjugation of feudatories. So far the earliest inscription is from 185 CE with a fragment of inscription in the pedestal of a full size human figure mentioning Jayadeva who was the ruler at this time according to historians.

2   The chronicles and Puranas are two genres of literature that give accounts about the past of the Kathmandu Valley. The chronicles, known as Vamsabali, specifically focus on the genealogy of the rulers and the events that centered on the rulers and major temples and shrines. Most currently available chronicles are from the beginning of the nineteenth century. There is one, the Bhasavamsabali, from the fourteenth century. Historians consider this chronicle as more reliable in its account of history than other chronicles. Vajracharya and Malla (1985) provides the original and its translation into English and Nepali. On the other hand, the Puranas are works from the fifteenth and sixteenth centuries that describe the glory of sacred places in Nepal. Among them, Swayambhu Puran extols the glory of Swaymabhu Caitya, while Nepal Mahatmya expounds the virtues of Pashupatinatha. J. R. Acharya (1992) provides an English translation of the Nepal Mahatmya, which is a Puranic work that extols the virtues of Pashupatinatha, the most revered shrine in Nepal.

3   See Sakai et al. 2000. This is a study of the geological layers from borings taken from three different places of the valley. The study mentions that Kathmandu Valley was a lake as recent as 6000 years ago.

4   Oral tradition says that the popular Newari name of Patan, Yalan, comes from Yalambar, the name of the first Kirata king in the valley. The palace site of the last king, Patuka, is called the Patuka mound and is located at the northwest quarter of the medieval palace square. Likewise there is also a story of battles relating the loss of Kirata fighters in the northeast quarter of the city.

5   From its early history, the word, Nepal, has indicated a region with the Kathmandu Valley as the centre or capital. The Kathmandu Valley was known as the Nepal Valley for all those living in other regions of present-day Nepal. The word, Kathmandu, is derived from the name of a wooden thirteenth century pavilion known as Kasthamandapa. The pavilion exists at the southwest corner of the palace square in Hanumandhoka, Kathmandu.

6   Pradhyumna Prabhavati is a legend from the Nepal Mahatmya, a work written in the sixteenth century. The legend, the Bhasavamsabali, also relates the event in detail. An English translation of this legend can be found in Brinkhaus (1987).

7   The connection between the Licchavi of Nepal and those of Vaishali in North India during the time of Buddha is not yet clear. It is thought that they might have migrated north in small numbers during later periods following Magadha king, Ajatasatru, who seized Vaishali. The first Licchavi ruler is thought to be Jayadeva I, sometime at the beginning of the third century (B. Acharya 1997). However, following the finding of the Jaya Varma inscription dated 185 CE, this date has been pushed one century back. Bangadel (2005) considers the Varma dynasty to have ruled the period prior to the fifth century rather than the Licchavi.

8   Gopalrajavamsabali notes the name of the cow as 'Nipa' in the legend of Pashupatinatha. A tribe with this name is mentioned in the Mahabharata and other Puranas. Gyanamani Nepal (1998 18; 321) mentions that they flourished in the Sindhu region and later migrated to various regions and eventually to Nepal. He further asserts the etymological link of this tribe with Nepal. In Nepali usage, the suffix 'ala' is found in numerous instance such as Himala, Panchala and Bengala, etc.

9   The Churia hills, also called Shivalik, are the southern most range of hills in Nepal with elevations from 700 to 1500 meters, which rise from the Terai plains (the lowland area bordering India in the south) and stretch from east to west. The Mahabharat range runs parallel to the Himalayas and meets the Churia hills.

10   The research of Bangadel (1982) on ancient images of Nepal (*Nepalka prachin murtiharu*) focuses particularly on the link between the Kathmandu Valley and Mathura, an important cultural center during the Mauryan and Kushana periods.

11   Hasrat (1970), citing Padmagiri's chronicle, gives a description of Manjupattan as a well planned town with a palace at the centre and eight gates at the four directions. According to another chronicle, Manjupattan was successively enlarged and later known as Bishalanagara, But, it was submerged later when Danasur stopped the drainage of the valley water (Wright 1972, 136).

12   Malla writes that in Licchavi inscriptions more than 80 per cent of the place names of rivers, hillocks, canals, and tax offices are of non-Sanskrit origin and that there is very little doubt that these nominals come from Tibeto-Burman languages (1981, 7).

13   Part of the inscription is illegible due to erosion. However, the context suggests the royal decree regarding the upkeep of some religious shrine (Vajracharya 1996, 490–1).

14   An inscription of Sundhara located at the east of the palace mentions the repair works in a temple and that the responsibility on the maintenance of the temple was given to the community of Matingrama (Matingrama-panchali). See Vajracharya (1973, 339).

15 Joshi, citing Dirghanikaya, also states the Koliya (of Ramagrama) belonged to the Naga clan. A number of ancient ruling dynasties of India such as Satavahana are known to be from the Naga clan (1998, 82; 94–6).

16 The location of the fifth stupa is in the Pimbahal area at the western part of the city.

17 The argument for the four stupas of Patan to be funerary monuments runs as follows. Stupas began as earth mounds that served as caitya. Caitya derives from the root *cita* 'funerary pyre' (Goswamy 1980, 1). This is also suggested by a passage of Mulasarvastivada Vinaya where a stupa containing relics is referred as *sarira-stupa* (Roth 1980, 185).

18 Shenyang, in northeast China, was an ancient settlement and a planned town during the Ming dynasty. In 1623, the Manchu established their rule and made Shenyang their capital. In 1643, four lamaseries were built outside the four city gates with a monumental stupa in each of these lamaseries. The Manchu practised Lamaism with Tibetan lamas as their priests. Thus, the planning of the city bears the ancient Chinese city concept with new Manchu layers of which the building of four stupas was a sign of Buddhist sanctity. By 1644, the Manchu assumed the throne in Beijing and Shenyang became the auxiliary capital (Guo 2000).

19 Kolver and Sakya (1985) published a large number of such palm leaf documents stored in Okubahal, one of the monasteries of Patan, in 1985 with photographs and interpretations of original documents written partly in Sanskrit and partly in Newari.

20 At the last day of the festival of Rato Macchendranatha, a ritual displaying of a vest said to have been offered by Karkotaka, the Naga king, to a Jyapu farmer for treating his queen suffering from an eye infection is observed. Legend says that the Jyapu farmer was from Bhaktapur. In the Mataya festival, groups gather in procession to visit all the Buddhist shrines including the caitya built at the residential courts following a fixed route. At the head of the procession, a Jyapu plays the role of Kirata Siva, accepts alms, and offers worship to the Buddhist shrines.

Chapter 3

1 Vajracharya points out that the inscription that mentions *astadasaprakriti*, is generally interpreted to mean various ethnic groups. He cites one inscription from Kashmir where the *astadashaprakriti* includes Kirata, Khasa, Kalinga, Dravida, Gauda, Huna…Chandala. The notion of ethnic group is sometimes mistakenly equated with the notion of caste, which is essentially a concept denoting societal divisions according to one's position in the Hindu professional and religious hierarchy. Other Licchavi inscriptions occasionally mention Bramhana and Kshetriya as well.

2 Sharma collates a list of 29 such titles from different sources mentioned in medieval documents with dates falling within his period of study, that is, from 879 CE, the beginning of Nepal Era, to 1482, before the division of the kingdom into three city states.

3 The term "maximal community" as used here is not entirely congruent with the concepts of maximal clan or maximal lineage that are anthropological terms where a number of clans trace their origin either to a known or a mythical ancestor. At the other end there is the notion of minimal clan or minimal lineage. In Newar society, a hierarchy in this lineage structure can be outlined from one extended family to the dewali group (Sharma 1997, 96–125). In a maximal community (Nepali: *brihad-samudaya* or *jati*), the clan communities belonging to this larger group do not claim a common ancestor.

We group them together because they identify themselves as belonging to a group such as Jyapu, or Shrestha, or Vajracharya/Shakya, etc., among which, by tradition, intermarriage was possible. Some sociologists may liken the idea of maximal community to caste. In the Bhasavamsabali (Lamsal 1966, 38–52), there is a classification that resembles the notion of maximal community as it is used in this study. It mentions 36 such communities (*jat*) among the Newar. In fact, it outlines the duties and obligations of the citizens according to this classification. With respect to the Jyapu, the Bhasavamsabali simply says that it consists of 32 jat. The surnames that we have noted in Patan and included in the Jyapu community may be assumed to be among these 32 jat. It should be noted that in the concept of *char jat chhattis-varna* 'four classes of thirty-six ethnic communities,' the jat consists of the four classic Hindu hierarchic divisions of a society and *chattis varna* stands for 'thirty six ethnic communities' recalling the 18 communities (*astadashaprakriti*) in Licchavi inscriptions. The Bhasavamsabali mixes up the 36 communities and its further divisions by using the same term "jat." The 32 jat of Jyapu mentioned there is different from the notion of the four classic Hindu divisions and should be understood as divisions in a community based on profession or family.

The clan community with the same surname or those who belong to a maximal clan is a valid category in the study of the spatial structure of Newar settlements, as shown in the study of Thimi (Pant and Funo 2001a; 2001b). In this study, however, our concern is limited to settlement clusters that correspond to the maximal community, a category higher than the clan community and maximal clan community, which are also workable concepts in the study of spatial clusters and equally applicable in Patan. It is probably in Shrestha communities where such clustering is less evident.

4   Interestingly, the number of tole in Bhaktapur during the period of Ranajit Malla (1720–1768) was also given as 24, while that of Kathmandu was 26 during the reign of Mahendra Malla (1617–1636). See Vaidya and Vajracharya 1998, 91.

5   Joshi identifies three other tole—Koshaltol, Yangalasyottaratol, and Nhagaltol—as mentioned in colophons dating back to 186 NS, 189 NS, and 275 NS respectively.

6   The *thyasaphu* record quoted by Vaidya and Vajracharya is not explicit about the 24 pramana being chiefs of the tole neighborhoods. However, we consider them to be the representatives of the 24 tole localities. As the number agrees with that mentioned by Kunu Sharma about fifty years earlier, the number of pramana mentioned here could reflect the number of tole.

7   According to Joshi, instances of tole as the centers of Sanskrit schools are still to be found in Bengal, Bihar, and Uttarpradesh in India.

8   In addition to the monasteries shown in the map, there are three bahil in Pulchok, a settlement area in the vicinity of the west stupa, a few hundred meters away from the city border.

Chapter 4

1   Since 1956, Sakya has published a series of monographs about individual monasteries in the Kathmandu Valley. For a list of his publications see Locke (1985). Some of Sakya's latest works are on Hiranyavarna Mahavihara (1992) and Rudravarna Mahavihara (1994).

2   There are variations between the lists of vihara given by Gutschow and Sakya (1980) and Locke (1985). Sakya gives a list of 145 vihara (119 bahal and 26 bahil) within Patan while Locke lists 163 within the traditional city neighborhoods.

3   This particular illustration comes from Kathmandu because it is known to have kept its basic original form intact (Korn 1979).

4   The inscription is about the foundation of the bahal. It describes in considerable detail the rituals performed during the construction of bahal, the guthi and various other aspects that highlight the medieval society of a bahal community. Locke (1985) provides its full translation.

5   A report on the restoration of Vabahal by Gutschow, Hagmuller, and associates delineate the clan households within the immediate wings of Vabahal. This illustrates an instance of the settlement cluster of Sakya and Vajracharya community around the bahal. However, the authors do not dwell upon the social nor historical aspects of the formation of such clustered settlements (Joshi 1992).

6   Some basic concepts in urban morphology, such as the genetic plan unit, morphological regions, and fringe belt have been put forward by Conzen (1988) in his morphological studies of British medieval towns. According to him, a genetic plan unit is a typical plan type of, for instance, a dwelling including its physical dimensions, and is representative of a period in the history of the development of the settlement.

7   The mandala is often carved on a circular gilded copper or brass repousse or on a stone slab and raised upon a pedestal. In the mandala at the centre, is depicted one of the five Buddhas of the Vajrayana pentad. The other four are placed in the four directions. This artifact is present in all monasteries of the valley.

Chapter 5

1   Acharya (1997, 72) mentions this characteristic of the distribution of Licchavi inscriptions in the settlement areas of Jyapu communities in other towns as well. For this reason he makes the bold suggestion that the descendants of Licchavi rulers became part of the farming class and merged with the Jyapu community after they were edged out of the aristocratic ruling class.

2   Gajalaxmi is the consort of the Hindu god, Vishnu. She, as Laxmi, is the goddess of prosperity. She was born when the ocean was churned by the *Daitya* and the gods in their search for an elixir. When Gajalaxmi appeared she was taken by Vishnu as his consort. In her iconic form Gajalaxmi is depicted with her voluptuous body in an erect posture standing on a lotus and holding a lotus flower in her hands. Two elephants (Sanskrit: *gaja*) flank her on the left and right. Each elephant pours water from a vessel held in his trunk as a sign of obeisance to her thereby bestowing her the epithet "Gajalaxmi." Bangadel (1982) finds similarities between the iconographies of Gajalaxmi from the second century BCE in Chyasal and those at museums in Kosambi and Mathura in India.

3   All these localities are known to have existed in the Licchavi period. Kumbhesvor is one of the primary religious sites dedicated to Siva, and Guita-tole is associated with the beginning of the *Panchadana* (offering of alms) ceremony, which is a sacred Buddhist tradition in Patan that is mentioned in the *Sarvanandavadana,* a Buddhist *jataka* that tells the story of one of his previous births.

4   The survey utilized the 1981 cadastral map that identifies property boundaries, architectural structures, and artifacts such as caitya and temples. However, it does not identify the specific nature of these artifacts, such as their ownership and structure type. The present study conducted a survey of the eight tole shown in Figure 5-2 to delineate the tole boundaries, community artifacts, and type of community as determined by surnames. The identification of each cluster in the Dupat tole was done by observing the entrance of each household in

the area and interviewing the residents. The survey was conducted on August 8–22, 1998 by Mohan Pant and on Jan 18–25, 1999 by Hom Rijal.

5 Rato Machhendranatha is worshipped as the god of rain, the most revered deity in the Patan. Also known as Aryavalokitesvara Padmapani, this deity is served by the Buddhist priests. As one of the celebrated Buddhist deities of medieval Nepal and India, Nepale—Bungama Lokesvara is depicted as a conventional Avalokitesvara in a Nepali palm leaf manuscript dated 1071. The deity dwells for six months in his hometown Bungamati, a small town about eight kilometres south of Patan, and for six months in Tabahal at the southern quarter of Patan. During the festival, the ratha or chariot of Machhendranatha is drawn through the prescribed routes of the town. The townspeople perform their worship when the ratha stops at certain points.

In the final day of the two-month festival, the presence of the king is customary. An eighteenth century Nepalese version of a legend about Rato Machhendranatha gives a background of this festival. The legend says that during the early medieval period (ninth to twelfth century) King Varadeva of Patan delegated three people to bring Machhendranatha to the valley from Kapotala Mountain to alleviate a long drought causing famine in the nation. He did so on advice of a Buddhist priest, Vandhudatta of Kathmandu. These three were Vandhudatta himself, his father, Narendradeva who lived in Bhaktapur, and Rathacakra, a Jyapu. When the deity arrived in the valley a dispute arose among these three regarding where the deity should reside as each one claimed their own place as the deity's residence. An elderly Jyapu from Patan was asked to arbitrate and he chose the city of Patan. Having given this verdict, the Jyapu was swallowed up by the earth. To this day many Jyapu participate in this festival. In fact, some Jyapu clans are addressed according to their roles in it. See Locke (1980) and Wright (1972).

6 Gutschow, Kolver, and Shresthacharya (1987) define livi as a courtyard or backyard of a monastery. Current usage, however, defines livi as a backyard which usually contains a vegetable garden. The root *li* means 'behind' as in *likha* 'the backside of a building' or *liga* 'the compost pit at the backyard.' The front yard is called *nhebi* (*nhe* 'front'). When the dwellings of a family begin to cluster, the backyards are turned into an inner court. Thus, *livi-chhen* (the house at the inner court) suggests an image of a series of courts in the early medieval times, a griha-mandala, or a nani seen in the tole of Patan today.

7 A palm leaf document dated 224 NS mentions a griha-mandala with one main door, which the lessee is entitled to use (Kolver and Sakya 1985, 112). For a detailed analysis of the social and spatial structure of a nani, see Pant and Funo (2001b).

Chapter 6

1 The field measurement work was done on July 1–4, 2003 by Mohan Pant and Ghana Raj Lohani with students from the Institute of Engineering, Tribhuban University.

2 The map with both the field measurement data and the measured drawings of the Nippon Institute of Technology (1981) shows average margin of error that is less than 2 per cent with respect to a length of 10 m. The measures primarily used in this study are greater than 9.6 m. The working accuracy increases as lengths increase (see the field measures in Figures 6-2 and 6-4), while the error of margin on individual data may increase to seven per cent with respect to measures of 2 m, close to the lowest measure (*danda* = 1.92 m) used for the analysis of the data.

3   A concept commonly known by the phrase *hayaphu niku* 'two cubits to eaves end' is applied here also for the plinth width. The field measurement taken in a number of places where plinths conspicuously show continuity across property boundaries and appear to have maintained their original widths shows the width close to 2 cubit (96 cm).

4   The earliest inscription for the Bhinche bahal is 1141 (NS 261); for Subahal it is 1142 (NS 262); and for Kwabahal it is 1082 (NS 202). See Locke (1985, 39; 80; 85).

5   Gutschow and Basukala (1997, 138–9) identify 105 Licchavi caitya or their fragments in Patan of which three are in Nakhachuk; five are in Nagbahal and Subahal; two are in the Bhinche bahal; and eight are in Guita bahil quarters.

6   The primary bahal are still identified by the local Newar communities as *mu-baha* while the branch bahal are called *kacha-baha*.

7   Sasano notes the regular form of the Bhinche bahal and Subahal quarter precincts and speculates that this regularity might possibly be due to the higher level of hierarchy of the two bahal in the locality compared to other monasteries.

8   See Chapter 5 for a discussion on the relationship of these two grid nets and the implication that the Jyapu neighborhood tole were settled earlier than those of the Bhinche bahal and Subahal.

9   Watanabe (1998) provides drawings of several other monasteries whose outer dimensions range from about 18–22 m in addition to those of Chabahil and I baha-bahi. See also Chapters 7 and 9.

10 Monier Williams writes of the Nivartana Stupa, a stupa erected at the spot where the charioteer of Buddha returned (Williams 1899, 560). Mahavamsa tika, a Buddhist literary work, mentions Nivattagiri. This is a city that was built on the spot where Kadamba, the elephant, turned back in order to capture Mahelanagara. Similarly, a caitya near Kadamba nadi is called *nivatta caitya*, which was built on the spot where Mahinda, at Devanampiya tissa's invitation, turned back on the way to Missaka parbata (Malalasekara 1983, 80). In Pali, *nivatti* also means to halt, as in *nivattitabham bhante*, 'you ought to tarry here, lord' (Childers 1909, 294).

11 *Corpus inscriptionum indicarum*, vol. 5, no. 12–25 cited in Dutta (1995). In the inscriptions, the Vakataka rulers of central India mention the donation of 400 to 2000 nivartana of land according to the royal measure. Various classical works give different values for nivartana. As it is also the same as the *danda* unit of measurement, it is difficult to ascertain the size of a nivartana (Dutta 1995, 42–4). In this study, however, since the values given by Kautilya are consistent with those of the grid system and the size of the quadrangle itself, his measures are considered to be of immediate relevance to our study.

Chapter 7

1   Nani has social and spatial connotations as a settlement cluster of one or several clans. Chok is best translated as a courtyard or a square. It is more a spatial feature than a social form. Many localities in the towns of the Kathmandu Valley are known by certain particular attributes with nani as suffix. For a more detailed study of nani, see Pant and Funo (2001b).

2   The field survey was conducted from June 10 to July 9, 2003.

3   The survey was conducted between June 20 and July 5, 2003. The survey team included Mohan Pant, Ghana Raj Lohani, and students from the Institute of Engineering, Tribhuvan University in Kathmandu. The authors are grateful for the support of Professor Sudarshan Tiwari, Professor Sudha Shrestha, Mr. Ghanaraj Lohani, and the students from the Institute

of Engineering who participated in the survey and preparation of drawings, and the residents of Nabahal, Elanani, Nakhachuk, and Nagbahal courts for their support in the survey works.

4   The central caitya is also known as Asoka caitya, a name usually given to larger caitya with the characteristic plain hemispherical domes usually whitewashed with lime. For a classification and detailed iconographic study of Nepalese caitya, see Gutschow and Basukala (1997).

5   The symmetry with narrow corner frontage is already apparent in the rock cut monastery caves of Pitalkhora, Maharastra (first century BCE), while the use of the swastika goes back to the remote past, that is, to the Indus civilization in the third millennium BCE. The swastika is a sacred symbol in Buddhism, often seen in Buddha's footprints as one of several auspicious signs. The distinct swastika pattern in the ground plans of a monastery in Sirpur, Madhyapradesh, India (seventh century) and the Great Stupa in Paharpur (Bangladesh) (eighth to ninth century) indicate that this symbolic figure was adapted to the planning of monasteries. See Huntington (1985, 23; 82; 391).

6   See Locke (1987, 85). For the Licchavi period caitya, see Gutschow and Basukala, (1997, 138, note 15).

7   Based on his analysis of existing dwelling forms in Thimi, Pant (2002, 84) proposes a standard street house that has 322-centimeter bays when measured from outer wall lines. For the dates of the two bahal, see Locke (1985).

8   The seven largest open courts of Patan and their measurements are as follows: Nakhachuk (58.88 m × 58.90 m); Nagbahal (70.28 m × 57.58 m); Elanani + Kwabahal + Sasunani (44.28 m × 58.20 m); Tabahal (76.80 m × 51.84 m); Subahal (55.86 m × 55.78 m); Bhinche bahal (59.54 m × 51.99 m); and Bubahal (32.64 m × 57.60 m). These measurements exclude plinth width (survey measurements by Mohan Pant and Ghana Raj Lohani, July 1–4, 2003).

9   The layout of the grid and divisions take into account the plinth width of 2 h (96 cm) that adds to the open court of 3 r wide. This width is assumed from a convention known as *hayaphu niku* 'two *hasta* to the end of the eave.' The widths of the plinths that exist at present show some variation from this standard. However, our field measurements in places where the plinths across property boundaries show continuity conform to this tradition.

Chapter 8

1   Bhandari (1989, 54) echoes other scholars citing Itihasa prakasha (Naraharinath. n.d., 158) that Manadeva was ruling from Patan during the fifth century CE and his palace Managriha was located where Patan Palace currently is. The Bhasavamshavali mentions another ruler, Manadeva, ruling from Patan (Poudel 1963). The date cannot be ascertained, but the context suggests sometime in the first half of the twelfth century (Vajracharya and Malla 1985, 216).

2   Three palace sites known from the Licchavi period inscriptions and from literary sources, such as those of Wang Hsuentse, are Managriha built by Manadeva (fifth century), Kailashakuta-bhavan built by Amsuvarma (early seventh century), and Bhadradivas built by Narendradeva (late seventh century). Scholars' opinions on the location site of these palaces differ. A number of researchers suggest the site of Managriha and Kailashakuta-bhavan to be at Hadigaon. Joshi (1998, 139) suggests the location of Bhadradivas to be somewhere in the neighborhood of Bhadravas, a village near Gokarna, east of Kathmandu.

3   Bhaktapur was first divided into Bhaktapur and Kathmandu. While Patan was under the rule of Kathmandu, it was more often under the control of the local feudal lords. It was around 1618–1620 that Siddhinarasingha Malla, son of Sivasingha Malla, the ruler of Kathmandu, began to rule from Patan as an independent kingdom.

4   Kurotsu also mentions the parallelism that exists in the planning of palace courtyard structures with the planning of Buddhist monasteries or bahal (Kurotsu 1991, 44).

5   The research papers were published in the *Journal of Architectural Planning and Environmental Engineering* and several other Japanese journals, which are partly listed in Nippon Institute of Technology (1985, 6–7). On temples and tower structures, see Watanabe (1985, 100–11; 1986, 114–9; 1993, 135–41). Of particular relevance to the dimensions and the grid of the floor plan are Kurotsu (1991a and 1993) and Watanabe and Kurotsu (1990a and 1990b).

6   Since its restoration, Keshavnarayan chok quadrangle has been turned into the Patan Museum. Illustrative drawings of the courtyard building are found in Hagmuller (2003).

7   The field survey was conducted on Jun 25–30, 2003 by Mohan Pant and Ghana Raj Lohani.

8   See Kurotsu (1991b) for structural considerations and iconographic studies of Mulchok and Sundari chok.

9   In addition to the unanswered question about Managriha (Note 2 above) and the existing Mangahiti, the oldest existing structure in the palace quadrangles is thought to be Keshavnarayan chok. The Patan Museum (Hagmuller 2003) reports that it was rebuilt on the earlier structure which could go back to the Licchavi period, and that the rebuilding in 1734 was on the site of Haka bahal. Bhasavamsabali discusses the construction of palatial courts (Sanskrit: *brikha*: bull, *varga*: square) during the rule of King Gunakamadeva in this way:

> … with the blessing of Adisakti isvari enshrined in the Patako palace of nine courts, the Adisakti goddess was brought from Brindavana and enshrined in the agam (the secret shrine) in one of the courts, naming it Mula-chhen, as the guardian deity of the world. The image of the goddess was made according to the standards of Bauddha and Saiva traditions….He built Manko-bahal, and a shrine dedicated to Varsesvor Mahadeva (Siva) in Lagankhel with a subterranean approach way for plentiful rain. He paved the streets in all directions with bricks and stones. To fulfil this task he also established a shrine of Maniganesa and an agam of trisakti. Then he built a royal court of name Manigal-bhatta with a shrine of Narayana 'Manikumara' covering an area of one karsha in the shape of *vrikha-varga* (emphasis added). He built kotagriha (fort/weaponry) and pond…. The city was built according to the traditions of 'u-damar-tantra'; including the existing settlements, the king made Lalitpattan famous as a 'city of twenty four thousands' and put his name in posterity (Lamsal 1966, 21–23; our translation).

According to historical sources, there were two Gunakamadeva during the Thakuri period (879–1200 CE). The first Gunakamadeva, whose inscriptional records date between 986 and 989, is credited with founding Kathmandu and numerous other works. While historical evidence is not yet available to prove this, the above account of the chronicle undoubtedly refers to Manikeshava Naryayan chok. The second Gunakamadeva (1184 CE) is known to have ruled three years but little else is known from the chronicles. Also see Nepal (2005, 26; 122).

10 According to a chronicle, the area or the neighborhood of Sundari chok is also said to have been the site of Haka bahal, a Buddhist monastery donated by King Laxmikamadev in the twelfth century. This bahal is now situated in a quarter about 300 m west of the palace. The locality immediately south of the palace is known as Haka tole. There is also a ritual tradition that commemorates the link of the present Hakabahal to its earlier site in the palace precinct (Wright 1972, 234).

11 The quadrangle of Keshavnarayan chok is thought to be the site of a structure known as *chaukwatha,* a fortified quadrangle built by Sivasingh, a de facto feudal ruler or *mahapatras,* before the re-establishment of direct rule by the Malla kings.

[12] The foundation for the Mulchok of Bhaktapur and Kathmandu is not known. What is certain is that the Mulchok of Kathmandu predates Pratap Malla (1641–1674). The history of Taleju enshrined in the Mulchok begins from Bhaktapur. It is only natural that Bhaktapur had this major court built by the time of Yaksya Malla (1428–1482 CE) following which the kingdom divided into three municipalities.

[13] The grid system applied by Gutschow in the placement of the window in the lower palace of Gorkha also refers to the outer wall line. However, in the absence of detailed measurements of the palace's dimensions, the authors have not been able to verify this independently.

[14] See Gutschow, 1985. Gutschow provides the ground plan of Bhaktapur Mulchok where the quadrangle block is 27.30 m (EW) and the open courtyard is 19.55 m × 19.75 m. The width of the wings is not given in Figures 3 and 4, but according to Gutschow, the width of the wings in the Mulchok of Kathmandu is 2.60 m, while in Bhaktapur, it is 2.80 m.

[15] It is important to note that Bhasavamsabali mentions one karsha of land for the courtyard. We are not certain whether or not the enclosed area includes the whole courtyard block or only the open courtyard. While karsha is not in use in present day land units, it was a unit of measure of weight and area in ancient times (Williams 1899). In area measure it is also defined as the area a pair of oxen can plough in a given time for a day. While this kind of measure does not give an exact measure, it shows certain relationship with nivartana, one of the definitions of which is the area six or eight oxen can plough in a day. If we assume that four pairs of oxen are required to plough one nivartana area, one karsha comes to be one fourth of a nivartana. A nivartana, as we have shown in Chapter 6, is 57.6 m × 57.6 m (3 r × 3 r), and one fourth of this size is 28.8 m × 28.8 m (1.5 r × 1.5 r). Thus, if we assume such a relationship of karsha with nivartana, the block of Keshavnarayan chok is exactly one karsha in area. However, from late medieval land deed documents, we learn that four karsha make one *ropani* (Rajbamshi, 2001). In today's standards, a plot of one ropani is equal to about 509 sq m that gives a square of 22.5 m × 22.5 m. However, it is not yet known how the size of the earlier medieval ropani unit corresponded in size to the late medieval karsha measure of the Mulchok type court.

[16] For measured drawing, see Hatano (1986). A ground plan of this bahal, also called Chaturvarna mahavihara, is also given by Gutschow (1985).

Chapter 9

[1] For a comparison in their plan layout, see Fig. 1-3-1 in Hatano (1998, 12).

[2] The survey work was conducted by Mohan Pant and Ghan Raj Lohani on June 29 to July 2, 2003.

[3] For floor plans and physical characteristics, see Korn (1979) and Nippon Institute of Techology (1998).

[4] For a comparison of the physical forms of bahil and bahal, see Korn (1979). M. Pant (1990) analysed the urban morphological significance of bahal and bahil. See also Hatano (1998) for more detailed divisions of the types of Buddhist monasteries and their historical relationships. On the ritual and social organization, see Locke (1987).

[5] The Bhasavamsabali notes that King Jayasthiti Malla of the fourteenth century changed the standard length of the measuring rod from 10.5 *hasta* to 7.5 *hasta* (Lamsal 1966, 38). Our studies so far have not revealed the use of the 10.5 *hasta* standard; however, the length of 7.5 *hasta* has been demonstrated in Khun bahal, that is, the *sishu hasta* standard (h). This

rod is exactly ⅓ of 1 r (19.2 m) when calculated by our reckoning of the ancient standard of measure. Furthermore, 22.5 h (½ r) is also a standard length in calculating the area of a house where 22.5 h × 4 h comprises a unit known as *java*. For more on this unit, see also M. Pant (2002).

6   The columns of bahal usually have floral patterns and images of deities that mark them as more elaborate versions of the basic column form found in bahil.

7   It is also necessary to point out that the dimension of 457.2 mm equals half of one English yard. Since I baha bahi and *Mulchok* of Patan Palace were both built in the fifteenth and early seventeenth centuries, the coincidence of these measures is difficult to explain.

8   In general, columns of traditional temples and monasteries, as well as palaces and common residential dwellings, are divided into two or three sections. Symbolic interpretation of this form of division refers to the square form at the lower part representing the earth; the octagonal section at the middle represents the sky; and the circular section at the top of the column represents the heaven. Such divisions are found in pillars for ritual ceremonies. In columns that support the upper structure, the top is usually of a square form. Examples of this may be found in the monasteries as far as Sri Lanka. For more details on this symbolism see Irwin (1980).

9   Manasara also defines the height of the column to be measured "from above the base (*adhisthana*) to below the fillet (*uttara*)". See Acharya (1980, 151).

10 The measurement data itself is precise up to 1 mm. Thus, the margin of error due to the measurement scale is between −0.5 mm to + 0.5 mm. The *angula* measure is calculated from the carved segments which are of the order of values greater than 70 mm. This leads to a maximum error of 0.7 per cent. This value against ⅓ of the *angula* is 8.3 per cent.

11 The criterion employed by Kurotsu (1998a) for the division of the segments is primarily the coincidence of the *angula* grid net with the line of divisions of the segments. In his method of division, the neckline and the differences in iconography are not important. Thus, the divisions made by Kurotsu differ from ours with respect to the segments (a), (b), and (c), while they coincide with (d) and (e). However, the finer internal divisions within each segment given in this paper can be combined to yield segments similar to those used by Kurotsu, and which then can be examined following his analytical approach. Our analysis has shown that the basic unit of *angula* given by Kurotsu fits to only about 20 per cent of the 48 measurement data ([a] to [f] of the eight bahil given in Table 8-2).

12 It is probable that the division of 1 a was further calibrated into smaller divisions. This is suggested by the case of Gujebaha where there is a discrepancy of 5.3 mm for Segment (a), which cannot be attributed to error due to carpentry. The width of the column of this bahal is also the smallest (165 mm) although the height (1916 mm) is close to the standard. Various proportions might have been attempted by the builders to obtain the desired aesthetics. In the segments of the column, a change of half an *angula* is sufficient to affect the proportional relationships. For instance, in Segment (a) there are two groups of columns with 8 a and 9 a. Similarly in Segment (b), differences of about one *angula* can be found. Such proportional variations occur in other instances studied. However, a larger sample is needed to classify the different groups and find the finer calibration. Studies of monastery columns of other cities and towns of the valley are necessary to understand this aspect of column proportions.

13 Kurotsu (1998a, 103–5) shows 420.6 mm to be the standard measure also in the determination of heights in the vertical section of the structure frame. Half a *hasta* is taken as the basic

module to get the length of the segments. When calculating percentile errors, he uses the total dimension of the segment in question as the base. This method becomes erroneous when calculating large measures as multiples of small units. Uniformity in the control of error can be achieved by 'margin of error' calculated with the minimum multiple in question as the base. In Kurotsu's case, the base should be half a *hasta*. The segments in the vertical section given by Kurotsu can be regrouped into four contiguous segments, the length of which then agree with the *hasta* of 480 mm and its quarter. Despite these confirmations, slight differences from the standard should be expected due to shrinkage or erosion of the timber as well as the masonry structure in the past centuries. Kurotsu (1998c, 77–8; 84–6) report that I baha bahi, which was first built in 1427, was reconstructed in 1661. Another repair work is noted to have been done in 1710 following an earthquake in 1681. The rooftop was repaired again in 1880. During the reconstruction in 1661, the brickwork on the external walls of the first and second floors was changed.

It should also be noted that to take above *hasta*, as a classic standard applicable in the vertical sections of other bahil requires measurement analysis of those bahil as is done in the analysis of columns and plans. See Kurotsu (1998, 103–8) for more details in the measurements and on the account of repair works of I baha bahi.

14   Interestingly, Raju and Mainker (1963) in their study of traditional measures in South India suggest the value of 1 a to be 17.79. According to them, this value is derived from the measures of *vitasti* (span = 12 digits) of 20 males, aged 25 to 50, from different provinces of India. Raju and Mainker could have elaborated their argument by showing grounds that this measure tallies with the measure of the ancients, particularly at the time of Kautilya, to whom the paper refers. They then modify this value to 17.86 mm to fit to the commercial *hasta* of south India that measured about 50 cm. This commercial *hasta* is assumed to be of 28 a, and suggest the standard of the *dhanurgraha hasta* of Arthasastra. However, Raju and Mainker (1964) also mention other *hasta* units of 48.5 cm as prevalent in South India.

15   That the height of a column was given the dimension of one *danda* is also suggested by a statement "a column is also called *danda*" when giving the definition of a column (Acharya 1979, 223).

Chapter 10

1   Acharya in 'Ashoka and Nepal', 2001 (first published in 1953) categorically rejects any such unfounded stories on Asoka's visit to the Kathmandu Valley on the grounds that there are no inscriptions and columns found in the valley to document his visit as are found in other regions. See Acharya (2001).

2   The map was prepared by the AERMAP, Firenze as commissioned by the United Nations Development Program and the Government of Nepal in the early 1970s for the Water Supply and Sewerage Project in Kathmandu Valley. The cadastral map of 1/1200 (1″ = 100′) scale was prepared by the Department of Land Survey, Government of Nepal in 1965.

3   Our field survey of the stupa positions, conducted in March 2004, has shown the harmika orientation of the East, South, and West stupas close to 18 degrees that shows slight difference with the value given by Herdick that ranges between 18 and 20 degrees.

4   "Grand Conjunction" is a term used in astronomy for a phenomenon when other planets—Mercury, Venus, Mars, Jupiter, and Saturn—in the solar system appear to be aligned with each other when viewed from earth as seen on May 5, 2000.

Chapter 11

[1] In a locality known as Jhatapol, north of the palace, there is a stone image carved in rough relief which is said to be of Lalita Jyapu. The masonry wall onto which the image is carved supports a raised plinth where a roughly hewn shaft of rock is erected along with other shrines. The shaft is known as the pole of *Lalita-jyapu* and which transformed into a Sivalinga. At present the image is regularly offered worship by the Tandukar community residing in the neighbourhood. The human-like figure, which closely resembles the facial structure of the Jyapu of Patan, suggests that the image is a true monument to a historical and popular hero of the past, whose story is only connected by the legend where he is remembered as the planner of Patan (Chap. 2).

Appendix 1

[1] For the records of the two Lichhavi inscriptions of Thimi, see Vajracharya (1973, 392–7). A recently discovered inscription in Deupatan dated 484 mentions "Themring," which refers to Thimi according to Rajbamshi (1995). Themring has the suffix 'pring,' which stands for settlement. A news article in the *Nepal Samachar* reported it is thought to be of Kirata origin (May 13, 2000 [Vaisakha 27, 2057 VS]).

[2] The data used in this study are primarily derived from a field survey of Thimi and its surroundings. The survey was conducted between 1994 and 2002. In the first stage, a base map was prepared using an aerial photograph of Thimi prepared by the Nepal Department of Land Survey in 1978. The map was corrected and verified through fieldwork; thus, we were able to obtain details identifying the individual dwelling blocks plus public and ritual artifacts such as temples, wells, and other structures. A sociological survey of the clan and neighborhood structures was conducted through interviews with the residents. Data thus obtained were tabulated or plotted on the maps. The data most pertinent to the analysis of dimensions were collected by measuring the frontages of all the dwellings on both sides of the main north-south street, including the width of its lanes. This process of measurement has been useful for noting the correspondence of building cluster lines and offsets, which are within the quarter blocks defined by the lanes. The measured area was limited to the area between Balakumari Square in the south and Hattimahankal in the north, including the old core of the town in order to restrict the quantity of data for the first stage of the study. The 'old core' was identified by Thimi residents. Our own analysis of the settlement clusters of the town later confirmed this.

[3] It is not known to which Hindu circles or Buddhist pantheons the deities belong, but the shrine is worshipped by farmers with cattle on the festival of *Ganesa-chaturthi* (observed on the fourth day of the bright half of the month of Bhadra). According to the families who offer worship at this shrine, chulanchi-dyo is the representative of Vajrabarahi of Chapagaon, Lalitpur. If they wish, they may also go to the Vajrabarahi shrine in Lalitpur. The day to visit this shrine is on *Ganesa-chauthi* (see Note 13 below). Further, one of the resident clans of the town, the Chapali-chhen, living in the quarter in the quarter west of Layaku, carry the fire lit in this shrine back to their homes on the festival of Sri-panchami, the first day of spring. Layaku offers its annual worship to the shrine on the day of Gathemangal, sravan Krishna chaturdashi (middle of July). For further details, see Pant (2002; 2003).

4   Pisacha chaturdashi is a ritual observed following the lunar calendar in Caitra krishna chaturdashi. In 2003, it fell on March 31.

5   Ghasya puja, which literally means 'devotional offerings of grass cutters,' is a ritual observed by those who traditionally tended cattle. In this ritual, the old core of the town is divided into two groups representing the upper and the lower quarters, the dividing line of which runs at the lane south of Layaku.

6   The Bhasavamsavali notes that during Gunakamadev's organization of Kantipura (Kathmandu) in the tenth century, he invoked Pachali Bhairava in the south of the town as the main *kshetrapala* 'protector of the area' (Lamsal 1966, 23–4). Likewise, King Bhupatindra Malla of Bhaktapur (1696–1722) built a three-storey temple of Bhairava in Taumadhi Square for the protection of the country, as well as for the removal of sin and distress from the people (Wright 1972, 194).

7   A similar instance from the modern period is known where a palace was taken as the reference point for measuring distances between localities. During the regency of Bahadur Shah (1777–1799), measured markers were set at two-mile intervals (*kos*) in all directions from the capital, taking Hanuman dhoka, then the royal palace, as the pivotal point (Slusser 1982, 198).

8   In this connection, there is a belief in the Prajapati community of Gancha-nani (west of Deguli) that their ancestors lived in this quarter at the west of Layaku. Furthermore, they believe that an existing vacant lot which borders the main street in the Chapali-chhen quarter (A9) contained their community house (*chapala*) in earlier times. Further, according to another oral tradition, a community from Nagadesha, a town to the north of Thimi, in earlier times, is said to have settled occupying parts of the block A3.

9   This study examines the communities of ancestral worship (known as dewali communities) and the antiquity of Deguli, one of the ancestral shrines of Thimi.

10 See the Kurudhamma Jataka cited in Agrawala (1953). *Rajjugahaka* is translated as 'royal surveyor' in Davids and Stede (1998, 562).

11 Nakagawa and Tsuchiya (2000) find an average value of 48.5 cm used for one *hasta*, which the authors describe as the unit 'u' in their measurement of the buildings of Angkor Wat.

12 The paper identifies two types of neighborhoods—the central and peripheral. Central neighborhoods are those whose their territories span both sides of the main street while the peripheral neighborhoods occupy only the peripheral areas away from or adjacent to the main street.

13 One important clue to the relationship between Lavadol and the upper town is seen in the oral tradition and ritual tradition of the Chapali-chhen clan (A9). This clan was among the earliest settlers in Thimi, a fact known from their ancestral temple site in Deguli and their precedence in the ritual of ancestral worship (Pant and Funo 2001a). Their oral tradition states that their ancestors moved from Lavadol to their present quarter in the town. The annual ritual of bringing home fire lit in Chulacchi-dyo of Lavadol during the day of Sri-panchami also suggests such a relationship with Lavadol. Several other residents of the town also speak of a relationship similar to those of Chapali-chhen. In contrast, another oral tradition tells of the movement of the Prajapati community in the southwest quarter of Deguli Square and the movement of a Jyapu community living in Nagadesha from the vicinity of Layaku to their present place of settlement. The two oral traditions coupled with rituals that link the past and present localities of each community suggest a reorganization of the settlement structure in Thimi at a certain point in history.

Appendix 2

[1] Banerjee concluded that the site belonged to the Chalcolithic age after finding seals with legends inscribed in Indus script during his dig for Buddhist remains in 1922. The discovery followed that of Harappa in 1921 by (Lal and Gupta, 1984, x).

[2] The work, published in three separate volumes, contains articles by researchers who led the excavation works in different areas of the city. The first volume gives a general introduction to the site and a description of the architecture, religion, figurines, and potteries in each area. The second volume is on coins, weights and measures, and the Indus script. Drawings of individual buildings, excavated sites, and photographs are presented in the third volume.

[3] MacKay, one of the excavators of Mohenjodaro writes the following on the town planning of Mohenjodaro:

> That the people of the Indus Valley civilization had some idea of town-planning is shown by the regularity with which the city of Mohenjo-daro is divided up, a regularity which is striking for an ancient city of the east, or for that matter, would be in a western city to-day. We find streets, both wide and narrow, on the whole successfully aligned, instead of winding in the way that was usual in most early cities. Indeed, from the very systematic way in which the city is laid out we must conclude that it was methodically planned and not just built haphazard.
>
> All the main streets, so far excavated, are oriented to the points of compass, and what little deviation there is so slight that this orientation is very conspicuous. Houses and public buildings correspond in their orientation with the streets...
>
> One of the two procedures must clearly have been followed: either the city must have been built on a definite scheme from the commencement of its history, which followed perhaps on a compulsory move from another site; or the arrangement of the city was the deliberate reconstruction on town planning lines by order of the city fathers or a higher authority.... In town-planning the peoples of the Indus Valley appear to have been superior to the early Sumerians ... (1931, 282–3).

[4] The strata of Sirkap are classified into six levels—I to VI from top to bottom. Marshall assigns the lowest two levels to the Bactrean Period, IV and III to Saka, and II and I to Saka Partheans and Kushana respectively.

[5] Kalibangan is located at about 1600 km southeast of Harappa. The excavation has revealed the settlement which is made up of two fortified areas. The upper area is thought to be a ritual center while the lower one is the main settlement area. The town is divided into sectors and blocks by north-south streets that are parallel and laid at regular intervals, while the east-west streets are not always throughways like the north-south streets. For Lothal, see Rao (1979). More recent excavations have brought into light yet another planned settlement—Rakhigarhi in Haryana. Based on the thick layers of Hakra Ware at Rakhi Garhi, the site may date back to about 2500 BCE to 3000 BCE.

[6] Mainakar studied the relationship of the scale found in Mahenjodaro and Lothal with respect to the size of bricks as well as with the plan of the Great Bath of Mohenjodaro and the Dock of Lothal. Vij makes a comparative analysis of weights and the dimensions of the Great Bath with respect to its implication of the knowledge of pi and astronomical instruments.

[7] Marshall first published *A Guide to Taxila* in 1918. The guide has had subsequent editions with its fourth edition published in 1960. It is probably due to the hypothesis on the catastrophic demise of the Indus civilization, or the wholesale destruction of the Indus people by the "invading Aryans" (Wheeler 1960) or other nomads from the north (Marshall, 1931 vol. 1) that any search on the relationship of Sirkap to Indus culture was foreclosed.

However, it is difficult to understand why Marshall, even when he was equipped with all the documents to speak on the planning features of Mohenjodaro and Sirkap by 1960, still preferred to remain silent on Indus tradition when writing on the town of Taxila.

8 The excavation in Sarai Khola, 2.5 km from Taxila, showed early Harappan or Kot diji type pottery (Halim 1972). On the finding of Indus cultural artifacts near Sirkap see Allchin (1980).

9 Baburam Acharya suggests that following the eastward thrust of Aryans, a segment of the local population moved northward or southwards towards the region of the Vindhychal range. The tribes were called *agneyadeshi* by the Aryans. The Kirata, who lived in the north were one such tribe. The Kumhal, potters of Newar communities, entered the hill regions of Nepal through the valleys formed by the Gandaki, Bagmati, and Kamala rivers. The Kumhal belong to the Kirata tribe and when they entered Nepal, which he suggests to be around eighth century BCE, they were familiar with the Aryan culture. Thus, they helped the communication and trade of the "Nipar" of the Kathmandu Valley with the southern Gangetic region. According to Acharya, the Nipar are one of the various tribes of Kirata. They were the earliest settlers in the Himalayan foothills. See Acharya (1997, 9–14).

10 Sindhuli (*Sindhu* = Indus), a district to the east of the Kathmandu Valley, has a Sindhuligarhi 'fort' that lies at the main connecting route of the valley with the southern plain. The etymological link of Sindhuli may be traced to the root, sindhu, that we find in other places such as Sindhu-palchok, another district that borders the Kathmandu Valley. In the Tibetan language the suffix *pa* is a nominal attribute signifying the inhabitant of a place, such as *Shyarpa, Dug-pa, Lhots-pa,* etc. (Acharya 1997, 79).

11 See Chapter 11. "s" is a unit of measure equivalent to 100 *hasta* which was used in the planning of Patan.

12 Wanzke also shows four axes in the east-west direction in the figure but not the measurement. Wanzke's definition of 'access axes' is similar to ours. A note might be added on the terrain feature that in Figure A2-5, a large number of contours are apparent. However, other topographic maps with heights show that the three areas—HR, VS, and DK Areas—are in a relatively gentle terrain of 170 m (Wheeler 1960). Dumarcay considers that in terrains with differing levels, horizontal projections might have been considered in the planning of settlement.

13 The margin of error is within ±5% from the ideal value. The margin of error is calculated with respect to the modular unit, which in this case is one *danda* (1.92 m). When calculated against the total length, the error is much smaller.

14 Dumarcay (2005, 15) suggests cubits of 51.56–52.83 cm and a measure of 33.02–33.52 cm, the equivalent in feet, originally suggested by Wheeler (1960, 66) to have been used in planning the city. It was desirable that the validity of these units be demonstrated through a detailed measurement analysis accompanied by relevant drawings. The multiples of suggested length of cubits do not coincide with the *danda* and *rajju* proposed in our study either in terms of the binary or decimal system known to have been employed in the Indus culture. The measure suggested by Wheeler (the foot equivalent of 33.02 cm) may lead to a cubit of 49.53 cm, which is relatively close to the *hasta* we proposed. However, the accumulated difference becomes significant in larger multiples such as the *rajju* when employed in town planning or field measurements. As we have demonstrated in this study, the coincidence of the grid of *rajju* with the cluster blocks and the streets in the settlements of Mohenjodaro and other towns precludes the possibility of these cubit measures having been used in the town planning scale of Mohenjodaro.

15   Haryana Online n.d., http://www.haryana-online.com/rakhigarhi.htm.

16   Taxila was the capital of the Achemedian Empire from the sixth century to the later quarter of fourth century BCE before Alexander the Great invaded it in 325 BCE. Alexander's viceroys ruled only for three years in Taxila before they were driven away by the forces of Chandragupta in 323 BCE. The Mauryan Empire from Pataliputra ruled Taxila for about one and a quarter centuries when it was the seat of the Viceroy Prince Ashoka and later his son, Kunala. In 189 BCE, the Bactrean came to rule the Gandhara region with Taxila as their capital. Following them, the Saka (90 BCE-78 CE) and Kushana (78-320 CE) ruled Gandhara until the advent of the Gupta Empire. Archaeological remains and artifacts as well as literary records all show that Taxila was an important centre of Buddhism. In the fifth century BCE, Panini, the celebrated Sanskrit grammarian and Kautilya, the teacher of Chandragupta, lived and taught in Taxila.

17   Many authors, following Marshall, continued to echo his view. However, Wheeler, following a report by A. Ghosh on the excavation made in 1945, made the following reference to Marshal's 1931 report, which according to him, needed modification:

> At one or two points in the northern part of the walled city, Marshall dug down in small areas to the natural soil. He found 'remains belonging to six successive periods of habitation … represented by clearly defined foundations of rubble masonry, with layers of debris above and below them. Of these successive strata of buildings, the fifth and sixth from the top belong to the period of Greek rule at Taxila (c. 190–85 BC).… The fourth city belongs to the time of the early Saka kings, probably of Azes I, many of whose coins were found buried in small hoards beneath the house floors. *It was this same Saka King who was responsible for contracting the city's perimeter and substituting well built walls and bastions of solid stone in place of the older fortifications of mud, and was responsible also for the symmetrical lay-out of streets and lanes which continued to distinguish it to the end of its history* [italics added]. The third city from the top, which is less clearly defined than the others, is also referable to the period of Sakas. The second city dates from Parthian times in the first half of the first century AD, and is characterised by the use of diaper masonry along with the ordinary local rubble. It is to this city that most of the structures exposed in Sirkap belong… (Ghosh 1948, 83–4).

18   The mention of Nepal comes in the chapter titled "The Activity of The Head of the Departments."

Glossary

Legend

Sanskrit (S)	Pali (P)
Nepali (Np)	Japanese (J)
Newari (Nw)	Chinese (Cn)

Abhilekha (S)	archival records (Np)
agan (Nw)	unapproachable; esoteric; (S) agam
agan-chhen (Nw)	shrine of esoteric deity or ancestor
Amitabha (S)	one of the five celestial Buddhas ruling the west direction
añgula (S)	digit
Arthasastra (S)	economics; ancient classic on state administration and economics thought to be the work of Kautilya, the prime minister of Chandragupta (4th c BC)
Aswin (S)	*see* Vaisakha
baha-bahi (Nw)	particular type of Buddhist monastery structure that combines features of bahal and bahil architecture
bahal (Nw)	type of Buddhist monastery; also called baha
bahil (Nw)	particular type of Buddhist monastery of the Kathmandu Valley; also bahi
Balakumari (S)	popular virgin cult belonging to the group of eight mother goddesses
Batuka Bhairava (S)	the young terrible destroyer, one of the 64 forms of Bhairava, the wrathful aspect of Siva
Bauddha (S)	[person or artifact] of Buddhist faith
Bhadradivas (S):	palace known to have been built by the Licchavi period king, Narendradeva of seventh century CE
Bhairava (S)	fiery form of Siva
bhiksu (S)	monk; religious mendicant
Bodhisatva (S)	Buddha-to-be who delays his emancipation so as to liberate the common mass from this world of ignorance
brahmacharya bhiksu (S)	celibate monk

Caitra (S)	*see* Vaisakha
caitya (S)	Buddhist shrine with relics or precious objects placed inside it; usually with four celestial Buddhas presiding in four directions
chapat (Nw)	community house; also chapa
chaukwatha (Nw)	fort with watch towers at the four corners
chhen (Nw)	house
chok (Np)	courtyard
churia Hills	hill range that extends from the east to the west of Nepal at the north of the southern plain
daksinakoligrama (S)	southern town of Kathmandu as known in the Licchavi period
dalan (Nw)	space on the ground floor which opens towards the courtyard of the monastery for gathering and ritual performance
danda (S)	unit of measure which is 108 digits long or 4 dhanurgraha hasta
dathu tole (Nw)	the middle neighborhood
de-bahu	ritual of making offerings to the town for its protection from evil spirits
deguli (Nw)	the shrine of ancestral deity
desha	town (in medieval Newari usage), country or nation (in present Nepali usage)
devata (S)	deity
devapattan (S)	(lit: the city of gods)
dewali (Nw)	ancestral worship
dhanurgraha hasta (S)	hasta of 27 añgula
dhanurmuhsti (S)	cubit of 26 digits
dharmacakra (S)	the Wheel of Law, usually the symbol of the Buddhist religion
dharmadhatumandala (S)	the realm of essential truth (dharma 'truth', dhatu 'essence'); The mandala is often carved in a circular gilded copper or brass repousse or in a stone slab and raised upon a pedestal. In the mandala at the centre is one of the five Buddhas of the Vajrayana pentad; the other four are placed in the four directions. In all the monasteries of the Kathmandu Valley, this artifact is present.
dhoka (Np)	gateway; door
digi (Nw)	space for ritual gathering in a Buddhist monastery, or built around it
fuki (Nw)	patrilineal clan (in Newar community)
gajalaxmi (S)	goddess of fertility, rain, and wealth
gandhuri-dyo (Nw)	main deity of Buddhist monastery
Ganesa (S)	deity of the Saiva cult whose image bears an elephant head

ghasya-puja (S):	offerings of the grass-cutters
Gopalarajavamsavali	a fourteenth century Nepalese chronicle
Gopala (S)	cowherd (lit.); an ancient community living in west and north India, and Nepal
grama (S)	village
grama-panchali (S)	village committee known in Licchavi Nepal (5th–9th CE)
griha-mandala (S)	cluster of dwellings such as that which forms a nani
gunila (Nw)	Newari month that falls between July and August
guthi (Nw)	trust with endowment of land or cash, (S) gosthi
Guyhesvari	esoteric goddess
harmika (S)	square cube over the hemispherical dome of a stupa or caitya
hasta (S)	cubit
hiti (Nw)	fountain
jataka (S)	a genre of Buddhist literature that tells stories about the Buddha's previous life
jing-tian-zhi (cn)	well-field system of field planning thought to have prevailed in ancient China
johrisei (J)	pattern of division where the field is divided in regular grids of standard measurement units
Jyapu	one of the Newar communities in the Kathmandu Valley
kacha-bahal (Nw)	branch of the main monastery
Kailasakutabhavan (S)	name of a palace built by Amsuvarma (seventh century CE), a king in the Licchavi period
karsha (S)	measure of land
Kirata	ethnic community in Nepal
kothu (Nw)	lower
kwapadyo (Nw)	main deity enshrined in a Buddhist monastery
Naga	ancient community that lived in Southeast Asia and in the northern part of India to the south of the Himalayas
lachi (Nw)	courtyard; square
Lalitasatah	community house named after Lalita, the legendary planner of Patan
layaku (Nw)	palatial/administrative court of medieval times (S: rajakula)
Licchavi	ancient clan that ruled in Vaisali during the Age of Buddha; ancient ruling dynasty of Nepal
livi (Nw)	backyard; courtyard
Lokanatha (S)	Natha cult of Saiva (lit: lord of the world)
Machhendranatha (Np)	legendary yogi of Natha cult absorbed in Vajrayana Buddhism (Sanskrit: Matsyendranatha)
Mahabharat Range	mountain range south of Himalaya
Mahadeva (S)	epithet of Siva (lit: the great god)
mahamandala (S)	larger mandala
Mahankal (S)	Time — The Great Devourer, an epithet of Bhairava

mahapatra (S)	feudal noble
mahavihara (S)	grand monastery (in Buddhist usage)
Mahisapala (S)	buffalo-herder (lit), a community in prehistoric Nepal
Managriha (S)	royal court named after King Manadeva
Manasara	Hindu classical text of architecture and town planning of ancient period
mandala (S)	structure with a strong element at its centre; in art and architecture, often represented by a circle or a square or both in juxtaposition with the primary entity at the centre and other entities at the periphery
mani	central axis
manigvaladhipati	lord of Manigval; [adhipati (S)]
Manjupattan (S)	city named after Manjusri
Manjusri	legendary Bodhisatva said to be from China
Manjusri-sthan	place where Manjusri dwelt or dwells, a particular place in Bhaktapur
mataya (Nw)	light festival of the Newar in the Kathmandu Valley
Mayamata	Hindu classical text on architecture and town planning of the medieval period
Minanatha (S)	one of the teachers of the Natha cult of Saiva and Buddhist esoteric yoga
mu-baha (Nw)	*see* mulbahal
mulachhen (Nw)	the main house/courtyard
mulbahal (Np)	main monastery; also called as mu-baha (Nw)
mulchok (Np)	main courtyard
Nagadaha	naga 'serpent', daha 'lake'; the Lake of the Holy Serpent
nagara (S)	city; town
nani (Nw)	quarter of dwelling clusters usually belonging to members of a clan with one main entry leading to courtyards and dwellings around them
nasa-dyo (Nw)	god of music and dance
Nepala Mahatmya (S)	(lit: The Glory of Nepal); a purana
Newar	one of the communities in the Kathmandu Valley which constitute a major population in cities and towns
Nipa	ancient tribe thought to be related to Gopala
nivartana (S)	unit of measure of land equal to the area of a square having one side that is 3 rajju
nrityanatha (Nw)	*see* nasa-dyo
pada (S)	block in the division of a city
pama (Nw: colloq)	*see* pramana
paridesha (S)	unit of length equal to 1 rajju or unit of measure of land equal to the area of a square having one side that is 2 rajju long
Pashupatinath	Siva, the temple of Pashupatinath
Pataliputra	Mauryan capital; present day Patna of Bihar State, India

pati (Np)	rest house; *see also* phalacha
phalacha (Nw)	*see* pati and dalan
pisacha-chaturdasi (S)	fourteenth day of the dark half in the month of Caitra when the evil spirits are propitiated for the protection of the town
Prajapati (S)	a community of Newar; epithet of Brahma
prajapatya hasta (S)	cubit of 25 digits
pramana (Nw)	administrators of a city quarter or a town in the medieval period; (S: pradhana)
Prastara (S)	particular model of a city with two major streets crossing at right angles. It is oblong or square in shape and it has an internal circumambulating street
pura (S)	fort; city
purana (S)	genre of literature that extols the virtue of a certain cult and its sacred places
rajguru (S)	[religious] teacher of the royal court
rajju (S)	rope; a unit of measure 10 danda long according to the Arthasastra of Kautilya
rajjugahaka (P)	bearer of rajju, the measuring rope
ratha (S)	chariot
rathayatra (S)	chariot festival [of a deity] (lit: the journey of the chariot)
Rato Machhendranatha	The Red Machhendranatha (Sanskrit: Matsyendra), a Buddhist-Hindu deity with a main shrine in Patan
Saivism:	cult of Siva
Saivite	person belonging to the Saiva cult
Sakta (S)	cult based on feminine power
sana guthi (Nw)	*see* si-guthi
sarira-stupa	caitya with corporeal relics of Buddhist saints
sarvasangha (S)	grand association comprising individual monastery associations (sangha)
Sarvatobhadra (S)	all auspicious; a model of building or town plan
si-guthi (Nw)	community trust for funeral ceremonies
sikhara (S)	summit; style of temple architecture with an elongated paraboloid conical form crowned over the sanctum
Sikhi Buddha	Buddha of an earlier era in the lineage of twenty-four Buddhas that preceded Siddhartha Gautam
sishu hasta (S)	cubit of 24 digits
sivalinga (S)	phallus of Siva
SriLaxmi (S)	goddess of prosperity and wealth
sri-panchami (S)	festival that falls at the beginning of spring
sthana (S)	place or locality
suvarna (S)	gold[en]
swastika (S)	sign of auspiciousness; one of the signs of Buddha; a model of building or town plan

Swayambhu (S)	Self-born
Swayambhu Stupa (caitya)	a Buddhist holy site in Kathmandu
Sweta-Bhairava (S)	One of the 64 forms of Bhairava (lit: the white Bhairava)
tole	neighborhood
Taleju (Nw)	ancestral deity of Malla kings of medieval Nepal
thatu (Nw)	upper [town]
tole-devata	deity of the neighborhood, most often the shrine of Ganesa
tretayuga (S)	*see* yuga
Uma-maheswora (S)	popular iconic image of Siva and his consort, Uma, sitting together with their family
Vaisakha (S)	month falling between mid-April and mid-May. The year begins with Vaisakha. The 12 months are Vaishakha, Jestha, Asadh, Srawan, Bhadra, Aswin, Kartik, Mansir, Paus, Magh, Falgun, and Caitra.
Vaishali	a republic in North India during the Age of Buddha; a Buddhist religious centre
Vaisnavi (S)	one of the mother goddesses in the cult of Eight Mother Goddesses – the astamatrika, the consort of Visnu
Vajracharya	those who have mastered the Vajrayana
Vajrayana (S)	one of the later schools in Buddhism that followed Theravada and Mahayana
vamanagar	city of/to the left of [the Bagamati River]
Vamsabali	chronicle that gives an account of past events (lit: genealogical account [of dynasties]
varna (S)	class divisions in Hindu social divisions; alternately, ethnic communities
vastusastra (S)	canons of architecture and town planning
Vajrajogini	goddess of the Vajrayana cult, also Vajrayogini (S)
viharas (S)	Buddhist monastery
Viswabhu	earlier Buddha
vitasti (S)	span; half a cubit
vrisha (S)	bull; virtuous
vrisha-varga (S)	a particular type of courtyard building which is square in shape
wanjala (Nw)	shrine of the Manandhar clan community corresponding to aga-chhen
Yalan (Nw)	popular name for Patan said to be from its first Kirata king, Yalambara
yata-chhe (Nw)	house at the south
yuga (S)	eon; age (There are four ages in the cyclic division of time: satya, dvapar, treta, and kali, sometimes glossed in English as Golden Age, Copper Age, Bronze Age, and Iron Age.)

Bibliography

Acharya, B. 1966 (2023 VS). *Nepalko sabbhanda purano sabhya vastiko sthapana ra bhinna bhinna samayaka namavali* [The establishment, development, and diverse names of the oldest civilized settlements of Nepal]. *Ramjham* 2: 10–21.

———. 1997 (2054 VS). *Nepalko sanskritik parampara*, Kathmandu: Kasthmandap Printing Press.

———. 2001 (2058 VS). *Ashoka ra nepala* [Ashoka and Nepal]. In C. Nepali, et al., eds. *Nepalko itihasaka vividh paksya* [Different facets of Nepalese history], p. 23–30. Kathmandu: Nepal Rajakiya Pragya Pratisthan [Royal Nepal Academy].

Acharya, J. R. 1992. The Nepala-Mahatmya of the Skandapurana: legends on the sacred places and deities of Nepal. Introduction and translation by Jayaraj Acharya. Jaipur: Nirala Publications.

Acharya, P. K. 1934. *Indian architecture according to Manasara-Silpasastra*, 2nd ed. Manasara Series, vol. 2. New Delhi: Oriental Books Reprint Corporation.

———. 1979a. *An encyclopaedia of Hindu architecture.* 2nd ed. New Delhi: Oriental Books Reprint Corporation.

———. 1979b. *Hindu architecture in India and abroad.* 2nd ed. Manasara series, vol. 6. New Delhi: Oriental Books Reprint Corporation. (Orig. pub. 1946 London: Oxford University Press.)

———, ed. 1980. *Architecture of Manasara/translated from original Sanskrit.* Manasara Series, vol. 4. New Delhi: Oriental Books Reprint Corporation.

Agrawala, V. S. 1953. *India as known to Panini: A study of the cultural material in the Ashtadyayi.* Lucknow: University of Lucknow.

Allchin, F. R. 1980. A note on the Asokan stupas of Patan. In *The stupa: Its religions and historical and architectural significance*, ed. A. Dallapiccola in collaboration with S. Zingel-Ave Lallemant, 147–56. Stuttgart: Franz Steiner Verlag Weisbaden.

———. 1982. How old is the city of Taxila? *Antiquity,* 56: 8–14.

Amatya, N. M. 1992. A Study on structure and formation of town in Patan. Master's thesis, Kyoto Univer.

Amatya, S. 1993 (2053 VS). *Kathmadaun nagarayana.* Kathmandu: Nepal Rajakiya Pragya Pratisthana (Royal Nepal Academy).

Anderson, M. 1971. *Festivals of Nepal.* London: Allen and Unwin.

Auer, G. and N. Gutschow. 1997. Domestic architecture of Nepal. *Art and Archaeology Research Papers* 12 (December): 64–9.

Bangadel, L. S. 1982 (2039 VS). *Prachin nepali murtikalako itihasa.* Kathmandu: Royal Nepal Academy.

Banerjee, N. R. 1980. *Nepalese architecture*. Delhi: Agam.

Barani, M. 1994. The residential unit: Symbolic organization. In *Kirtipur: An urban community in Nepal*, eds. M. Shokoohy and N. H. Shokoohy, 63–74. Monographs on Art, Archaeology, and Architecture, South Asian Series. London: Araxus Books.

Barre, V. et al. 1981. *Panauti, une ville au Nepal*. Collections Architectures. Paris: Berger Leverault.

Becker-Ritterspach, R. O. A. 1987. *Water conduits in the Kathmandu Valley*. New Delhi: Munshiram Manoharlal.

Begde, P. V. 1978. *Ancient and medieval town planning*. New Delhi: Sagar Publications.

Bendall, C. 1903. The history of Nepal and surrounding kingdoms (AD 1000–1600), pt. 1. *Journal of Asiatic Society of Bengal*, n.s., 72: 1–32.

Bernier, R. M. 1977. Wooden windows of Nepal: An illustrated analysis. *Artibus Asiae*, 39 (3–4): 89–108.

Bhandari, D. 1989 (2046 VS). *Nepalko udbhav tatha vikasko vislesanatmak itihas* [An analytical history on the formation and development of Nepalese nation]. Kathmandu: Prakash Prakashan.

Bhattacharya, B. 1927. Origin and Development of *Vajrayana, Indian Historical Quarterly*, 3: 733–46.

———. 1968. *The Indian Buddhist iconography*. Calcutta: K. L. Mukhopadhyaya.

Bisht, R. S. 2000. Urban planning at Dholvir: A Harappan city. In *Ancient cities and sacred skies*, eds. J. M. Malvillle and L. M. Gujral, 1–10, New Delhi: Indira Gandhi National Centre for the Arts.

Bista, S. D. 1982 (2039 VS). *Nepal gadh* [Forts of Nepal]. Kathmandu: Sajha Prakashan.

Blake, S. P. 1991. *Shahajahanbad: The sovereign city in Mughal India, 1639–1739*. Cambridge: Cambridge University Press.

Brinkhaus, H. 1987. *The Pradyumna-Pravabati legend in Nepal: A study of the Hindu myth of the draining of the Nepal Valley*. Stuttgart: F. Steiner Verlag Wiesbaden.

Burgess, E. et al. 1925. *The city*. Chicago: University of Chicago Press.

Carter, H. 1972. *The study of urban geography*. London: Edward Arnold.

Childers, R. C. 1909. *A Dictionary of Pali language*. London: Kegan Paul.

Cimino, R. M. 1986. Simarongarh: The forgotten city and its arts. *Contributions to Nepalese Studies*, 13 (39): 277–88.

———. 1990. The Labyrinth of Simaraungarh. In South Asian archaeology 1987: proceedings of the Ninth International Conference of the Association of South Asian Archaeologists in Western Europe, vol. 2, ed. M. Taddei with the assistance of P. Callieri, 1151–63. Rome: Istituto Italiano per il Medio Ed Estremo Oriente.

———. 1995. A short note on a new Nepalese labyrinth. *East and West*, 45 (1–4): 381–5.

Clark, T. W. 1957. The Ranipokhari inscription, Kathmandu. *Bulletin of the School of Oriental and African Studies*, 20: 167–87.

Coburn, T. B. 1982. *Devi-mahatmya: The crystallization of the goddess tradition*. Delhi: Motilal Banarasi Das.

Conzen, M. R. G. 1962. The plan analysis of English City Centre. In *Proceedings of the I. G. U. symposium in urban geography, 1960*, ed. K. Norborg, 383. London: Edward Arnold.

———. 1968. The Use of Town Plan in the Study of Urban History. In *The study of urban history*, ed. H. G. Dyos, 113–30. London: Edward Arnold.

———. 1988. Morphogenesis, morphological regions and secular human agency in the historical townscape as exemplified by Ludlow. In *Urban historical geography*, eds. D. Denecke and D. A. Shaw, 253–72. Cambridge: Cambridge University Press.

Coulanges, N. D. F. D. 1980. The ancient city: a study on the religion, laws, and institutions of Greece and Rome; with a new foreword by A. Momigliano and S.C. Humphreys. Baltimore: John Hopkins University Press.

Dagens, B., trans. 1985. *Mayamata.* New Delhi: Sitaram Bharatiya Institute of Scientific Research.

Dallapiccola, A. 1980. *The stupa: Its religious, historical and architectural significance.* In collaboration with S. Zingel-Ave Lallemant. Stuttgart: Franz Steiner Verlag Weisbaden.

Dani A. H. 1999. *The historic city of Taxila.* Lahore: Sang-e-Meel.

Deng Yi et al. 2002. A study on the block formation and its subdivision into the housing lots in the inner city of Beijing: An analysis of Qianlong Jingcheng Quantu, map of the capital city of Qianlong Period (1750). *Journal of Architecture and Building Engineering* (November): 209–17.

Dennecke, D., and D. A. Shaw, eds. 1988. *Urban historical geography.* Cambridge: Cambridge University Press.

Deo, S. B. 1968–69. Glimpses of Nepal woodwork. *The Journal Of Indian Society of Oriental Art* 3 (5): 1–67.

Dohorty, V. S. 1978. Notes on the origin of the Newars of Kathmandu Valley. In *Himalayan anthropology,* ed. F. Fisher, 433–45. The Hague: Mouton.

Dumarcay, J. 2005. *Construction techniques in south and southeast Asia: A history.* Trans. B. Silverstone. Raphaelle: Dedourge.

Duncan, J. S. 1990. *City as text: The politics of landscape interpretation in the Kandyan Kingdom.* Cambridge and New York: Cambridge University Press.

Dutta, S. 1995. *Land system in ancient India (400 AD–700 AD).* New Delhi: Munshiram Manoharlal.

Dyos, H. J., ed. 1968. *The study of urban history.* London: Edward Arnold.

Eliade, M. 1954. *Myth of the eternal return.* New York: Pantheon Books.

——1959. *The sacred and the profane: The nature of religion.* Trans. W. R. Trask. New York: Harcourt Brace & World.

Finley, M. I. 1977. The ancient city: From Fustel de Coulanges to Max Weber and beyond. *Comparative Study in Society and History* 19 (3): 305–27.

Finsterwalder, R. 1980. *Patan City Map, 1: 7500.* Munich: Arbeitsgemeinschaft fur vergleichende Hochgebirgs-forschung.

Finsterwalder, R. 1989. *Kathmandu Valley, 1: 50,000.* Munich: Arbeitsgemeinschaft fur vergleichende Hochgebirgs-forschung.

Fleming, A. 1987. Coaxial field systems: Some questions of time and space. *Antiquity* 61: 188–202.

Friedman, D. 1988. *Florentine new towns: Urban design in the late medieval ages.* Cambridge: MIT Press.

Funo, S. et al. 1997a. Street pattern and block system of Cakranegara City, Lombok, Indonesia: Spatial structure of Cakranegara, pt. 1. *Journal of Architectural Planning and Environmental Engineering,* no. 491 (January): 135–39.

——. 1997b. Street pattern and block system of Jaipur City, Rajasthan, India—an analysis on city maps (1925–28) made by Survey of India, pt. 1. *Journal of Architectural Planning and Environmental Engineering,* no. 499 (September): 113–99.

——. 1998a. Ritual facilities and community organization of Cakranegara City, Lombok, Indonesia: Spatial structure of Cakranegara, pt.2. *Journal of Architectural Planning and Environmental Engineering,* no. 503 (January): 151–6.

————. 1998b. Building types and block pattern of Jaipur City, Rajasthan, India: An analysis on city maps (1925–28) made by Survey of India, pt .2. *Journal of Architectural Planning and Environmental Engineering*, no. 508, (February): 121–7.

————. 1998c. Characteristics of habitat segregation in Cakranegara City, Lombok, Indonesia: Spatial structure of Cakranegara, pt. 3. *Journal of Architectural Planning and Environmental Engineering*, no. 510 (August): 185–90.

————. 2001. Consideration on transformation of street blocks in Jaipur City, Rajastan India: An analysis on city maps (1925–28) made by Survey of India, pt. 3. *Journal of Architectural Planning and Environmental Engineering*, no. 539 (January): 119–26.

————. 2002a. Space formation of Jaipur City, Rajasthan, India: An analysis of city maps (1925–28) made by Survey of India. *Journal of Asian Architecture and Building Engineering* (March): 261–9.

————. 2002b. The spatial formation in Cakranegara, Lombok. In *Indonesian town revisited*, ed. P. J. M. Nas, 201–29. Muenster/Berlin: LitVerlag.

————. 2006. *Mantolo toshi: Hindou toshi no kukan rinenn to so no henyou* [The City as mandala: Spatial formation and transformation of Hindu cities]. Kyoto: Daigaku Gakujutsu shuppankai [Kyoto University Press].

Gellner, N. 1992. *Monk, householder and tantric priest.* Cambridge: Cambridge University Press.

Gellner, N., and D. Quigley, eds. 1999. *Contested Hierarchies: A collaborative ethnography of caste among the Newars of the Kathmandu Valley, Nepal.* Delhi: Oxford University Press.

Ghosh, A. 1948. Taxila (Sirkap), 1944–5. *Ancient India*, no. 4: 41–84.

Giuseppe, F. 1807. *Account of the Kingdom of Nepal, 1768–71. Asiatick researches*, vol. 2, 3 07–322. Repr., Delhi: pub. unknown, 1970.

Gorse, G. 1988. A family enclave in medieval Genoa. *Journal of Architectural Education* 41(3): 20–4.

Gosling, E. M. B. 1983. The History of Sukhothai as a Ceremonial Centre: A Study of Early Siamese Architecture and Society. Phd diss., University of Michigan.

Goswami, B. N. 1980. Introductory speech: Some uninformed questions about terminological equivalents. In *The stupa: Its religions and historical significance*, ed. A. Dallapiccola in collaboration with S. Zingel-Ave Lallemant, 1–11. Stuttgart: Franz Steiner Verlag Weisbaden.

Guo, Ching Hua. 2000. Shenyang: the Manchurian ideal capital city and imperial palace, 1625–43. *Urban History*, 27 (3): 345–59.

Grunendahl, R., and H. P. Sastri. 1989. *A concordance of H. P. Sastri's Catalogue of the Durbar Library and the microfilms of the Nepal German Manuscript Preservation Project. A catalogue of palm-leaf and selected paper MSS. belonging to the Durbar Library Nepal.* Vols. 1 and 2. Stuttgart: Steiner Verlag, Wiesbaden.

Gutschow, N. 1976. The Pujahari Math: A survey of Newar building techniques and restoration methods in the valley of Kathmandu. *East and West* 26: 191–204.

————. 1980. The urban context of the stupa in Bhaktapur/Nepal. In *The stupa: Its religious, historical and architectural significance*, ed. A. Dallapiccola in collaboration with S. Zingel-Ave Lallemant, 137–46. Weisbaden: Franz Steiner Verlag.

————. 1981a. Kathmandu: Historical development, spatial structure, social and ritual topography. *Khumbu Himal* 13 (3): 247–57.

————. 1981b. Patan: Historical development, spatial structure, and ritual topography. *Khumbu Himal* 13 (4): 262–72.

————. 1985a. Courtyard buildings of Nepal: The palaces, temples and monasteries. In *Vijayanagara–city and empire: New currents of research*, ed. A. Dallapiccola in collaboration with S. Zingel-Ave Lallemant, 362–79. Wiesbaden: Steiner.

______. 1985b. Gorkha: The architectural documentation of two palaces from the 18th and 19th century. *Journal of the Nepal Research Centre* 7: 3–24.

______. 1993. Bhaktapur: Sacred patterns of a living urban tradition. In *Urban form and meaning in south Asia: The shaping of cities from prehistoric to precolonial times*, eds. H. Spodek and D. M. Srinivasan, 163–83. Hannover and London: University Press of New England.

Gutschow, N., and B. Kolver. 1975. *Ordered space concepts and functions in a town of Nepal.* Weisbaden: Steinerverlag.

Gutschow, N., and M. Vajracharya. 1977. Ritual as mediator of space in Kathmandu. *Journal of Nepal Research Society*, I (Humanities): 1–10.

Gutschow, N., and H. Sakya. 1980. The monasteries (Baha and Bahi) of Patan: A contribution towards the cultural topography of a Newar town. *Journal of Nepal Research Centre* 4: 161– 74.

Gustchow, N., and A. Michaels, eds. 1987. *Heritage of Kathmandu Valley.* Proceedings of an International Conference in Lubeck, June 1985. Sankt Augustin: VGH Wissenschaftsverlag.

Gutschow, N., N. B. Kolver, and I. Shresthacharya. 1987. *Newar towns and buildings: An illustrated dictionary, Newari-English.* Nepalica 3. Sankt Augustin: VGH Wissenschaftsverlag.

Gutschow, N., and V. Basukala. 1997. *The Nepalese caitya.* Lumbini International Research Institute Monograph Series, 1, Stuttgart and London: Axel, Menges.

Hagmuller, G., ed. 2003. *Patan Museum: The transformation of a royal palace.* London: Serindia Publications

Halim, M. A. 1972a. Excavations at Sarai Khola, pt. 1. *Pakistan Archaeology* 7: 23–89.

______. 1972b. Excavations at Sarai Khola, pt. 2. *Pakistan Archaeology* 8: 1–112.

Hasrat, R. J. 1970. *History of Nepal, as told by its own people and contemporary chroniclers.* Hoshiarpur, Punjab: V. V. Research Institute, Book Agency.

Harutaka, S. et al. 2000. Climatic changes and tectonic events recorded in the paleo-Kathmandu lake sediments. *Chigaku Zashi* 109 (5): 759–69.

Hatano, J. 1986. Historical changes in the plan of Buddhist monasteries and royal palaces in Nepal. In *The royal buildings and Buddhist monasteries of Nepal*, 81–7. Saitama-ken: Nippon Institute of Technology Research Mission.

______. 1998. A history of Buddhist monasteries, Part 1, Chap. 3. In K. Watanabi, ed., *Buddhist Monasteries of Nepal*, pt. 3, 11–13. Tokyo: Chuo Koron Bijitsu Shuppan.

Herdick, R. 1985. Urban residential quarters of the Newar in Nepal: A symbolic and spatial-social unit. In *Vijayanagara—city and empire: New currents of research*, ed. A. Dallapiccola in collaboration with S. Zingel-Ave Lallemant, 380–98. Wiesbaden: Steiner.

______. 1993. Remarks on the orientation of the large stupas of the Kathmandu Valley: A discussion on principles of lunar calendaring. In *Anthropology of Tibet and Himalayas*, eds. C. Ramble and M. Brauen. 101–23. Zurich: Museum of Anthropology.

His Majesty's Government of Nepal. 1969. *The Kathmandu Valley Plan.* Kathmandu: Department of Housing and Physical Planning.

Hoek, B. van den. 1993. Kathmandu as a sacrificial arena. In *Urban symbolism*, ed. P. J. N. Nas, 360–77. Leiden, New York, and Koln: E. J. Brill.

Howard, N. 1995. An introduction to the fortification of Central Nepal. *European Bulletin of Himalayan Research*, no. 9: 28.

Huntington, S. 1985. *Art of ancient India: Buddhist, Hindu, Jain.* Tokyo: Weatherhill.

Irwin, J. 1980. The axial symbolism of the early stupa: An exegesis. In *The stupa: Its religious, historical and architectural significance*, ed. A. Dallapiccola in collaboration with S. Zingel-Ave Lallemant, 12–38. Weisbaden: Franz Steiner Verlag.

Isavorapant, C., and T. Nakagawa. 2004. A study on architectural documents of viharn (Buddha hall) in Lanna, Northern Thailand: Studies on traditional architectural manuals in Thailand. *Journal of Architectural Planning and Environmental Engineering,* no. 577 (March): 189–93.

Ishii, H. 1980. Structure and change of a Newari festival organization. In *Himalayan anthropology,* ed. J. Fisher, 505–27, Hague/Paris: Muton.

———. 1999. Caste and kinship in a Newar village. In *Contested hierarchies: A collaborative ethnography of caste among the Newars of the Kathmandu Valley, Nepal.* N. Gellner and D. Quigley, eds., 109–57. Delhi: Oxford University Press.

Jansen, M. 1984. Architectural remains in Mohenjodaro. In *Frontiers of Indus civilization,* eds. B. B. Lal and S. B. Gupta, 55–86. New Delhi: Indian Archaeological Society.

Joshi, G. and V. Basukala. 1992. *Restoration of Vabaha.* Kathmandu: Gutschow, Hagmuller & Associates.

Joshi, H. R. 1973 (2030 VS). *Nepalko prachin abhilekh* [Inscriptions of ancient Nepal]. Kathmandu: Royal Nepal Academy.

———. 1992. The contribution of Nipa tribe in the origin of Nepal. *Rolamba* 12 (3): 3–6.

———. 1996. Tols. *Rolamba* 16 (1): 1–3.

———. 1998. *Forgotten pasts of Nepal.* Lalitpur: Joshi Research Institute.

Kane, P. V. 1973. *History of Dharmasastra: Ancient and mediaeval, religious and civil law,* vol. 3, 2nd ed. Poona: Bhandarkar Oriental Research Institute.

Kangle, R. P. 1972. *The Kautilya Arthasastra.* Repr., Delhi: Bombay University, 1992.

Khandalwal, K. 1950. A note on two Nepalese wood sculptures. *Marg* 4 (1): 50–2.

Kharel, G. 1997. Chhusya bahal (viharas) ko kala vastukala: ek adhyayan [A study on the art and architecture of Chhusya bahal], *Contributions to Nepalese Studies* 24 (1): 87–112.

Kirkpatrick, F. 1969. *An account of the Kingdom of Nepaul, being the substance of observations made during the mission to that country in the year 1793.* In *Bibliotheca Himalayica,* vol. 3, series 1. Repr., New Delhi: Manjusri Publishing House. (Orig. pub. 1811, 1st ed.).

Koirala, K. 1985. *Indrajatra.* Kathmandu: Guthi Sansthan.

Kolver, B. 1976. A ritual map from Nepal. In *Folia Rara: Festchrift,* 68–80. Weisbaden: W. Vogt.

Kolver, B., and H. Sakya. 1985. *Documents from the Rudravarna-Mahavihara, Patan, 1. Sales and Mortgages.* Nepalica 1. Sankt Augustin: VGH Wissennschaftsverlag.

Korn, W. 1979. *The traditional architecture of the Kathmandu Valley.* Kathmandu: Ratna Pustak Bhandar.

Kosambhi, D. D. 1960. At the crossroads: Mother goddess cult-sites in ancient India, pt. 1. *Journal of Royal Asiatic Society* (April): 17–34.

———. 1960. At the crossroads: Mother goddess cult-sites in ancient India, pt. 2. *Journal of Royal Asiatic Society* (October): 135–44.

Kramarisch, S. 1976. *The Hindu temple.* New Delhi: Motilal Banarasidass.

Kulke, H. 1980. Legitimation and town planning in the feudatory states of Central Orissa. In *Ritual space in India: Studies in architectural anthropology,* ed. J. Pieper, 30–40. Art and Archaeology Research Papers 17. London: AARP.

Kurokawa, K. 1997. *Neparu syujuchi kukan kosei genri ni kan suru kenkyu.* Master's Th., Department of Architecture, Kyoto Univ.

Kurokawa, K. et al. 1998. Space formation of Hadigaon, Kathmandu, Nepal: Distribution of holy places and ceremonies. *Journal of Architectural Planning and Environmental Engineering,* no. 514: 155–62.

Kunwar, R. B. et al., eds. 2002 (2058 VS). Index of ancient Nepal. *Ancient Nepal* 149: 7–53.

Kurotsu, T. 1991a. Grid of floor planning for Chok: Quadrangular architecture of the royal buildings of Nepal, pt. 3. *Journal of Architectural Planning and Environmental Engineering*, no. 426: 149–56.

______. 1991b. *The study on quadrangle architecture of the old royal buildings of Nepal.* Special issue, Reports of Researches, nos. 91–02. Saitama: Nippon Institute of Technology.

______. 1993. God image and space design of Sundara Chok: Quadrangular architecture of the royal buildings of Nepal, pt. 5. *Journal of Architectural Planning and Environmental Engineering*, no. 447: 129–34.

______. 1998a. Design dimensions: Vertical section, chap 3. In *Buddhist monasteries of Nepal*, ed. K. Watanabe, pt. 3, 103–8. Tokyo: Chuo Koron Bijitsu Shuppan.

______. 1998b. Results of the survey of the structural remains undertaken in the course of the restoration work, chap 6. In *Buddhist monasteries of Nepal*, pt. 2, ed. K. Watanabe, 44–75. Tokyo: Chuo Koron Bijitsu Shuppan.

______. 1998c. A discussion of repairs and remodeling carried out on I baha bahi 1661–1995 and some plans of execution on conservation work in general, chap 7. In *Buddhist monasteries of Nepal*, ed. K. Watanabe, pt. 2, 76–89. Tokyo: Chuo Koron Bijitsu Shuppan.

Kurotsu, T., and K. Watanabe. 1990. Structures of Chok: Quadrangle architecture of royal buildings of Nepal. *Journal of Architectural Planning and Environmental Engineering*, no. 408: 101–9.

Lafrenz, J. 1988. The metrological analysis of early modern planned towns. In *Urban historical geography*, eds. D. Deneck and D. A. Shaw, 273–84. Cambridge: Cambridge University Press.

Lal, B. B., and S. B. Gupta, eds. 1984. *Frontiers of Indus civilization.* New Delhi: Indian Archaeological Society.

Lamsal, D., ed. 1966 (2023 VS). *Bhasavamshabali*, pt. 2. Kathmandu: Nepal Rastriya Pustakalaya.

Levi, R. I., and K. P. Upadhyaya. 1992. *Mesocosm: Hinduism and organization of a traditional Newar city in Nepal.* Berkley: University of California Press.

Levi, S. 1905. *Le Nepal: etude historique d'un royaume hindou*, 3 vols. Paris: Leroux. Translated in 2006 into Nepali by D. Upreti as *Nepal—hindu adhirajya ko itihasa (1)*. Lalitpur: Himal Association.

Locke, J. K. 1980. *Karunamaya: The cult of Avalokitesvara-Matsyendranatha in the Valley of Nepal.* Kathmandu: Sahayogi Prakashan.

______. 1985. *Buddhist monasteries of Nepal.* Kathmandu: Sahayogi Prakashan.

Mainaker, V. B. 1984. Metrology in Indus civilization. In *Frontiers of Indus civilization*, eds. B. B. Lal and S. B. Gupta, 141–51. New Delhi: Indian Archaeological Society.

Mackay, E. J. H. 1931. Architecture and masonry. In *Mohenjodaro and Indus civilization*, vol. 1, ed. J. Marshall,. London: Arthur Probsthein.

Malla, K. P. 1981. Linguistic archaeology of Nepal Valley: A preliminary report. *Kailash* 7 (1–2): 5–23.

Malvillle, J. M., and L. M. Gujral. 2000. *Ancient cities, sacred skies.* New Delhi: Indira Gandhi National Centre for The Arts.

Manandhar, T. 1986. Newari-English dictionary, ed., A. Vergati. Delhi: Agam Kala Prakashan.

Marshall, J. 1931. *Mohenjodaro and Indus civilization*, 3 vols. London: Arthur Probsthein.

______, ed. 1951. *Taxila*, 3 vols. London: Cambridge University Press.

______. 1960. *A Guide To Taxila*, 4th ed. Cambridge: Cambridge University Press.

Muller, U. 1981. *Thimi: Social and economic studies on a Newar settlement in the Kathmandu Valley.* Liebig-Universitat Giessen: Selbstverlag des Geographischen Instituts der Justus.

Munankarmi, L. 1989 (2046 VS). Tantrik devi-devatama matrikagana [The mother goddesses in Tantrik Pantheon], *Nepali Sanskriti* 5 (3): 8–19.

Nakagawa, T., and T. Tsuchiya. 2000. Planning method of Angkor Wat. In *Challenges and Roles of Asian Architecture for the Millennium, Proceedings, Third International Symposium on Architectural Interchanges in Asia.* Third International Symposium on Architectural Interchange in Asia, February 23–25, 2000, 175–85. Cheju: Cheju National University.

Naraharinath, Y. n.d. Itihasaprakasa, vol. 2/1.

Nepal, G. 1998 (2044 VS). Nepal nirupan [Nepal: An exegesis], *Prachin Nepal* 103: 1–14.

———. 1983 (2040 VS). *Nepal nirukta* [Nepal: An etymological study]. Kathmandu: Royal Nepal Academy.

Nepal, G. 2005 (2062 VS). *Nepalko madhyamik kalako itihasa* [Medieval History of Nepal]. Kathmandu: Makalu Books and Stationers.

Nepal Heritage Society. 1993. *Kathmandu upatyaka—bhautik vatavaran tatha sanskritic sampada samrakshyanatmak suchi*, A1-A3, Aa1-Aa4 (2050–2052 VS). Trans. by Uttam Jha of *Kathmandu Valley: The Preservation of Physical Environment and Cultural Heritage, A Protective Inventory*, 2 vols. UNESCO, 1975.

Nepali, C. et al., eds. 2001 (2058 VS). *Nepalko itihasaka vividh paksya* [Different facets of Nepalese history]. Kathmandu: Nepal Rajakiya Pragya Pratisthan [Royal Nepal Academy].

Nepali, G. S. 1965. *The Newars: An Ethno-Sociological Study of a Himalayan Community*. Bombay: United Asia Publications. Repr., Kathmandu: Madhab Lal Maharjan, Himalayan Booksellers, 1988.

Nippon Institute of Technology. 1981. *The royal buildings in Nepal.* Saitama-ken: Nippon Institute of Technology Research Mission.

———. 1985. *The royal buildings and Buddhist monasteries of Nepal.* Saitama-ken: Nippon Institute of Technology.

———. 1986. *The royal buildings and religious remains of Nepal.* Saitama-ken: Nippon Institute of Technology Research Mission.

Oldfield, H. A. 1880. *Sketches from Nepal.* 2 vols. Repr., New Delhi: Delhi: Cosmo Publications, 1974.

Ohji, T. 1990. The "ideal" Hindu city of ancient India as described in the Arthasastra and the urban planning of Jaipur. *East Asian Cultural Studies* 27 (1–4): 55–73.

Oliphant, L. 1852. *A journey to Kathmandu, The capital of Nepal.* London: Murray.

Sakya, A. et al., ed. 1995. *Padmavati mahavihara—Na-bahal ko samksipata parichaya ra pragati vivarana* [A brief introduction and progress report of Padmavati Mahavihara: Nabahal]. Lalitpur: Na-bahal.

Pant, M. 1990. Bahal Mandal: A study of traditional settlement pattern of Patan City, Kathmandu Valley. Masters Th., Tongji Univ.

———. 1994. Buddhist monasteries of Kathmandu Valley towns. *Ekistics* 61 (368/369): 306–15.

———. 1995. Periodisation in the urban history of Thimi, Kathmandu Valley. *Ne-Star* 2 (September): 45–56.

———. 1996. Ceremonial centre, sacred city and ritual space: A review of recent works on traditional cities of South and East Asia. *Rolamba* 16 (2): 8–12; 16 (3): 10–4.

———. 2002. A study on the spatial formation of Kathmandu Valley towns: The case of Thimi. PhD diss., Kyoto Univ.

Pant, M. and S. Funo. 1998a. Socio-spatial environment of a Buddhist monastery quarter of the city of Patan, Kathmandu Valley. In *Proceedings of the second international symposium on architectural interchange in Asia, September 1998*, 441–44. Kobe: Kobe University, Architectural Institute of Japan.

——. 1998b. Spatial structure of a Buddhist monastery quarter of the city of Patan, Kathmandu Valley. *Journal of Architectural Planning and Environmental Engineering*, no. 513: 183–9.

——. 2000. Spatial structure of the Jyapu community quarter of the city Patan, Kathmandu Valley. *Journal of Architectural Planning and Environmental Engineering*, no. 527 (January): 177–84.

——. 2001a. Ancestral shrine and the urban structure of Kathmandu Valley towns: The case of Thimi. *Journal of Architectural Planning and Environmental Engineering*, no. 540: 197–204.

——. 2001b. Analysis of settlement clusters and the development of the town of Thimi, Kathmandu Valley. *Journal of Architectural Planning and Environmental Engineering*, no. 543: 177–85.

——. 2002. A morphological analysis of neighborhood structure—toles and the artifacts of the Kathmandu Valley towns: The case of Thimi. *Manusaya, Journal of Humanities*, Special issue, no. 3: 40–65.

——. 2003. Considerations on the layout pattern of streets and settlement blocks of Thimi: A study on the planning modules of Kathmandu Valley Towns, pt. 1. *Journal of Architectural Planning and Environmental Engineering*, no. 574: 83–90.

——. 2004a. A study in the pattern of plot divisions of courtyard residential blocks of Patan, Kathmandu Valley. *Journal Asian Architecture and Building Engineering* 3 (1): 197–205.

——. 2004b. Considerations on modular measures in the layout of courtyard settlement quarters of Patan: A study on the planning modules of Kathmandu Valley Towns, pt. 2. *Journal of Architectural Planning and Environmental Engineering* 580 (June): 83–90.

——. 2005. The grid and modular measures in the town planning of Mohenjodaro and Kathmandu Valley: A study on modular measures in block and plot divisions in the planning of Mohenjodaro and Sirkap (Pakistan), and Thimi (Kathmandu Valley). *Journal Asian Architecture and Building Engineering* 3, no.1: 51–9.

Pant, M. R. 1978. Kasahi sambandhi, tadpatrama lekhieka dasawata likhatpatra [Ten palm leaf documents related to Kasahi]. *Purnima* 75 (3): 5–11.

Pant, N. 1964. Hanuman sthapana garnama hetu [The reason for erecting images of Hanuman]. *Purnima* 3 (3): 1–13.

Peng, G. 1972. The philosophy of the city design of Peking. *Ekistics* 33 (195): 24–9.

Pieper, J., ed. 1980. *Art and archaeology research papers*. Bombay: Max Mueller Bhavan.

Piggott, S., 1945. *Some ancient cities of India*. London: Oxford University Press.

Port, M. le. 1991. Traditional Newar building practices in the Kathmandu Valley. In *Man and his house in the Himalayas: Ecology of Nepal*, ed. G. Toffin, 8–144. New Delhi: Sterling Publishers.

Poudel, N., ed. 1963, (2020 VS). *Bhasavamshabali*. Part. 1. Kathmandu: Nepal Rastriya Pustakalaya.

Pradhan, R. 1996 (2053 VS). Historical background of the Kathmandu world heritage sites with special reference to Patan Monument Zone. *Prachin Nepal*, 139: 49–59.

Prajapati, S. 1989. Newar kumhale. *Rolamba* 9 (1): 6–17.

——. 1993 (2050 VS). Bhaktapur Chandesvari Kshetra. In *Chandesvari*: Special issue of Banepa Municipality, ed. H. Joshi, 12–8. Banepa: Banepa Muncipality.

Proksch, A. 1995. *Images of a century: The changing townscapes of the Kathmandu Valley*. Kathmandu: Gesellschaft for Technische Zusammenarbeit (GTZ) GmbH.

Pruscha, K., ed. 1975. *Kathmandu Valley: The preservation of physical environment and cultural heritage, a protective inventory*, 2 vols. Prepared by His Majesty's Government of Nepal in collaboration with the United Nations and UNESCO. Vienna: Schroll.

Quigley, D. 1999. Shresthas: Heterogeneity among Hindu patron lineages. In *Contested hierarchies*, eds. N. Gellner and D. Quilgley, 80–108. Delhi: Oxford University Press.

Rajbamshi, Shankarman. 1983 (2040 VS). *Vastulaksyana. Prachin Nepal* 78: 38–47.

———, ed. 1984. *Bhumi sambandhi tamsuk-tadapatra*, pt. 2. Kathmandu: His Majesty's Government of Nepal, Department of Archaeology

———. 1983 (2040 VS). *Vastulaksyana. Prachin Nepal* 78: 38–47.

———. 1987 (2044 VS). Bhumi sambandhi kehi aitihasik tamsuk tadpatra [Some palm leaf land deed documents]. *Abhilekh* 5: 5–15.

———. 2001 (2058 VS). Karsa ko artha [The meaning of karsha]. In *Nepalko itihaska vividh paksya* [Diverse facets of Nepalese History], eds. C. Nepal et al, 195–7. Kathmandu: Nepal rajakiya pragya pratisthan [Royal Nepal Academy].

Rajbamshi, Shyamsundar. 1995. Itihasaka kura-liccavikalin abhilekh [Some notes from history: An inscription from Liccavi period], *Rolamba*, 15 (3): 29.

———. 1996. Itihasaka kura [Some notes from history]. *Rolamba* 16 (2): 29–30.

Raju, L., and V. B. Mainker. 1963. Development of capacity measures in South India, pt. 1. *Metric Measures* 6, (July): 3–12.

———. 1964. Development of length and area measures in South India, pt. 3. *Metric Measures* 7: 12–23.

Rao, S. R. 1979. *Lothal.* Vols 1 and 2. Memoirs of Archaeological Survey of India, No. 78. New Delhi. Archaeological Survey of India.

Rao, T. A. G. 1914. *Elements of Hindu iconography*, 2 vols. Madras: Law Printing House.

Rangarajan, L. N. 1992. *Kautilya—The Arthasastra*. New Delhi: Penguin Books.

Regmi, D. 1965. *Medieval Nepal*, pt. 1. Calcutta: Firma K. L. Mukhopadhyaya.

———. 1966. *Medieval Nepal*, pts.2 and 3. Calcutta: Firma K. L. Mukhopadhyaya.

Regmi, M. C. 1978. *Land tenure and taxation in Nepal.* 4 vols. Kathmandu: Ratna Pustak Bhandar. (Orig. pub. 1963–8.)

———. 1989. The Newars of Patan. Regmi Research Series, 21/3. Mimeographed paper with limited circulation. Kathmandu: Regmi Research (Private) Ltd.

Rosser, C. 1966. Social mobility in the Newar caste system. In *Caste and kin in Nepal, India and Ceylon*, ed. C. Von Furer-Heimendorf, 68–139. London: Bombay: Asia Publishing House.

Roth, G., 1980. Symbolism of the Buddhist stupa. In *The stupa: Its religions and historical and architectural significance*, ed. A. Dallapiccola in collaboration with S. Zingel-Ave Lallemant, 183–209. Stuttgart: Franz Steiner Verlag Weisbaden.

Rovato, G. 1801. An account of the Kingdom of Nepal. *Asiatic Researches* 2: 307–22.

Rykwert, J. 1976. *The idea of a town.* Princeton: Princeton University Press.

Rhys-Davids, T. W., and W. Stede, eds. 1972. *Pali-English dictionary*. New Delhi: Oriental Books. (Orig. pub. 1921–5).

Sakai Harutaka, et al., 2000. Climatic changes and tectonic events recorded in the paleo-Kathmandu lake sediments. *Chigaku Zashi* 109 (5): 759–69.

Sakya, A. et al., ed. 1995. *Padmavati mahavihara—Na-bahal ko samksipata parichaya ra pragati vivarana* [A brief introduction and progress report of Padmavati Mahavihara: Nabahal]. Lalitpur: Na-bahal.

Sakya, H. 1998. Jhigu baha, bahi mhasikegu jhichyagu laksyana [Some characteristic differences between baha and bahi]. In *Buddha jayanti smarika* [Souvenir issue of Buddha's birth anniversary], 53–5. Lalitpur: Bhinchebahal.

Sakya, H. R. 1994 (2051 VS). *Sivadeva sanskarita Rudravarna Mahavihara chhagu adhyayana* [A Study on Sivadeva sanskarita Rudravarna Mahavihara]. Lalitpur: Ukubaha—Buddha jayanti Samaroha Samiti.

Sakyabhikshu, S. 1999 (2056 VS). Bhumi sambandhi tadapatraharu [Palm leaf land documents]. *Abhilekh* 17: 56–82.

______. 2000 (2057 VS). Bhumi sambandhi tadapatraharu [Palm leaf land documents]. *Abhilekh* 18: 56–76.

______. 2002 (2059 VS). Bhumi sambandhi tadapatraharu [Palm leaf land documents]. *Abhilekh* 20: 58–79.

Sekler, E. F. 1987. *Urban design at Patan Durbar Square. A preliminary inquiry.* Sankt: VHG Wissenschaftsverlag.

Sharma, B., ed. 1969. Kathmandu-upatyakako-ek-rajvamsabali. *Ancient Nepal,* 4: 1–15; 5: 1–17; 6: 1–29.

Sharma, B. P., ed. 1964 (2021 BS). *Sri Nepal Rajakiya Virapustakalaya Vrhatsucipatram, Bauddhavisayakah, 3 khanda.* Kathmandu: Vir pustakalaya.

Sharma, K. 1961 (2018 VS). *Kirtipataka.* Trans. Yogi Naraharinath. Patan: Jagadamba Prakashan.

Sharma, P. R. 1983. The land system of the Licchavis in Nepal. *Kailash* 10 (1–2): 11–62.

______. 1997. *Kula, bhumi ra rajya* [Lineage, land and the state]. Kirtipur: Centre for Nepal and Asian Studies, Tribhuvan University.

Shepard, J. W. 1985. Symbolic space in Newar culture. PhD diss., Michigan University.

Shokoohy, M and N. H. Shokoohy. 1994. *Kirtipur: An urban community in Nepal.* Monographs on Art, Archaeology, and Architecture, South Asian Series. London: Araxus Books.

Shrestha, B. L. 1999. *Land-registration in Nepalese perspective.* Kathmandu: Nepal Survey Society,

Shrestha, C. P. et al. 1986. *Historic cities of Asia: Kathmandu.* Kathmandu: Centre for Nepal and Asian Studies, Tribhuvan University.

Shrestha, H. 1974 (2031 VS). *Newari lokagita* [Newari folksongs]. Kathmandu: Nepal Rajakiya Pragya Pratisthan [Royal Nepal Academy].

Shrestha, K. 2001 (2058 VS). Kirata jatiko nalibeli. *Pragya* 94 (1): 60–92.

Shrestha, S. 1994. Historic Public Buildings. In *Kirtipur: An urban community in Nepal,* eds. Shokoohy, M and N. H. Shokoohy, 75–122. Monographs on Art, Archaeology, and Architecture, South Asian Series. London: Araxus Books.

Sjoberg, G. 1960. *The preindustrial city.* New York: Free Press.

Slater, T. R. 1981. The analysis of burgage patterns in medieval towns. *Area* 13: 211–6.

______, ed. 1990. *The built form of western cities.* Leicester: Leicester University Press.

Slusser, M. S. 1979. Indresvara Mahadeva, a thirteenth century Nepalese shrine. *Artibus Asiae* 41(2–3): 185–225.

______. 1982. *Nepal mandala: A cultural study of Kathmandu Valley.* 2 vols. Princeton: Princeton University Press.

Slusser, M. S. and G. Vajracharya. 1973a. Some Nepalese stone sculptures: A reappraisal within their cultural and historical context. *Artibus Asiae* 35 (1–2): 79–138.

______. 1973b. Some Nepalese stone sculptures: Further notes. *Artibus Asiae* 35 (3): 269–70.

______. 1974a. Two medieval Nepalese buildings: An architectural and cultural study. *Artibus Asiae* 36 (3): 169–218.

______. 1974b. The wooden sculptures of Nepal. *Arts of Asia* 4 (5): 51–7.

Snellgrove, D. L. 1957. *Buddhist Himalaya.* Oxford: Bruno Casirer.

Snodgrass, A. 1988. *The symbolism of the stupa.* Ithaca: Cornel University.

Tachikawa, M. 1984. *Materials for iconographic studies of the eight mother-goddesses in the Kathmandu Valley,* pt. 1. Anthropological and linguistic studies of the Gandaki Area in Nepal. Monumenta

Serindica 12. Tokyo: Institute for the Study of Languages and Cultures of Asia and Africa (ILCAA), Tokyo University of Foreign Studies.

————. 1986. Materials for iconographic studies of the eight mother-goddesses in the Kathmandu Valley, pt 2. Anthropological and linguistic studies of the Gandaki Area in Nepal. Monumenta Serindica 15. Tokyo: Institute for the Study of Languages and Cultures of Asia and Africa (ILCAA), Tokyo University of Foreign Studies.

Takahasi, Y. 1983. *Kyoto chusei toshi kenkyu* [A study on the medieval urban history of Kyoto]. Kyoto: Shibunkaku Shuppan.

Takahasi, Y. et al., eds. 1993. *Zushyu Nihon toshi shi* [An illustrated urban history of Japan]. Tokyo: Daigaku Shuppan Kai.

Tandukar, J. 1994 (2051 VS). Tandukara jati: Ek chinari [Tandukar community: An introduction]. In *Nepal Tandukara samaja smarika*, eds. S. Tandukar et al., 1–9. Kathmandu: Nepal Tandukar Samaj

Tandukar, S. 2002. Lalitapuri nagari tandukar jatiko chinari [An introduction of Tandukar community of Lalitpur]. In *Nepal Tandukara* samaja 2059, eds. Tandukar, S. et al., 1–6. Kathmandu: Nepal tandukar samaja.

Tevere MacFadyen J. and J. W. Vogt. 1977. The city is a mandala: Bhaktapur. *Ekistics* 44: 307–9.

Tewari, R. et al., eds. 1963 (2020 VS). Abhilekh sangraha, pt. 9. *Itihas samsodhan mandal.*

Tiwari, S. R. 1989. *Tiered temples of nepal.* Kathmandu: S. Tiwari.

————. 1996 (2053VS). Ancient towns of Kathmandu Valley: A survey of legends, chronicles and inscriptions. *Ancient Nepal,* no. 139: 25–35.

————. 2000. The architecture of Nepal in the ancient period. *Vaastu* 2: 67–72.

————. 2001. *Ancient settlements of Kathmandu Valley.* [Place of Publishing]: Centre for Nepal and Asian Studies, Tribhuvan University.

————. 2002. *The brick and the bull.* Kathmandu: Himal Books.

Theolfile, E. and P. Joshi. 1992. *Historical Hiti and Pokhari: Traditional solutions to water scarcity in Patan.* Kathmandu: Gutschow, Hagmuller & Associates, UDLE.

Toffin, G., ed. 1991. *Man and his house in the Himalayas: Ecology of Nepal.* New Delhi: Sterling Publishers.

————. 1992. The Indrajatra of Kathmandu as a royal festival: Past and present. *Contributions to Nepalese Studies* 19: 73–91.

————. 1994. The farmers in the city: The social and territorial organization of the Maharjan of Kathmandu. *Anthropos* 89: 433–59.

————. 1996. The moiety system of Newars. *Journal of Centre for Nepal and Asian Studies (CNAS)* 23 (1): 65–88.

Vaidya, T. R., and B. Vajracharya. 1998. *Madhyakalin nepalko prashasanik itihas* [A history of medieval Nepalese administration]. Kathmandu: Centre for Nepal and Asian Studies, Tribhuvan University.

Vajracarya, G. V. 1967. Thyasaphuko aitihasik vyakhya [Historical explanation of Thyasaphu]. *Purnima* 13 (4): 15–25.

————. 1976. *Hanuman Dhoka Rajdarbar* [The Hanumandhoka royal palace]. Katmandu: Center for Nepal and Asian Studies, Tribhuvan University.

Vajrachara, G. 1976 (2033 VS). *Hanumandhoko rajdarbara* [Hanumandhoka royal Palace]. Kirtipur: The Institute of Nepal and Asian Studies, Tribhuvan University.

Vajracharya, D. 1964a. Mallakalma desa raksayako vyavastha ra tyasaprati prajako kartavya [The conduct of the country's defense in Malla times and the citizens]. *Purnima* 2 (1): 20–33.

________. 1964b. Caukotdarbara [The Fortress Palace]. *Purnima* 3 (1) 51–7.

________. 1968. Licchavikalka vasti [Settlements of the Licchavi Period. *Purnima* 18 (5): 87–101.

________. 1969. Licchavikalako sasan paddhati [The administration system of Licchavi period], pt. 4. *Purnima,* 24 (6): 223–32.

________. 1972. Dranga vyaparako kendra [Dranga, a regional centre of commerce]. *Madhuparka* 4 (10): 23–7.

________, ed. 1972 (2029 BS). *Triratna Saundarya Gatha.* Kathmandu: Nepal Sanskritik Parisad.

________. 1973. *Licchavikalka Abhilekh.* Kirtipur: Centre for Nepal and Asian Studies, Tribhuvan.

________. 1999 (2056 VS). *Madhyakalaka abhilekh* [Medieval inscriptions]. Kathmandu: Center for Nepal and Asian Studies, Tribhuvan University.

Vajracharya, D. and K. P. Malla. 1985. *The Gopalarajavamsavali.* Nepal Research Centre Publications, No. 9. Kathmandu: Franz Steiner Verlag Wiesbaden GmBH.

Vajracharya, P. 1986 (2043 VS). Acharyakriyasamuccaya. *Abhilekh* 4 (4): 87–90.

________. 1993 (2050 VS). Bhumisambandi tadapatra tamsuk [Some Palm leaf land deed documents]. *Abhilekh* 11 (1): 110–18.

Vajracharya, R. 1996. Geographical, historical and cultural background of Patan. *Rolamba* 16 (2): 4–7; 16 (3): 2–6.

Van den Hoek, B. and B. G. Shrestha. 1992. Guardians of the royal goddess: Daitya and Kumar as the protectors of Taleju Bhavani of Kathmandu. *CNAS Journal* 19 (2): 191–222.

Verardi, G. et al. 1988. Harigaon Satyanarayan, Kathmandu—1984–88. Rome: ISMEO.

Vij, B. B. 1984. Linear standard in the Indus civilization. In *Frontiers of Indus civilization,* eds. B. B. Lal and S. B. Gupta, 153–6. New Delhi: Indian Archaeological Society.

Wanzke, H. 1983. Axis systems and orientation at Mohenjo-Daro. In *Interim Reports,* vol. 2 Pakistan, eds. Jansen and Urban, 33–44. Roma: IsMEO.

Watanabe, K. 1985. Functions of Mandir and Bhawan: Towers of the royal buildings, pt. 1. *Journal of Architectural Planning and Environmental Engineering,* no. 335 (September): 100–11.

________. 1986. Structure of Mandir: Towers of the royal buildings, pt. 2. *Journal of Architectural Planning and Environmental Engineering,* no. 369 (November): 114–19.

________. 1993. Structures of Bhawan: Towers of the royal buildings, pt. 3. *Journal of Architectural Planning and Environmental Engineering,* no. 447 (May): 135–41.

________, ed. 1998a. *Buddhist Monasteries of Nepal.* Tokyo: Chuo Koron Bijitsu Shuppan.

________. 1998b. Design dimensions for the floor plan, Part III, Chap. 2. In *Buddhist monasteries of Nepal,* ed. K. Watanabe, 100–2. Tokyo: Chuo Koron Bijitsu Shuppan.

Watanabe, K., and T. Kurotsu. 1990a. Structures of Chok: Quadrangular architecture of the royal buildings of Nepal, pt. 1. *Journal of Architectural Planning and Environmental Engineering,* no. 408 (February): 101–9.

________. 1990b. Functions of Chok: Quadrangular architecture of the royal buildings of Nepal, pt. 2. *Journal of Architectural Planning and Environmental Engineering,* no. 412 (June): 97–107.

Williams, M. 1899. *A Sanskrit English dictionary.* Oxford: Clarendon Press.

Wilson, H., trans. 1983. *Matsyapuranam,* Pt. 1. Delhi: Nag Publishers.

Wheeler, M. 1960. *The Indus civilization.* Cambridge: University Press.

________. 1966. *Civilizations of the Indus valley and beyond.* London: Thames & Hudson.

Wheatley, P., 1967. Proleptic observations on the origin of urbanism. In *Liverpool Essays in Geography,* eds. R. Steel and R. Lawton, 315–45. London.

________. 1969. *City as symbol.* London: Lewis.

————. 1971. The pivot of the four quarters: A preliminary enquiry into the origins and character of the ancient Chinese city. Edinburgh: Edinburgh University Press.

Wright, D., ed. 1972. *History of Nepal.* Trans. by M. S. Shunker and P. Gunananda. Repr., Kathmandu: Nepal Antiquated Book Publishers. (Orig. pub. 1877.)

Wu, Jin. 1993. The historical development of Chinese urban morphology. *Planning Perspectives* 8: 20–52.

Yamane, S. et al. 2000. *Amedabado (Gujarato, Into) kyu shikai ni okeru gaiiku kukan no kousei* [A study on the neighbourhood districts of the old city area of Ahmedabad (Gujarat, India)]. *Journal of Architectural Planning and Environmental Engineering,* no. 538 (December): 141–8.

Yogeshraj. 1998. Pikhalakhu: muladhoka bahirako rakshyaka [Pikhalakhu: The guardian deity outside the Maindoor]. *Pragya* 87 (28): 125–8.

Yokoi, K. 1998. *Katomanzu bonchi ni okeru bunka zai no hozon syufuku ni kan suru kenkyu* [A study on the conservation and restoration works of the built cultural heritage of Kathmandu Valley. Master's th., Kyoto Univ.

Yokote, S. I. 1992. *Neparu minka no keitai bunseki: Patan ni okeru minka no jissoku chyosa dezain sabei to sono toku-I* [An analysis of the characteristics of Nepalese vernacular dwellings: A survey of vernacular dwellings of Patan]. Master's th., Kyoto Univ.

Yonechi, F. 1966. A preliminary report on the geomorphology of Kathmandu Valley. In *Science Report of Yamagata University,* 7th Series (Geography), 23(2), 153–61.

Zanen, Sj., M., 1986. The Goddess Vajrayogini and the kingdom of Sankhu. *Purusartha* 10: 125–64.

Index